BY FRANK FREIDEL

Franklin D. Roosevelt: *The Apprenticeship*

Franklin D. Roosevelt: *The Ordeal*

Franklin D. Roosevelt: *The Triumph*

Franklin D. Roosevelt
The Ordeal

Franklin D. Roosevelt
The Ordeal

by
FRANK FREIDEL

With Illustrations

Little, Brown and Company · *Boston*

The author wishes to thank Duell, Sloan & Pearce, Inc.,
for permission to quote from *F. D. R.: His Personal
Letters,* Vol. II, copyright 1948, by Elliott Roosevelt

*Published simultaneously
in Canada by McClelland and Stewart Limited*

PRINTED IN THE UNITED STATES OF AMERICA

For
Linda Beth

Contents

Contents

List of Illustrations

Franklin D. Roosevelt
The Ordeal

Spectator at Paris

> President Wilson's gallant appeal . . . meant little to the
> imagination or the hearts of a large number of the so-called
> statesmen who gathered in Paris to assemble a treaty of
> so-called peace in 1919. I saw that with my own eyes. I
> heard that with my own ears. Political profit, personal
> prestige, national aggrandizement, attended the birth of
> the League of Nations, and handicapped it from its infancy.
> — FDR, *December 28, 1933.*

NEW YEAR'S DAY, 1919, found Franklin and Eleanor Roosevelt
aboard the U.S.S. *George Washington*, heading for Paris. Roosevelt, who was not quite thirty-seven years old, had made a splendid reputation for himself during the war as one of the best-liked and most
energetic young men in Washington. His two years in the New
York State Senate, and nearly six years' service as Assistant Secretary
of the Navy under President Woodrow Wilson, had done much to
wear off the political taint of his origin in the Hudson River aristocracy and his education at Groton and Harvard. Although he began
his public career as a blue-stockinged foe of Tammany, by the summer of 1918 he had so effectively made his peace with the organization that it had dangled before him the nomination for Governor
of New York. He had declined, because he wanted to get into uniform and to see the war at first hand. He went overseas as a civilian
in July; by the time he returned, it was too late to get into the armed
forces. Now with the war at an end, he was bound overseas again.
His official task was to supervise naval demobilization, but he was
even more excited over the opportunity to catch a glimpse of the
Paris Peace Conference.

Although the voyage was stormy and rough, the Roosevelts enjoyed
it. They had a comfortable suite; Franklin took setting-up exercises
daily with Walter Camp, played shuffleboard, and made a thorough
inspection of the ship. In spite of the exciting talk aboard among
the delegates to the Peace Conference, for Roosevelt the trip was a

resumption of familiar patterns of activity. Yet for the Roosevelts as much as for the delegates, this crossing was far more symbolic of the new than of the old. While Franklin gloried in being strenuous, Mrs. Roosevelt spent long hours reading a new book she had given her husband for Christmas, *The Education of Henry Adams,* a saga of disillusionment heralding the new cynical spirit that followed the war. "Very interesting," she commented, "but sad to have had so much and yet find it so little." [1]

Suddenly, on January 6, a radio message brought startling news: Theodore Roosevelt was dead. He had been in a hospital when they left, but had not seemed seriously ill. Grieving, Franklin saw in this only the personal loss of a beloved relative. "My cousin's death was in every way a great shock," he declared, "for we heard just before leaving that he was better — and he was after all not old. But I cannot help think that he himself would have had it this way and that he has been spared a lingering illness of perhaps years." At the moment he did not see in the event another portent of the extent to which the Roosevelts were sailing into a new era. But Eleanor saw the death of her uncle in the larger perspective of history — "Another great figure gone from our nation — " and felt keenly that "a great personality has gone from active participation in the life of his people." Of course she also did not grasp the momentous significance for her husband's career. The great oak had crashed, and sunlight flooded through to the growing sapling.[2]

On the day after the Armistice was signed — November 12, 1918 — Roosevelt's mercurial mind had jumped easily from war to demobilization. Always quicker to shift mental gears than those around him, the Assistant Secretary chafed at the red tape and delays; and just as he had long expressed impatience over the slowness of Secretary of the Navy Josephus Daniels in prosecuting the war, so he now felt equal irritation over the leisurely fashion in which his superior proposed to wind it up. As earlier, when Roosevelt felt war production was lagging, he gave vent to his feelings in a memorandum for his files. This time it was because Daniels, at a meeting of the Council of the Navy Department, ignored unanimous advice to continue building warehouses in New Jersey to store the vast quantities of war supplies that now would be surplus. Secretary Daniels declared that the Navy could build warehouses later on its own land; but Assistant Secretary Roosevelt protested to himself, "When will

the shortage become so acute that it secures *action* by the Sec'y?" [3]
So it went, with Roosevelt restless for action.

A far larger and more pressing matter generated still greater impatience in Roosevelt. He violently opposed the Secretary's decision to allow Admiral William S. Sims in London to demobilize naval installations in Europe. Since Congress would hold Secretary Daniels responsible, he should send a civilian representative with the rank of Assistant Secretary to direct the task. So argued Roosevelt. This was, of course, a continuation of his earlier theme that the Navy must establish a well-organized administration under a civilian head to supervise its huge, varied, and often confused business interests overseas. Nor was Roosevelt's observation that Congress would hold Daniels responsible an argument without weight. The loss of Congress to the Republicans in the November elections meant that after March an investigation of the naval conduct of the war was almost inevitable. Of course, Roosevelt had in mind something more than protecting the Secretary from congressional charges of maladministration. Although too adroit to say so outright, he believed that the one civilian with the requisite intimate knowledge of European naval activities was he himself. [4]

There was, of course, another consideration which the Assistant Secretary may not have confessed to himself: Washington was turning dull, and the focus of excitement was shifting to Paris. He could not expect to keep his office for more than the two remaining years of the Wilson administration, nor did he want to, now that the war was over and public interest sure to veer away from naval affairs. The one spectacular task remaining was to close up the Navy in Europe. That errand would give him an opportunity to visit Paris while one of the world's most crucial diplomatic episodes was unfolding. Since Secretary Daniels had ordered Admiral William S. Benson to represent the Navy at the Peace Conference, Roosevelt could hope for no more than to be physically present on the spot while great decisions were in the making. This was not much, but it was better than nothing.

Still the Secretary hesitated to let him go. Daniels had full confidence in his supply officers in Europe, and he believed that he could direct demobilization adequately from Washington. Furthermore, he needed his Assistant Secretary to supervise the delicate negotiations involved in returning vessels to their private owners, while he himself worked to obtain enabling legislation from Congress. Therefore they must both remain in Washington, he maintained, until Congress adjourned on March 4.[5]

Both in writing and in conversation, Roosevelt kept expressing his very strong reasons for wanting to go abroad. Even when Daniels firmly said "No," the Assistant Secretary stubbornly refused to accept it as final. On December 7, in his Washington home lying in bed with a cold, he penned an unusually vehement plea. In it he threatened, in order to keep his own record clear, publicly to shift to Daniels all responsibility for possible demobilization errors.[6]

This bold letter accomplished its purpose. An officer who served under Daniels once likened the Secretary to a large block of ice: one could chip and chip with no apparent result, until suddenly the whole cake would break in half. Roosevelt's irate jab split the block. Roosevelt drafted, and Daniels signed, dispatches informing Admirals Benson and Sims that the Assistant Secretary of the Navy would arrive to supervise demobilization.[7]

At first Roosevelt had planned to leave on December 15, but he had not entirely recuperated from the attack of influenza and pneumonia which had kept him in bed much of the fall. Consequently, he obtained permission to take his wife with him; she hastily packed, and they embarked on New Year's Day, 1919.

On the voyage, they enjoyed the companionship of a remarkable group of notables. President Wilson had sailed earlier, but with them were Charles Schwab, Bernard Baruch, Walter Camp, and the Mexican and Chinese delegations to the Paris conference. In addition, Roosevelt had with him a considerable party of his own: once again, as special assistant, his longtime playmate Livingston Davis; as legal counselor, a genial Irish Democratic politician, Thomas Spellacy; and to carry out most of the actual work, Commander John M. Hancock of the Supply Corps, who had made a splendid record as head of Navy Purchasing during the war.[8]

On the voyage, Roosevelt's interest centered more on peacemaking than on naval matters. On January 10, when the *George Washington* dropped anchor off Brest, he gave a luncheon in honor of the Chinese and Mexican Peace Commissions. At its conclusion, he addressed them, and for the first time in years said nothing about increasing armaments. Instead, he elaborated upon the great task that confronted them at the Paris Conference. His attention had shifted from warmaking to peacemaking, and he espoused the new cause with all the vigor and singleness of devotion with which he had served the old.[9]

But Roosevelt's official assignment was to supervise demobilization, not to help design the peace. Once ashore he began immediately by inspecting an uncomfortably overgrown camp at Brest, where, under the supervision of General Smedley Butler of the Marine Corps, soldiers were pouring in to await transportation home. It had rained almost constantly; the camp was deep in mud despite quantities of duckboards which Butler had commandeered. Although its maximum capacity was 40,000 men, 60,000 were already there, and more were arriving at a faster rate than the Navy could ship them out. Thousands were dying of influenza that winter, and although Butler had kept the sicklist to 1⅛ per cent, Roosevelt feared that if the Army further overcrowded the camp there would be danger of an epidemic. He discreetly cabled his warning to Daniels * with the hint that the Secretary of the Navy might show it to Secretary of War Newton D. Baker.[10]

Paris was crowded with soldiers and diplomats; everyone was relating rumors and anecdotes about Wilson, the peacemakers, and the formal conference about to open. Eleanor Roosevelt relayed some of these to her mother-in-law: the French were very anxious, it was whispered, that Wilson should visit the devastated areas before he made decisions on the settlement with Germany; American soldiers were somewhat disgruntled because he had not visited them; and Mrs. Wilson, people complained, had gone to an Army hospital only twice.† Roosevelt picked up other tales about German atrocities and equally revolting Bolshevik horrors, some of which he retold after his return to America.

The Assistant Secretary must have felt frustrated to be confined to gathering scraps from the fringes of the conference rather than negotiating sweeping policies at its center. Limited as he was to indirect accounts and untrustworthy gossip, preoccupied as he had to be with his own naval tasks, he was in no position to grasp fully the desperation of the moment. Hunger and Communism swept westward. Herbert Hoover dramatically declared, "The wolf is at the door of the world." This, in addition to the urgency of domestic problems in the war-weary Allied countries, placed almost unbearable pressures upon the

* At Brest, FDR offered to send home Secretary Daniels's son, Josephus, who was stationed with the Marines, but the upright Secretary insisted that Josephus stay until his regiment came home. Earlier, Daniels had refused when FDR offered to get Josephus a commission.[11]

† Mrs. Roosevelt, established in a suite in the Ritz, followed the conference as closely as her husband. She enjoyed a pleasant social round with the wives of the leading dignitaries; Bernard Baruch sent her roses.[12]

exhausted, wrangling leaders of the conference. Prime Minister David
Lloyd George told Parliament: "I am doubtful whether any body of
men with a difficult task have worked under greater difficulties —
stones crackling on the roof and crashing through the windows, and
sometimes wild men screaming through the keyholes." [13]

While this tragedy was unfolding, Roosevelt was absorbed in no
easy task: the negotiation of property settlements with France. As
he had found the previous summer, the Navy in its haste to establish
bases had made faulty contracts, or sometimes none at all.* Now he
was anxious to clear up the claims of the French, and above all to dispose of the Navy's property on the most advantageous possible terms
before the Army began to dump its enormous holdings, which inevitably would depress the market. Naval officers in Europe had already
made considerable headway in demobilization before Roosevelt's arrival, and rather resented his presence as unnecessary. Admiral Benson
in Paris crowed to Daniels: "I think Mr. Roosevelt was surprised to
find that such great progress had been made." But in his next remarks,
Benson unwittingly described the situation which made the presence
of a high-ranking civilian most desirable: "Due to the peculiar ideas of
our French friends, who in my opinion can give the worst kind of
a Yankee points and then beat him on a bargain, it is difficult to settle
any of the financial questions involved. It may be uncharitable to say
so, but I cannot escape the feeling that they are trying to force us to
leave as much of our equipment in France as possible, and give it to
them; or, in other words, leave it so that they can make any use of it
they want without having to pay for it." As these comments from the
conservative Chief of Naval Operations indicate, the Americans were
negotiating claims settlements in a fairly tense atmosphere. They were
all too willing to believe fabrications like the widespread story that the
French were charging the United States rental for graveyards in
which American troops were buried. The French for their part were
equally suspicious. [14]

A prerequisite for successful negotiations was the rebuilding of cordial relations, and no one was better qualified for this task than the
affable Roosevelt. He could act both pleasantly and authoritatively,
as Hancock once put it, to "lubricate the discussions [so] that there

* Hancock, fearing much the same sort of snarl might result from nebulous
contracts in the Second World War, warned Donald Nelson in advance. When
a tangle developed anyway, Hancock was brought to Washington — though not
by FDR — to head an interdepartmental board to handle contract settlement. He
also drafted contract re-negotiation legislation.

would be a better basis of dealing." This done, the diligent Hancock could arrange airtight details of settlement. While Roosevelt carried on the top-level conversations, Hancock did the bulk of the work. He prepared most of the policy letters and, after his return to Washington, a sixty-eight-page official report for Roosevelt's signature. They made a perfect team, which, in the finest Roosevelt tradition, got things done — and in a hurry.[15]

From Admiral Benson and other naval officers at Paris, Roosevelt gathered data on all bases and stations in France. From President Wilson he obtained permission to sell matériel directly, under authority of a wartime statute, rather than by the customary thirty-day advertising for bids, which would have made sales in Europe difficult if not impossible. As a basis for setting a fair price on installations, he tried unsuccessfully to get figures on their cost. Because the Navy had not operated a central accounting office in Europe, it had no accurate records of costs, and after the war the Bureau of Supplies and Accounts could do no better than make estimates for the naval records.[16]

Through André Tardieu, Roosevelt sought the permission of the French Government to sell surplus property. Tardieu had already asked that no property of a foreign government be sold in France, but when Roosevelt assured him that the Navy's stores were quite small, he gave his approval.

The Assistant Secretary's "biggest deal" with the French involved the partly completed Lafayette Radio Station near Bordeaux. Three or four departments of the French Government each wanted the station, but since they had no appropriations, would make no definite commitments. Despite continued conferences, the question hung fire until Roosevelt arrived. Somewhat mixing his metaphors, Roosevelt explained to a Navy officer: "Our French friends have to 'fish or cut bait' and I am willing to be the goat in getting them to do this." The French, he told Daniels later, "had backed and filled for over six weeks, and I finally put it up to Tardieu and told him that if they did not wish to keep the LaFayette Station themselves, I would have to take the material down and ship it home for use at the new Monroe station. They agreed to take it the next day." * Then the same kind of delay followed as the French tried to make up their minds whether or not to have the Americans finish the station. Again Roosevelt set a dead-

---

* Despite his firmness, FDR managed to retain Tardieu's good will. In 1932, Tardieu expressed his delight over the success of his "très cher ami." [17]

line; again the French capitulated. They agreed to pay the actual cost if the United States would complete construction.[18]

While Roosevelt was able to expedite major transactions like this, small claims — from individual holders of land the Navy had occupied, or from those who had suffered damages from Navy negligence — would obviously be submitted over a considerable period of time. Consequently, Roosevelt set up claim boards in both Paris and London. These functioned with remarkable smoothness. While a few of the claimants may have asked for exorbitant damages, most of them were more than fair. A Belgian priest was struck one night by a Navy car; his robe caught on the bumper and he was dragged along beneath the car for some distance on the rough cobblestones. Although he was injured, he asked no more than a new robe — a claim for only about fifty francs.[19]

The Italian Government, which had caused Roosevelt so much concern the previous summer, demonstrated an even stronger spirit of generosity when, to Roosevelt's delight, it assumed all expenses incurred by Naval Aviation in Italy.[20]

Twice Roosevelt conferred at the Hotel Crillon with Herbert Hoover, who was back in Europe to head postwar relief. Roosevelt tried with only moderate success to work out arrangements to dispose of surplus naval supplies to Hoover's commission. Hoover would not take Navy uniform cloth, because the quality was too high and he could purchase a satisfactory cloth at a considerably lower price. Nor would Hoover arrange to purchase fancy tinned provisions — he wanted only condensed milk, beans, and flour. Besides, the Relief Commission was not itself buying supplies, but merely acting as a clearing-house for financial arrangements between buyer and seller. To do business with it, the Navy would have to accept the municipal bonds of Vienna, Bucharest, or Warsaw,* and this, of course, was impossible.[21]

While demobilization proceeded smoothly in France, Roosevelt left Paris for London by way of the now silent battlefields. Eleanor Roosevelt accompanied him, and was as impressed by the grisly scenes as her husband had been earlier. The days were bright and sunny, not too cold, but she felt wretched from an attack of pleurisy. There were

---

* Hancock recalls, nevertheless, that the Navy turned over many items of food to Hoover, some of which were of value less as nourishment than as morale builders. It also tore down many of its temporary buildings, transported them to Belgium and re-erected them for the homeless.

many mementos of recent battles — "On the way to Ham, saw a wrecked German gun close to the road," one member of the party noted. "The crew had been buried nearby, and their bones were showing through the dirt which had been washed away in places." They stopped and examined the clothing of the Germans, a heavyweight fabric made from rather coarse wool.

At Cambrai, Roosevelt later wrote, he "wandered into a side street and met a French sergeant with the Croix de Guerre with Two Palms. He had with him his two little children who he had not seen since August 1914. They were caught in the Boche rush, carried off to Belgium, and now the family is reunited in the wreck of what is still their home — the roof gone but the lower story inhabitable — and they are beginning again at the beginning." At Amiens, Roosevelt sardonically reported, "We found a very much upset British Lieutenant who had expected us in the morning and had definite instructions that Mrs. Roosevelt was under no circumstances to visit Bapaume or Cambrai. When I told him that we had already visited the entire battle area he almost fainted and had visions of court-martial." [22]

As protocol demanded, Admiral Sims, a striking-appearing, vigorous, egocentric leader, met Roosevelt at London. Like Admiral Benson, he demonstrated no particular enthusiasm when Roosevelt explained the purpose of his mission. Sims assembled a number of his staff at the office to meet the Assistant Secretary; they listened embarrassed to what ensued. Roosevelt told Sims that he had come over personally to supervise demobilization, because there might shortly be a Republican President, and, with a Republican Congress already elected, an investigation of the Navy was likely. Since Roosevelt would be responsible, he wanted to make sure that everything was handled properly. Sims retorted that if this was the reason why he had come, he might much better have stayed home, since if Roosevelt played no part in the disposition of goods in Europe, he could refer congressional investigators to Sims as the man responsible. Roosevelt flushed but did not argue.[23]

In point of fact, Sims had almost completed demobilization of the air stations and most other Navy holdings before Roosevelt arrived. Only a few problems of final settlement with the British remained. However, Roosevelt feared that the sums involved might be quite large. The United States Army had entered into an agreement with the Air Ministry which he considered "perfectly wild" because it might mean negotiations for several years. Hancock and Spellacy helped him draw up an entirely different sort of arrangement to wind up financial obligations for the air bases. This gave the British options on them until June 1, 1920, since it would take some time to obtain Acts of Parliament to take them over. The British could, and did, acquire several of the smaller bases under the Defense of the Realm Act. For example, Roosevelt persuaded the Air Ministry to purchase the Killingholme Air Station for forty pounds plus the proceeds from the sale of twenty-seven permanent and two portable barracks.[24]

Other transactions and arrangements for closing hospitals and air-fields in England were almost routine. While Hancock handled most of these, Spellacy went on a jaunt to Ireland. Roosevelt himself, as Eleanor reported, spent his days at the office, but came home for lunch and for tea about 5:30. "He's really not overworked," she said.[25]

Indeed, Roosevelt had time to worry about the rapid deterioration of friendly relations between the United States and Great Britain. The wartime spirit of camaraderie and co-operation was giving way to suspicion that each might try to build its sea power to the point where it could dominate foreign trade. The United States, which even before its entrance into the war had seized a large part of the former German foreign trade, and by default much of the British, was interested in maintaining its new dominant position. As early as 1916, Navy League realists, envisaging this sort of outcome of the war, insisted this was the most important reason why the United States must build and maintain an all-powerful Battle Fleet.

Roosevelt, too, in 1916 espoused this view of sea power; but by 1919, even though there was no longer the menace of a German Fleet to bind the two powers together, he considered maintenance of Anglo-American friendship to be of greater worth. So, while big-navy men in Washington advocated a three-year naval-building program, Roosevelt in London disparaged the "wholly unfounded alarms" of the British. "The United States has no intention of challenging anybody's naval supremacy," he told reporters; it merely intended to keep its new large merchant marine, and to maintain a Navy adequate to protect it. This must have been small comfort to the British shippers — since, in effect, Roosevelt was affirming that the Americans intended, by force if need be, to hold on to the large share of the world's trade which they had acquired during the war, but that neither the United States shipping nor Navy were in the least a menace to Britain, the greatest of maritime powers.[26]

Within two weeks Roosevelt finished his work in London and returned to the Continent. Since he was going to the occupied Rhineland, where American women were not as yet allowed, he sent his wife directly to Paris. With a small party, he embarked at Dover for Ostend on an American destroyer, the U.S.S. *Yarnell.* It turned out to be a tense crossing; he had to place his faith in the skipper — who became one of the most famous of his admirals in the Second World War — William F. Halsey. "At seven Sunday morning we left the harbor," he later described the voyage, "smooth sea but hazy & ran across to Calais, thence up the swept channel past Dunkirk. . . . Here the fog shut down very thick and just before we reached a point off Ostend we failed to pick up one of the buoys, and because of a mine field off shore which had not yet been swept up we anchored. After two hours of waiting for the fog to lift I decided to make an attempt to reach shore as it was absolutely necessary to get to Brussels for the King's [luncheon]." At this point Roosevelt's account tantalizingly stopped; but he did get safely ashore in a motorboat.[27]

The visit to Brussels, Roosevelt commented later, was "one of the most delightful things in my life." He dined with the King, and with the American Minister, Brand Whitlock; he visited the forts at Liége; and he reviewed "a magnificent Canadian division." [28]

As he went into the Rhineland, Roosevelt was returning to an area he had known as a boy. He was thrilled to see the Allied troops occupying this German area, and especially looked forward, as he approached the American sector, to seeing the United States flag flying over that formidable fortress and symbol of German pride, Ehrenbreitstein. But when the fortress came into sight, to his keen disappointment he saw that the flagpole was empty. When he angrily asked the occupation authorities in Coblenz what the reason was for this, they told him they did not wish to humiliate the Germans unduly. Roosevelt, who earlier would have preferred a drive on Berlin to an armistice, felt that the Germans must be taught in no uncertain terms that they had lost the war. As soon as he reached Paris, he complained to General Pershing, who felt likewise. Pershing immediately ordered the American flag raised over the citadel.[29]

While he was in Germany, Roosevelt spent the night across the Rhine with General John A. Lejeune, the Marine commander, and inspected his brigade, which was attached to the Army Second Division. Although stories had spread back to Paris that the Germans were treating the troops with marked hospitality, the men were more than eager to return home.[30] A yarn went the rounds that when Roosevelt inspected the Marines, he elaborated upon the great privilege they enjoyed in occupying Germany; he patted his pocket, and told them that within it were steamship tickets to the United States, which he would gladly exchange for a Marine uniform. This was more than one private could stand, and he shouted, "I'll swap you!" *

On the way back, Roosevelt again crossed the battlefield, stopped to gather German trophies — helmets, shell cases and the like — and reached Paris so laden down that he had to employ two enlisted men to pack his souvenirs.† He spent a week more in the French capital while the Peace Conference was in full swing. He was fascinated by the debates over the Covenant of the League of Nations, but had to stay on the side lines. He did not even see a draft until he was on the train to Brest where he was to embark for the United States, when a New York *Times* correspondent showed it to him. He was exceedingly excited and interested.[32]

President Wilson was on the *George Washington* on the return voyage. He was bringing the Covenant to discuss with the Senate. Roosevelt hoped very much that the President would talk to him about it, but was fearful that he would not have the opportunity, since Wilson, aside from ceremonial occasions, kept very much to himself. Finally, to Roosevelt's delight, the President did invite him to his cabin to discuss the Covenant. Later, at a luncheon which both Mr. and Mrs. Roosevelt attended, he again talked about how much the League would mean and how essential it would be for the United States to participate in it. Eleanor Roosevelt recorded in her diary a remark which her husband in the future quoted repeatedly in his speeches. The President had said, "The United States must go in or it will break the heart of the world, for she is the only nation that all feel is disinterested and all trust." [33] Roosevelt agreed completely, and at once became a strong public advocate of the League.

As the *George Washington* approached Boston, it had a near mishap which strangely contributed to the Roosevelt legend. The ship and its

---

* In point of fact, FDR was so keenly aware how homesick the men were that he would not have been likely to taunt them, even inadvertently. Remembrance of this sort of sentiment may in part account for his remark to Stalin at Yalta that American occupation troops were not likely to stay in Germany for more than two years.[31]

† The trophies are now in the Roosevelt Library.

escort of destroyers nearly went aground in the fog off Cape Ann. Both Ray Stannard Baker and Josephus Daniels in their autobiographies give credit to Roosevelt, with his intimate knowledge of these waters, for identifying the location and navigating the *George Washington* to safety. However, Roosevelt, who was on the bridge with his friend, Captain Edward McCauley, did no more than guess they were in the vicinity of Marblehead, which was very nearly correct. When the weather cleared, an officer identified the exact location, Thacher Island, and they headed southward into port.[34]

At Boston, Roosevelt participated in the parade in honor of Wilson through streets jammed with wildly enthusiastic crowds, and lunched with the laconic Governor of Massachusetts, Calvin Coolidge. In the afternoon, he heard the President make his first speech on behalf of the Versailles Treaty, and receive a strong acclamation. There seemed no hint of trouble ahead; even the Republican Coolidge said he felt sure the people would back the President. The war was won, demobilization was proceeding rapidly, and there seemed every reason to envisage a bright future in which the League of Nations would make wars impossible.[35]

CHAPTER II

Toward More Efficient Government

> I firmly believe that unless we set our own house in order,
> and, by American constitutional means, make our govern-
> ment as efficient as we would conduct our own private
> individual businesses, . . . it will simply mean the spread of
> doctrines which seek to effect change by unconstitutional
> means.
>
> — FDR, *February 26, 1920.*[1]

AS spreading disillusion kept pace with demobilization, Roosevelt
by word and deed asserted his new faith that more efficient government at home and more vigorous participation in affairs abroad
would assure prosperity and peace. This he repeatedly labeled "progressivism," although the domestic side of it — the less government
interference in business, and the more businesslike the functioning of
government, the better — was a formula more in keeping with the program of the National Association of Manufacturers than with the
New Freedom. Nevertheless, few people challenged the new content
that Roosevelt placed behind the "progressive" label.

Before the war, the great majority of progressives had already
achieved their rather limited goals. They had long since gained all the
legislation they wanted. By 1919, unparalleled industrial production
and prosperity dulled at least temporarily their dislike of corporate
monopoly, while strikes sharpened their prejudices against powerful
labor organizations. They disliked the many strikes for higher wages,
even though they themselves suffered also from the high living costs
which helped create labor unrest. They feared the many changes the
war had brought about, especially the specter of militant Communism
in eastern Europe. Consequently, they condemned both organized labor
and radicalism, and they longed for old days and ways.

As the program of many former progressives became essentially conservative, so too did Roosevelt's, as he talked repeatedly on the two
themes of American leadership abroad and business leadership at home.

Shortly after Roosevelt's return from Paris, he delivered a series of speeches on the League in which he outlined America's new role in world affairs. Popular enthusiasm for the League was still at a peak, and it seemed certain that the United States would enter it on some basis. Nevertheless, Roosevelt made a serious effort to meet the attacks of Senator Henry Cabot Lodge and other critics by warning repeatedly that the only alternative to the League was heavy armament. For the first time in his life, he told an inquiring college student, he did not favor a larger United States Navy — providing the United States joined the League. Consequently, the United States could not draw up its postwar naval policies until the Senate decided whether or not it would ratify the Versailles Treaty, Roosevelt explained. "Our very rules of life are dependent upon a decision yet to be made."

Roosevelt was frank to admit how recent his own conversion had been. "Last spring I thought the League of Nations merely a beautiful dream, a Utopia," he confessed. "But in June I went abroad, in those critical days. I found in Europe not only the desire to beat the Hun but also a growing demand that out of it all must come something else. When our glorious offensive began this demand for something greater than peace grew larger." Again: "This is a time of idealism, a time when more ideals are properly demanded of us, and over there on the other side, every man, woman and child looks to us to make good the high purpose with which we came into this war." [2]

This did not mean that Roosevelt was ready to make a doctrinaire defense of the League Covenant against those followers of Lodge's who demanded various modifications. It was an experiment, he granted, and one could perfectly validly raise objections against various details. This had been equally true of the United States Constitution at the time of debate over its ratification. "It is important not to dissect the document," he insisted, but "first to approve the general plan." Although he did not say so explicitly in public addresses, his frame of reference was obviously that of the practical politician who regarded the ultimate end as so important that he was ready to compromise away details in order to attain it. This was in marked contrast to Wilson's demand that the Senate accept the Covenant without the slightest change.

During the year that followed, as Wilson and Lodge refused to make the slightest concession to each other, Roosevelt continued to feel that the question of reservations was of little real significance, and wearied of the furor. He was still optimistic enough to expect a compromise and ratification. At a dinner given by Senator and Mrs. Charles S.

Thomas of Colorado, his friend Mrs. Hamlin, who was a strong League advocate, sat beside Lodge. Roosevelt, every time she looked his way, caught her eye and winked.[3]

The vital issue, Roosevelt consistently believed, was for the United States to maintain world leadership. This it could best do through the League. Without the United States, he warned, the League would degenerate into a new Holy Alliance, hostile toward the United States, rather than become the sort of concert of powers he wished, one that would serve as a bulwark against the spread of revolutionary ideas from Russia.[4] Enemies of the League were denouncing it for its "internationalism"; truly, he granted, it would promote the sort of internationalism that would prevent future wars, but would eschew that of the "red flag and the black flag." *

Like many another liberal, Roosevelt felt that the Allied victory and continued American leadership should mean the spread throughout the world of the type of civil liberties and self-government enjoyed in this country. While other nations learned democracy from the United States, it in turn must learn to assume positive leadership in meeting world crises. In June, 1919, he told the graduating class at Worcester Polytechnic Institute that America's entrance into the war had signaled a new relationship toward the rest of humanity. "The United States would commit a grievous wrong to itself and to all mankind if it were even to attempt to go backwards towards an old Chinese wall policy of isolation." Even more than wrong, it would be a folly, he thought — indeed, an impossibility, since "though we may consider the actual fighting as ended there will be many crises in international affairs for many years to come. In them the United States cannot escape an important, perhaps even a controlling voice." [6]

The same realism which led Roosevelt to this conclusion caused him, as months of debate over the League went by, increasingly to feel that even though the United States need not arm heavily, it should maintain substantial armaments and some form of compulsory military training. Whether or not the United States entered the League, it must remember the lesson of preparedness. Americans must "not forget that some kind of . . . universal national service is the surest guarantee of national safety." "After a war there is a reaction and we do not want to talk of future wars, but I want to say that with all deference to W. J. [Bryan] that I do not count on the million men who

* In his remarks of March 1, 1919, FDR apparently went so far as to charge the Soviet government with the nationalization of women for immoral purposes.[5]

would spring to arms overnight. We have to have training." In addition to all the arguments he had used before the war — that it produced better, healthier citizens — he added new ones appropriate to the anti-Red state of mind of 1919: "It stands against anarchy and Bolshevism, against class hatred, against snobbery; it stands for discipline, good fellowship, order, and a broader Americanism."

Despite the widespread American fear that the contagion of revolutionary Bolshevism might cross the Atlantic, those in the armed forces clamored to get out, and most citizens demonstrated no enthusiasm for universal military training. Going against general opinion, Roosevelt made yet another emphatic plea before a New York State Convention of the American Legion, in October, 1919. In addition, he wrote privately, "I can still honestly say that I hope one of my four boys will go to the Naval Academy in spite of the general situation in the U.S.N. at the present moment!" As Overseer at Harvard, he pressed a military training course upon President A. Lawrence Lowell, and as Acting Secretary of the Navy, he announced a program to establish Naval Reserve officer training corps in colleges and universities throughout the country.[7]

But the reaction against all things military was even stronger than Roosevelt had feared it would be. By January, 1920, even he was trimming before the contrary gusts of public sentiment. "I am not keen for universal military training just now," he hedged, "but I do believe that we should have universal training with the military cut out. We should have universal training for good citizenship, to improve our government, national, state and municipal. We must have discipline and effort. Every man should take his part." Thus, despite his advocacy of the League of Nations, he tenaciously clung to his fundamental trust in adequate armament, or, failing that, in any training the public would accept.[8]

This was only one indication of how strongly he still placed his faith in armed force.

Within the Navy Department, high-ranking officers urged upon him vigorous postwar policies in which they took little or no account of the League of Nations. Perhaps it was only coincidence that they did so especially when Secretary Daniels was in Europe and Roosevelt was Acting Secretary.

There came to his desk for signature in April, 1919, for instance, a particularly significant secret communication to the State Department inquiring what its policies in various areas would be, so that the

Navy could plan to back them with force if necessary. Foreign policy, this statement declared, depended for its acceptance by other nations upon the power behind it. "It is probable that certain policies are of such importance to our national interests that they must be defended at all cost. On the other hand certain policies are not, by the expense that would entail, justified if they lead to war." Consequently the State Department should know what its policies might cost, and the Navy should know what it might be called upon to uphold by force. There was foreboding of the future in this concrete example: "With present equipment of naval bases in the Pacific, and lack of scouting vessels, it will not be possible for our naval forces to be sent beyond Hawaii in case of war with Japan. Yet we cannot succeed in such a war unless we are able to carry the war into Japanese waters and cut off her commerce. Does our policy with regard to the Philippines and the Far East warrant the Navy Department in devising plans to carry the war to the western Pacific?" In order to carry out policies like this, the letter concluded, the Navy, War and State Departments should form a Joint Plan Making Body. Close co-operation between these departments was necessary at all times, and "of supreme importance in the present condition of world affairs." While Roosevelt did not prepare this letter, he did sign it, and it undoubtedly gave him cause for reflection.[9]

In keeping with its doctrine, William V. Pratt, recently Assistant Chief of Naval Operations, and one of the keenest naval planners, wrote flatteringly from a battleship to the new "big boss," suggesting that he send a respectable fleet to the Mediterranean areas. "I realize that . . . in view of our stand on the Monroe Doctrine, we could hardly afford to be butters in so to speak, but isn't the time rapidly coming, when we will be almost forced to interest ourselves in Eastern European affairs?" Pratt inquired. "When that happens, as you know, one of the diplomat's strongest assets is the backing of a goodly number of men-of-war." [10]

Roosevelt displayed his readiness to accept suggestions of this nature when Rear Admiral W. B. Caperton suggested a similar squadron to promote trade and friendship in Latin America. "It has long been a pet hobby of mine that we ought to re-establish the old South American Squadron," Roosevelt commented. He recommended that the Navy follow the example of the British — who, according to rumor, were sending some of their best light cruisers. Perhaps, Roosevelt added, the United States should establish two squadrons, one in the Atlantic and another in the Pacific. The Chief of Naval Operations concurred, since he had "always been a strong supporter of the doctrine that the trade follows the flag," and put the Planning Committee to work on the proposals of Caperton and Roosevelt. Similarly, in the summer of 1919, when relations with Mexico were again strained and the possibility of new United States intervention arose, it was Roosevelt who sent plans for naval preparations to Secretary of State Robert Lansing, who showed them to President Wilson.[11]

The public saw none of this side of Roosevelt's work during his final eighteen months in the Navy Department, but it did hear much about him as a vigorous, efficient young administrator. In 1919, unlike the war years, no security restrictions hampered newspapermen from giving full publicity to many of his administrative activities, and this they did, especially during two long interludes in 1919 when Daniels was away and Roosevelt in his glory as Acting Secretary.[12]

Like a realistic parent admonishing his offspring to stay away from the cookie jar, Daniels made his departure. Naval demobilization was almost complete; aside from delicate negotiations with the new Republican Congress, there seemed few serious responsibilities to face the Acting Secretary, or pitfalls for him to avoid; but Daniels gave him instructions to cover almost any contingency that might arise. Roosevelt was to beware of accepting the recommendation of the Bureau of Supplies and Accounts to buy steel rails from Bethlehem Steel at a price which Daniels considered exorbitant. Above all, he must avoid being trapped by Congress. Most of the bureau chiefs would present Roosevelt with letters for him to sign and send to the new Republican Naval Affairs Committee chairmen. These he must not send, but hold in the traditional Daniels fashion: "It would be very well . . . for you to have a drawer and put them all in it so that we can make a study of them, and we will discuss them when I get back." Even after he had left, in March, 1919, Daniels sent a reminder from mid-Atlantic. "I wish you to know how glad I am that you so earnestly recommended my making the trip," he wrote Roosevelt. "I felt such confidence that all was going well in Washington that I have not tried to think about it and have succeeded very well." [13]

Acting Secretary Roosevelt reassured his chief: "Ever since you left, things have been so quiet here as to be almost terrifying. Literally nothing has happened outside of the routine work, which, however, has been positively voluminous, and all I can say is that I have the deepest sympathy for what happened to you when I was away on both of my trips to Europe."

However well Roosevelt functioned, there was little opportunity for startling innovation, which undoubtedly was why Daniels was willing to leave him in charge. One of the few differences between his actions and those of his chief was his quickness to accept resignations of underpaid officers who wished to take high-paid business positions. Daniels had released these men only grudgingly or not at all.[14]

The work load was indeed heavy, since not only was the Secretary gone, but also the Chief of Naval Operations and three of the bureau chiefs. By his own account, Roosevelt had to work fourteen hours a day; but he thrived on it, and just before Daniels returned boasted to a friend, "I have had a perfectly delightful two months, running things with a high hand and getting things done that were never done before." [15]

"You ought to see the change in the carrying on of the Department work," Roosevelt confided to another friend. "I see civilians at the old building from 9 A.M. to 10:30,* then I see the Press, and then dash down to the new building in a high-powered car, and from that time on — 11 A.M. — see no outsiders, Congressmen, Senators, or anybody else. The Department mail is signed at regular hours, and absolutely cleaned up every day, with the result that nothing is taken home, mislaid, lost, et cetera, et cetera!" [17]

Despite this incessant rush (or perhaps because of it), Roosevelt was as gay as ever. To his friend Herbert Bayard Swope of the New York *World* he wrote:

HIGHLY ESTEEMED STRANGER!

It is good to know that you have returned to the land where Democracy is still safe, and I trust that you have discarded your Paris accent, English clothes and Lisbon habits. I really want to look you over and see for myself whether you are still the same

* FDR once facetiously described what seeing a civilian might sometimes involve: "I shall be very glad to see Mr. Ripley L. Dana when he comes down here. I know nothing about the Squantum contract but will be glad to have him talk to me for five minutes. It would be just as agreeable to me if he were to use the Chinese language, as I am so thoroughly accustomed to looking pleasant and intelligent about matters I have never heard of before that I can do it just as well if the explanation is made in a tongue of which I know not one word. After all this is over, I will shoot the poor devil along to your much esteemed friend, Admiral Parks, who will probably then shoot him along to Admiral Capps, and where he goes from there, the Lord only knows and I don't care." [16]

good old Swope or have taken on the manners and customs of a Billy Bullitt.[18]

Mostly, Acting Secretary Roosevelt kept in the public eye in a pleasant sort of way. He stirred up widespread controversy (in all of which his name figured) by proposing that the United States emulate the British who had preserved Lord Nelson's flagship *Victory* in a permanent concrete berth. The Navy should similarly moor the *Constitution* and *Constellation* on the Potomac at Washington. Of course, this angered civic organizations in the ports where these vessels already were docked; but the flurry did Roosevelt more good than harm. His old love of parades and displays had not abated, and these were even better ways to maintain public interest in the Navy. He promised a "real naval parade" for New York City, and candidly explained, "I know the Navy needs recruits and I feel sure a parade such as the people of the city evidently want would have a wonderful effect in stimulating recruiting." In April, standing on the Ellipse by the White House, he reviewed the Yeoman (F) Battalion (as the women in the Navy were then designated); and in August, after winning a sharp controversy with the War Department, he arranged a parade of eight thousand Marines. As Acting Secretary, Roosevelt stood beside President Wilson and Secretary of War Newton D. Baker to review the troops as they marched past.[19]

As for the pitfalls Daniels had warned him against, Roosevelt seemed capable of avoiding them. He did function more vigorously than his chief, but he had no better luck, when he tried to beat down the price of steel. The companies submitted new bids almost identical to the old ones. Consequently, he invoked a wartime statute still in force, and commandeered 14,000 tons from the Carnegie Steel Company — for which the Navy would pay later, on the basis of prevalent market quotations. This was a drastic action to take in 1919, but Roosevelt felt it necessary in order to start building two new battleships before congressional authorization lapsed.[20]

In the realm of labor relations, Roosevelt was equally forceful in words, but less so in action. When a tugboat strike in New York Harbor threatened to cut off coal, and thus paralyze the public utilities of New York City, he first offered to get the coal through, then declined on the ground that it was the proper task of the Fuel and Railroad Administrations.[21]

The New York *Times* tartly criticized his timidity; undoubtedly it would have chastised him more vigorously had it known that one of five candidates for honorary degrees whom he informally recommended to Harvard University was Samuel Gompers, the President of the American Federation of Labor. Gompers, he wrote President Lowell, "has done more than any other to foster the whole-hearted efforts of Labor during the war and . . . has, in my judgment, displayed remarkable leadership and the highest kind of patriotism." But Lowell and the Harvard Corporation ignored this, as well as Roosevelt's other recommendations.[22]

At about the same time, Roosevelt inevitably incurred the wrath of many union men through cutting the working force in the navy yards. He told the employees that the Navy would have to drop 30 per cent of them by July in order to meet the demands of the Republican Congress, but the Republican New York *Tribune* claimed that he was "passing the buck" to cover up the fact that the yards were seriously overstaffed with "deserving" Democrats holding down sinecures.[23]

Clearly, Roosevelt would have difficulty in 1919, a year of strikes and labor unrest, in formulating some sort of position through which he could retain union support and yet mollify growing public sentiment against organized labor. First of all, both publicly and in his conduct of departmental affairs, he took an unassailable position against labor radicalism. An orderly solution to labor problems, he asserted, was "another way of hitting the Soviet method." He declared typically, in the summer of 1919, "We need a constructive program in labor matters. We wish to give labor a larger share of the profits, successes and improved conditions of the country, but we can't stand for any small group in a community holding up a community." He pointed out that "half a million men can tie up the whole country," and that "the vicious cycle keeps spiralling higher and higher until it collapses." Referring to the striking steel workers, who, according to a fact-finding committee, were suffering from deplorable conditions — most of them working sixty-nine hours a week — he said: "If conditions in the steel industry are not right they will be improved, but the improvement ought not to come by means of a strike." He put it more strongly in November after the government had acted quickly to block a coal strike led by John L. Lewis. Miners' pay had remained the same since September, 1917, while the cost of living had risen drastically. But Roosevelt said:

"The United States cannot afford to stop and sit back to wait until the next trouble . . . We must realize that the doctrine of the American people must come first, and while this trouble has been settled by resort to war statute, men and women employed at essentials vitally connected with the life of the nation must realize they enjoy a different status than those in private employment. The employees of railroads, in the mines, in public service corporations, must understand they owe a duty to the people and that they cannot of necessity be the same free agents as those working for private interests." *

He had a solution. He proposed establishing local and national labor courts of equity or arbitration, which would have power not only to investigate but also to act. This clearly indicated his paternalistic view of labor relations. He felt that frank and open conferences with labor leaders, of the sort in which he participated during his seven years in the Navy Department, would eliminate 99 per cent of the disputes. As for the remaining 1 per cent, these should come before local and national labor courts which would function on an equity basis. Had such courts been in operation, he posited, both the steel and coal strikes could have been avoided.[25]

Whatever labor leaders may have thought of these proposals, in the campaign of 1920 those connected with naval labor were vociferous in their endorsement of Roosevelt. Hence, through placing his emphasis upon public interest, Roosevelt, rhetorically at least, succeeded in squaring the circle. He maintained the enthusiastic support of both labor and capital.

The Acting Secretary also engaged in controversy much more to his liking, and injected himself into foreign policy questions, when he talked with reporters about a possible postwar naval construction policy for the United States. This, of course, was in quite a separate compartment in his thinking from his parallel discussions about the League of Nations. He hinted that he favored a super battle cruiser, of a type that would make all existing battleships obsolete — and ignored entirely, in his comments to the press, the profound reaction a ship of this sort would create in the British Admiralty. Quite contrary to his instructions from Daniels, he conferred with Senator Poindexter, who was expected to be the Republican Chairman of the Naval

---

* In the spring of 1920, FDR advocated drastic national action to end an outlaw railroad strike because, he said, the nation was impatient at having the wheels of industry threatened at the slightest provocation.[24]

Affairs Committee, to seek his endorsement of a new building program. Poindexter refused to commit himself, on the grounds that while he favored an adequate fleet he opposed a "paper navy" for the purpose of bluffing Europeans. This was aimed less at Roosevelt than at Daniels, who, it was rumored around Washington, favored continuing the building program in order to bargain more effectively at Paris for disarmament.[26]

As yet, no one in the Navy Department was talking seriously about the possibility that air power might make battleships obsolete, but Roosevelt did assert strongly that in the postwar era the United States must maintain its air power as well as its sea power. Control of the air he deemed essential — both for American commerce and for defense.

He received private warning from Paris that the British were projecting flights to Constantinople, India, and elsewhere, in order to pioneer global air routes through which to dominate the air as completely as they did the sea.* As an American answer, he strongly backed the flight of four naval NC planes eastward across the Atlantic in May and June, 1919. While the flying boats were being readied for the trip, he visited the naval air station at Rockaway Point, Long Island, and went up for a ten-minute flight in the NC–2, along with a group of officers that included his warm friend Lieutenant Commander Richard E. Byrd.[28]

After several of the seaplanes successfully reached England, Roosevelt explained at length the significance of this first American transatlantic flight. It was, first and last, entirely the work of naval aviation, he emphasized; and its purpose was to gather scientific information to be used in future Atlantic crossings. And, he took occasion to emphasize, naval aviation was "so very much an integral part of the navy, so entirely nautical in its application and functions and in the problems concerned," that the proposal to take it away from the Navy "borders

---

* FDR's feeling of rivalry toward the British did not carry over into his personal life. He was proud to introduce Admiral Jellicoe at a luncheon, although he was careful to give a double meaning to his remarks on Jellicoe's role in the Battle of Jutland. At a dinner for General Sir Robert Baden-Powell, he sat next to Lady Baden-Powell and talked enthusiastically about the Boy Scouts in the war. On Christmas, 1919, the Roosevelts entertained the new British Ambassador, Edward Grey, Viscount of Fallodon, who had been Foreign Minister during the war. The Roosevelts were, as earlier, friendly with a number of members of the British colony in Washington. On a lovely spring Sunday in 1920, when Mrs. Hamlin called at the embassy, she found FDR just starting a game of hockey with Sir Arthur Willert of the London *Times*.[27]

on the ridiculous." * Aviation could keep up with the rapid technical advance in the Navy only by being a vital branch of it. Similarly, the Army must have control over its air arm. For these reasons, Roosevelt, both in talking to reporters and in testifying before a congressional committee, strongly opposed the creation of a separate air force. Quest for "rank and emolument," and the "glorification of self-seekers," he hinted, might motivate the advocates of consolidation. While he did not mention General Billy Mitchell by name, he charged: "The height of ambition of some individuals is to be caught in the limelight of publicity . . . or to be known as the man who tore wide open existing governmental organizations."

There were also objections of another sort. Establishment of a separate air force, he warned, might serve as a blow to free enterprise if it involved taking the manufacture of airplanes away from private industries and concentrating control in a centralized governmental board. This would "at once paralyze the entire industry at its source." Roosevelt powerfully stated his faith in American industry:

"Competitive genius is the key to the manufacturing world; stifled by over-regulation, or confiscated by law, industry dies. Industry may be assisted by governmental benevolence when such industry is in its infancy, but when expanded to its full strength industry is the nation's backbone. Our industries have been the index of our development and our mainstay in peace and war. In Heaven's name, do not brain industry with the club of politics, especially the youthful and growing industry of aircraft manufacture. Let us give the manufacturers and experimentalists full scope. The bread of encouragement cast on the waters of industry will return a thousand-fold in the guise of progressive development and productive economy." 29

In his feeling that the United States should lead the world, Roosevelt was no more than following the direction of President Wilson's thought. Owen D. Young of General Electric Company recollected a decade later that in the spring of 1919, when General Electric was negotiating the sale of an important radio patent to the British Marconi Company, Admiral W. H. G. Bullard, the head of naval communications, told him that Wilson opposed the sale because he wished the

---

* FDR described the role of naval aviation as being "co-operation with the fleet . . . : bombing enemy's men-of-war and bases; protection of its own fleet from hostile craft; scouting, reporting movements of enemy over smoke screens, in low visibility, and over the horizon; detecting mine fields, torpedoes, and submarines; spot-shooting, and escort and convoy work."

United States to maintain an international communication system.[30]

Admiral Bullard himself strongly took this position, and in further conversations with Young and other General Electric executives, outlined a scheme "to retain in American hands the complete domination of radio communication in the United States, Central and South America" through establishment of a new American radio corporation. They wished the Navy to sell its wartime radio stations to this private company. Commercial broadcasting for entertainment purposes did not exist; radio was a means of transmitting messages comparable to telegraph and cable, and the Naval Radio Service controlled 85 per cent of the nation's facilities. If a corporation owned these, it would possess a near monopoly.[31]

Young and his associates quickly accepted Admiral Bullard's suggestion, and in response to a letter signed by Roosevelt, came to Washington to open negotiations for the purchase of naval holdings by a Radio Corporation of America. However, when Roosevelt discovered that the British Marconi interests would be influential if not dominant within the proposed company, he refused to sell. Instead, he cabled Daniels in Paris to inquire whether or not he should approve a tentative contract. The Secretary requested him to delay the matter until he returned. "Even before you got back," Roosevelt assured Daniels ten years later, "I had told Mr. Young definitely that the Navy Department could not even consider the sale of any of its war-acquired patents or stations to any company which was not wholly under American ownership." [32]

Daniels after his return decided to favor continued government operation rather than sale to a private monopoly, and Roosevelt agreed with him. But there was strong opposition even to allowing the Navy to carry commercial messages through its radio service; Congress, zealous to restore government facilities to private enterprise, paid no attention to a bill providing for continued Navy ownership. Consequently, the Navy Department reluctantly accepted a proposal to sell out to the totally American-controlled Radio Corporation of America, which had bought out the British interests.[33]

While Roosevelt was consistent in favoring American domination in both aviation and radio, he apparently advocated a government monopoly of radio communications at the very time that he opposed government control of aircraft manufacture. Secretary Daniels must have strongly shaped Roosevelt's thinking on radio, for through most of the Assistant Secretary's public statements on other matters there ran a thread of opposition to government ownership or control. When the powerful RCA came under sharp attack as a monopoly, a decade later, it was easy for Roosevelt to recollect how emphatically he had supported government ownership. But even had he fostered the sale of naval radio to the company, he would have had little to do with the creation of a private radio monopoly, since in practice that came largely through patent control.*

Private enterprise of a sort in which all Americans worked and participated seemed to Roosevelt the best possible answer to radicalism — and radicalism worried him greatly. He had a personal encounter with it which might well have made a confirmed Red-baiter out of a more timid or perturbable man. At 11:15 on the evening of June 2, 1919, he and Eleanor Roosevelt drove into his block on R Street just a moment after a bomb blasted the house of Attorney General Mitchell Palmer, directly across the street from their home. Had they arrived a minute earlier, they might both have been killed — for the force of the explosion shattered the front of the Palmer home, tore off doors, and smashed windows within a radius of a hundred yards. Roosevelt drove Mrs. Palmer and her daughter to safer lodgings for the night, then told reporters, "It was a terrible explosion. We saw nothing of the man who was planting the bomb. No wonder, as we now understand his body was blown to bits." [35]

A month later, serious rioting between Negroes and whites broke out in Washington and continued for several days. Police could not cope with the disorder, and finally the Army Reserve had to quell it. "The riots seem to be about over today," Roosevelt wrote on July 23. "Luckily the trouble hasn't spread to R Street and though I have

* Further indication of FDR's general feeling that the government should get out of competition with business and foster private enterprise were his proposals for use of government-owned merchant vessels:

> Early in 1919 I submitted to the President a memorandum in opposition to a continuation of the Shipping Board or E[mergency] F[leet] C[orporation]. I suggested, and with the concurrence of a number of naval officers, that the government should keep 10 or 12 of the best passenger vessels; turn them over to the Navy and operate them on trade routes not served by private American companies. In other words, my idea was to develop new routes and to withdraw the ships from any one of these routes as soon as any American company offered to provide the same service.
>
> The Navy could have put a nucleus regular U.S.N. crew on each ship, filled up the rest of the crew with candidates for the naval reserve and we would have turned out in this way 4,000 or 5,000 fairly well-trained officers and men for the Navy and Merchant Marine each year. The plan, of course, got nowhere, but I am sure it was fundamentally sound." [34]

troubled to keep out of harm's way I have heard occasional shots during the evening and night. It has been a nasty episode and I only wish *quicker* action had been taken to stop it." As much as possible he made a joke out of this nerve-racking episode. To a Harvard classmate in Little Rock, he wrote, "With your experience in handling Africans in Arkansas, I think you had better come up here and take charge of the Police Force." [36]

Outbursts of this sort were no laughing matter. Roosevelt told the Knights of Columbus:

"Today there is unrest in the whole world — more in other countries than here. And in this unrest is the element of trying to get something for nothing, of trying to rush law and order off its feet, of seeking to put into effect new doctrines without consultation, without thought, without consideration of the whole mass of the people. Every one of us would like to see a state of perfection on earth. . . . But we know too that every great reform takes time and good judgment, and that too great haste often defeats its own ends." [37]

The key to economic stability was easily within grasp, Roosevelt believed. It was the war-fostered habit of savings and investment, which he termed "the best insurance against future business depression which has ever been devised. . . . I do not think that any great people which has acquired this habit need ever fear a return of the old-fashioned panics which used to disgrace the United States. If every family owned even a $100 bond of the United States or a legitimate corporation there would be no talk of bolshevism, and we would incidentally solve all national problems in a more democratic way." [38]

At other times, he seemed to feel that assimilation and education of immigrants was a significant means of preventing radicalism. The so-called melting pots in the industrial centers of the Middle West were pots "which did not melt," he told a women's patriotic organization. "Most of the anarchists are people who have no education or have been educated along false lines." [39]

While Roosevelt thus firmly placed himself on the side of law and order, he displayed no disposition to bait Reds or harry Pinks. In private, he took to task the Commandant of the Boston Navy Yard for discharging several machinists on loyalty grounds. All four who had been investigated, Roosevelt felt after examining the records, had been disturbing elements, and might well be subject to discharge for efficiency reasons. But three of the number were no more than Socialists. "Now, my dear Admiral," Roosevelt wrote (at about the time both

Congress and the New York Legislature were expelling Socialists from their membership), "neither you nor I can fire a man because he happens to be a Socialist. It so happens that the Socialist Party has a place on the official ballot in nearly every State in the Union." As for the fourth man, "He was alleged to have actually circulated revolutionary literature in the shop, literature which advocated the Soviet form of government and which, therefore, constituted, in my judgment, an attack on our own form of government. This is a very different thing." [40]

When on September 11, 1919, Governor Calvin Coolidge of Massachusetts wired Acting Secretary Roosevelt, asking that the Navy hold itself ready in case he should ask President Wilson for Federal aid to break the Boston police strike, Roosevelt gave no more than a routine reply: "The navy will, of course, keep with the army in carrying out such orders as may be given by the President." This was in lukewarm contrast to President Wilson, who from Montana strongly commended Governor Coolidge's decision to deal harshly with the strikers. A Wall Street alumnus of Harvard exhorted Roosevelt, as an Overseer of the University, to fire one of the instructors who had compounded his incendiarism in advocating government ownership of railroads by condoning the Boston police "mutiny." The instructor was Harold Laski, whom President Lowell had rebuked but refused to dismiss. Roosevelt replied laconically that he would be glad to take the matter up at the next Overseers' meeting. What his position would be, he did not say. Whatever he may have recommended concerning Laski, few liberals could find fault with his mild stand against radicalism, for this was the era in which President Wilson himself sternly refused to liberate the Socialist leader, Eugene V. Debs, whose only crime had been opposition to the war.[41]

Few among either liberals or conservatives could fail to applaud Roosevelt's major postwar objective: to operate the government in a more sound, efficient, and businesslike way. Both a leading Republican, Henry L. Stimson, and Roosevelt's Democratic chief, Daniels, had a similar basic attitude. Roosevelt took advantage of frequent opportunities to develop facets of this theme. He especially did so when Congress in the fall of 1919 held hearings on a project which many members of both parties had sponsored for years — the establishment of a Bureau of the Budget. This bureau was to prepare an annual budget for the entire government, have the power to investigate or inspect within each department, and thus to eliminate the hit-or-miss system, as old as the government itself, by which each department separately requested appropriations from Congress.[42]

When Roosevelt appeared before the House Select Committee on the Budget, he not only heartily endorsed the proposal to create a national budget system, but strongly recommended a greater centralization of authority within the Navy Department. The bureau chiefs generally held themselves responsible for expenditures to Congress rather than to the Secretary of the Navy. For the sake of efficient management, Roosevelt suggested, the Secretary should have complete authority over the chiefs and their expenditures. As the Navy Bureau system existed, there was too much "dog-in-the-manger policy" and competitiveness among the bureaus; more centralized authority and delegation to the Secretary of the authority to transfer money from one bureau appropriation to another (with the consent of a congressional committee) would lead to a greater efficiency.

Representative John Nance Garner challenged Roosevelt and asked him whether, if a bureau chief were unsatisfactory, the Secretary could not remove him. Roosevelt granted this was true. "The difficulty is, though," he explained, "that when the average Secretary of the Navy and Assistant Secretary come into the office they are pretty new at the game, and are saddled with a system; they work along with that system for a while while they learn about it, and the chances are that during a short term of office they will not make any change." The Chairman commented that Roosevelt had put his finger on the difficulty, that the inexperience of the civilian Secretary caused him to rely on the bureau chiefs and made them more powerful than Congress had intended. Roosevelt pointed out that the British eliminated this difficulty through a system of permanent undersecretaries, paid as high as $15,000 or $20,000, who were highly qualified, nonpolitical experts, responsible for running the department. "I consider," he explained, "that while the general British business methods are inferior to the American, the business of the Government is on the whole a more efficient machine than in our Government."

Far from having a high-paid undersecretary system, the United States Navy Department, Roosevelt explained, could offer its top career civilian only three thousand dollars per year; the next highest six or eight positions paid twenty-four hundred. As a result, the Navy lost nine out of ten of its efficient civilian workers. At the same time, the Civil Service system functioned too much on a basis of seniority, with the result that high civilian positions became filled with dead timber. One of the Representatives pointed out the tendency to appoint men to non-Civil Service jobs as a reward for political services rendered, rather than because of their technical ability. Roosevelt agreed this often happened, but pointed out the way in which the Navy during the war had hired experts without reference to their politics; if it could continue to do so, "we would do mighty well." [43]

Before the Congressional Committee, Roosevelt prudently restrained his language, but in a series of public addresses he pungently derided the mismanagement in Washington. The government, he said, was the largest business in the country, and because of the archaic system under which it was functioning, the worst-managed: "Congress is running its business in such a way that if it was a private business it would be in the hands of a receiver in a week." It was "just about 100 years behind modern American conditions." [44]

With delightful candor, Roosevelt in an address before Harvard students in February, 1920, explained exactly what he meant. First he paid his respects to Congress. He recommended reading the *Congressional Record* as one would a comic magazine, since "There is more humor in . . . [it] every morning than there is to be found in any other comic paper in this country . . . and next to . . . [it], the hearings form the greatest source of amusement that we have in Washington. Congressional hearings meet and talk and talk endlessly, and then adjourn to allow the stenographers to catch up with the records." After the lengthy hearings on the proposed budget system, he pointed out, "The result was a compromise in the bill which has practically wiped out its value." A number of separate committees would still consider appropriations. What this could mean to the Navy Department was exemplified the previous year when the Naval Affairs committee "because of the superior knowledge of civilian congressmen over naval officers, decided that the appropriation for the Bureau of Steam Engineering, which handles the insides of ships, should be materially cut down, at the same time allowing the appropriation for the Bureau of Construction, which handles the hulls of ships, to remain the same. The result was that in the case of numerous ships the hulls were ready, but there was no money left to make the machines turn over." As for the legislative process as a whole: "They have a privilege called Prerogative, and that is the right to talk us to sleep. . . . Today proceedings drag along. . . .

Today every move that is made by both sides is a move touched in some way with the question of party or political advantage. It would be a perfectly simple thing if they could forget prerogative, precedent, parliamentary law and Magna Charta, to put into effect — any businessman could do it — a system by which the legislative branch of the government would move along American lines."

The executive departments were equally open to criticism. As an example of overlapping functions, he described how four different departments had jurisdiction over various species of bears in Alaska, and how four different navies were being operated outside the jurisdiction of the Navy Department: two in the Commerce Department, one in the War Department, and one in the Treasury Department.* Consolidation of these as a unit and use of the same repair facilities would save millions of dollars a year. Throughout the executive branch of the government, there must be "re-organization and re-apportionment of work . . . along lines of simple business sense." In addition, salaries should be raised sufficiently to attract capable men who would run the government more effectively. If he were given a free hand in the Navy Department, Roosevelt asserted, he would increase the pay of employees five million dollars, and thus "through increased efficiency I would save the government at least fifteen million dollars, making a net saving of ten million." By this he meant in part that fewer numbers of competent men could achieve more than larger numbers of incompetents. On another occasion he said, "I am employing in the navy department, and am compelled to do so by law, 2,000 people out of about 10,000, who ought to be either in the hospital or in the grave."

On one occasion, Roosevelt later recalled: "The Acting Secretary of the Navy was solemnly summoned before the [Appropriations] Committee of learned Representatives — he was asked with scowls and frowns why, in his estimate, he had dared to ask for an additional second class clerk at $1600 a year and an additional messenger boy at $900 a year. He said that the work of the office had expanded and that he really needed them. The scowls and frowns continued, and in this way an hour or two was taken up going into each and every Bureau of his Department. He knew full well that the Appro-

---

* In September, 1919, FDR had reluctantly complied with an executive order turning the Coast Guard back to the Treasury Department, and engaged in a caustic exchange of correspondence with Secretary of the Treasury Carter Glass. The Coast Guard had been under the Navy Department during the war, and Roosevelt and Daniels both wished to keep it there.[45]

priations Committee had decided beforehand to allow no increases at all in his Department, but the solemn farce continued. Towards the end of the cross-examination he was asked whether there was not some way in which he could cut down the number of employees in his Department. His answer caused somewhat of a commotion at the time, for the simple fact that it was extensively reprinted throughout the country." The answer was Roosevelt's formula: to promote only for merit, pay higher salaries, to establish pensions and, by weeding out the parasites, to cut the working force by one third. "Continued employment by the government is not a constitutional right," he declared. "It should depend in Washington, as in properly conducted private concerns, on the worth of the individual."

What this would mean for all departments, Roosevelt suggested to a group of businessmen: "Any man with common sense could save 10 per cent of our government expenses, and based on even the old figures this would mean an annual savings of one hundred million dollars. You are paying for it in taxes and you will continue to do so until you put your government on a business basis." [46]

In discussing these matters forthrightly and even emphatically in 1919, Roosevelt generally seemed above politics; and yet the very earnestness of his appeal — as the businesslike young administrator, ready to place statesmanship above partisanship — was in itself excellent politics. Large numbers of self-styled "progressives," not confirmed members of either major party, were ready to accept a program like Roosevelt's as being "progressive," or in other words, what they wanted for postwar America. The program of the Wilson Administration was almost of the past; that of Roosevelt was of the future.

CHAPTER III

A Search for Scapegoats

> Frankly, I must decline to be made in any way the scape-
> goat for things which had their inception among the
> regular navy officers concerned.
> — FDR TO JOSEPHUS DANIELS, *March 1, 1921*.[1]

NOT everything went smoothly for Roosevelt after the war. He suffered occasionally from the defects of his very virtues: his quickness to accept new schemes, willingness to do favors for friends, and zest for achieving big things in a small amount of time. As always, he leaped before he looked. Ordinarily, he landed on his feet with amazing regularity; but several times, during his last months in the Navy Department, he did not fare quite so well.

In one of these precarious leaps, involving an oil deal, Roosevelt was lucky enough to land without a public scandal. The end, cheap oil for the Navy, was, for a man of his political aspirations, by no means worth the serious and needless risks he took in the spring of 1920. While he was, as Daniels remarked again and again, "as clean as a hound's tooth," this sort of enterprise almost inevitably led to stories casting doubts on his honesty. Years later, a retired Admiral wrote that it was "what we in the department considered at the time to be a 'crooked' deal." [2]

The world-wide shortage of oil in the years following the war was growing increasingly acute. While domestic production increased 78 per cent, consumption went up 104 per cent. Standard Oil and a group of large independents, which altogether controlled about 84 per cent of the refined oil, took advantage of the seller's market to send prices soaring. The price of oil to the Navy at Boston increased from $1.80 per barrel in the 1917 fiscal year to $3.40 in 1921. Even at this high price, the Navy could not get as much oil as it wished; most oil companies refused even to bid on Navy contracts, although the Navy promised that the United States Shipping Board would provide them with tankers on a priority basis. Roosevelt explained later, "We were politely told by the great oil interests, which were making fabulous profits in selling commercial oil to mills and private establishments generally, that they could not renew contracts except at figures which were prohibitive. We advertised for bids not once but three times. The best we could get was the promise from the great oil combinations of a little — a very little — not 10 per cent of our total needs, at a price of over $4.00 per barrel." [3]

Since the Navy had largely shifted from coal to oil, this impasse, Daniels testified, was so serious that it "made almost all of us turn gray." The Secretary used his war power to commandeer oil at 75 per cent of the market price; the oil companies could apply to the courts for whatever additional sum might be adjudged fair. This technique was unsatisfactory enough, but Roosevelt's substitute proposal was much worse. He recommended to Daniels on April 3, 1920, that the Navy advance from its oil funds a sum of three and a half million dollars to a group of promoters who held contracts for the purchase of cheap Mexican crude oil. With the sum advanced, plus other money they would obtain from sale of stock, the promoters would erect a refinery at Fall River, Massachusetts. Transportation was tight; that was one of the ways in which Standard Oil and the other companies maintained monopoly prices although they controlled only 60 per cent of the crude oil production. The Navy would have to break that bottleneck for the new company by providing tankers either directly or through assignment from the Shipping Board. Then, when the refinery was in production, it would repay the loan in fuel oil at $3.25 per barrel, for a total saving to the Navy, estimated on the basis of prices at the time of the contract, of $1,610,337.84. [4]

Behind Roosevelt in presenting the proposal was Louis Howe — Fall River was Mrs. Howe's home town — and behind them both was a group of respectable New England businessmen. Some of these were old friends of Roosevelt's.* But the key figure was Arthur P. Homer, that affable promoter who had been active on behalf of small patrol boats (and Sterling Motors) in 1916 and 1917. Homer had since participated in various other projects. Although he shifted from one scheme to another, he remained on such cordial terms with Roosevelt that in February, 1920, he used Roosevelt as a reference in applying for a position with the great J. P. Morgan. Among other things, Homer was speculating in oil. He formed the Washington Oil Syndi-

* FDR tried unsuccessfully to get them to give the contract for construction of the refinery to another friend of his, Elliott Brown.

cate in the fall of 1919 to purchase properties in Oklahoma, and persuaded Roosevelt to invest five thousand dollars in it.[5]

By the beginning of 1920, Homer saw possibilities for making huge profits out of the difference between the cost of crude oil in Mexico and the selling price of refined oil in the United States.* He interested Roosevelt, who in turn tried to induce the Morgenthaus to participate in the venture. They declined because tankers were impossible to get, the supply of Mexican oil was decreasing rapidly, and the cost of building a refinery on the Mexican coast, as Homer planned, would be between one and two million dollars. Next Homer persuaded Roosevelt to take the scheme to the Navy in a form which circumvented two of the Morgenthaus' objections. The Navy was to obtain the tankers for transportation, and to provide the capital to build a refinery in the United States.[6]

At first the proposal made little headway in the Navy Department. Admiral Robert S. Griffin, the Chief of the Bureau of Steam Engineering, warned Daniels against it; others alleged that Homer would make $250,000 out of the deal. Some persons even hinted that Assistant Secretary Roosevelt also had some financial interest in it. There is no evidence that he ever had any investment in Homer's new company; documents indicate that in 1920 he sold his interest in the Washington Oil Syndicate, which Homer merged into the New England Oil Corporation.† On April 10, Roosevelt again urged Daniels to accept the deal, on the grounds that it would provide the Navy with oil a third cheaper than any other plan. The Secretary postponed a decision in order "to secure guarantees & look further into it," then five days later rejected the contract because it would require the Navy to furnish tankers to bring the oil out of Mexico. Roosevelt remained persistent, sold Admiral Griffin and several others on the scheme, and brought it up before Daniels for a third time. Although the Secretary still felt the Navy should commandeer oil instead, he capitulated. "I hae me doots," he wrote in his diary, "but Griffin & all others

---

* One of the component companies made a contract for oil from the Panuco area of Mexico at 12½ cents per barrel.

† FDR wrote "Sold 1920" on the corner of the receipt for five thousand dollars invested in the Washington Oil Syndicate. A very careful search by the staff of the Roosevelt Library of all the pertinent Roosevelt papers there has failed to turn up any evidence that Roosevelt ever had any financial interest in the New England Oil Corporation.

agreed and I assented [,] voting against it, but saying I have only one vote." [7]

In this way, the New England Oil Corporation came into existence. That fall, Roosevelt proudly told an audience at New Bedford how the oil monopoly had tried to hold up the Navy, and had been thwarted. The Navy, he said, had worked out a process for refining the heavy Mexican crude, and had searched until it found "a company not connected with the big interests, with skill and energy enough to accept our plan and to furnish us with refined Mexican oil. Our plan was put up to every plant of this kind. . . . We finally found one." As a result —

New England has an independent refinery which, when entirely completed, will represent Ten Millions of dollars of investment, and your mills right here in New Bedford are going to get no inconsiderable amount of oil for your furnaces — coal shortage or no coal shortage. Every tax-payer in the United States gained by the saving the Navy made in buying oil this way. . . .

Now that is what the Government has done right here to help you — I think I might almost say what I have done to help you, because this whole matter came under me as Assistant Secretary of the Navy. [8]

Roosevelt spoke too soon, for the short sad history of the New England Oil Corporation was marked by delays and difficulties of all sorts, and by an additional factor which no one seems to have expected: a drastic fall in the price of oil. As a result, when the Navy finally did get this oil, it was not cheaper, but substantially more expensive. The transactions, however, were all absolutely honest.[9]

A combination of administrative zeal and desire to help out friends contributed to this first episode; ambition led to the next. Since childhood, Roosevelt had loved naval heroes; in addition, politics led him to identify himself with Admiral Sims, even when Sims began to display himself as a quite sour, disgruntled hero ready to open a heavy barrage of criticism against the Secretary. Roosevelt had always made himself popular with the enemies of Daniels. He sympathized with Sims in his irritation at the Secretary's refusal to let naval personnel accept foreign decorations. Later, when Sims complained to Roosevelt against the embarrassing brevity of the Navy's own list of awards, then publicly aired his acute dissatisfaction, Roosevelt wrote Mrs. Sims,

"Strictly between ourselves, I should like to shake the Admiral warmly by the hand." [10]

Soon Sims broadened his onslaught into a general charge of inefficiency. He addressed a letter to the Secretary on "certain naval lessons of the Great War," which he wove around an eleven-point indictment of the Navy Department. Since it was the beginning of 1920, an election year, Republicans in the Senate seized with delight upon Sims's letter as the outline for a thoroughgoing investigation. Obviously, charges of maladministration were likely to encompass the Assistant Secretary as well as the Secretary. At this point Roosevelt quickly changed his mind about Sims, expressed his irritation to friends, and counseled Daniels to defend himself aggressively before the Senate Naval Affairs Committee.* Labeling the investigation as "scandalous," he commented, "It does seem a pity, does it not, that really fine, interesting men seem so often to lose their heads completely. The net result of all this will be, of course, to hurt the Navy, including Sims, Benson, Wilson, etc., etc. The hurting of a Secretary or an Assistant Secretary, who, after all, are but birds of passage, is very incidental and very unimportant, but the Navy has gone on for nearly 150 years, and, we hope, will always go on; therefore its reputation is of importance." [11]

This altruistic viewpoint notwithstanding, Roosevelt did lose his own head, apparently from fear that the investigation would ruin his reputation along with that of the Secretary. At this critical point he made a speech in which he corroborated the charge of Sims that the Navy was by no means ready for war in 1917, and made public how much more militant he had been at that time than either Secretary Daniels or President Wilson. [12]

This of course was an unfortunate gesture, which Daniels, and probably even Wilson, resented; Roosevelt had to issue a press statement to explain it away. [13] More than that, it was foolish, for his fortunes were linked, for better or worse, with the Wilson Administration. Almost immediately Roosevelt, too, came under fire, and became the object of charges which, if proved, would have been ruinous. Whether or not

---

* Daniels was especially upset because Sims in his letter attributed an anti-British statement to someone in the Navy Department. Daniels wrote in his diary, January 18, 1920, "FDR came to see me and said he and Frank Polk thought I ought not to wait till called before the committee to say that the Department & I had made no such statement. . . . So I sent for Coontz & Taylor and wrote letter to Senator Page. Showed it to FDR who approved. So did Tumulty. It was sent to all the papers. Letter explains everything."

Roosevelt knew it, Admiral Sims felt contempt for him as well as for Daniels, and abetted the attack.*

Before the naval investigation hearings were over, several Republican Senators went so far as to accuse Roosevelt of undermining the morals of sailors!

Nothing could have been further from Roosevelt's objectives, for the whole unfortunate, complicated mess grew out of the joint desire of Daniels and Roosevelt to make the Navy a clean, wholesome institution which would build the character of recruits. Roosevelt both in word and action had emphasized this theme. Soon after he came to Washington in 1913, he sharply denounced a judge who had supposedly sentenced a criminal to a term in the Navy. He was anxious to do all he could to destroy this old concept of the Navy as a dumping ground for the dregs of both the United States and Europe, and in its place sell the Navy as a most sound and valuable training school for those who did not go on to universities. He even took his case to the mothers in the June, 1917, *Ladies' Home Journal*, in an article on "What the Navy Can Do for Your Boy." When demobilization in 1919 left the Navy far below its authorized strength, Roosevelt renewed his exhortations. He sent recruiting officers to address high school graduating classes in order to point out the many opportunities which the Navy offered for those who could not go on to college.[15]

Moved by the same desire to make the Navy attractive to young men of high caliber, Secretary Daniels in 1917 had determined to reorganize the Naval Prison at Portsmouth, to make it an agency of rehabilitation rather than punishment. Further, in 1919, Assistant Secretary Roosevelt had tried to clean up deplorable moral conditions existing among naval trainees at Newport. These two separate, apparently unrelated, reforms exploded into a single scandal in 1920.

* In time, FDR became quite scornful of Sims. He wrote Daniels in 1922 that he was thinking of commissioning a British painter to make him another copy of "Rodman's Squadron at the Surrender of the German Fleet." His only objection to it would be "the presence of Sims standing alongside of Rodman on the quarterdeck." Sims, he granted, had done "a mighty good job" as principal naval representative in London, "without the authority over Operations or policies which Pershing had in the Army," but FDR disliked the movement then under way to make him a full Admiral. "When I think that during my two months abroad I saw more sea-service with the American Navy than Sims did in two years, it makes me anxious to apply to Congress for a life appointment as a Lord High Admiral or at least something one grade better than what Sims is seeking. If Sims is made an Admiral what rank are they going to give to the Rear Admirals who actually commanded ships?"[14]

Daniels was horrified when he visited the Portsmouth Naval Prison before the war to find it had more Marine guards than prisoners, and had as its aim to punish, not to rehabilitate. "They would break a man instead of making him," Daniels once reminisced. One of Roosevelt's stories at the time incidentally illustrated the prevailing system: A young officer giving a grammar lesson to some enlisted men asked, "What are the two principal parts of a sentence?" A sailor replied, "Bread and water and solitary confinement." Yet most of the prisoners were disciplinary rather than criminal offenders; 65 per cent were deserters, serving out three-year terms — a number had done nothing more serious than to overstay their leaves with girl friends. Daniels immediately ordered their sentences reduced drastically, and decided upon a thoroughgoing reform of the system. The man to do this, he felt, was Roosevelt's friend and political ally, Thomas Mott Osborne, who had made remarkable achievements (and stirred up a furor) as warden of Sing Sing Penitentiary. Daniels found Roosevelt enthusiastic, so he commissioned Osborne a Lieutenant Commander in the Naval Reserve to take charge of the prison.[16]

Osborne became commandant in the summer of 1917, just when the enormous expansion of the Navy was about to bring a huge influx of new prisoners. When he arrived, he found 170 prisoners and 160 Marine guards. He immediately sent most of the guards elsewhere, dispensed with walls, established a self-governing association among the prisoners, and even encouraged theatricals. On the whole, his system worked remarkably well, although a few prisoners did take advantage of him. During his three years at Portsmouth, about six thousand men passed through the prison, and only eight escaped. Osborne's objective, as he expressed it to Daniels before taking command, was to make a fundamental change at Portsmouth. "It has been a scrap heap; you wish me to make it one of humanity's repair shops." [17]

Consequently, when prisoners completed their sentences, he wanted to return them to the Fleet rather than give them dishonorable discharges from the Navy. Many naval officers objected sharply, because they were afraid that in the close living conditions at sea, the ex-convicts would contaminate the other enlisted men. Nevertheless, Osborne appealed to Daniels and Roosevelt, who backed him up. Of the six thousand prisoners, he returned approximately four thousand to active service. But Daniels remembered that his own customary support of the Commandant led some officers to sneer, "Go to see Daniels about Osborne — he'll give him the place." Unfortunately, Osborne took too great advantage of this; he quarreled vigorously with any officers who stood in his way, and habitually took his complaints, both big and small, directly to the top. Daniels was proud that "Osborne changed that prison from a hard place into a human place — one of the brightest spots of the Navy's administration," but he and Roosevelt had to reap the animosities that Osborne stirred up.[18]

The most important consequence of these reforms to Roosevelt was a bitter quarrel between Roosevelt and one of the most brilliant of the younger officers, Captain Joseph K. Taussig, Director of Enlisted Personnel.* Taussig felt that Osborne's methods were making serious inroads into the discipline of the enlisted men. He was upset over accounts of "the most outrageous things" taking place at Portsmouth, and complaints "from the Commanders afloat that the discipline of the service was being undermined owing to the return to the service of men convicted of criminal acts who boasted about the splendid time they enjoyed in confinement. Also, prisoners were writing to men in the Fleet that life was much pleasanter at Portsmouth than on board ship."

Taussig felt so strongly that these conditions were harmful that, when he could not change them, he asked to be relieved of his supervision of enlisted men, and be sent to the Naval War College at Newport, where Admiral Sims was President. Shortly after his arrival there, he read an article in the *Army and Navy Journal* which asserted that younger officers, especially destroyer commanders, approved of the Navy's policy of restoring Portsmouth graduates to active duty. Taussig indignantly retorted to the *Journal* that, as a former destroyer commander and subsequently as officer in charge of enlisted personnel, he knew this was not so. He did not know that he was replying to the Assistant Secretary of the Navy.[20]

The service magazine printed Taussig's letter, and added the comment that it was in answer to Roosevelt. The Assistant Secretary in turn became angry, and sent a strong refutation in which he singled out Taussig's assertion that among the ex-convicts back with the Fleet were some convicted of homosexuality. Roosevelt claimed that Osborne had restored to service only two such men, and there were special circumstances in both cases. He granted that men guilty of

---

* Taussig commanded the first division of destroyers sent to Queenstown in 1917. When he arrived after nine days of buffeting in a storm, Admiral Bayly asked when they would be ready to go to sea. Taussig replied, "We are ready now, sir; that is, as soon as we finish refueling." [19]

moral offenses, whether reformed or not, were not wanted in the Navy. "There can be no two opinions on that score," he commented. "There is, however, one broad question about which two opinions can legitimately be held: Should men guilty of purely military offenses be given a dishonorable discharge and sent back to civil life, or should they be given an opportunity to 'come back' and make good in the Navy?" As for Taussig, his charges could "only be of harm to the service in that they give a wrong impression of actual facts." Roosevelt concluded with the hope that Taussig had, "merely through lack of knowledge, made a false statement." [21]

Publication of this letter caused Taussig, an ambitious officer, to feel that his career was being placed in jeopardy. In an effort to clear his name, he sent an official letter to the Secretary of the Navy, requesting a Court of Inquiry to redress his wrongs. Roosevelt's letter, he asserted, "questions my veracity, impugns my motives, and tends to publicly discredit me." As for the return of morals offenders to the service, he claimed that the number was nearer to a hundred than two, and that on one occasion — on or about April 12, 1919 — Roosevelt as Acting Secretary signed an order restoring ten to service. [22]

Roosevelt in turn feared his own future was endangered. With his usual faith in his ability to reconcile differences on a person-to-person basis, he decided to send for Taussig before taking action on a Court of Inquiry. Daniels gave no advice, except to tell Roosevelt he doubted the wisdom of conferring with Taussig. As Daniels had expected, the conference accomplished nothing. After Roosevelt and Taussig talked for two hours, at the close of their conversation, when Taussig was in a hurry to catch a train, Roosevelt dictated a joint statement that he intended should settle the matter. Taussig, who insisted it should contain a declaration that he had not made a false statement or given a false impression, left before the smooth copy was ready, and when it appeared in the *Army and Navy Journal*, he was by no means ready to accept any part of it. A few days later, Roosevelt wrote him pleasantly about some changes at Portsmouth, and expressed the hope that they could talk again about getting the prison operation on a permanent basis. "By the way," Roosevelt added, "Major Leonard has just come in from the Jag's [Judge Advocate General's] office and wants to know what had better be done about your formal request for a Court of Inquiry. He suggested that it be either withdrawn by you, or that it be pro forma refused by the Secretary on the ground that the matter was one of misunderstanding and has been satisfactorily ended.

Will you let me know which you think is the best thing to do?" [23]

Taussig declined the choice offered him, and replied firmly that he considered the public statement Roosevelt's, not his. "The truth of the matter . . ." — Taussig wrote — "which fact was more impressed on me during our conversation, is that you apparently do not understand my attitude in this matter, and that it was impracticable, under the conditions, for you to make a statement that would have been satisfactory to me." Taussig stood on his request for a Court of Inquiry. Roosevelt kept this official letter in his personal file and never gave him an answer.[24]

Altogether, Roosevelt disposed of the matter rather easily. He also had little trouble refuting the charges of lax management at Portsmouth that had grown out of a Department of Justice investigation. Secretary Daniels appointed his own board to investigate general conditions at the prison. Its three members were Rear Admiral A. S. Halstead, Commandant of the Portsmouth Navy Yard, Rear Admiral Herbert O. Dunn, Commandant of the First Naval District — and, as senior member, Roosevelt himself. Roosevelt wrote Admiral Dunn, with whom he was on cordial terms,* "I feel certain that we can work out that Portsmouth Prison trouble if we of the service can only get together on these things and not air our dirty linen in public." On January 14, 1920, they inspected the prison and discussed the allegations with Osborne. A man had absconded with 9449 dollars of prisoners' money, and several other unfortunate episodes had occurred. Nevertheless, the board gathered considerable evidence indicating that most of the charges originated with a lying ex-convict, that they were untrue, and that the prison was operating smoothly and efficiently. Roosevelt immediately upon his return to Washington told newspapermen, "Well, there isn't very much to it." The official report of the board was in agreement with this, and even mildly favorable to some organizational changes Osborne wished to make.[25]

Surprisingly, Osborne, not content with his vindication, resigned in a huff because Daniels would not follow his recommendations to the last detail. A retired commodore continued his general policies until Daniels left the Navy Department in 1921, but the new Administration

---

* Admiral Dunn not only sat on this board of investigation, but headed the Court of Inquiry which checked into a scandal at Newport in which FDR was interested. In July, 1918, FDR had spent several pleasant days in the Azores with Admiral Dunn. In January, 1920, Dunn was interested in securing an appointment to the Naval Academy for a nephew of his wife's. Roosevelt obligingly wrote Henry D. Flood of Virginia, and obtained the appointment.

then restored Marine control, increased the guards from a half dozen to 160, and announced, "We'll have a prison here instead of a boardinghouse." Undoubtedly there had been some truth in the contention of many officers that life had been more pleasant in Osborne's prison than aboard naval vessels, particularly when the latter involved sea duty on the North Atlantic in the winter. That was no longer true in the Harding Administration.[26]

Roosevelt did not extricate himself so easily from the strangely interwoven Newport difficulties, which came to a head at about the same time. During the war he had assisted Daniels in a vigorous effort to clean up vice around the training camps. As early as June, 1917, Roosevelt announced that the Navy was secretly investigating unwholesome conditions at Newport, one of the most troublesome of these areas. In spite of this investigation, two years later conditions were still very bad.[27]

At this point, in the spring of 1919, Roosevelt as Acting Secretary established a naval squad to gather evidence in order to clean up vice — which he later claimed had been described to him only broadly as including bootlegging, drugs, and immorality. He had known nothing, he said, of the methods to be used to gather evidence. The squad was known as "Section A — Office of Assistant Secretary," but subsequently Roosevelt declared that this title was no more than an administrative device, which the Chief of the Bureau of Navigation recommended and the Judge Advocate General approved — "that their actual work was at no time under the supervision of the Assistant Secretary, but was solely a personnel matter." Several naval officers later disputed this. Roosevelt insisted emphatically afterwards that the responsibility rested with the Bureau of Navigation and other officers, who were trying to make him a scapegoat by claiming that it had been his. The shocking fact was that the investigators, while acting as decoys to trap perverts, had several times engaged in sodomy. When the Acting Secretary learned this early in September, he instantly ordered the squad to stop work. Subsequently, a Court of Inquiry began investigation.[28]

This, unfortunately, was only the beginning. It developed into a public scandal; and, early in December, 1919, following customary procedure, Admiral Sims sent word to Roosevelt, by way of Mrs. Sims and Mrs. Roosevelt, that a high-ranking officer in Washington was placing the responsibility upon Roosevelt. Through the month of January, John R. Rathom, a vigorous newspaperman friendly to Sims, aired the matter in the Providence *Journal*. At first his attack was only upon "Navy officials" in general; later he focused his attention upon Roosevelt. Two factors led to this: about this time, at the suggestion of Sims, Captain Taussig took his quarrel with Roosevelt to Rathom; also, Roosevelt drew Rathom's fire by leading in a warm rebuttal of his general charges. Rathom protested to Roosevelt against the "unwarranted and amazing attack on the Providence *Journal* and myself"; Roosevelt retorted that, since Rathom was well aware that the Navy Department was establishing a competent Court of Inquiry, his charges were "disingenuous and dishonorable" and "morally dishonest." [29]

Rathom vigorously counterattacked in kind by mailing to newspapers throughout the country copies of an article from the *Journal* entitled "Vicious Practices in U.S. Navy Denounced by Clergy of Newport." Roosevelt protested not only to editors who published articles of this sort, but sent one of the reprints to the Senate Naval Affairs Committee with the request that it investigate, and if at all possible stop the Providence *Journal* from disseminating them. The effect of Rathom's reprints, he feared, would be that "Any mother reading the headlines . . . would very properly hesitate before allowing her son to enlist in the Naval Service. In fact, it is believed that any average citizen reading this article must be led to believe that the Navy as a whole is a pretty rotten institution, and that it is not a proper place, either on its ships or in its training camps, for young Americans to be." [30]

As for the accusation that "Navy officials . . . [used] highly objectionable methods in collecting evidence," Roosevelt asserted to the editor of the Boston *Herald*, "If that is true I will not only apologize to you, but take great pleasure in resigning my present office." None of this had any effect in stopping a torrent of articles denouncing Roosevelt with which Rathom flooded the Providence *Journal*. These Rathom circulated in pamphlet form during the campaign of 1920. [31]

The Naval Court of Inquiry made Roosevelt an interested party to its proceedings, and he testified before it; but for the time being the Senate Naval Affairs Committee did not conduct the investigation which Roosevelt had requested. It was quite occupied in the spring of 1920 with the over-all inquiry into naval conduct of the war which Admiral Sims's letter of January had inspired. [32]

The Senate hearings began in March and ran into June. During the weeks that Sims and his cohorts attacked, and Daniels and officers loyal to him counterattacked, an interesting change took place in Roosevelt. He showed no disposition to go back into his files and dig out the tart memoranda against Daniels he had placed there in the months before and after the declaration of war in 1917. Quite the contrary, he was ready to defend publicly and emphatically the role of the Navy in the war. He declared, at a Democratic dinner toward the end of March, that he did not wish to claim that the party had won the war, for that was the achievement of all the American people. "But I will say," he added, "that in spite of ninety-seven investigations, costing more than $2,000,000, they still have to unearth an embalmed beef or paper shoe scandal," such as those that plagued earlier Republican administrations.[33]

A little later, Roosevelt made direct answer to the Sims-inspired investigation. He declared that the Navy was a pretty fair organization despite the Admiral's charges, and "it will receive due credit from the Nation when history is written — not what we call 'three-to-two history' in Washington, written by three Republican and two Democratic Senators."

Senator Frederick Hale, the Republican Chairman of the Senate Investigating Committee, had planned to ask Roosevelt to appear, but, to Daniels's pleasure, Roosevelt sent word that if he testified, Hale would regret it, and again referred to the "three-to-two" history. The committee did not call him; since it could have asked him quite embarrassing questions about his earlier attitude toward the Secretary, he was quite correct in considering himself "somewhat lucky." Instead the investigators asked him, along with several others, to submit his proposals for a reorganization of the Navy Department.[34]

As Roosevelt mulled over a possible reply, he confided to an intimate, "I think I shall drop a bomb into the committee by saying that nobody in the Navy, either Washington or London, was in any way to blame for anything at any time, but that the whole blame for anything and everything that went wrong rests squarely on the shoulders of the Senate and House of Representatives. I think this would make a hit besides being largely true." [35] He softened this somewhat in his letter to Hale. "Frankly," he wrote, "what is the most serious trouble with the Navy now, as it has been in the past, is Congress." He went on with his familiar views that the existing system of making legislation and appropriations was both archaic and unbusinesslike. A Navy appropriation bill too often became a local "pork barrel" issue. As a result,

"The Navy has always had to lead a hand-to-mouth existence, interspersed with investigations, hastily gotten up plans, make-shift policies, and a general spirit of time-serving to meet the political conditions of the hour."

As for the organization of the Navy Department, Roosevelt said that the establishment of the office of Chief of Naval Operations had been a step in the right direction toward centralization of controls. He reiterated his belief in the principle of establishing direct lines of responsibility — but this should center in civilian control under the Secretary of the Navy.* He not only scoffed at the possibility of putting an admiral in charge of the department, but paid his explicit respects to Sims and Taussig at the War College in Newport, by criticizing "the present tendency to build up a 'holier-than-thou' small organization or aggregation of officers at Newport," when there was an "imperative need of tying the War College into more close touch with the actual life of the Navy." [36]

Roosevelt's deliberate attack attracted considerable newspaper notice, and served even more effectively to separate him in the popular mind from the admirals, who, because reaction from the war was already setting in, were rapidly losing their prestige. Always a sensitive barometer of public opinion trends, he may well have intended this separation. Probably he hoped the "holier-than-thou" thrust would incite a reply. In any event, one shortly came forth, more to Roosevelt's political profit than loss. Rear Admiral Benton C. Decker, Commandant of the Seventh Naval District, denounced Roosevelt to the *Army and Navy Journal* in a letter widely reprinted: "These may be the same officers who were scornfully referred to as 'gold laced gentlemen' when on a previous occasion Mr. Roosevelt sought to ingratiate himself with the workingmen, and the same to whom his confidential secretary writes letters, giving instructions that they dare not give in public with regard to the laboring men. But they are not scorned as 'gold laced gentlemen' when he meets them in rich clubs of New York and Washington." [37]

In effect, Roosevelt, forced to choose between Daniels and Sims, had chosen Daniels. He may have done so because he had to share the imaginary lion's den which newspaper cartoonists created for Daniels, or because in his own days of trouble he enjoyed the full faith and

---

* As President, FDR strongly favored civilian control. He facetiously sent word to the Navy Department in 1937, "anybody caught lobbying for a General Staff will be sent to Guam!"

support of his chief. In any case, from this time on his criticisms of his superior gave way to warm appreciation and admiration.

From a perspective of many years, Eleanor Roosevelt reviewed her husband's relations with Daniels, and concluded: "In the early years, when he was Assistant Secretary of the Navy, you very often see a young man's impatience with the way older men thought and worked. At times he was critical of his chief, Josephus Daniels, but he learned as time went on to have a deep admiration for the qualities of character and to value the high ability of Mr. Daniels. It was his own experience that taught him it was one thing to understand and get on with naval officers, and another and perhaps even greater quality which enabled Mr. Daniels to understand and get on with Congress. What he spoke of slightingly at first, he came to admire inordinately because of all the difficulties he himself encountered." [38]

Candidate for Vice President

> Franklin's nomination . . . really didn't require much shoving from anyone. . . . He had played a fine part all through the convention and when Cox was nominated as President, sublime availability geographically as well as from every other standpoint was so apparent . . . he went through in quick time.
>
> — GRENVILLE T. EMMET TO LANGDON MARVIN, *July 8, 1920.*

ON May 22, 1919, one of the most conservative newspapers in the United States, the New York *Sun*, looked over the field of Democratic presidential possibilities. In its leading editorial it proclaimed, "If it were the job of THE SUN to suggest to the Democratic party the man who, in the absence of Mr. WILSON's candidacy, might prove a standard bearer to be reckoned with by the opposition party in 1920, it would name FRANKLIN D. ROOSEVELT, the brilliant young Assistant Secretary of the Navy." [1]

It is ironic that a voice of Wall Street was nominating the man who fifteen years later became the focus of conservative loathing. More important, this was a clear indication of how thoroughly Roosevelt's skillful course had ingratiated him with numerous groups possessing sharply conflicting political objectives. In a word, he was "available." At the same time, Roosevelt was too young and too lacking in national reputation to be a serious contender for the nomination. No one knew better than he that he should not take the *Sun's* editorial seriously. It "is very delightful," he wrote an admirer, "but one of the largest jokes on record." [2]

Roosevelt, bearing the name that he did, and possessing a high degree of ambition, would not have been human if he did not have the Presidency in the back of his mind as an ultimate goal. People were still coming into his office as they had for years, gazing out the window with him at the White House, and pointing the parallel to Assistant Secretary Theodore Roosevelt. There was not much he could do but blush and perhaps say something about not seriously deluding himself that lightning would strike twice in the same place.[3]

Certainly, though, Roosevelt was not going to erect any political lightning rods. On the contrary, he was painstakingly trying to create conditions which would send another bolt toward a Roosevelt. This was a long and tedious task, into which he invested a considerable part of his efforts during 1919 and 1920. How much he hoped to achieve is not clear, and probably was not clear to him at the time. Suffice it to say that his attitude was frankly opportunistic — he wished to advance his political name and reputation as much as possible while he built for a somewhat distant and unforeseeable future. No especial gifts of prophecy were necessary to see that public favor was swinging strongly away from both the Democratic party and progressivism; Roosevelt was ready to base his operations on the premise of a Republican victory in 1920. After that, he expected to engage in law practice, for he had five children to support, prices were soaring, and he felt a financial pinch. As early as March, 1919, he wrote, "In many ways I wish it were possible for me, now that the war is over, to return to something a little more lucrative than this position." Meanwhile he made the low-paid position of Assistant Secretary as politically profitable as possible. He believed in tides of public opinion (even as his own attitudes seemed to float on their surface), and as surely as they were ebbing for the Wilsonians in 1919, they would subsequently flow back again. Roosevelt maneuvered adroitly to place himself in a position to ride that flood.[4]

To do so, for the time being he would have to limit his following somewhat, by proclaiming himself the young spokesman for the losing cause of progressive Democracy. He clung to the useful "progressive" label at the same time that some of his concepts of progressivism had veered well to the right. In effect, he wished to establish himself as the Dauphin of the Wilson administration. His opportunity to do so came only a week after the *Sun* editorial, and he seized upon it brilliantly. The occasion was a meeting of the Democratic National Committee at Chicago; the keynote speaker was Attorney General Mitchell Palmer, who was hopeful that his war on radicals would bring him to the White House. Roosevelt was also to speak. According to newspapermen, he did not prepare his speech until after he had arrived in Chicago, but it was such a stinging attack upon the Republican Old Guard in Congress, and such a striking reaffirmation of the Democrats as the party of progressivism, that it stole the headlines from Palmer and marked Roosevelt as a coming leader. James Cox of Ohio, another presidential aspirant, was highly impressed; Roosevelt's friend, Robert R. McCormick, reported it on the front pages of the Chicago *Tribune* under the headline, "Palmer Loses Place in Sun to Roosevelt." It was a fighting speech — the first of Roosevelt's great political addresses.[5]

For twenty-five years, Roosevelt began, the liberal and conservative forces had been battling each other within each party. But the die was now cast: the Republicans had so thoroughly purged themselves of liberal influence that "by next year it will be clear to the American people that the Republican party is the conservative party of the United States and that the Democratic party is the progressive or liberal party." The Republicans were "devoted to the policies of conservatism and reaction, to the principles of little Americanism and jingo bluff, to the old hypocrisy of Penrose and Mark Hanna and Blaine." The new Republican Congress was concerned only with raising the tariff "for pet groups of manufacturers," and lowering taxes "to lighten the burden of those unfortunate individuals who have incomes of $1,000,000 a year or more." Republican foreign policy had, as its sole objective, opposition to anything Wilson might propose: "I asked a prominent member of that party who happens to be an intimate personal friend of mine what is the purpose or policy of Senator Lodge as Chairman of the Committee on Foreign Relations. He said 'That changes from day to day. When Mr. Lodge reads his morning paper at the breakfast table and sees what the President has said or done, his policy for the next 24 hours becomes the diametrical opposite.' "

The Democratic party also, Roosevelt granted, had "gone through a struggle between conservatism and liberalism." He gave a concise interpretation of its history in the previous quarter of a century:

It was swept too far in one direction perhaps in 1896 and in 1900, but we must remember that many of the ideals and principles enunciated by Mr. Bryan and his associates of those days are now the law of the land, principles considered visionary then but accepted whole-heartedly today. The campaign of 1904 was an unsuccessful attempt to reconcile the conservative wing of the party, but from that day on, it became evident that the Democracy of the United States was and is and must be a progressive Democracy. Beginning with the Congressional elections of 1910, followed by the triumphal selection of a progressive Democrat

to lead the Ticket at Baltimore in 1912, the party has become established on definite principles. During its first four years, it has
carried through more great measures for the good of the whole
population than any other party in any similar period. During
the past two years, it has been responsible for guiding the Nation
through the most stupendous war in history. And in so doing, it
did not fail to call upon the best brains in the country, irrespective of party. In the crisis, the Democratic Party has remained
the party of progress.

So we are approaching the campaign of 1920 — approaching it
with the broad principles settled in advance; conservatism, special
privilege, partisanship, destruction on the one hand — liberalism,
common sense idealism, constructiveness, progress, on the other." [6]

Like any effective political speech, these fine-sounding generalities
cloaked schisms that would develop over almost any point of a concrete program. It was designed to evoke a warm emotional response
from those who were still progressive, and the many more who still
considered themselves progressive. As a piece of political analysis,
the speech was only partly accurate. Roosevelt was correct in pointing
out how completely the liberals had lost control within the Republican party, but he was mistaken — as events in the 1920 Democratic
National Convention proved — in declaring that progressives dom-
inated the Democratic party. Nevertheless, as a testament of political
faith, the speech was highly successful. It placed its author well toward
the front of the liberal minority within the Democratic party, and
gave him additional strength among that still smaller minority to
whom the name "Roosevelt" had more glamor than a party label.

The speech brought to an abrupt end the editorial bouquets of
papers like the Sun, but they had been of dubious political worth,
if not downright harmful. Now that he appeared both partisan and
formidable, the Republican press opened fire on him.*

Among the Democrats, the speech aroused great enthusiasm. The
editor of the Detroit News wrote his Washington correspondent

---

* One of the most energetic thesaurus searchers among American editors,
Arthur Vandenberg of the Grand Rapids Herald, wrote under the heading, "Oh,
Franklin!": . . . "Even so good a man . . . occasionally falls into sophistry when
he turns into plain, every-day 'politician.' . . . for this eminent Democrat to charge
that the whole Republican party has gone to the demnition, reactionary bow-
wows — in a 'dying spasm,' as he said — is for him to resort to demagogy so trans-
parent and so thin that it is almost pathetic in its confession of a lack of better
ammunition." [7]

that he was printing it, although it was several days old. "It was a humdinger!" — he exclaimed — and it marked Roosevelt as the coming man. "I already can see the Democrats in this state running around in circles trying to discover whether the new bird is an eagle or a hawk, or merely the usual political bat accidentally emerging for a moment into the daylight." [8]

It was an eagle all right, but still a fledgling one, which must undertake numerous trial flights before it was ready to soar. Even had Roosevelt been ready for the presidential nomination, he probably would not have made a serious fight for it in a year when he could not possibly win the election. He certainly could have had no desire to be another Bryan. On the other hand, "Roosevelt for President" talk could help start people thinking of him in those terms. A minor boom could be of long-range value, and there were enthusiasts ready at a word to start one.

In Massachusetts, politicians working to obtain the senatorial nomination for his friend Mayor Andrew J. Peters of Boston, at the same time quietly suggested Roosevelt for President. "The game's about as clever a one as ever seen in the old Bay State," a newspaperman commented. It was an "adaptation and improvement upon the German propaganda methods," which involved "no note more loud than a murmur into a receptive ear or a whisper." A New York City adherent, Judge Henry M. Heymann, was less discreet. After a trip to Washington to see Roosevelt, he sent out "Roosevelt for President" publicity to newspapers. Unfortunately, it was unsigned, and the envelopes containing it bore a Washington postmark. The New York *Herald* embarrassingly pointed out the city of origin. Roosevelt realized the obvious inference would be that he was booming himself from the Navy Press Bureau, and wired Heymann to stop. Heymann obligingly persuaded editors of other newspapers to kill the story. "Thanks for your action in nipping my Presidential boom in the bud," Roosevelt wrote him. "Being early on the job is sometimes wise and sometimes not. I sometimes think we consider too much the good luck of the early bird, and not the bad luck of the early worm." [9]

If not a serious contender at the moment for the Presidency of the United States, Roosevelt was a very real possibility for Governor of New York State if Al Smith should decide not to run for a second term. He was, besides, the most likely nominee for United States

Senator, to run against James Wadsworth. Since he was at peace with Tammany, there was no major obstacle in his way.

However, he strongly discouraged all talk of the governorship by commenting, typically, "What is the matter with the re-nomination of Governor Smith? People as a whole throughout the State think that he has done well." His demurrers that he was not interested in the senatorial nomination were slightly weaker; he confined his comments to an insistence that he was too busy with naval demobilization (long since completed), or that it was too soon to talk about candidates.[10]

January, 1920, seemed politically and personally a bleak time for Roosevelt. Mrs. Hamlin wrote in her diary: "As I was walking along R. St. . . . I met Franklin Roosevelt — he has had his tonsils out and has been ill too — he looks rather poorly for him. He had two of his boys and a dog with him and we walked along together. Several of the children have had or are having chicken-pox — James is to have his appendix out — Eleanor was getting out 2000 invitations for Navy teas. He said he did not expect to run for the Senate — that even if he wanted it or could get it — he thought it stupid." [11]

Yet New York politicians seemed likely to bestow the nomination upon him. Tammany chieftains were not overly friendly, but thought he would make a strong candidate in the Dry rural areas, especially if the Wet Senator Wadsworth were to run. Prohibition was just going into effect that month, and was at the peak of its popularity.* But Roosevelt hedged, partly for fear that, in what promised to be a bad year for the party, he would also have to overcome the handicap of a weak presidential candidate. He commented, "I am perfectly frank in saying that I would not run this autumn for Dog-catcher if the Democrats nominate a party hack or a reactionary or a Bryan at San Francisco." Because he feared that even McAdoo, a leading contender, was not strong enough, he declined a proffered political alliance with him.[13]

There was one possible candidate that Roosevelt early in 1920 did feel might be strong enough: he was sufficiently progressive, had

---

* The advent of Prohibition did not make FDR Dry in his personal life, although he could not afford to stock his cellar as adequately as many of his friends. He was critical of Wadsworth as openly advocating "what comes pretty close to being nonenforcement of the law. Quite aside from the broad issue of Prohibition or no Prohibition, any approval of nonenforcement or of lax enforcement of any statute is a dangerous suggestion for the Republic." [12]

an unparalleled reputation as an administrator, and had come out of the war and into the period of disillusion still so tremendously popular that he might save the Democrats from disaster. That was Hoover. "I had some nice talks with Herbert Hoover before he went West for Christmas," Roosevelt wrote their mutual friend, Hugh Gibson. "He is certainly a wonder, and I wish we could make him President of the United States. There could not be a better one." [14]

Numerous Democrats and liberals besides Roosevelt were turning in desperation to Hoover, without bothering to find out much about either his party or ideology. When Hoover announced publicly that he favored taking the Versailles Treaty out of politics and ratifying it with mild reservations, he became the choice of large numbers of intellectuals. It clinched the matter with them when one of the irreconcilable foes of the Treaty, Senator James A. Reed, labeled him a "dangerous internationalist," and sneered that he would be the ideal candidate under a British-controlled League of Nations. Enthusiasts of both parties tried to enter Hoover's name in the primaries.[15]

During the war, Roosevelt had become acquainted with Hoover through their mutual friend from California, Secretary of the Interior Franklin K. Lane, and had come to have warm admiration for his ability. While Hoover had never been in politics, his background and leanings were Progressive Republican. Since he had contributed to Theodore Roosevelt's Bull Moose campaign funds in 1912, it was entirely logical for Franklin Roosevelt to dream of winning him over to the Democratic party.*

As Roosevelt told the story of the attempt ten years later, it had so gained in embellishments, if indeed it had any factual basis, that Hoover could not recall the episode as ever having taken place. Hoover was in 1920 a man of relatively far greater importance than Roosevelt, and like Winston Churchill in London in 1918, he made much more of an impression upon Roosevelt than Roosevelt did upon him. After dinner one night, as Roosevelt recalled, he and Lane sought to sell Hoover on a plan of action. Hoover should mention incidentally in some statement that he was a true Jeffersonian Democrat, and the political writers would do the rest. Then, he could obtain a respectable number of delegates for the convention so that

---

* While Hoover had been "nonpartisan in both word and deed" during the war, he was known to his colleagues to be Republican. He writes: "(a) I was a registered Republican in California from 1898 on; (b) I was a member of the National Republican Club from 1912 on and (c) I publicly supported Theodore Roosevelt in 1912." [16]

while he would not win the nomination in 1920, he could become the logical candidate, and win both the nomination and the election in 1924. Roosevelt thought he and Lane had convinced Hoover; consequently he recounted that he was shocked when Senator Lodge's daughter, Mrs. Augustus P. Gardner, told him at a dinner party a few days later that Hoover was about to announce himself a Republican. Roosevelt retorted he knew positively that Hoover would do nothing of the sort; Mrs. Gardner replied that she was equally certain, for her father and Boies Penrose had sold Hoover on the Republican party.* It was a keen disappointment to Roosevelt when events proved she was right.[19]

With the end of this forlorn hope, there was nothing in Roosevelt's subsequent actions to indicate that he expected a Democratic victory in either the nation or the state. Whether through astuteness or indifference, he took a rather strong independent position. This would gain him little in 1920, but strengthen him for the future. New York political observers assumed, of course, that he was tied to President Wilson and, since the truce of 1917, to Tammany as well. But Roosevelt's repeated public onslaughts against the inefficiency of administration in Washington were certainly not complimentary to the President.† Probably Wilson was little aware of them, since he had made only a limited recovery after his breakdown in September, 1919, and Mrs. Wilson and his secretary, Tumulty, carefully screened the news that went to him. At the end of February Wilson was not in a very pleasant mood; he dismissed Secretary of State Lansing for holding an unauthorized cabinet session during his illness, although Daniels tried to get him to put the dismissal on other grounds. That very day, Daniels noted in his diary, concerning Roosevelt's appeal at Harvard for government reorganization: "FDR persona non grata with W. Better let speech pass."[21]

---

* In 1931 Roosevelt told this story to the ablest of his campaign biographers, Ernest K. Lindley, but subsequently asked Lindley to delete it from his book.[17]

Hoover comments: "So far as I recollect, Lane never mentioned the Presidency to me. It is unlikely, as he was a warm supporter for Mr. Baker. Mrs. Gardner's supposed statement is also apocryphal. Both Penrose and Lodge bitterly attacked me over my whole period in public life — until I became Secretary of Commerce. They both opposed my appointment. I never even met Penrose prior to that time and Lodge only twice and then on unfriendly occasions. So you will see it is unlikely that they sold me the Republican Party."[18]

† The Republican platform in 1920 called for reorganization of the Federal administration on a more businesslike basis. The Democratic platform did not mention the subject.[20]

The public knew nothing of this, of course, but at the beginning of May observers did note with interest that Wilson passed over the candidate that Roosevelt and the State Democratic Chairman strongly recommended for a Federal District judgeship, and instead appointed a man sponsored by Mayor George R. Lunn of Schenectady. Lunn, a former Socialist who had remained at outs with Tammany, was a contender for the Democratic nomination for United States Senator.[22]

Roosevelt chose this exact time to take a slap at Tammany. Ignoring both the strong advice of a supporter, and his own better judgment of a few weeks earlier, he decided not to defer the fight against the unit rule until the Democratic Convention assembled, but to send a strong protest to the delegates before they assembled in conference on May 7. He did so although he knew in advance that Tammany would control the delegates and overwhelmingly vote for the New York delegation to function as a block at the convention. He was also sure that the convention would follow precedent, and vote down the unit rule. It was not like him to court certain defeat unless he had a purpose, and the clue lay in a letter he wrote, but did not send. "If I understand the temper of the voters this year at all, 'having an organization' is going to be more of a handicap than a help," he declared. "I never saw a time when there was such a universal disgust at 'organization in general' as the present, and if I run it will be because I am honestly persuaded that people who are tired of mere machine politics prefer me to Wadsworth, who is hopelessly, irrevocably and chronically a machine man, first, last and always." [23]

In his attack on the unit rule, Roosevelt declared that he was somewhat humiliated by the little respect New York delegations received at conventions, because managers of candidates regarded them as "merely a parcel of 'straw' men with strict orders to sign on the dotted line." This in turn led to apathy on the part of Democratic voters within the state. In order to choose a better candidate with more appeal to the independent voters (and Roosevelt erroneously predicted their number would be large in 1920), the delegates should bury the unit rule along with the dodo. As he himself could have predicted in advance, it was his proposal that the delegates relegated with the dodo; but he could not have expected the devastating vote of 64 to 8. The severity of the whipping came in part because, at the meeting, Lunn and Seabury launched a vehement attack upon the unit rule and Roosevelt stayed away. According to one intriguing report, Boss Murphy wanted to avoid a showdown with them, but Al Smith insisted "that the Tammany chieftain snap his whip and 'lick' Lunn and Roosevelt at one stroke." [24]

Roosevelt was glad he did not attend, as he had no desire to be a tail to the kite of Lunn and Seabury; but had he gone, he would have tried to prevent the acrimonious discussion they precipitated.[25] Had the unit rule been broken, McAdoo would have been the beneficiary at the convention. Consequently, the main purpose of the overwhelming vote was to kill off the McAdoo boom, and thus repudiate the Wilson Administration. But those who arranged it were glad, in the process, to demonstrate the pathetic weakness of the "Federal Crowd," and to tell off Roosevelt for presuming to dictate to them.

Whether intentionally or not, Roosevelt had killed off two booms in the state: McAdoo's and his own. For the time being there was no more talk of Roosevelt for Senator. He had by no means completely eliminated himself as a potential candidate, but reporters did not again predict his nomination until the beginning of the National Convention. The principal beneficiary of the maneuver was Al Smith; the delegates would presumably caucus on the train, and in the opening ballots give him a complimentary "favorite son" vote.[26]

"I am a little amused," Roosevelt commented, upon reading newspaper reports that he had cost himself the senatorial nomination. "There would be no use in telling them that I really do not give a continental damn about . . . [it] one way or another, and that even if I did I would not want it at the price of keeping my mouth shut." He might well be amused, for he had not seriously damaged himself, and had even retouched his slightly faded reputation as an independent.[27]

What Roosevelt really wanted was the governorship, anyway. There was slight chance of that, since Al Smith would certainly run again. Nevertheless, to mend his fences among Hudson River Valley neighbors, Roosevelt held an informal meeting for all committeemen from adjacent counties at his home on June 5. Rain kept most of the guests away, but to those that came, he fed a fine buffet luncheon, while his friends circulated the hint that they would much prefer to see Roosevelt run for Governor, if only Smith were to run for Senator.[28]

While he was fishing, he put down a slender line for the Vice Presidency too. During the winter his friend Louis Wehle had tried to promote a Hoover-Roosevelt ticket. Even after Hoover declared himself a Republican, Wehle continued to promote Roosevelt for the vice-presidential nomination. In addition, Roosevelt apparently had listened to some quiet suggestions that there might be a John W. Davis-Roosevelt ticket. Davis, a wealthy lawyer, and at the time Ambassador at London, previously had been a West Virginia Congressman. Roosevelt requested and acquired a copy of his voting record on labor issues shortly before he left for San Francisco. While Roosevelt was ostensibly for McAdoo, he seemed to hope that if the three leading contenders — McAdoo, Palmer, and Cox — deadlocked, he could engineer the nomination of Davis.

By the time the convention neared, there were many rumors, emanating from no one knew where, that Roosevelt would make a fine candidate for Vice President. In mid-June, Roosevelt's law partner, Langdon Marvin, reported "much enthusiasm" among his amateur friends, mostly Republicans. Of course Roosevelt replied: "I am wondering who started this fool Vice-Presidential boom. I have seen nothing about it in the papers and I am not at all sure that I care for it." 29

Nevertheless, for a man going to San Francisco to the Democratic National Convention ostensibly only as a delegate, to vote for the best possible presidential candidate, Roosevelt brought with him quite a little entourage. Should some unexpected opportunity suddenly arise, he would be ready. He urged Daniels to go, on the grounds that he could help bring about unity, since Daniels, rather remarkably for an administration figure, was on good terms with both Bryan and Tammany. Roosevelt took along his secretary, Camalier, and two of the Dutchess County friends who had started him in politics ten years earlier, Thomas Lynch and John E. Mack. He wired Mack it was "really important" to go to the convention. Mack said afterwards that he had no idea what was going to take place, but a labor leader in Washington was optimistic enough to write a union official at Mare Island Navy Yard on June 4, "There is every indication that the Hon. Franklin D. Roosevelt will be on the National Ticket." 30

At the convention, things went far better for Roosevelt than he could possibly have hoped. The spirits of the Democrats had risen somewhat by the time they assembled in San Francisco, for the seemingly overconfident Republicans at Chicago had nominated a little-known mediocrity, Senator Warren G. Harding. The strongest of the Democratic candidates was McAdoo, who had Dry support, and who as Secretary of the Treasury had built a considerable following among officeholders. (During a critical McAdoo rally, his opponents sang, "Every Vote Is on the Pay Roll.") But McAdoo lacked the endorsement of his presidential father-in-law, and there was a rumor with some basis in fact that Wilson, despite his feeble condition, wished a third-term nomination. Attorney-General Mitchell Palmer controlled another group of the administration delegates, but was too unpopular with labor and liberals throughout the country to muster sufficient votes. Then there was the carefully chosen candidate of the bosses, James Cox — progressive enough as Governor of Ohio, and pro-League enough to be fairly acceptable to the liberals, yet possessing two assets the bosses regarded as essential if they were to carry their own individual domains in November: he was a Wet, and he had not been associated with the unpopular Wilson Administration.[31]

Roosevelt was busy on his long transcontinental train ride, and arrived at the convention hall once again on friendly terms with Tammany. The New York delegates applauded him when he invited them to visit the battleship *New York*, riding at anchor in San Francisco Harbor. Word went around that, after all, Tammany would support Roosevelt for United States Senator. Rumors also circulated that Tammany would fight to invoke and maintain the unit rule. The beneficiary of this big block of votes, Murphy implied, would be the Wet candidate, Cox.

It was the bone-Dry Lunn, not Roosevelt, who immediately organized the anti-Tammany New York delegates in a fight against the unit rule. Lunn was anxious to hold the leadership of these delegates anyway, since he very much wanted to run for United States Senator. There was a rumor that he was so exasperated with Roosevelt's conduct that he was considering entering the senatorial primaries against him. But when the convention Rules Committee took up the question of the unit rule, Roosevelt joined in the protest against it; the committee invalidated the rule — and Roosevelt's followers gave him all the credit. More important, because the unit rule no longer applied the New York delegates were not bound by the majority, and could vote their individual preferences.[32]

At the opening session, Roosevelt impulsively scored another coup, which spectacularly called attention to him, and dramatized to the convention his independence of Tammany and loyalty to Wilson. The sudden display of a huge oil painting of the President touched off a demonstration in Wilson's honor. The delegates of state after state grabbed their standards and paraded around the convention hall, looking scornfully at the New York delegates who remained seated while a stalwart Tammany man, Jeremiah T. Mahoney, held the state placard. William W. Farley, Chairman of the State Committee, had refused to allow New York to join the procession, but at its height, when Roosevelt and Lunn again asked permission, Farley granted it. Charles T. White of the New York *Tribune* reported, "Messrs. Roosevelt and Lunn, imbued with zeal and clothed with authority as they thought, swooped down upon the standard and in the melee jerked it away from Judge Mahoney. There was a sharp interchange and more or less jostling, but no blows were struck. Roosevelt and Lunn, through sheer impetuosity, bore away the New York standard in triumph and joined in the procession of standards, much to the joy of the Wilson men from the Southern States. Within five minutes the tale was circulating outside the Auditorium that the first session of the national convention was treated to a fist fight between New York delegates." Farley, seeking to cover up the bad impression of Tammany that the incident created, later told reporters that it was "just a scuffle." But Roosevelt made it sound even more dramatic: "When I wanted to take the standard I was told that New York would remain seated. I didn't like that and I grabbed the standard.* About half a dozen men grabbed me and we had a jolly fight, but I got the standard and it was paraded." [33]

Once more, Roosevelt seemed slated for Tammany punishment. Several days later, Farley announced the name of someone else as the probable nominee for Senator; but at about the same time, Roosevelt was seen in the auditorium, seated next to Murphy and engaged in animated conversation with him. Tammany was supposed to be disgusted with the way Roosevelt had kicked over the traces at every opportunity, yet when the great Irish orator, Bourke Cockran, mellifluously nominated Al Smith for the Presidency, it was Roosevelt who came to the platform and made a seconding speech. This was a short, pleasant address which attracted as favorable attention toward Roosevelt himself as toward Smith.† One of Roosevelt's law partners wrote,

* The New York standard wound up, properly inscribed, on the wall of FDR's study at Hyde Park.

† Henry L. Mencken was looking darkly through anti-New Deal glasses when he reminisced years later that it effectively killed off enthusiasm for Smith. FDR had said:

> The past half hour has shown that the great Democracy of the state of New York is an integral part of the Democracy of the nation [*Applause*], and that is another reason why we from New York sent to this Convention

at the time, that he delivered it "in an admirable way." It "was very good and brought him publicly before the whole convention so that the delegates all saw and heard him. The impression he made could not have been better." [35]

When the balloting began, Roosevelt joined the New York delegation in voting for Smith. The delegation remained united for the first seven ballots. Then, when Tammany gave the word to swing to Cox, seventy did so; while a block of twenty, led by Roosevelt and Lunn, switched to McAdoo. The rule that the winning candidate must gain two thirds of the votes in the convention again blocked a quick nomination, and for several days the balloting went on indecisively. Some forty-seven of the New York delegates left for home; most of them were Cox men. Before they left, Murphy secured a promise from Roosevelt and Lunn that they would not interfere with their proxy votes for Cox. On this basis the New York voting continued; Roosevelt steadfastly stood by McAdoo. [36]

In his speech seconding Smith, Roosevelt had taken a poke at Harding by remarking that the nominee of this convention would not be chosen in a hotel room at two in the morning. But, of course, the Democrats also engaged in much quiet maneuvering. The subsequent story that Roosevelt received the nomination for Vice President as a result of a sudden, spontaneous gesture on the part of the delegates was good politics but poor history. It was the product of careful groundwork. Many people subsequently took credit for its successful consummation, and that in itself is a key to one of the means of nomination — a large number of delegates and figures behind the scenes, for one or another reason, felt that Roosevelt would be the ideal vice-presidential nominee, and their combined efforts triumphed. Two other factors

---

the name of our beloved Governor. I love him as a friend; I look up to him as a man; I am with him as a Democrat, and we all know his record throughout the nation as a great servant of the public.

Come back with us to the old Empire State, and if you will do so and learn to know our Al Smith, there won't be any question about what action you will take. [*Applause.*] Yes; the Democracy of New York is united — united behind our Governor, from Montauk Point to Niagara Falls, from the Delaware to the St. Lawrence, and so knowing that he has been a Governor in the open, we know, too, that this Convention is a Convention in the open. [*Applause.*] The nominee of this Convention will not be chosen at 2 A.M. in a hotel room. [*Applause.*]

In the Navy we shoot fast and straight. Governor Smith, in that respect, is a Navy man. [*Applause.*] Help us in New York. Let us help you in the other forty-seven states by lending to his good right arm more power. [*Applause.*] [34]

were also essential — Roosevelt's complete acceptability, and the deliberate, studied approval of Boss Murphy. In the final analysis, Roosevelt was a pawn in Murphy's larger game.

On the evening of July 4, Murphy, Brennan and Taggart tried to break the impasse in favor of Cox by urging McAdoo to accept the vice presidential nomination. McAdoo refused, so early the next morning the word went around to the delegations to stand firm, and push through Cox regardless of McAdoo. Murphy next dangled the prize of the Vice Presidency before Roosevelt, perhaps to try to create a split between the Roosevelt and Lunn factions of upstate New York delegates, both of which groups were voting for McAdoo. He spread the word that Roosevelt was to be Cox's running mate.* But this was no more than a suggestion which Murphy need not subsequently honor. If his tactic was used for creating dissension, it failed, simply because Lunn was so anxious to have a clear field in running for Senator that he wished to boost Roosevelt into the vice presidential nomination. Late that night Lunn maneuvered Murphy into such a tight spot that the Boss, in order to get out of it, gave Roosevelt definite assurance of support.

By midnight, a Cox drive was gaining momentum among the exhausted delegates; a few more votes and he would be nominated. At this critical point, just before the forty-third ballot, Lunn challenged the votes of the New York delegation. This meant breaking the gentlemen's agreement on proxy votes he had made with Murphy, since the Chairman of the Convention, Senator Joseph Robinson, had ruled earlier in the day that delegates could not vote by proxy. Cox would have lost more than forty votes, and the drive probably would have stalled.† Lunn's request caused a violent argument among the New York delegates, and after a few minutes' discussion with Murphy, Lunn withdrew it. Immediately after the ballot, Lunn moved an adjournment, which the convention overwhelmingly voted down. He conferred again with the Tammany leaders; they pledged their support

---

* Some indication of how widespread this belief became is Sara Delano Roosevelt's letter of congratulations to her son: "It was a surprise tho' Mr. Newbold, Uncle Warren & others telephoned me as soon as the nomination of Gov. Cox was known, that you were likely to be the Vice Presidential Candidate." 37

† Had the drive stalled, the result might well have been a deadlock with an opportunity for John W. Davis. FDR later wrote Davis, "We nearly put you across at San Francisco but it became apparent after the Sunday recess that the delegates were going to either McAdoo or Cox and the break came late Monday night." 38

to Roosevelt for any office he might want, and Lunn did not again challenge the vote.[39] On the next ballot, Cox was nominated.*

By the time the convention reassembled at noon to nominate a Vice President, Roosevelt support was snowballing. The nomination did not seem a very important matter; the delegates had not given it much thought, were anxious to get home, and were easy enough to sway whatever way the leaders wished. A number of different politicians were independently lining up delegates and pressuring Murphy on Roosevelt's behalf; Mack, Lathrop Brown, and others in Roosevelt's coterie met with a warm response as they went about soliciting votes.[41]

Meanwhile, after Cox won the nomination, it occurred to one of the Ohio leaders, Judge Timothy T. Ansberry, that Roosevelt would make a good candidate for Vice President. He called Cox and obtained his approval.[42]

As for Cox, in his autobiography he recounts that at dawn in Dayton he received a telephone call from his manager, Edmund H. Moore, inquiring his preference for Vice President: "I told him I had given the matter some thought and that my choice would be Franklin D. Roosevelt of New York. Moore inquired, 'Do you know him?' I did not. In fact, so far as I knew, I had never seen him; but I explained to Mr. Moore that he met the geographical requirement, that he was recognized as an Independent and that Roosevelt was a well-known name." Moore got in touch with Murphy, but was ready, if the Boss objected, to transfer his support to Secretary of Agriculture Edwin T. Meredith. Murphy declared, "I don't like Roosevelt. He is not well known in the country, but, Ed, this is the first time a Democratic nominee for the presidency has shown me courtesy. That's why I would vote for the devil himself if Cox wanted me to. Tell him we will nominate Roosevelt on the first ballot as soon as we assemble." [43]

When the delegates returned to the auditorium at about noon, they knew nothing of Cox's choice, and Murphy talked as though he had no commitment. As Roosevelt's friends lined up delegates, their main

---

* Lunn explained the next day that he had made the challenge, despite the arrangement with Tammany, upon the insistence of the McAdoo managers. At that point, "Mr. Murphy told us that he would give his support to Mr. Roosevelt for any office, whether the vice-presidential nomination or the nomination for United States senator. We agreed to stand by the agreement we made with him when the delegates left and told the McAdoo managers that we would not insist upon a poll of the New York delegation." [40]

fear was that Cox might prefer some other candidate. Meanwhile small conferences were going on here and there, and a major caucus among the big leaders continued under the platform even while nominating speeches were being made overhead.[44] Some of the Cox leaders still favored Meredith, but he was from Iowa, and the big three bosses decided that, because Cox was a Wet, they would have to concentrate on the East and needed an administration man from that area to balance the ticket. The Tammany men felt they should be rewarded with a New York nominee for their steadfastness in casting seventy votes for Cox even when his fortunes lagged, but Westerners insisted that the candidate for Vice President should not be a member of Tammany. Murphy leaned toward Secretary of State Bainbridge Colby — who like Cox was damp, and who would bring the useful support of the Hearst newspapers — but Colby was lukewarm toward the nomination.[45]

When Roosevelt's name came up, John J. Fitzgerald remembered much later, Murphy said that Roosevelt would be as objectionable to Murphy as to any of the other Democratic leaders. But he was not objectionable to the others. Tammany men argued with Murphy that he would bring more votes to the New York ticket than Colby, anyway. Brennan of Illinois and Pat Harrison of Mississippi joined with Judge Ansberry to pressure the reluctant Murphy. Ansberry declared less than a week later that finally Wilbur W. Marsh of Iowa, Treasurer of the Democratic National Committee, said to him, "You name the man." Ansberry looked directly at Murphy and replied, "If I am left to name him, it will be Franklin D. Roosevelt." Murphy gave a wink and a nod.[46]

Ansberry suddenly recalled the constitutional requirement that the President and Vice President must be at least thirty-five years old, and feared that the youthful-appearing Roosevelt might not qualify. While someone else was putting in a call to the Navy Department to inquire, he encountered Roosevelt.

"How old are you?"

"Thirty-eight. Why do you want to know?"

"I'm going to nominate you."

"Do you think I ought to be around when you do?" *

---

* FDR meticulously maintained the air of modest surprise, so useful in politics. When a reporter told him he looked like a possibility for the nomination, he replied, "I can't afford the honor. I have five children." Upon his return to Hyde Park, he declared he had not known in advance he would be nominated, which, in view of the last-minute conference under the platform, was true enough. "Personally, I had no idea of being nominated until about thirty seconds before it was

"No, I'd leave the hall." [48]

California had just finished nominating Edward L. Doheny, and two other states had already put up the names of favorite sons when Florida yielded to the District of Columbia, and Ansberry came to the platform. "The young man whose name I am going to suggest," he began, "is but three years over the age of thirty-five prescribed by the Constitution . . . but he has crowded into that short period of time a very large experience as a public official." The war had given him as much as "in ordinary times could not be attained in a generation." Ansberry mentioned his naval service, emphasized his family, and concluded, "His is a name to conjure with in American politics . . . Franklin D. Roosevelt."

Kansas and Indiana seconded the nomination. A few minutes later Al Smith came to the platform on behalf of New York to repay Roosevelt's courtesy of a few days earlier, but unlike Roosevelt, did not stick to his subject. He did not mention the nominee until the end of the speech, and then in a single long sentence. A woman from Washington and Joseph E. Davies of Wisconsin added their seconds. The other candidates began withdrawing; Governor David R. Francis of Missouri then moved that, since all the vice-presidential nominations but one had been withdrawn, the rules be suspended, and Roosevelt be declared the nominee. The motion carried, and Roosevelt was nominated by acclamation.[49]

There were cries from the floor, "Roosevelt! Roosevelt! We want Roosevelt!" But Roosevelt observed propriety and left the hall. In his stead, Daniels came to the rostrum, and praised his assistant so fulsomely that he swept out of consideration any gossip of discord in the Navy Department.* The convention then adjourned *sine die.* Western Democrats were especially happy over the choice.[51]

---

actually done," he wrote. And at the home-coming, he told a crowd that the unexpected had happened:

"I was sent from the floor of the convention to meet a man under the speaker's platform. The man whom I was supposed to meet was not there. Someone rushed up to me and said, 'They are nominating you.' I replied, 'Quit your kidding.' No one was more surprised than I was to get the Vice-Presidential nomination." [47]

* FDR received countless letters and telegrams of congratulations. His chief passed on to him one from Mrs. Daniels to demonstrate that " 'the whole D — aniels family' is behind you." Walter Lippmann of the *New Republic* wired, "Your nomination is the best news in many a long day. When cynics ask what is the use we can answer that when parties can pick a man like Frank Roosevelt there is a decent future in politics." Richard E. Byrd telegraphed the single word "Good," and followed it with a letter explaining, "You will probably think it

Afterwards there was some discussion as to why Murphy had not blocked the nomination of this young man whom he so obviously disliked. There was, of course his remark to Moore, but more than this there was the important reason that it served to keep the upstate independent Democrats docile. It immobilized a dynamic figure, who was habitually insurgent, in a losing year when Murphy would logically concentrate more on purging dissidents than on winning victories. Roosevelt would bring as much strength to the ticket as vice-presidential nominee as he would if he ran for the Senate. Still another possible motive of Murphy's was this: he may have been demonstrating himself to be the biggest man in the convention, and at the same time gratuitously insulting President Wilson by taking one of the President's junior administrators, not in good standing, and putting him onto the ticket without Wilson's having had anything to do with it.[52]

The one unexplainable factor was that Murphy should have been willing to allow this young man such a superb opportunity to acquire a national following. For that was obviously what impelled Roosevelt to accept the nomination. His potent name — the symbol of progressivism — had much to do with his receiving the nomination; the campaign would give him an opportunity to display to the nation a personality to match.

---

queer that I did not get any stronger than the word 'good.' I am reserving the word 'fine' to use at some future convention when there won't be any 'Vice' in front of the 'President.' " Herbert Hoover wrote, "The fact that I do not belong to your political tribe does not deter me from offering my personal congratulations to an old friend. I am glad to see you in the game in such a prominent place, and, although I will not be charged with traitorship by wishing you success, I nevertheless consider it a contribution to the good of the country that you have been nominated and it will bring the merit of a great public servant to the front. If you are elected you will do the job properly." President Wilson had conventionally wired Cox, "Please accept my hearty congratulations and cordial best wishes"; to fit the lesser importance of the vice presidential nomination, he watered down his telegram to FDR: "Please accept my warm congratulations and good wishes." [50]

The First Presidential Campaign

> I am dictating this just before leaving for the big trip to
> the Coast, and I am glad that I had that 1920 experience,
> otherwise I should be worried by the prospect.
> — FDR TO JOSEPHUS DANIELS, *September 12, 1933.*[1]

T HE HOPELESS CAMPAIGN of 1920 was an exhilarating rather
than a depressing experience for Roosevelt. He conducted it on
a fairly idealistic level, with vigor, intelligence, and unflagging good
humor. After all, he had everything to gain and nothing to lose, since
obviously no one votes for or against a candidate for Vice President.
For the first time in his life he had an opportunity to build a substantial national reputation and to convince scores of state and local
Democratic leaders that he was a rarity among contenders for the
Vice Presidency: a man with a future. There had not been a
comparable candidate since the Rough Rider Roosevelt in 1900. For
Franklin D. Roosevelt, therefore, the foredoomed fight for Wilson's
League and the New Freedom was not so much a lost crusade as a
dress rehearsal. It was his first presidential campaign.

For the most part, it was good fun, although at times exhausting.
There was the bustle and excitement which he loved so well, the flags
flying, bands playing, crowds cheering around bunting-draped plat-
forms, the reporters and photographers, and midnight poker and
speech-writing sessions aboard the special train. The nerves of others
became frayed, but his remained steady. With remarkable aplomb he
learned what for him henceforth would be the greatest of sports,
national campaigning. By the end of three months' intensive practice,
he was a skilled player.

Although, as Roosevelt was well aware, an overwhelming majority
of American newspapers were Republican, his nomination met with a
shower of editorial bouquets. But before the campaigning began, there
were a few brickbats mixed in. The New York *Sun*, which only a
little more than a year before had nominated him for the Presidency,

now saw no merit in him as a vice-presidential candidate, and McCormick of the Chicago *Tribune* reversed his former flattering attitude to dub his onetime schoolmate "The One-half of One Per Cent Roosevelt," who had been nominated solely to lure the votes of former Bull Moosers. "He is to put the honey of a name on the trap of a ticket," the *Tribune* declared. "Franklin is as much like Theodore as a clam is like a bear cat. . . . If he is Theodore Roosevelt, Elihu Root is Gene Debs, and Bryan is a brewer." [2]

Some other Republican friends also rushed to change their minds about Roosevelt. Henry Cabot Lodge, who had used Roosevelt as a tool against Daniels, was quick to abandon his former ally. When Senator Ball inquired if the investigation of the unsavory Newport affair should be dropped, for fear implication of Roosevelt would appear a political move, Lodge replied he could see no reason for doing so.[3] Indeed, he felt that the Senate Committee would be subject to severe criticism unless it proceeded.* To a supporter, Lodge crisply commented on Roosevelt:

"He talked well in the early years of the [Wilson] Administration. He is a pleasant fellow whom I personally liked, but now that the Administration is coming to a close we can see that when it came to the point, he did exactly what Daniels wished him to do. He is a well-meaning, nice young fellow, but light. As Harvey said in his last number, he has been talking lately very 'freely and foolishly.' His head evidently turned and the effect upon a not very strong man is very obvious." [5]

This flurry of attention heralded the emergence of Roosevelt as a major public figure. It soon died down, but while it lasted it foreshadowed the period when his family could claim even less of his time than during the previous years. Even his mother seemed aware of this. When she wrote in excitement of plans for a home-coming, she remarked, "If & when you are elected, you will belong to the nation; now you are 'our boy' of Hyde Park & Dutchess." During a lull in the

* Nevertheless, during the campaign, Senator Ball's committee remained silent. Rathom, the Providence newspaperman, spread scandalous statements in the press and in pamphlet form. FDR countered by suing Rathom for libel, and the matter failed to become a campaign issue of any significance. However, it worried FDR sufficiently for him to send for Arthur Krock to come to Hyde Park from the Democratic headquarters to advise him. Krock, who sat with FDR before the fire and helped work out the solution, has reminisced, "I'll never forget how young and handsome he was and how young and charming his wife was. . . . I was very much for him." [4]

campaigning he did squeeze in a few days with his family. A woman reporter visited him at Campobello, and described gushingly the happy and successful manner in which he functioned as head of a household of five children.[6]

Yet this interview itself represented an intrusion into their private life of a sort which Eleanor Roosevelt did not particularly enjoy. Although she had vigorously participated in war work, and had behind her seven years of Washington social functions, a rather gossipy Washington correspondent regarded her as still "essentially a home woman," who "seems particularly to dislike the official limelight, and to resent the pitiless publicity given the private and personal affairs of people who are prominent in official life. Just how she'll ever endure the Vice-Presidential status . . . remains to be seen."

One of her friends commented, "She is too much a Roosevelt to be anybody's prize beauty, but she's pure gold!" She was still rather self-conscious about her appearance. The day her husband was nominated, Howe wired her for a photograph; she replied, "Are no pictures of me." As a result, newspapers enlarged a photograph of the Roosevelts at a baseball game, but through error cut out Mrs. Roosevelt and included the woman sitting on the other side of Roosevelt as "the candidate's wife." Finally, at the end of August, Mrs. Roosevelt capitulated, and told her husband's New York campaign manager where he could obtain a picture of her. She explained, "I take such bad photographs that I've not had any taken for years." At the same time she confessed she was not overjoyed at her husband's nomination: "Personally I had wanted Franklin out of government service for a few years at least. So in spite of the honor I really feel rather unselfish when I wish for his success." In the months that followed, she loyally aided him to the utmost.[7]

As for Roosevelt, he slowly traveled East from San Francisco, laying plans and conferring with politicians on the way. Numerous returning delegates, and leaders in Utah, Colorado, Kansas, and Missouri, all promising they would work vigorously, discussed possible campaign issues with him. On the day of his nomination, Howe wired him to make "efficient government" his keynote. But the Republicans were already making much of that, and even before Roosevelt crossed the Rockies, he discovered the far greater interest in the League. When he broke his trip for a day at Glenwood Springs, Colorado, the Republican mayor unexpectedly transformed a nonpartisan public appearance into a political rally by telling the crowd that he would vote for Roosevelt and Cox in order to support the League. Even some New York leaders, despite the League's unpopularity among the Irish, urged Roosevelt to advocate it aggressively. "Keep them on the defensive," William W. Farley, the State Chairman, counseled; "keep the League of Nations to the fore as the main issue of the campaign." [8]

At Columbus, Roosevelt conferred with Cox for some hours, and impressed him as being alert and "keenly alive to the conditions that would bear on the campaign." Demonstrating his confidence in Roosevelt, Cox returned to his office, and left Roosevelt to speak for him at a press conference. For the most part, the vice-presidential candidate, in this interview, was pleasantly vague, but with two words he set the theme of the campaign.

A reporter asked, "Do you regard the League of Nations as the dominant issue of the campaign?"

"Yes," Roosevelt firmly replied.

"And you will treat it as such in your campaign speeches?"

"Undoubtedly." [9]

Harding immediately snatched at this: "The Republican party and candidates gladly accept the challenge. We are more than willing to make the election a national referendum on the question whether we shall have four years more of Democratic readiness to surrender the Republic." [10]

Roosevelt replied that he was "quite willing, as I know Governor Cox is, to let the American people decide whether they will go back to the conditions of 1914, or whether they will join with civilization and humanity in this great step forward."

At the same time, Cox announced that he and Roosevelt would confer with President Wilson on campaign issues the following Sunday. This added corroboration to the readiness of the Democrats to center the fight about the League, for surely the main purpose of a "pilgrimage to the White House" would be to use it as the occasion to proclaim faith in the Covenant. It also underscores the inaccuracy of the long-popular legend that Cox's decision to campaign on the League issue was a sudden, impulsive gesture toward the ailing President.[11]

The visit to the White House was indeed dramatic. During the Second World War, Roosevelt reminisced to Claude Bowers:

I accompanied the Governor on the visit to Wilson. A large

crowd greeted us at the station and we went directly to the White House. There we were asked to wait fifteen minutes as they were taking the President to the portico facing the grounds. As we came in sight of the portico we saw the President in a wheel chair, his left shoulder covered with a shawl which concealed his left arm, which was paralyzed, and the Governor said to me, "He is a very sick man."

The Governor went up to the President and warmly greeted him. Wilson looked up and in a very low, weak voice said, "Thank you for coming. I am very glad you came." His utter weakness was startling and I noticed tears in the eyes of Cox. A little later Cox said, "Mr. President, we are going to be a million per cent with you, and your Administration, and that means the League of Nations." The President looked up again, and again in a voice scarcely audible he said, "I am very grateful" and then repeated, "I am very grateful." [12]

After leaving the President, Cox gave a statement to reporters committing himself to campaign for the League. A hostile Republican present described the scene to Lodge: "Young Roosevelt acted as a sort of master of ceremonies, ushering Cox into Tumulty's room where the correspondents had assembled; the candidate for vice president was bright and boyish and a little silly in his exuberance — the thing has gone to his head." Roosevelt also issued a statement. "I wish that every American could have been a silent witness to the meeting between these two great men," he declared. "Their splendid accord and their high purpose are an inspiration." To his wife he wrote that it was "a very wonderful experience." [13]

With the main subject for campaign debate set, Roosevelt spent the next several weeks winding up affairs at the Navy Department, planning his speaking trips, and writing his acceptance speech.* At the request of President Wilson, he remained as Assistant Secretary until just before the notification ceremonies. But Daniels urged him to rest, while Howe remained in the Department and conducted the routine business of the Assistant Secretary's office.[15]

Roosevelt took advantage of these few remaining days to take one last short ride on a destroyer. He left Boston at 8:40 one morning

* When FDR first appeared in Washington after receiving the nomination, workers at the Navy Gun Factory marched from the Navy Yard to the Navy Building to present him with a gavel made from the handrail of the President's yacht *Mayflower*, and to thank him for the friendly attitude he had always taken toward labor.[14]

aboard the *Hatfield*, and personally piloted it through the treacherous Lubec Narrows into Passamaquoddy Bay. When they anchored at 7:06 that evening at Campobello, he boasted not only that it was his fourth destroyer trip through the narrows, but that he had made it in record time. This was great sport, but politically it was an unwise amusement for a vice-presidential candidate. He had used a government ship as a private yacht, and had burned up enough coal to last fifty families all winter in order to carry his 165 pounds to a summer resort, Hearst's New York *Journal* pointed out. It asked what right he had to use "a warship for commuting purposes." In this respect, the end of his seven years as Assistant Secretary was very much like the beginning. As William Allen White once wrote him, "Ships arouse your noblest visions, something like 'Mr. Dick' who had 'King Charles in his head.' " [16]

There remained officially only his resignation; this was an elaborate ceremony. Some two thousand employees assembled at the main entrance of the Navy Building to watch Daniels present him with a silver loving cup on their behalf. He sent a letter of resignation to President Wilson, in which he wrote, "To you, personally, I can only repeat that all my life I shall never fail to remember the splendid principles you have kept to the fore and the devotion to unselfish service which you have given us as an example." Wilson in an informal reply expressed his "sincere regret," but, singularly enough, had Daniels draft for him a formal letter accepting Roosevelt's resignation. Counterbalancing this somewhat cool treatment, Roosevelt and Daniels exchanged notes of a warmth of mutual affection that more than erased any lingering animosities.[17]

In his happiest and most generous spirit, Roosevelt wrote in longhand:

MY DEAR CHIEF:
This is not goodbye — that will always be impossible after these years of the closest association — and no words I write will make you know better than you know now how much our association has meant. All my life I shall look back, — not only on the *work* of the place — but mostly on the wonderful way in which you and I have gone through these nearly eight years *together*. You have taught me so wisely and kept my feet on the ground when I was about to sky-rocket — and in it all there has never been a real dispute or antagonism or distrust. . . .[18]

Daniels, touched, replied in kind, and in his diary wrote his most revealing thought on his delightful but sometimes exasperating assistant: "He left in afternoon, but before leaving wrote me a letter most friendly & almost loving which made me glad I had never acted upon my impulse when he seemed to take sides with my critics."

As he prepared to leave Washington, Roosevelt, Daniels noted, was "full of campaign." He embarked immediately after his resignation upon three months of strenuous speaking. Many a vice-presidental candidate has filled no more than an ornamental place on the ticket. Roosevelt's Republican opposite, Governor Calvin Coolidge, for the most part maintained a traditional dignified silence, but Roosevelt was ready once again to take his cue from Theodore, and to use the campaign to make himself better known, particularly in the West, where embers of progressivism still glowed and Theodore Roosevelt was still remembered as one of the greatest American presidents. He described the Republican plans for a "throttled or backporch campaign" as "wholly foreign to my conception of a candidate's clear duty." It was satisfactory neither to the electorate nor to the candidate for the nominee to sit in an armchair, while highly paid publicity men gave the country an inaccurate impression of his dignity and wisdom.* "It is just as important for the candidates to get in touch with the United States as it is for the voters to have a chance to see and hear them." [19]

"We will drag the enemy off the front porch," Roosevelt proclaimed, and Arthur Krock added that if Harding were to defend himself from both Cox and Roosevelt, "he will have to swap his rocker for a revolving chair. He requires one anyway, if he is to face in every direction in his attitude on the League issue and other factors." [20]

Roosevelt tried to make his appeal "largely to the young voters" through an approach at least outwardly frank. "I am not given to pussy-footing and evading," he asserted, "and . . . am totally incapable of the old-fashioned oratorical speech, which clothes definite issues with glittering generalities." A candidate, he declared, should speak in terms understandable to the average person, not merely to the

---

* FDR's personal acquaintance with Harding, he later declared, "was really only a casual one, though it is true that I used to play golf with him on several occasions before he was nominated for the Presidency. After May, 1920, I never saw him again. As a golf companion he was always most agreeable and a good sport whether he won or lost." Once, many years later, FDR paid Harding a back-handed compliment by comparing Washington's "somewhat ponderous" style of writing with his. "No one else that I know of could write quite like Washington, unless Warren Harding."

philologist. His delivery of a section of a speech, recorded at the time, was crisp and incisive. One feature writer, comparing him with Coolidge, said that, while neither was a classical style orator, "Roosevelt's style is more direct and downright, he manages to give a peculiar impression of knowing all that he is talking about and more, too, that is extremely effective. . . . With all this there goes an ease and directness that saves the driest subject from seeming heavy." [21]

In his emphasis upon progressivism, Roosevelt made a good partner for Cox. The two men conferred amicably several times before the active campaigning began, and subsequently Roosevelt ably abetted Cox at a rather hectic meeting of the National Committee. "I have been greatly impressed with the really splendid qualities of Cox," Roosevelt wrote on July 24. "I never knew him well before, but have spent several days with him during the past week. Incidentally, they were the kind of days that tried men's souls and he measured up." Although Cox was the choice of the bosses at San Francisco, he had a sound progressive record both in Congress and as Governor of Ohio. He had fostered much reform legislation, including the reorganization of Ohio prisons, and had demonstrated marked ability as an administrator. At the Convention, Southern reactionaries as well as Wilsonians had opposed him. Although he was not widely known, he was rather well qualified to be chief executive.[22]

Ellery Sedgwick wrote that he was trying to persuade Harvard President Emeritus Charles Eliot, who was not very favorably disposed toward either candidate, to come out for Cox in the *Atlantic Monthly*. Roosevelt replied that Cox was the sort of man Eliot might well support: "He is a true liberal and while of course he lacks many of the 'literary' qualities of President Wilson, he has, in my judgement, far greater ability as an Executive." As for himself, Roosevelt continued, "I shall do my best to make the principal issue of the campaign the question of progress versus reaction. That, after all, is the fundamental, and I feel certain that the country does not want to revert to the leadership of a man who is, essentially, McKinley-minded." [23]

This was the theme of Roosevelt's acceptance speech. He delivered it on August 9 from the front steps of his Hyde Park home to a large crowd gathered on the lawn. It was an excellent speech, a clear, well-phrased, logically organized exposition of the campaign issues.*

"Two great problems will confront the next administration," he

---

* FDR had asked Franklin K. Lane, a felicitous stylist, to help him put the finishing touches on it.[24]

began: "our relations with the world and the pressing need of organized progress at home." In the realm of foreign policy, either the United States must prepare to live in monastic seclusion behind a wall of heavy and expensive armaments, or come to realize that "modern civilization has become so complex and the lives of civilized men so interwoven with the lives of other men in other countries as to make it impossible to be in this world and not of it." In domestic affairs Roosevelt pledged better organized, more efficient government. "The golden rule of the true public servant is to give to his work the same or even higher interest and efficiency than he would give to his private affairs. There is no reason why the effectiveness of the National Government should not at least approximate that of well-conducted private business."

Throughout the speech Roosevelt emphasized youthfulness and progress, as contrasted to age and conservatism. "Some people have been saying of late: 'We are tired of progress, we want to go back to where we were before; to go about our own business; to restore "normal conditions." ' They are wrong. This is not the wish of America. We can never go back. The 'good old days' are gone past forever; we have no regrets. For our eyes are trained ahead — forward to better new days. . . . To this future I dedicate myself." [25]

On the whole, the audience was captivated. McAdoo was disappointed because Roosevelt did not once mention Wilson, but Daniels was approving. The New York *Post* reporter was so swept away by Roosevelt's vigor and air of confidence that he predicted that if he did not "win thousands of votes for his ticket this fall by his charm and ability, as a campaigner, the . . . speech . . . must have been a fluke." F. W. Taussig, the Harvard economist, declared that "in comparison to Harding's performance [it was] like Hyperion to a satyr." [26]

The acceptance speech set a standard which was difficult if not impossible to maintain. With the trend so strongly Republican, a statesmanlike — hence dull — campaign would have done little to bring out a Democratic vote. Within a few days, Roosevelt was attacking the Republicans so trenchantly — for their efforts to raise a multimillion-dollar campaign fund — that no one henceforth could call him above partisanship. [27]

Immediately after the speech Roosevelt left on a swing through the country as far West as Seattle. While Howe remained temporarily at the Navy Department, a former secretary, Charles McCarthy, managed the headquarters in New York. Roosevelt took with him in his private railroad car his more recent secretary, Renah F. Camalier, and the Navy public relations man, Marvin McIntyre, who took charge of speech writing and publicity on the train. An observant and capable reporter who had covered the Navy Department for the Associated Press, Stephen T. Early, traveled ahead as Roosevelt's advance agent. Early gave out publicity in cities where Roosevelt was to appear, and sent back detailed reports of local political conditions to guide him in preparing his speeches. These covered warnings of factional differences and other dangerous matters Roosevelt should avoid, together with analyses of the sentiment of farmers, laborers, and large foreign groups, and appraisals of predominant feeling on Prohibition, the high cost of living, and above all the League of Nations. Through Early, local leaders sent suggestions to Roosevelt on what to soft-pedal or emphasize in different speeches. Early and McIntyre carried out their assignments admirably; the teamwork was excellent.[28]

On this first campaign trip, Roosevelt talked on a diversity of subjects, but especially on the League. The issue, thanks to the interchange with Harding, seemed fairly well set, with the Democrats favoring it and the Republicans opposed. The biggest question seemed to be to what extent Roosevelt could interest voters in this issue, which they had heard debated for so many months. They had wearied of the subject without, in most cases, ever really grasping what all the noise was about. Their confusion was matched by their indifference. Early wired from Chicago what, on the whole, applied to the entire nation: that the educated classes favored the League, but they were decidedly in the minority. Leading newspapers vigorously fought the League; the rank and file of voters were opposed if not indifferent, and did not understand it.* To farmers, the League was a remote factor compared with the precipitate drop in produce prices; laborers were far more concerned over the high cost of living. In keeping with this information, Roosevelt followed the general formula of telling each group

---

* Early stated this even more clearly from Minneapolis: "There is a general lack of interest in the League of Nations and a good many Democrats openly assert their dissatisfaction that the League was made the big issue. The rank and file of the people want to know what they are going to get. The war is over — for them. They are not fighting even though peace has not been declared. They are thinking closer to home, [of] their bread baskets and not of their war allies. The big issues to them are those which will bring them something personally and individually and not nationally." [29]

what the Democrats would do for them. Usually he concentrated most upon the League issue when he addressed audiences of women or professional men.[30]

At Chicago, on August 11, Roosevelt opened on a note of high and fulsome oratory. "Tonight," he declared, "we are firing the opening gun of a battle of far-reaching importance, and once again the shots are going to be heard around the World — for the action of the American Nation this year will be watched with anxious eyes by all civilization." The meeting was "a wonder," he informed his wife. The next day, as he headed northwest, was "*very* strenuous." He may have been referring to his language in addition to his activities, for at Waukegan he sounded like a parody on Theodore Roosevelt as he denounced the Old Guard Republicans for their slanderous talk about "democratic maladministration, about sinful squandering, about a saturnalia of extravagance, about a cataclysm and a betrayal." [31]

In a St. Paul speech, he promised much to farmers, labor, and school-teachers. Early joined Roosevelt at Minneapolis, and while he spoke, circulated through the audience to get comments. He informed Howe, "Without exception they were excellent for the Boss. He is speaking easier, going good and will be a finished product of oratory before we see New York again." [32]

Up to this point Roosevelt had done splendidly. Cox wired approval and encouragement. But in Montana, he overreached himself. It was the home state of Bruce Kremer, Vice-Chairman of the Democratic National Committee. Kremer arranged several large audiences, and sent word that at Deer Lodge he wanted a "rough peppy Americanism speech, bringing in [the League]," and a "snappy appearance at Anaconda with typical Roosevelt conduct." Roosevelt delivered — complete with typical conduct — but what he said that day carried far beyond the borders of the state.[33]

August 18 was a beautiful day and Roosevelt was in an expansive mood. As he went from Deer Lodge to Butte to Helena, he repeated the same speech with, at least at Deer Lodge, a few extemporaneous flourishes. A decade later, one of the Democratic leaders reminded him of "a heavy-roofed barn of a place in Deer Lodge, Montana, a farmer's picnic, and a strong forceful young man standing on a stairway addressing an audience under rather difficult conditions, but with an extended arm and sharp pointed finger driving home each of his thoughts." Obviously playing for the vote of Theodore Roosevelt supporters, he reminded his audiences of "the men in 1912 who thwarted the will of the majority of the Republican party." These were the "wolves who preyed upon the broad interests of the American people and represented special interests — they are the same wolves who have tried to do so again this year, but the American people can see through the thin disguise. They know the Penroses, the Lodges, the Smoots and the Watsons are still licking their chops for another killing."

Then Roosevelt proceeded to take the same sort of vigorous approach to the League of Nations, with a hard-boiled realism that proved more truthful than politic. He sought to refute "one of the many representations which have been handed out by these same wolves — that relates to the so-called six votes of Great Britain and her colonies in the secondary body of the League — the Assembly. As a matter of fact, I have always felt that President Wilson slipped one over on Lloyd George when he was in Paris, because while England and her colonies are apparently getting six votes to our one, the United States has a lot more than six votes which will stick with us through thick and thin in any controversy. For instance, does anybody suppose that the votes of Cuba, Haiti, San Domingo, Panama, Nicaragua and of the other Central American States would be cast differently from the vote of the United States? We are in a very true sense the big brother of these little republics. We are actually acting as trustee at the present time for many of them. They appreciate our disinterested policy toward them. Their lot is our lot, and in the final analysis the United States will have far more than six votes which will stick with us through thick and thin." [34]

At about this point he digressed from his text and boasted, "You know I have had something to do with the running of a couple of little republics. The facts are that I wrote Haiti's Constitution myself and, if I do say it, I think it a pretty good constitution."

These words bounced back upon him sharply. Harding picked up the boast and proclaimed a few days later that when he became President, "I will not empower an Assistant Secretary of the Navy to draft a constitution for helpless neighbors in the West Indies and jam it down their throats at the point of bayonets borne by United States Marines." [35]

The digression about the Haitian Constitution was, of course, both untrue and unfortunate.* There is no doubt that Roosevelt

* Perhaps this was what FDR had in mind, when in 1939 he consoled Frank Knox (who had said many vehement things against FDR in 1936): "I, too, was

said it, although he issued emphatic denials from time to time for years afterwards. Both the Democratic and Republican papers in Montana carried the statement, and when Roosevelt charged the Associated Press with disseminating a false story, more than a score of reporters of both parties signed a statement that they had heard him make the remark. Clipped and pasted in Roosevelt's own scrapbook was the most damning evidence of all, a published account of a speech he had delivered in Newburgh, New York, the previous January, in which he had made the same boast.* The manner in which this campaign slip came back to haunt him in years to come can be regarded as simply funny.

When the *Nation* in 1928 referred to the "Roosevelt Constitution," he indignantly protested to Villard against publishing this "old stuff and nonsense," and stated categorically:

1. I never admitted in a public speech that the constitution of Haiti was the best ever.
2. I never said I had written that constitution.
3. It is a deliberate falsehood to call it the Roosevelt Constitution.[36]

What was not so funny was that Roosevelt, in his Montana speeches, was describing how the League would function in entirely accurate terms of power politics, without bothering to clothe his description in the delicate terms of good-neighborliness. Again and again, and as late as in his speech at San Francisco on August 23, he declared that the United States controlled outright at least two nations to the South — "Why I have been running Haiti or San Domingo for the past seven years" — and the United States could control twice the six votes of the British Dominions in the League Assembly.[37]

The Republican New York *Tribune* pointed out that these remarks would not help American relations with Latin America. They came "too near to justifying the suspicions they entertain of the United States." Roosevelt, the New York *Telegraph* concluded, "is not a Malay running amuck to be taken seriously and handled accordingly. He is a spoiled child to be spanked." The retiring director general

---

inexperienced in national campaigns in 1920 and later regretted many of the things I said at that time!"

For a discussion of FDR's actual relationship to the Haitian Constitution, see *The Apprenticeship*, pp. 283–284.

* " 'I wrote a constitution for them,' said Mr. Roosevelt laughingly, 'which was accepted without a dissenting vote.' "

of the Pan-American Union, John Barrett, declared that Roosevelt had made a grave diplomatic mistake, if he were correctly quoted. Roosevelt took his cue from Barrett's expressed hope that he had been misquoted, and claimed in a belated denial, on September 2, that Republican reporters and editors had given quite an unfair twist to his words.[38]

But this was not the end of the matter. Equally belatedly, Harding from his front porch in Marion, Ohio, denounced Roosevelt's statement as being, to the best of his knowledge, "the first official admission of the rape of Hayti and San Domingo by the present Administration." He added, "To my mind, moreover, it is the most shocking assertion that ever emanated from a responsible member of the government of the United States." *

Since July, the *Nation* had been running a series of articles by Herbert Seligmann exposing Marine rule in Haiti. Villard sent a copy of one of them to Roosevelt, with the comment that the charges were clear and specific and added up to "one of the blackest records of dishonor in the history of military imperialism the world over." He invited Roosevelt to have the Navy Department issue a statement in its own defense. Howe asked the Marine Corps "to get up something." Daniels commissioned a Marine general to prepare a full account on Haiti with which to answer Harding, but when the report was forthcoming in October, the general (who had no love for Daniels and Roosevelt) confirmed the wanton killings. The Republicans seized upon this with alacrity, and for the moment Roosevelt was thrown so far off balance that he wrote Daniels his willingness, if need be, to abandon the campaign, then at its most intensive stage, and come to Washington to defend the Navy. But the Negroes who would be most affected by exposures of this sort were still traditionally Republican; the handful of readers of the *Nation* and the *New Republic* had long been told that neither party was liberal and the Democrats simply more interested in capturing progressive votes. So, altogether, Roosevelt's indiscretions and the Administration mistakes in Haiti had only a negligible effect on the vote.[40]

For the rest, on his first swing through the West, Roosevelt dem-

---

* Harding said concerning FDR's self-vaunted role in Haiti: "Practically all we know is that thousands of native Haitians have been killed by American Marines, and that many of our own gallant men have sacrificed their lives at the behest of an executive department in order to establish laws drafted by the Assistant Secretary of the Navy, to secure a vote in the League and to continue at the point of the bayonet a military domination." [39]

onstrated those qualities so irritating to doctrinaire liberals and to historians seeking consistency, but seemingly so requisite to successful campaigning – ambiguity and expediency. He talked as a realistic, he-man progressive in touch with the West and its problems. Governor Riggs of Alaska had warned him how unpopular "Pinchotism," the Eastern brand of conservation, was throughout the Northwest. Consequently at Billings he tried to overcome local dissatisfaction over the refusal of the Secretary of the Interior to allow construction of a dam for irrigation purposes within Yellowstone Park. What the West needed, he stressed, was not so much "conservation" as the next logical step, "development." This seemed rather vague anti-conservationist talk, but at Spokane he spoke brilliantly in terms of reclamation on a scale that would foreshadow a Columbia Valley Authority.*

Upholders of the civil rights of unpopular minorities had generally admired Roosevelt. The *Nation*, at the same time that it criticized Roosevelt's imperialism, praised him for being basically an old-fashioned liberal who could not condone the persecution of radicals that followed the war. Yet on a single day, Roosevelt talked at Tacoma as a progressive enemy of Republican special interest, and at Centralia as a super-patriot determined to rid the nation of subversives. Only a year before, American Legion men at Centralia had engaged in a bloody battle with the I.W.W. Roosevelt said he regarded his visit there as "a pilgrimage to the very graves of the martyred members of the American Legion who here gave their lives in the sacred cause of Americanism."

In a manner reminiscent at some points of the words, if not the spirit, of Lincoln's Gettysburg Address, Roosevelt declared at Centralia: "Their sacrifice challenged the attention of the Nation to the insidious danger to American Institutions in our very midst. Their death was not in vain for it aroused the patriotic people of the Great Nation to the task of ridding this land of the alien anarchist, the criminal syndicalist and all similar anti-Americans. Here in the presence of your honored dead, I pledge to the Nation our determination to carry on this patriotic work – to make certain that the land, throughout its breadth and width, shall be made unsafe for those who seek by violence to destroy the Constitution and the Institutions of America." He affirmed his faith in the ability of the American Legion to carry on

---

* FDR proposed great projects which would involve long-range planning and financing through annual congressional appropriations or perhaps even revolving funds.

this great cause, "to put into public life that new blood, that new courageous and independent thinking, and that high form of red-blooded patriotism that will keep us on the high road to better things." [41]

Consistency in politics is a rare luxury; if Roosevelt did not always indulge in it, his supporters possibly were not disturbed by his lapses, and probably not even aware of them. Over-all, he made an excellent impression. He expounded effectively those things in which Westerners were most interested, and most of the time sounded like a militant progressive. Before he left Montana, one of the most ardent of the former Bull Moosers, Harold L. Ickes, issued a statement endorsing the Democratic ticket. Roosevelt's nomination, said Ickes, emphasized the progressive character of the Democratic party. When Cox toured the same area subsequently, he found political leaders all full of praise for Roosevelt. Perhaps the most flattering indication of his effectiveness was the Republican decision to send Theodore Roosevelt, Jr., on his trail. "He is a maverick," said young Theodore at Sheridan, Wyoming. "He does not have the brand of our family." * If that were so, Westerners seemed to like the maverick better than the regular line, and in years that followed they were one of Franklin Roosevelt's strongest sources of support.[43]

At the end of August, Roosevelt returned to New York. Beginning with his speech in Chicago, he had traversed twenty states in eighteen days and averaged a fraction more than seven speeches a day. Some he delivered as early as seven in the morning, others as late as midnight. In the State of Washington, he made twenty-six speeches in two days. Well-pleased with the impression he had made, he misgauged the people of the West as "still very progressive" and "with us in our stand on the important issues."

* Several times during the campaign, FDR, without mentioning names, attacked Theodore Roosevelt, Jr. Finally, on October 27, he made a strong outright bid for the votes of T.R.'s former followers:

"I wish Theodore Roosevelt were alive today. He at least had definite convictions. He was not afraid to take a position and maintain it. He never wobbled. He never sought to evade even when members of his own party disagreed with him. To me his memory will always stand for one characteristic more than another — fair fighting. He hit hard, but he taught young America to hit above the belt. During his life he was first to make objection to unfair political methods of misrepresentation. At all times he acknowledged the respect due to the Presidency of the United States. He understood the distinction between fair criticism and disrespectful vilification." [42]

On the other hand, Roosevelt was not too pleased over the relatively little attention he had received in newspapers throughout the rest of the country. The vice-presidential candidate on a losing ticket was not especially newsworthy; the Associated Press had not considered him important enough to bother to assign a staff man to accompany him.[44]

At New York headquarters, things were alarmingly dead. McCarthy complained that he could not get so much as a desk or a typewriter without personal effort, and that the publicity bureau would not spend any money until further orders. The party leaders were not even bothering to solicit the would-be contributors whose names George Foster Peabody suggested, and were brusque to William Church Osborn and other would-be campaign workers. "I am frankly disappointed at the slowness in getting the business organization going," Roosevelt wrote the National Chairman, George White, and went on to suggest various effective and aggressive tactics similar to those of the Republicans. The sad fact was that the self-generating vigor and optimism of Roosevelt and Cox remained almost the only bright spots in the murky gloom. "The real work around Headquarters here," wrote McCarthy on October 8, "is being done by the revolving electric sign which has the pictures of Cox and Roosevelt on it. There is about as much life in this place as there is in the man in the moon. . . . When all is said and done you cannot win an election without money." [45]

Nevertheless, Roosevelt continued to work as hard as though a handful of additional Democratic votes could tip the balance. Through most of September, he campaigned in New England and up-State New York — hopelessly lost territory. He took off September 21 in order to enter his oldest son, James, in Groton, but otherwise through the latter part of the month maintained his vigorous tempo. The emphasis was still upon progressivism and the League, but several times he introduced new notes, interesting less because of their bearing upon the campaign than their implications for his own future. At Manchester, New Hampshire, he followed Calvin Coolidge, who he claimed had assumed that "the great accomplishments of our history are due to the preponderating wisdom and power of the Congress of the United States," and that during the next four years the President should be a sort of chief clerk to carry out the policies announced by the Senate cabal. "As I recall history," Roosevelt asserted, "most of our great deeds have been brought about by Executive Leaders, by the Presidents who were not tools of Congress but were true leaders of the Nation, who so truly interpreted the needs and wishes of the people that they were supported in their great tasks."[46]

In October the campaign went into high gear; Roosevelt headed West again on a schedule even heavier than before. This time Eleanor Roosevelt, who had stayed home until her son Jimmy entered Groton, accompanied him. They had gone no further than West Virginia when word came that the boy was ill, but his grandmother went to visit him, and Mrs. Roosevelt continued on the trip. Much of the time she was the only woman on the car, although here and there other women campaigners joined them. She felt decidedly a novice, but learned a great deal. As for her husband, he averaged about ten speeches a day and his voice became like "that of a crow," but he kept on. The strain told on most of the entourage; the tempers of several grew short and Roosevelt once had to intervene to prevent a fist fight. Sometimes Roosevelt was impatient, Camalier remembers, but he never uttered a cross word.[47]

As the campaign drew to a close, Roosevelt marshaled the arguments on the League, which he had held to as the central theme. So much had been said that little could be new. The central point of discussion was Article X, the collective security provision of the Covenant,* which the Republicans claimed would mean sending American boys to fight on foreign soil, and which Roosevelt said would not. The argument became as barren as the little story he related about a Kansas Senator's description of Lodge as "a case of thin soil intensively cultivated."

When the respected Republican elder statesman, Elihu Root, declared that Article X was what Cox would insist upon, and Harding reject,[48] it was Roosevelt who answered him.

"Mr. Root knows that the question of force of arms would not be raised unless various other measures, such as international ostracism of the country making the threat, had first wholly failed. In other words, force of arms, which Mr. Root drags up as a bogy, would only be recommended in case of a threatened world-conflagration such as that through which we have just passed. Every sane man knows that in case of another world-war America would be drawn in anyway, whether we were in the League or not."[49]

* Article X provided: "The Members of the League undertake to respect and preserve as against external aggression the territorial integrity and existing political independence of all Members of the League. In case of any such aggression or in case of any threat or danger of such aggression the Council shall advise upon the means by which this obligation shall be fulfilled."

Roosevelt reiterated his wish to add reservations to the Versailles Treaty providing that nothing in it should be "in any way superior to our Constitution or in any way interfere with the rights of Congress to declare war or send our soldiers overseas." [50]

Earlier he had resorted to the homely simile he had used before (and would use again), by comparing the League to a fire department. People no longer sat on their front porches when they saw a neighbor's house catch fire; they had organized a department with equipment. What it still needed was a chief, and the United States should be the fire chief. [51]

Another facet of the League issue was the "hyphenated vote." The Irish and Germans, large numbers of whom were normally Democratic, according to Early and everyone else, were going to vote Republican because of the League. For this reason, some added, every German-American newspaper in the United States was supposedly Republican. Roosevelt tried to capitalize upon this by charging that the Republicans unscrupulously were trying to secure the German vote by "making special appeals to the very small but dangerous element in our Country which was not loyal, or was of doubtful loyalty during the war." As an example, he cited George Sylvester Viereck's support of Harding. [52] This attack caused Roosevelt some little embarrassment in 1928 when he ran for Governor. Yet there is nothing to indicate that anti-League Irish and Germans deserted the Democratic party in any greater proportion than the population as a whole.*

During the first part of October, the Republicans seemed to be swinging more and more toward an anti-League position; most informed people were favorable to the League, and the Democrats hoped that if more people could be educated on the subject, they would vote for Cox and Roosevelt. Politicians from West Virginia to Colorado and back again and again sent word to Roosevelt to keep on the League subject. Early in the month, Harding engaged in anti-League double talk at Des Moines, Iowa, and Roosevelt felt there was a glimmer of hope. [53] For a few days, newspapers reported that the Republicans were losing ground.

It is doubtful whether Roosevelt at any point seriously thought he could win; Eleanor Roosevelt has said that he never held any hope. He was too optimistic by nature not to indulge in the dream of

* An unpublished statistical analysis by Robert Friedman of the University of Illinois, of various foreign elements in the election of 1920, shows no significant correlation.

victory, however. "The old idea about the vice-presidency is going to be knocked into a cocked hat this time if our ticket is elected, and I think it will be, after my trip to the west," he had written on September 18; "four years from now the vice-presidency is going to be a highly respected and live wire office." Certainly Harding's negative implications on the League added to this buoyancy. "Things are really going vastly better," he wrote Tumulty on October 17. "The President's judgement that the League would be the only true issue is wholly borne out." *

The evidence, as Roosevelt years later came to view it, was to the contrary: the League issue did not change many votes. Surveys bear this out. While most rural people, for instance, could not fathom the intricacies of the Covenant, they did not care much one way or the other. Most of them in the North read Republican newspapers, but few of these bothered to attack the League; instead they fired their editorial ammunition at the larger target of Wilsonianism.† Early had written from Sioux Falls, South Dakota: "The bitterness toward Wilson is evident everywhere and deeply rooted. He hasn't a friend." At the same time — "There is good sentiment in favor of *a* league of nations." But whatever enthusiasm existed was hard for Cox and Roosevelt to capitalize upon. The voters considered them tied to Wilson; hence their election would be a continuation of the disliked regime. Republican campaign orators never opposed "*a* league" but always had instructions to refer to "*the* League" as "Mr. Wilson's League." Roosevelt cut loose as far as possible. He seldom mentioned Wilson's name, but did have to defend repeatedly the acts and achievements of the Wilson Administration.[55]

If Harding's Des Moines speech did drive any well-informed liberal voters toward the Democrats, it was easy enough for the Republicans to retrieve them. Their lure was the statement of some thirty-one

* But when FDR remarked to his friend, Tom Lynch, that he would want him in Washington after the 4th of March, Lynch, who had been circulating among the audiences, replied that while people liked FDR personally, they would not vote for Cox and the League.[54]

† An unpublished survey by James Murray, University of Illinois, of twenty-nine downstate Illinois newspapers, indicates that only one paper interpreted Harding as opposing outright American membership in the League. Even after his Des Moines speech of October 7, which seemed anti-League, few Republican leaders opposed it. On the other hand, no papers, Democrat or Republican, even published the manifesto of thirty-one prominent Republicans favoring the League, which followed it in a few days. As developed in all the papers, the issue was not so much the League as Wilsonianism.

prominent members of the party that they favored a League, but would vote for Harding. Roosevelt's moment of hope waned. Every straw poll in the North showed Harding leading by wide margins, and the *Literary Digest* poll, which had great prestige, gave him a margin of three to one in six key states. Boss Murphy's men scarcely bothered to campaign in New York City. "This good for nothing Tammany bunch," McCarthy wrote to Roosevelt, was "doing absolutely nothing. If they have not sent out the word to lay down they might as well do it." They concentrated so exclusively on efforts to pull Al Smith through to re-election as Governor that they placed Smith's picture on campaign posters opposite that of Cox, where custom demanded Roosevelt's should have appeared.[56]

Yet, at the close of the campaign, the candidates tried to appeal to a bandwagon psychology, and sent heartening telegrams to each other, presumably to read to audiences.* After that, there was not much to do except to issue a final pre-election statement — "Four months of a long uphill fight have come to a close" — and go to Hyde Park to await the results. When the figures began to come in, the fact that they meant a Republican victory could have been no surprise, but the proportions of the landslide must have been a sharp jolt. Harding received 61 per cent of the popular vote, 16 million to Cox's 9 million, and 404 electoral votes to 127 for Cox.[58] Roosevelt wired congratulations to Coolidge, and issued a statement calling upon Americans of all parties to give their wholehearted support to the new Administration.[59]

If Roosevelt was depressed, he did not show it. "Curiously enough," he wrote three days later, "I do not feel in the least bit down-hearted. It seems to me that everything possible was done during the campaign, and no other would have been either honorable or successful. As long as the other people were going to win I am glad they have such a clear majority. The whole responsibility will be theirs, and I hope they will be able to make good for the sake of the country." The one criticism he made had a peculiarly Theodore Roosevelt flavor: "My only fear for the country is that the old reactionary bunch will so control things that many Liberals will turn Radicals, and that

---

* In part they were doubtless still too optimistic because they seldom saw or heard anyone except their own warm adherents. "We are having the most remarkable meetings I have ever seen. The fight is won," Cox wired FDR on October 20. FDR replied three days later that the swing to the Democrats that he had noticed in the Middle West applied to New York as well, and predicted they would carry the state.[57]

the heavy majority will end in a period of utter confusion. Let us all hope that this will not take place." [60]

A few days later, Roosevelt made light of the debacle by styling himself at the head of a letter, "Franklin D. Roosevelt, Ex. V.P., Canned. (Erroneously reported dead)." There was reason for him to feel gay as he began to analyze the results, since for him the net result of the campaign was considerable gain, not loss. He had won national stature. Numerous politicians in various sections of the country knew him personally, and liked and admired him well enough to write him their morning-after thoughts.[61]

Roosevelt entered into correspondence with all these new and important allies. They were a significant asset. To all of them he had the same message: that they should begin at once reorganizing and building toward the next campaign so that they would be in a strong position to take advantage of Republican mistakes by the time of the congressional elections of 1922. Within New York, he felt that he had excellent opportunities, since although Tammany had almost abandoned the national ticket, they had not been able to pull Al Smith through. He pointed out, "Even the worst of our leaders recognize that an overwhelming majority in New York City for Governor Smith was insufficient to elect him." On both the state and national levels, he was not through, but just beginning, even though it might be a long fight. "Thank the Lord," he wrote Steve Early, "we are both comparatively youthful." [62]

Infantile Paralysis

> I have renewed my youth in a rather unpleasant manner
> by contracting what was fortunately a rather mild case of
> infantile paralysis.
>
> — FDR, *September 16, 1921.*

I N November, 1920, for the first time in ten years Roosevelt was
out of public life. The Republican landslide was an indication of
the shift in the times as well as in his personal fortunes. The era of
political reform was long since over, and one of speculative business
activity was about to open. The center of gravity of the nation swung
back from Washington to Wall Street. Many former progressives
were left dazed or disillusioned, but not Roosevelt. He went to Wall
Street.

This was a major readjustment. Within a few months he was forced
to make an even greater one.

After a short vacation spent in duck hunting in Louisiana,[1] Roosevelt returned to New York City to embark upon new activities as
a lawyer and businessman. Van-Lear Black, a wealthy Baltimore finan-
cier and sportsman, hired him at a salary of $25,000 per year to become
vice president in charge of the New York office of the Fidelity and
Deposit Company of Maryland, the third largest surety bonding
concern in the country. The directors of the company had wanted
"an executive with legal training, an alert mind and a soundness of
judgment which had not been warped by specialization." These undoubtedly were less important criteria in choosing Roosevelt than
his famous name and his flair for the spectacular. Black himself was a
man who took tall chances on yachts and in airplanes; Roosevelt was
the sort that appealed to him.[2]

Roosevelt's function in his new job, as he himself explained, was
to help maintain business stability. The Fidelity and Deposit Company made investigations before it issued the surety bonds that guaranteed the holders against loss. Thus it helped prevent individual

dishonesty and corporate speculation. The company served as "a balance wheel in industry" and was in effect a public utility, Roosevelt declared. Thus he felt it encouraged "real progress and constructive work." [3]

In his new role as a Wall Streeter, Roosevelt expressed his views on the sharp depression which the country was suffering. Business was reconciled to heavy losses, he stated, since deflation was inevitable. "It requires more than a few months for the vast industry and commerce of this country to resume prices which compare favorably with the pre-war values," he said. "The entire cycle of revision must be accomplished before business will again function normally." [4]

This was the sort of talk that generally came from financiers. To underscore finance as his profession, on January 7, 1921, he received a most auspicious send-off — a testimonial dinner at Delmonico's. The Governor of the Federal Reserve Board, William P. G. Harding, in the main address, congratulated the nation upon reaching a more normal state of mind, and predicted sane business conditions, with neither wild orgies of extravagance nor irrational pessimism.[5] The presence of many dignitaries highly respected among businessmen and financiers still further proclaimed Roosevelt's soundness: Justice Augustus N. Hand; Frank A. Munsey, the magazine and newspaper publisher; Adolph S. Ochs, publisher of the New York *Times;* Edward R. Stettinius of United States Steel; Daniel Willard of the Pennsylvania Railroad; and Owen D. Young of General Electric — all were there.[6]

Roosevelt spent only his mornings working as, in his own phrase, one of the "younger capitalists." Afternoons he took active part in a new law partnership into which he had entered the previous spring with his old friends, Grenville T. Emmet and Langdon P. Marvin. It was not very exciting, and received no fanfare. Altogether, he liked his new activities. "I am delighted to get back to real work again," he wrote Felix Frankfurter. "The two varieties of work seem to dovetail in fairly well." [7]

As was his habit, Roosevelt also dovetailed in an astonishing variety and quantity of political, charitable, and social activities. He served as one of the Overseers of Harvard University, director of the Seamen's Church Institute, President of the Navy Club (a recreational organization for sailors), Chairman of a two-million-dollar fund drive for Lighthouses for the Blind, Chairman of the Greater New York Committee of the Boy Scouts of America; he was a prime mover in establishing the Woodrow Wilson Foundation, a member of the Near East Relief Committee, the Council of the American Geographic Society, and the Executive Committee of the National Civic Federation.[8]

Public appearances served to keep him known, and gave him further opportunity to appear as a sound young businessman. His engagement book for the spring months of 1921 was jammed with speaking dates. But these were speeches of a different sort from those he had delivered in the progressive era. Reform was not popular, and he did not publicly advocate it. Indeed, when the National Civic Federation planned a committee on political matters, he warned, "You will get off on the wrong foot if you call it a 'Department of Political Reform.' The word 'reform' still brings visions of pink tea artists who dabble in politics one day a week for perhaps two months in the year." [9]

In private, Roosevelt addressed himself to the professional politicians, and based his appeal to them not on ideologies but on techniques. He repeated his long familiar refrain that the Democratic organization in upstate New York must be built from the district level. Within a week after the disastrous 1920 election he was expressing his indignation to Al Smith that the Republicans had been able to turn out majorities of three to one and even five to one in many rural areas. During the campaign he had seen the remarkable organization that Will Hays had built in Indiana in only four years; certainly the Democrats could do likewise in New York State. He was eager to rebuild for the 1922 election both on a state and on a national level, and was ready to back any group that would undertake this in upstate New York, provided it did not challenge the city machine. It was rumored that when Al Smith joined Roosevelt's long-time upstate ally, William Church Osborn, in an alliance against Tammany Boss Murphy, Roosevelt would have no part of it. Yet he wrote Osborn a charming note supporting him for the state Democratic chairmanship. His aim was simple: to prevent the sort of city–country rift in the party which would lead only to further Republican victories. He preferred party unity under the firm rule of Boss Murphy to insurgency and defeat. That kind of unity prevailed at the State Convention in June, 1921. Roosevelt's personal stake in maintaining it seemed obvious. Already he appeared to be a major contender for the 1922 nomination for United States Senator, and he would need competent organizations behind him if he were to win.[10]

Roosevelt retained his faith in the League of Nations and his affection for the Navy; however, his views continued to evolve with the times. Realistically accepting the fact that the Republican victors refused to take the United States into the League, he advocated precisely the substitute for League membership that the new Harding Administration in a few months seized upon as its own. The United States should first make peace with Germany and then seek agreement with other countries to start reducing "the terrible burden of armaments from which all nations are suffering," he wrote in March, 1921. "I am wholly out of sympathy with this talk about our having the greatest Navy in the world." [11]

This did not mean that he advocated "Utopian disarmament" without regard to other nations — as a member of the Harvard Board of Overseers he was insisting upon proper facilities for the Reserve Officers' Training Corps. He meant, rather, that the Democratic Party should ask President Harding to call a meeting between the United States, Great Britain, and Japan, to stop the costly naval competition. But it was Senator William E. Borah, not Roosevelt, who asked Harding to do so, and the Republicans made the cause of limited naval disarmament their own. On Armistice Day, 1921, the great powers began conferring in Washington; soon they agreed upon a naval ratio, and pledged themselves to build no more capital ships for ten years. [12]

At the time this was hailed as a noteworthy achievement; but, from the perspective of several decades, big-navy advocates later regarded the Treaty of Washington as a disastrous blunder through which the United States gave away the naval supremacy with which it might have maintained world peace during the unstable thirties. Blunder or not, it was a program which Roosevelt favored at the time. [13]

While ideologically Roosevelt was growing away from the Navy Department, he had to tie up several unfinished bits of naval business. In principle, he was opposed to accepting legal commissions in which he would benefit from his recent position as Assistant Secretary.* Yet in November, 1920, he shocked some of his former associates by appearing at the Navy Department on behalf of the New

---

* In 1925, FDR declined to prosecute claims for a prospective client because it "would seem like capitalizing public service for private gain. There is no legal reason why I should not appear on behalf of clients against the government, yet I am convinced that for my own self-respect I should prefer not to do so." [14]

England Oil Corporation, which he had done so much to foster while he was in the Department. Secretary Daniels sent him to Gordon Woodbury, the new Assistant Secretary. Woodbury treated him so curtly that Roosevelt, who was a little obtuse in matters of this sort, complained that he must be "either crooked or pinheaded!" [15]

There still remained, besides, the painful aftermath of the Newport trouble. A subcommittee of the Senate Naval Affairs Committee, consisting of two Republicans and one Democrat, had slowly gone ahead with an investigation of the sordid affair. In the summer of 1921 it violated its promise to give Roosevelt an opportunity to testify, and prepared to report. Overwrought, Roosevelt dashed to Washington, which was sweltering hot, and "found all the cards stacked" against him. The two Republican committee members told him they thought it unnecessary to let him testify on his own behalf, since he had already appeared before the Navy Board. Finally they did agree to give him a few hours to examine the fifteen volumes and six thousand pages of testimony before the committee, and to allow him to submit a statement. They promised to wait until eight in the evening for his statement, but even before that hour they gave their unamended majority report to the newspapers for release the following afternoon. It was so scurrilously denunciatory of Roosevelt and Daniels that the usually austere New York *Times* ran a headline:

> LAY NAVY SCANDAL
> TO F. D. ROOSEVELT
>
> • • • •
>
> DETAILS ARE UNPRINTABLE [16]

The Republican majority report quoted the finding of the Navy's court-martial on the question of Roosevelt's knowing that vice investigators were engaging in sodomy in order to trap homosexuals. The court-martial had held Roosevelt's actions to be "unfortunate and ill-advised" — a statement quite objectionable to Roosevelt. The majority report went further, and labeled them "a most deplorable, disgraceful and unnatural proceeding." [17]

For hours Roosevelt worked with pencil on legal foolscap, preparing an emphatic refutation of the charges. The subcommittee paid no attention to it, or to his request for an open hearing before the entire Naval Affairs Committee. However, the lone Democratic Senator on the subcommittee issued a minority report criticizing that of his colleagues as being unjust. In addition, Roosevelt with the aid of Steve

Early prepared a press statement which in part vitiated the very unfavorable publicity. "As an American, one deplores bad faith and a conscious perversion of facts on the part of any Senator," he asserted. "As an American, irrespective of party, one hates to see the United States Navy . . . used as the vehicle for cheap ward politics." [18]

The Republican Senators had overreached themselves. The violent and preposterously partisan nature of their report dulled its effect. "That Senate business is pretty lowdown stuff, but as a matter of fact," Roosevelt privately predicted, "in the long run, it will only hurt those mean and dishonorable enough to stoop to deliberate falsification for the sake of politics." The charges were, indeed, soon forgotten; but understandably they deeply upset Roosevelt at the time. In words of a sort he normally never used, he expressed the feeling that those who had smeared him "will be duly rewarded for this kind of dirty work after they pass on to the next life." [19]

At least outwardly, Roosevelt sloughed off his anger quickly. A few days later he went in a skylarking mood with a group of notables on a Boy Scout outing up the Hudson. Their announced purpose was to visit the Scout Camp at Palisades Interstate Park, but their horseplay took a rather adult form. A former internal revenue collector brought along a large hollow cane filled with what was apparently an alcoholic beverage. The men passed the cane from one to another and drank from it. When it reached the Police Commissioner, they immediately arrested him and brought him to mock trial for possessing liquor in violation of the Volstead Act. Roosevelt served as "prosecuting attorney." He tasted the fluid, smacked his lips, and declared, "May it please the court, I find that the liquid in this container is nothing more than vanilla extract, and I move that the case be dismissed." It was. The outing was of the type Roosevelt always would particularly enjoy. But no one knew until later what distinguished this one from many others — it was the last occasion when newspaper photographers took pictures of Roosevelt walking alone, unaided.[20]

Despite his appearance of vitality and excellent health, Roosevelt was, as he later granted, thoroughly fatigued. The unpleasantness in Washington had forced him to cut short his vacation at Campobello; at the end of July he returned there. "I thought he looked tired when he left," his secretary, "Missy" LeHand, wrote Mrs. Roosevelt a few days later. But Campobello vacations to Roosevelt meant substituting long days of sports and physical exertion for his usual strenuous regimen in the city. His way of resting would have worn out most men.[21]

Van-Lear Black took Roosevelt back to Campobello aboard his yacht, the *Sabalo*. When they ran into dirty weather, Roosevelt took over the navigation, since Black's captain did not know the Bay of Fundy waters. For hours he remained at the wheel, battling the fog, until he brought the yacht safely into Welchpool Harbor.[22]

The next day was sunny, and they fished for cod from the *Sabalo's* tender. "I baited hooks, alternating between the fore and aft cockpits of the motor-tender, crossing beside the hot engine on a three-inch varnished plank," Roosevelt once recalled. "I slipped — overboard. I'd never felt anything so cold as that water! I hardly went under, hardly wet my head, because I still had hold of the side of the tender, but the water was so cold it seemed paralyzing. This must have been the icy shock in comparison to the heat of the August sun and the tender's engine." [23]

Although Roosevelt did not feel well, he continued his usual active routine. Wednesday, August 10, 1921, was no exception. In the afternoon, while the Roosevelts were sailing in their small yacht, the *Vireo*, they saw a forest fire on one of the islands and went ashore to help put it out. Roosevelt cut evergreen branches for himself and his children, and for several hours they flailed at the flames. "Late in the afternoon we brought it under control," he recalled. "Our eyes were bleary with smoke; we were begrimed, smarting with spark-burns, exhausted." The remedy, Roosevelt thought, would be a swim. So with his children he dog-trotted two miles along the hot, dusty roads across the island of Campobello, swam across a narrow fresh-water lagoon inside the beach, and dipped into the frigid waters of the Bay of Fundy. Then they ran back in their bathing suits.[24]

"I didn't feel the usual reaction, the glow I'd expected," Roosevelt recalled. "When I reached the house the mail was in, with several newspapers I hadn't seen. I sat reading for a while, too tired even to dress. I'd never felt quite that way before." [25]

During supper, Roosevelt quietly remarked that he thought he had a slight attack of lumbago, excused himself and went upstairs to bed. "The next morning when I swung out of bed my left leg lagged but I managed to move about and to shave. I tried to persuade myself that the trouble with my leg was muscular, that it would disappear as I used it. But presently it refused to work, and then the other." [26]

When Anna Roosevelt carried a tray into her father's room, he

FDR with James and Elliott, at Campobello, N.B., July 27, 1920

FDR, as President of the Boy Scout Foundation of Greater New York, visits the Scout Camp at Lake Kanowahke, July 27, 1921. (This is the last picture showing Roosevelt walking unassisted.)

greeted her with a cheerful smile, and even a wisecrack. There was nothing to be cheerful about, for his temperature was 102. Mrs. Roosevelt was worried, and the children alarmed. She sent for their old friend, Dr. E. H. Bennett in Lubec, who, despite Roosevelt's pain and paralysis, diagnosed the illness as no more than an ordinary cold. In order that the house might be quiet, Mrs. Roosevelt sent the children and some guests off on a three-day camping trip. Even with the reassurance of Dr. Bennett, she was too concerned about her husband to go with them.

The next morning, Friday, August 12, Roosevelt could not stand up, and by evening had even lost the power to move his legs. They were numb, but very sensitive to the touch. He ached all over, was at least partly paralyzed from the chest down, and his thumb muscles had become so weak that he could not write.[27]

By Saturday, Mrs. Roosevelt and Dr. Bennett decided they must call in a consultant. Louis Howe, who was visiting at Campobello, helped them canvass the resorts. They located a famous elderly specialist, Dr. W. W. Keen of Philadelphia, who was staying at Bar Harbor. He diagnosed the paralysis as due to a blood clot in the lower spinal cord, prescribed heavy massage, predicted that Roosevelt would recover, though perhaps not for a long time — and sent a bill for six hundred dollars. Mrs. Roosevelt sent to New York for a masseuse; meanwhile she and Howe massaged her husband as best they could. The heavy kneading of his feet and lower legs was exceedingly painful to him, since they were hypersensitive. Still worse, it was exactly the wrong treatment, and further damaged the muscles.

For several days, he continued to have a serious fever and to show no improvement. It was difficult to get a nurse, so Mrs. Roosevelt herself took care of him and slept on a couch in his room.[28]

A week after the first chill, his temperature returned to normal, and despite the acute depression that normally accompanied this illness, Roosevelt's spirits bobbed upward. "I think he's getting back his grip and a better mental attitude though he has of course times of great discouragement," Mrs. Roosevelt wrote. "We thought yesterday he moved his toes on one foot a little better which is encouraging." She added, referring to the specialist's prediction that it might take a long time for her husband to recover, "I dread the time when I have to tell Franklin and it wrings my heart for it is all so much worse to a man than to a woman." [29]

Whatever the dark feelings Roosevelt must have had, he kept them to himself at the time. Years later he confided to Frances Perkins that for the first few days he had been in utter despair, feeling that God had abandoned him. Then his buoyancy and strong religious faith reasserted themselves; he felt that he must have been shattered and spared for a purpose beyond his knowledge. As he had been brought up to do, he displayed none of the black side of his feelings to his family; incredibly soon he was making light of his affliction. Only a week after he was taken ill, he wrote, "Thanks to a severe chill which I lay to vagaries of the Bay of Fundy climate, which has more tide and more kinds of weather than any other place in the globe, I am spending a considerably longer vacation than I intended under the stern eye of a doctor who refuses to allow me to more than look at my mail and sign a few letters each day." [30]

Roosevelt's uncle, Frederic A. Delano, meanwhile was consulting several specialists, who from Delano's description felt certain that the disease was infantile paralysis. They recommended that the massages and manipulations stop, since the patient must have time to rest and rebuild slowly. On August 25, Dr. Robert W. Lovett, a Boston specialist on poliomyelitis, arrived and confirmed this. He stopped the massaging and suggested hot baths. Fortunately for Roosevelt's morale, Dr. Lovett considered it a mild attack, and thought Roosevelt might recover completely.[31]

On the first of September, Sara Delano Roosevelt, who had been in Europe, arrived at Campobello, and immediately entered into the gay spirit of the sickroom. She wrote her brother:

"I got here yesterday at 1:30 and at once . . . came up to a brave, smiling, and beautiful son, who said: 'Well, I'm glad you are back Mummy and I got up this party for you!' He had shaved himself and seems very bright and *keen*. Below his waist he cannot move at all. His legs (that I have always been proud of) have to be moved often as they ache when long in one position. He and Eleanor decided at once to be cheerful and the atmosphere of the house is all happiness, so I have fallen in and follow their glorious example. . . . Dr. Bennett just came and said 'This boy is going to get all right.' They went into his room and I hear them all laughing. Eleanor in the lead." [32]

The first stage of the illness was over, and Roosevelt was ready to begin working to regain the use of his legs. Even more important to him than this was the question of whether he would be able to return to his career. Sara Roosevelt firmly believed that for him to do so would kill him, and strongly voiced her opinion that he should not. Her son was an invalid; an invalid he would continue to be. Therefore he should give up all thought of future participation in business and politics. He had had a brilliant career already, even though he was only thirty-nine, and was well entitled to retire. He should return to Hyde Park, which he loved, to the life of a country gentleman, and a collector of books and stamps. In effect, he would have been returning to her full domination, and would have been assuming the way of life of his elderly ailing father, her beloved James, whom she had nursed twenty years before.

Roosevelt would have none of this. The struggle against his mother's wish for him to retire went on for months, but fortunately he did not have to fight it alone. Eleanor Roosevelt thinks that if it had been a necessity for him to retire he could have done it and not been unhappy. However, it was not necessary; she, Howe, and Dr. George Draper, who was taking over the treatment, felt that for Roosevelt to retire would be "a terrible waste," and fortified him with spirits as indomitable as his own. Even before Roosevelt was sure he had infantile paralysis, he was impatient to return to his career. Within two weeks after the attack, Mrs. Roosevelt was planning to move him to New York City for treatments because, "if, as he hopes, he can carry on his various business activities it can only be done there." On August 22, he authorized President Henry Noble MacCracken of Vassar College to name him on a committee for an endowment drive, and on September 12, he accepted membership on the Executive Committee of the Democratic Party in New York State. Thus, there was literally no period when he was out of public life. He came to a determination to go on and make a further career for himself, Mrs. Roosevelt has said, at a time when he was lying in bed and working for hours to try to wiggle a big toe.[33]

At the same time, Howe, who had spent years building a reputation for square dealing with newspapermen, fed vague explanations to a press association correspondent who came over from Eastport almost every day. He managed to keep the news that Roosevelt was seriously ill out of the newspapers until August 27, when he could couple with it the information that "he is now improving." Thus, from the outset Howe helped create the illusion — so important if Roosevelt were to continue active in politics — that there was nothing vitally wrong.[34]

Howe's greatest difficulty came on September 13 when a private railroad car arrived at Eastport to take Roosevelt to New York. The crowd of well-wishers and reporters would have been shocked to see Roosevelt helpless on a stretcher. Besides, the invalid was a shy man who would have been keenly embarrassed over displaying his weakness in public. Consequently, Howe started a rumor that Roosevelt would land at a dock at the far end of town, then signaled the motorboat to bring him in at the near end. His stretcher was loaded onto a luggage cart and bumped up a long, sharp incline to the train. It was a physical as well as a mental ordeal, for every jolt caused him excruciating pain; yet when he spied eight-year-old Franklin, Jr., he managed to smile, wave, and convey the impression that nothing very much was wrong. His stretcher was passed through the window of the railroad car, and he was comfortably settled before the crowd spied him. When the New York *World* correspondent saw him in the car, "Mr. Roosevelt was enjoying his cigarette and said he had a good appetite. Although unable to sit up, he says he is feeling more comfortable." [35]

Thus Roosevelt returned to New York City without letting the public learn that he was suffering from anything more than a passing illness. After he had arrived at the Presbyterian Hospital, Howe gave the story to the newspapers that Roosevelt was suffering from poliomyelitis and had lost the use of his legs below the knees. But he quoted Dr. Draper, who had been Roosevelt's school chum: "He will not be crippled. No one need have any fear of permanent injury from this attack." After the New York *Times* ran this news on its front page on September 16, Roosevelt wrote Adolph S. Ochs, the publisher:

> While the doctors were unanimous in telling me that the attack was very mild and that I was not going to suffer any permanent effects from it, I had, of course, the usual dark suspicion that they were just saying nice things to make me feel good, but now that I have seen the same statement officially made in the New York *Times* I feel immensely relieved because I know of course it must be so.
>
> I am feeling in the very best of spirits and have already been allowed to take up part of my somewhat varied interests. [36]

If anything, Howe had succeeded too well in creating the impression that Roosevelt had suffered only a slight handicap from which he was quickly recuperating. Herbert Pell sent a note asking him to attend a meeting of the Democratic Executive Committee on October 11. Howe scrawled on the margin, "Mr. Pell had better wake up & hear the birdies!" Even Roosevelt had to admit to another political associate that the newspaper accounts were "a trifle optimistic." [37]

Undoubtedly Howe was aiming his emphatic forecasts of quick and complete recovery at Roosevelt as well as at the public, for the sad fact was that Roosevelt was still a very sick and badly crippled man. Dr. Draper, who was a skillful specialist, now found his former optimism (based on Dr. Lovett's diagnosis) quite unjustified. Roosevelt continued to suffer from agonizing sensitivity. It hurt him even if someone touched the sheet on his bed. Over a period of weeks he would now and then run a temperature as high as 102. He made little or no improvement. At the same time that Roosevelt was determined that he was going to leave the hospital on crutches in two or three weeks, Dr. Draper was confiding to Dr. Lovett that he feared the back muscles were so seriously damaged that his patient might not even be able to sit erect. He felt that the maintenance of Roosevelt's morale was paramount, and in co-operation with Mrs. Roosevelt and Howe he worked diligently to sustain it. Dr. Draper wrote, "He has such courage, such ambition, and yet at the same time such an extraordinarily sensitive emotional mechanism, that it will take all the skill which we can muster to lead him successfully to a recognition of what he really faces without crushing him." [38]

Yet slowly Roosevelt did make progress, and because he did, it is questionable whether he ever faced up completely to his condition. He still had sufficient power in his arms to pull himself up by a strap over his bed and thus turn himself over. Dr. Draper did not examine his arms, in order not to disturb his belief that they were unaffected; indeed, Roosevelt took considerable pride in their strength.* When Daniels visited him in the hospital, he beckoned his former chief close to the bedside, then suddenly launched a blow that sent him reeling. "You thought you were coming to see an invalid," Roosevelt laughed, "But I can knock you out in any bout." [40]

He did recover the entire strength in the muscles of his arms, and as he developed them, they became very powerful. His back muscles too recovered, and despite Dr. Draper's forebodings, there came a day when he was able to sit up. On October 28, 1921, he went home to his 65th Street house, able to pull himself up by a strap and, with some assist-

* Ernest K. Lindley wrote that after over ten years, the close friends and business associates who visited FDR in the hospital still reminisced about it "eagerly and with tones of wonder." "In essence they are all the same. Roosevelt gaily brushed aside every hint of condolence and sent them away more cheerful than they could make a pretense of being when they arrived. None of them has ever heard him utter a complaint or a regret or even acknowledge that he had had so much as a bit of hard luck." [39]

ance, to swing himself into a wheel chair. His state of mind was excellent, and his hope for the future boundless. "I . . . am getting along well and expect to be walking on crutches in a very few weeks," he wrote on December 8. "The doctors say that there is no question but that by the Spring I will be walking without any limp." [41]

But the months of pain and strain were by no means over. In January, 1922, the muscles behind his knees began to tighten and pull his legs up under him. Dr. Draper had to put both legs into plaster casts. During two weeks of agony, wedges, driven a bit deeper each day, stretched the tendons back.[42]

In February, Roosevelt was able to put on braces of steel, weighing seven pounds each, and stretching from his hips to his shoes. With the aid of these, he slowly learned to stand up once more and to walk with crutches. He was not really walking, but maneuvering himself with his hips; he was never again able to walk or even stand without support. He had no balance and no power in his legs. However, at the time, he still either did not know, or did not choose to believe, that he was hopelessly crippled. With determination and enthusiasm, he began gentle exercises that he hoped in time would rebuild the strength of his leg muscles.[43]

It was a most tense, unpleasant winter in the house on 65th Street. Everyone had outwardly to maintain a semblance of cheerfulness when there was nothing to be cheerful about. Roosevelt would get down on the living room floor with the younger children, but since they failed to realize his weakness, there was the danger that they would rough-house with him too hard. The house was so overcrowded that Mrs. Roosevelt had to sleep on a cot in one of the boys' rooms. Through it all, Sara Delano Roosevelt, with her usual dogged vigor, worked unceasingly toward her goal to get Roosevelt to accept his invalidism as permanent and return to Hyde Park to retirement. She poked and prodded at every weak point in the family relationship — she was sure she knew better than the doctors and that her son must be kept quiet; the house was too noisy. She even worked to convince fifteen-year-old Anna that it was unjust for the girl to have a small fourth-floor room, while Louis Howe had a large third-floor room with bath. To do so was not difficult, since Howe, whose humor and interests were entirely adult, was not liked by the Roosevelt children. Also, Anna was at a difficult age and quite unhappy already. Sometimes at the dinner table she was so annoying to her father that he spoke severely to her and she left in tears. Consequently her grandmother was able to persuade her that her mother was not interested in her. Finally, Anna went to her mother and demanded a switch in rooms. Eleanor Roosevelt, preoccupied with her husband's illness, did not realize Anna's agitated state of mind, and rebuked her sternly.[44]

Every bit of Mrs. Roosevelt's thought and energy was going into the fight on behalf of her husband. As had always been her habit, she maintained a phenomenal degree of outward composure. It never occurred to her to take Anna into her confidence and "consult with her about our difficulties or tell her just what her father was going through in getting his nerves back into condition." In retrospect she wrote, "I have always had a very bad tendency to shut up like a clam, particularly when things are going badly; and that attitude was accentuated, I think, as regards my children." [45]

Even Eleanor Roosevelt's magnificent reserve could withstand only so much attrition. One afternoon in the spring, while she was reading to her two youngest sons, she began to sob uncontrollably, and cried for hours. When Elliott came home from school and found her crying in the living room, he fled; Howe tried to find out what was wrong and failed. Finally, she went into an empty room, locked the door, and slowly pulled herself together. It was the only time that she lost emotional control of herself, but it seemed to have a salutary effect upon Anna, who began to draw closer to her mother, and soon was confiding in her. As for Mrs. Roosevelt, "From that time on I seemed to have got rid of nerves and uncontrollable tears, for never again have either of them bothered me." [46]

There has been much speculation about the effect of the illness and suffering upon Franklin D. Roosevelt. He did demonstrate immediately a truly incredible fortitude — but he had possessed it in large measure since childhood. His own reserve, the buoyant mask with which he hid his inner feelings, was so uncracked at the time and in following years that it is hard to gauge his emotions.

"Now, I don't want any sob-stuff in the relation of my experience," he warned a newspaperman in 1928. "Of course, it was a great shock to be stricken down at a time when, except for natural exhaustion after a hard campaign, I felt myself to be in the pink of condition. And it was rather humiliating to contract a disease of which 75 per cent of the victims are children. But I am thankful that my children were spared." [47]

CHAPTER VII

The Comeback Begins

> Except for my legs I am in far better physical shape than
> ever before in my life, and I have developed a chest and
> pair of shoulders on me which would make Jack Demp-
> sey envious.
>
> — FDR, *December 8, 1922.*

THE MENTAL rehabilitation of Roosevelt began by the end of
the first week of his illness at Campobello Island. The physical
recovery could not really start until the spring of 1922, but by then
he was already making a striking adjustment to his new condition of
life.

Previously he had been highly mobile, darting like a waterbug from
one function to another, going everywhere and doing everything. He
had been seldom out of the public eye; wherever it focused, there he
was. This almost frantic existence had seemed essential to his political
ambitions — and now it was gone. For the time being, he could no
longer appear at the dinners, meetings, rallies, and other gatherings
which had been so time-consuming but so useful. He could not even
attend political and business conferences unless they met at his own
home.

Roosevelt determined to meet this situation not with surrender but
with readjustment. He must learn to delegate most of the tasks which
he used to perform for himself. This called for an organization, and
within a very few months he had assembled a small, effective one.
Its chief of staff was Louis Howe, who functioned much as he had
when Roosevelt was Assistant Secretary — as press agent, political
guide, and administrative assistant. His long experience in operating
many enterprises in the name of Roosevelt made it easy for him, beginning in the fall of 1921, to continue many of Roosevelt's business
and civic activities. At the time that Roosevelt became ill, Howe had
recently finished winding up affairs in the Navy Department, and was
debating whether or not to accept a lucrative business position. He

immediately declined it, and thereafter gave his full time and devotion to Roosevelt.[1]

The task which faced Howe was to maintain Roosevelt's morale and (partly for this reason, and partly for its own sake) to maintain Roosevelt's eminent position in politics. One of the minor but most delightful means Howe had of keeping Roosevelt in high spirits was to make use of his own flair for amateur theatricals, which coincided with Roosevelt's love of spoofing and partying. At the close of the 1920 campaign, Roosevelt had given a pair of cuff links for Christmas to each of his entourage; the following January they assembled to celebrate his birthday. Thus began the Cuff Links Club. Under Howe's management, it provided Roosevelt annually with a sort of Gridiron dinner of his own. As major-domo for the meeting at Roosevelt's home, January 26, 1924, Howe planned to rig the dining room "to represent the ward-room of the Battleship *Colorado* and making it a complimentary dinner given by the employees of the Brooklyn Navy Yard, still maintaining the fiction that we were on our campaign trip" —

> We might start things with an amusing dialogue between Admiral [William V.] Pratt and the Master Mechanic in which Pratt insists that all the boys come aboard whether they have washed their hands or not. To carry this out get [Marvin] McIntyre to get sailor suits from the Department for our four sweetest singers. They can dress in my room before dinner, and appear as the Colorado Star Quartette. Also, some other goat must represent the Marines. Apropos of Hayti, he should present Franklin with a couple of skulls of Haytians which he dug up from the local graveyard for amusement. You will probably remember the unfortunate incident.
>
> The more I think of it, the more possibility this seems to give, and I am getting quite keen for it as I write. A special radio from "Little Ted" [Roosevelt] has infinite possibilities in it.
>
> Get the gang together and go to it, and let me know the date for the big drunk.[2]

Howe helped Roosevelt decide which of his many functions he wished to salvage, and which to jettison. Some were of a hobby nature which did not require physical exercise, and these of course he could keep up — collecting stamps and naval books, manuscripts, and pictures. He could, himself, make purchases by mail, but he often sent Howe as his representative to auctions.

At one auction Roosevelt acquired for eighty-five dollars the minutes of the Council of Appointment of New York City, for 1778–1779. He arranged for the New York Historical Society to publish it as a volume of their collections, and reprinted fifty copies under his own title page, which carried the information, "From original manuscript in possession of Franklin D. Roosevelt." Also, he edited and published the *Records of the Town of Hyde Park*.[3]

Colonial Dutch houses interested him even more. In 1923, he wrote an article for *De Halve Maen*, the publication of the Holland Society, recommending that the Society sponsor a book of photographs of houses essentially of Dutch origin. He served as chairman of the Publication Committee of the Society, raised a fund of $7000 to underwrite the project, and obtained the services of a competent photographer and of an excellent local historian, Helen W. Reynolds. The result was a handsome book,[4] for which he wrote the introduction:

> The genesis of my interest in *Dutch Houses in the Hudson Valley before 1776* lies in the destruction of a delightful old house in Dutchess County, New York, when I was a small boy; for, many years later, in searching vainly for some photograph or drawing of that house, I came to realize that such dwellings of the colonial period in New York as had stood until the twentieth century were fast disappearing before the march of modern civilization and that soon most of them would be gone.[5]

In the winter of 1921–1922, Roosevelt had to decide which offices in civic organizations he would be able to retain. He began by dropping several. One day, when Howe was going over a list of them with Roosevelt, crossing off one after another, they came to the Boy Scouts. Roosevelt balked, because he wished to help complete its reorganization. Indeed, in March, 1922, he made one of his first public statements after his illness, calling upon patriotic veterans to serve as scoutmasters. There were only 20,000 Scouts in New York City, he asserted, when there should be 100,000. Every new scoutmaster made possible an additional Scout troop. He could not resist pointing out the military significance: every new troop meant that much additional training for better citizenship and defense.[6]

For Roosevelt the Boy Scouts also represented a means of promoting racial tolerance. When an expatriate in Paris wrote him an anti-Semitic, anti-immigrant tirade, and implied that the Scouts should be of pure "Nordic" and "old American" stock, Roosevelt replied indignantly:

"If you were familiar with the Boy Scouts you would realize that thousands of Scouts are of Jewish origin. This is true not only in New York City but in many other parts of the country. Thousands and thousands of the Scouts themselves are what you call 'second generation Americans.' . . . I want to suggest that you come back home and spend the next few years in getting to know your own country." [7]

Religious tolerance likewise was a theme upon which Roosevelt liked occasionally to expand. His vehicle for doing so was his position as chairman of the campaign to raise funds to construct the Cathedral of St. John the Divine. Both he and his half-brother, James Roosevelt Roosevelt, took the keenest interest in this project. More than his deep pride in and devotion to the Episcopal Church motivated him, for he felt strongly that the Cathedral must be built above creed and faction. The debate between fundamentalists and modernists was already at a high pitch. It was to reach its rather ludicrous climax several years later — when William Jennings Bryan, the fundamentalist, jousted with Clarence Darrow in a Tennessee trial over a state law forbidding the teaching of evolution. Roosevelt, in the winter of 1923, proclaimed:

"People as a whole realize that the Cathedral will be something above and beyond any disagreement of one generation. This great temple is, to be sure, a creation of man, but as far as human knowledge will allow it, is being built to last and endure through the centuries. In its lifetime countless generations of ministers and laymen will come and go, agreeing not always on matters of doctrine or the interpretation of the true teaching of the Christian religion, yet through all this the Cathedral will remain and grow strong as the outward symbol of the permanency of faith. There need never be fear that the Cathedral will represent a narrow or blind doctrine." [8]

This was typical of the way in which Roosevelt was holding on to many of his old interests and old ideas, expanding them to meet the new demands of the 1920's. Unless he continued to be prominent in this way in well-known causes, and unless he continued to make public pronouncements (banal or hackneyed though they might be), the electorate would soon forget him, and a comeback would be even more difficult. Under Howe's guidance, he worked this vein as energetically as he dared. By the end of 1925, he felt he should go more slowly. "I want to tell you frankly that my name as a Chairman of campaigns is getting worn out," he wrote in declining a new venture. "I have recently been the Chairman of the Cathedral Building . . . fund and also of the American Legion drive, and am constantly sending out appeals as the President of the Boy Scout Foundation." [9]

Without leaving his home or office, Roosevelt could thus lend his name to drives or even political enterprises; but for several years it remained difficult for him to appear in person at the countless dinners, rallies, and meetings that an active politician is expected to attend. Someone else must represent him at these affairs, someone of personal charm and prestige. Howe's skill was unsurpassed, but his unimpressive demeanor made it essential that he keep hidden from public view. To fill this need, Howe with remarkable foresight turned to a person who at the time seemed a most unlikely candidate for the role: Mrs. Roosevelt. Not only could she make appearances for her husband, but she could appeal to that fairly new and as yet not fully known half of the electorate, the women. Women's divisions of the party were starting to grow rapidly in size and prestige. A woman of Mrs. Roosevelt's latent talent could assume a key position in a remarkably short time.

Eleanor Roosevelt, who until fairly recently had shunned publicity, now forced herself into quite different habits. She did so at Howe's insistence, and with a will, since like Howe she recognized the necessity of keeping her husband actively in politics if he was to retain his interest in life.

The metamorphosis of Eleanor Roosevelt had begun several years earlier. After 1917, when she worked so long and arduously in a Washington canteen for soldiers, she gradually became more active outside her home. In the winter of 1920–1921 she had started to build a life of her own by studying shorthand, typing, and cooking. Soon she was writing reports on national legislation for the New York State League of Women Voters, and traveling throughout New York as its vice-president. From these experiences, from her many trips with her husband, and from years of attentive listening, she undoubtedly had come to know far more about the workings of politics than she realized.

Eventually, she began to rise in the Democratic party of the state. After presiding at a luncheon for the women's division of the Democratic state committee, she became finance chairman of the division — during the only period when it raised its own money. This made it necessary for her to appear in front of audiences. With Howe sitting in the rear as critic and teacher, she forced herself to make political speeches and learned to restrain her nervous giggle.

By 1924 she had made herself, as a New York *Times* reporter commented, an experienced and expert campaigner. She had also acquired numerous political acquaintances who were useful to her husband, and she was influential among the women voters. She displayed an integrity and a sustained enthusiasm for progressive reform that were comparatively rare in the politics of the twenties. In her own right she was a significant political leader.

Roosevelt took a keen interest in his wife's new tasks. "At home we discussed politics violently," she has said. And yet she refused to participate in the making of his political decisions. She felt it was better to let a man run his own business and avoid being regarded as the instrument of someone else, particularly his wife.[10]

As early as January, 1922, Roosevelt demonstrated an understanding of how to build the distaff side of the Democratic party. He advised Mrs. Roosevelt's friend, Caroline O'Day, who was head of the state women's division:

"Get the right kind of women in every election district in the various rural counties. . . . There are thousands of election districts upstate where it is not only unfashionable to be a Democrat, but even where Democrats are rather looked down upon. It is absolutely necessary for us to restore in these country districts . . . the prestige of the party. Democratic women have too often in the past been rather apologetic for calling themselves Democrats. This should end, and they should let the world and their neighbors know that they take great pride in their Party." [11]

While his wife made public appearances, another woman served as a less conspicuous but none the less significant member of the little group around Roosevelt. This was his personal secretary, Marguerite A. LeHand, whom he called "Missy." He had become acquainted with her while she was working at his New York headquarters during the 1920 campaign. She was a strikingly attractive woman who combined intelligence with absolute devotion. Throughout the rest of her life she was to serve Roosevelt loyally.[12]

Roosevelt himself captained this team. He depended upon those around him for assistance, not direction.

Even before he returned to New York from Campobello, he was dictating political letters. As soon as he arrived at the Presbyterian Hospital — in the autumn of 1921 — he began corresponding with Democratic leaders in Hyde Park, Dutchess County, and elsewhere in the state. Within a week after leaving the hospital for his own home in New York City, he jumped again into national politics by writing to the newly elected Chairman of the Democratic National Committee, Cordell Hull, and proposing that the party overhaul its "archaic and outgrown machinery." As a start, he suggested in another letter, which he made public, that the Democratic leaders hold annual conferences. Reaction was favorable. "You have hit the nail squarely on the head," the editor of the Nashville *Tennessean* told him. Hull, after expressing his warm and friendly interest by mail, called at Roosevelt's house to confer with him.[13]

Meanwhile Roosevelt was formulating issues that would bring votes to the Democratic party — and to himself. He addressed himself to small-business, middle-class Americans, who had formed the backbone of the progressive movement and, though no longer as keenly interested in progressive reform, still harbored for the most part a prejudice against Wall Street. At the end of 1921, in a letter to be read at a Jackson Day dinner at Portland, Oregon, he declared that the significance of Jackson for the 1920's lay in his "earnest determination to keep the control of our government out of the hands of professional moneymakers and to keep it, as was always the intention of our forefathers, in the hands of the people themselves." [14]

Roosevelt's efforts brought immediate results. In January, 1922, when his legs were in casts and his pain excruciating, the New York *World* reported that Tammany considered him the ideal nominee for United States Senator the next fall. At the end of May, when he had advanced to crutches, Arthur Sears Henning of the Chicago *Tribune* found the New York organization favoring him for Governor. He was "a good man with a great name," one of the political higher-ups told Henning. "We couldn't do better." An upstate Republican paper dubbed him the "Boy Scout of Democracy," in a scurrilous editorial which must have warmed Roosevelt's heart — since the enemy would not be likely to waste ammunition on a man considered hopelessly ill.[15]

The fact that his name was so current in politics in 1922 was most heartening. It meant that he could center his attention upon physical recovery, secure in the knowledge that at the proper time he would have no trouble in running for office. "Though I am very much better and improving every day I am still forced to get about on crutches and could not possibly run a campaign this fall," he wrote a well-wisher in July, 1922.[16] "There is no possibility of my running for the Governorship *this year.*" *

* The italics are mine.

This optimism helped him to view his affliction in a rather detached fashion — most of the time. But one day, sitting in his wheel chair in his Hyde Park library, he was supervising his daughter Anna while she stood on a ladder moving books. Suddenly she dropped an armload. He winced, then upbraided her. She ran off crying, and sobbed to her mother that she did not see why her father need be so angry with her over a mistake.

"Mother talked of the battle Father was fighting against great odds; of the naturalness of his nervous reaction; how lucky we were to have him alive and to be able to help him get well; how much more patience and grit he had to have than we; until I felt very sheepish and even more ashamed — but in a different way, a more adult, understanding way. Back I went to the library where, of course, I not only found forgiveness but also a sincere and smilingly given invitation to resume my place on the library ladder." [17]

The outburst had relieved rather than created tension, and it was of a rare sort. Most of the time, Roosevelt was so unself-conscious that around his children he bared his legs, which, because of the failure of the muscles to function, were becoming pathetically thin. He would identify the various muscles by name and explain which ones he was concentrating his exercises on. Thus he accustomed them to his condition. When he went to Boston in June, 1922, to be fitted for braces, he told Mrs. Hamlin that his hips were normal, but his legs less and less so the farther down he went, and his toes only 15 per cent of par. But he insisted that "he was gaining very surely." [18]

Most of that summer he worked on his legs at Hyde Park. Dr. Lovett had recommended that he take only gentle massage, keep in warm sunshine, and swim in water of a temperature of at least seventy degrees. It proved to be excellent advice. "Sunlight seems to do more than anything else to restore the motor nerves," Roosevelt wrote two years later, "and swimming is the best exercise, because the body is practically sustained by the water and the legs have a perfectly free motion without any weight being put on them." In the summer of 1922 Vincent Astor gave him the use of a nearby pool, and Roosevelt was pleased to find that he could move his legs in the water far better than he expected. Determinedly, he set himself the task of increasing their movement. "One day, he hollered to me — he was out there swimming," Sara Roosevelt's chauffeur, Louis Depew, recalled — "and he says, . . . 'The water put me where I am and the water has to bring me back.' " [19]

In his eagerness to recover, Roosevelt was impatient with mild exercise, and forced himself through a routine so strenuous that he ran the risk of damaging rather than rebuilding his leg muscles. He had parallel bars set up in the garden, and, bearing most of his weight on his arms and shoulders, made his way back and forth on these. Once he slipped, painfully tore some of his leg ligaments, and set back his recovery by several weeks. But he persevered. Almost every day he tried the still more rigorous exercise of setting out on his crutches down the long drive toward the front gate. Chatting, joking with those who accompanied him, as though what he was doing were a pleasure, he inched along his perspiring way until he was too exhausted to go further. He seldom reached the road.

He improved his legs somewhat, and he developed his arms and shoulders and chest to such an extent that his physical appearance was altered from slender to stocky. To demonstrate his self-reliance, he would sometimes drop himself off his chair and crawl across the floor, his legs trailing behind him. By autumn it should have been manifest that he could not force his legs back into shape, and, yet, patient and smiling, he kept on with his strenuous and painful regimen.[20]

Not everything at Hyde Park that summer was grim exercise. Roosevelt spent part of his time in pleasant relaxation, reading or engaging in the hobbies which he enjoyed. For instance, for several years he had enjoyed making model boats and sailing them on the Hudson River.* He now found that with balsa wood he could build craft with which to "beat all my rivals . . . because of the lightness of my hull compared with theirs." He was proud of these miniature sloops and schooners, so freakish and yet so fast.[22]

In 1923 he wrote a detailed description of this absorbing hobby:

> My first interest in building small boats came through my older children and I built 1 or 2 in the beginning that were fairly accurate models of the *Resolute* and the *Reliance*. I then became interested in the question "How fast can a small boat be made to sail?" I discarded all so-called rules of the model yacht enthusiasts affecting displacement, depth of keel, sail area etc., and devoted myself to the problem of how to make the fastest possible small boat of a given size. I early adopted a standard of 38" overall length, and have tried almost every kind of experiment

---

* In June, 1921, FDR had raced a toy yacht across the Hudson in competition with those of Howe, his son Elliott, and two of his friends. Elliott's yacht *Resolute* won by covering a mile in fourteen and a half minutes.[21]

from the English cutter to the skimming dish, and even double-keeled boats and catamarans.

These boats we race on the Hudson River every summer, and it has brought forth some very interesting data in regard to weights, sails, etc. I might add that the construction of each boat becomes simpler — the first boats I made were real models, complete down to the last detail [.] [N]ow, however, in order to get the necessary lightness of construction, I use balsa wood for the hull, balsa wood or oiled silk for the deck and aluminum for the spars . . . The first year the boats took nearly 16 minutes to cross the Hudson, a distance of ⅜ths of a mile. Since then some of them have done it in 10 minutes and 15 seconds. This is not bad for a tiny craft only 38 inches long. The maximum sail area was reached this year in a boat which successfully carried a mast 6 feet long. You can imagine that the sport produces not only a vast amount of discussion from all who take part in it as to the respective merits of the various types of boats, but produces also keen rivalry in the mechanical skill and appliances for the saving of weight, new forms of rigging etc.

It goes without saying that all the children of the neighborhood are tremendously interested, though I am not sure that their interest is any greater than that of the older generation." [23]

That summer and fall, Roosevelt's political role was more like his sailing of model boats than like the yachting he would have preferred. Yet he found his political activities gratifying. He kept a firm grip on even the most minute functions of the Dutchess County Democratic organization. In order to do so, he had to fend off Edward E. Perkins, who had never liked him since his start in politics in 1910. His old allies, John E. Mack, Tom Lynch, and a few others, stood by him firmly against Perkins, as they had for many years.

In Dutchess County matters, Roosevelt especially enjoyed working with Henry Morgenthau, Jr., son of Ambassador Morgenthau, who had long been one of the most generous contributors to Roosevelt's campaign funds. Roosevelt had first met the younger Morgenthau in 1915, when Dutchess County Democrats arranged for him to come to Hyde Park for lunch. Roosevelt, much taken with his guest, then only twenty-four, had tried to persuade him to run for sheriff, but Morgenthau felt he should devote most of his time to running his farm. "He is an awfully nice fellow," Roosevelt reported to the Democrats, "and one who will be a tremendous asset to us in the county." They should put him on the county committee — "Certainly we ought to do everything possible to keep him interested." Roosevelt continued to keep in touch with him, especially during the war, when Morgenthau served as an officer in the Navy. And Mrs. Roosevelt worked with equal pleasure with Elinor Morgenthau. Similar upper-class background and interests in farming, as well as common political goals, bound the two families together in an enduring friendship.[24]

In state affairs, Roosevelt in 1922 tied himself to Al Smith's coattails. With a good vote-getter like Smith, the Democrats had a fine opportunity to take advantage of unfavorable economic conditions and recoup their losses. Unemployment was still heavy, and the country was not as yet really recovering from the sharp depression of the previous year. The Harding Administration, despite its emphasis upon policies favorable to big business, had failed to bring the sort of "normalcy" for which voters were looking. In New York State, the Democrats might well return to power if they could remain united and run a strong leader for governor. The main obstacle was William Randolph Hearst, who was in one of his perennial office-seeking moods. Hearst had the Mayor of New York under his thumb, and through lavish spending was persuading numerous Democrats to support him for the nomination for either governor or senator. Inevitably this would mean another trouncing for the Democrats in November. Only Smith, who loathed Hearst, was strong enough to prevent the publisher from dominating the ticket. Unfortunately, Smith had a sizeable family, and was reluctant to leave the presidency of a trucking firm at 50,000 dollars per year to return to the governorship, which paid only 10,000.[25]

Without consulting Smith, Roosevelt sent a letter of advice to a state Democratic conference which met early in July. He warned them they would risk defeat if they sought out "false gods and political nostrums." They should turn to the man who stood for honest, vigorous administration and progressive Democracy. "I appreciate keenly that this particular man in every way deserves a rest from public service in order to attend to his personal affairs," Roosevelt declared, "yet I believe that the need of the State of New York for his services is so great that he would put this first." And he named the man — Alfred E. Smith.[26]

Roosevelt wrote privately to Smith (who had thanked him for the letter to the conference), "I realize full well the extremely difficult position you are in." He pointed out that the public letter was carefully worded so as not to call upon Smith for any commitment, and he reiterated his fear of the Hearst drive. "There is no danger about this County or any other County that has an effective organization," he told Smith, "but, as you know, there are some dreadfully weak sisters upstate and the promise of the Hearst iron men looks mighty good." [27]

In the next few days, as Hearst continued to gain momentum, numerous delegations of politicians visited Smith and urged him to declare his candidacy. Only a week before the deadline for filing designating petitions for the primary, Smith finally capitulated, with the proviso that the leaders of the party call upon him publicly to run. Roosevelt, next to Smith the best-known Democrat in New York State, wrote the desired open letter,[28] asserting that Smith was the hope of the "average citizen":

"Something must be done and done now. In every county the chief topic of political conversation is 'Will Al Smith accept if he is nominated?' Already unauthorized agents are saying that you will not accept, and many are being deceived and beginning to lose interest as a result. It would surprise you to know what enthusiasm would spring up overnight if we knew you would accept the nomination." [29]

Roosevelt's letter was front-page news, even though Samuel Seabury had written a similar plea three months earlier. Newspapers predicted that Smith would quickly answer Roosevelt's appeal. And he did. "During the past twenty years," he wrote, "I have been so honored by my Party that even the members of my family would be dissatisfied if I did not answer the call." He promised to run, if nominated.[30]

This was a political coup of the first importance for Roosevelt. Friends and newspapers congratulated him; Hearst's baffled ally, Mayor John F. Hylan, remarked in exasperation, "Yes, I read Al's letter, but I can't figure out who Frank Roosevelt represents." Someone retorted in a letter to the New York Times that Roosevelt represented "Democrats not demagogues," and added that he had picked a winner in Smith. Roosevelt viewed his own handiwork with satisfaction. "It appears to have rather punctured the Hearst boom," he commented, "but eternal vigilance is necessary in Politics, and Al will not be nominated until the votes are actually cast in the Convention." [31]

Within Dutchess County, Roosevelt worked hard to prevent a defection to Hearst before the convention met. On September 8 he held a reception for Smith at his Hyde Park home — an excellent occasion for displaying himself as well as Smith before the party workers. He wrote a formal endorsement of Smith to be read at the meeting of the county committee — at which, for the first time, women (including Mrs. Roosevelt) were allowed to participate as full members. The county sent a strong Smith delegation to the convention.[32]

Roosevelt himself was not yet in physical shape to attend, but Mrs. Roosevelt and Morgenthau went. When Smith was nominated, these two led the Dutchess County delegates in a procession three times around the hall.* Howe, of course, was there too, and he reported that Hearst's name was "chogged in" once, by a Queens orator, but the result was "not over five handclaps and at least 50 loud hisses." Nevertheless, to the very end, Hearst fought for the nomination for United States Senator, then lost because of Smith's refusal to run on the same ticket with him. Smith wanted Roosevelt as the senatorial candidate. Roosevelt declined, and tried to get the nomination for his upstate ally, George Lunn, the eager aspirant of two years earlier. But Lunn, Howe reported to Roosevelt, "accepted [a] seat on [the] back end of [the] band wagon while we were fighting for a front place"; he accepted nomination as Lieutenant Governor. This was lucky for Roosevelt. He could not be blamed for letting Lunn down, and he could gain some merit with Murphy by acquiescing in the nomination of Hearst's friend, the Commissioner of Health of New York City, Dr. Royal S. Copeland.[34]

Once the convention was over, Roosevelt was ready to close ranks with Hearst against the Republicans. He allowed himself to be named honorary chairman of Dr. Copeland's campaign committee. When the Doctor came to Poughkeepsie to speak, and appeared depressed because of newspaper hostility, Roosevelt encouraged him to carry on. "I often think of that night at Hyde Park," Roosevelt reminded him a few years later — "of how you wondered if it was worth while to even try to make a real fight, and how I told you that no fight was lost in advance if it was entered into with all one's mind and heart." [35]

Only in this humble way was Roosevelt able to participate in the 1922 campaign. He did little more except to write a strong letter of endorsement for Smith late in October: "Governor [Nathan L.] Miller is an obstruction to navigation. . . . It is time to clear the channel."

---

* Smith wrote FDR later, "Everything went along first rate, I had quite a session with our lady politicians as Mrs. Roosevelt no doubt told you. I was delighted to see her taking an active part and I am really sorry that you could not be there but take care of yourself — there is another day coming." [33]

His active participation was not essential, since, as he had predicted, it was a Democratic year. Smith was elected by the largest plurality a gubernatorial candidate had ever received in the state. He carried his entire ticket (including Dr. Copeland) to victory. In doing so, he won a remarkable number of upstate votes. Roosevelt, hailing this "reawakening of the Rip Van Winkle upstate Democracy," emphasized to Smith his strong interest in making "matters still better, especially in a good many counties where the leadership is either antiquated or of the type which is controlled by the Republican machine." He suggested to Smith a number of upstate Democrats whom he thought worthy of appointment.[36]

Roosevelt boasted to Joseph E. Davies, "I had quite a tussle in New York to keep our friend Hearst off the ticket and to get Al Smith to run, but the thing went through in fine shape." He was, of course, overstating his own role somewhat. Still, he had exerted a good deal of influence for a man who could not physically participate in the campaign.[37]

By December, 1922, he was able from both a political and a personal standpoint to take a much more heartening view of his future. "I am just back in New York after a very successful summer at Hyde Park," he informed James Cox. "The combination of warm weather, fresh air and swimming has done me a world of good. . . . The legs are really coming along finely, and when I am in swimming, work perfectly. This shows that the muscles are all there, only require further strengthening. I am still on crutches but get about quite spryly, and, in fact, have resumed going to my office down town two or three times a week." And he went on to outline to Cox, who at least nominally headed the Democratic Party, what he had achieved in New York, and what he hoped the Democrats could do in the nation.[38]

Already he had begun to reappear at the office of the Fidelity and Deposit Company at 120 Broadway. He did not yet visit his law office at 52 Wall Street, because of the high front steps — he could not bear the thought of being carried up them in public. At 120 Broadway he could manage, by himself, the one little step up from the sidewalk. At first, with painful pride, he would come slowly walking down the corridor on his crutches. One horrible morning the crutches slipped on the polished marble of the lobby, and he plunged to the floor. But, as Basil O'Connor remembers, he pulled himself to a sitting position, and almost gaily called to the bystanders to lift him to his feet. Later he allowed himself to be whisked in by wheel chair. He came two days a week, then three, and finally four. This required a new routine. Between 8:30 and 10:30 he saw Howe and particular intimates at home in bed. Then he went to the Fidelity and Deposit office, took lunch at his desk, and remained until 1:30. "I used to go occasionally to lunch with him there, sitting across the desk from him — he couldn't move from the desk," his law partner, Langdon P. Marvin, remembered. "We used to have lively and pleasant luncheons together — he was always excellent company and he hadn't let his terrific disease depress him. He never mentioned it and he was always buoyant and optimistic." In the afternoon he would work at his personal business (occasionally the law) until five o'clock, then come home for tea, exercises, and conferences until dinner.[39]

Gradually he adjusted himself to his limitations so well that he could work more effectively than ever before. Ernest K. Lindley, writing in 1931,* declared:

> He soon began to find that his inability to run around had compensating advantages which, in time, became a really powerful asset. He had always been a restless worker, frequently jumping up and down and dashing here and there through sheer excess of physical energy. He had always been vigorous in his exercise. He had seldom shown fatigue simply because he had been endowed with unusual vitality. Now that he was compelled to sit in one spot, all of his energy was of necessity concentrated upon the work before him. A bit removed from the hurly-burly, he was relieved of many petty irritations and the nervous wear and tear which is one of the most exhausting things about city life. He had an excellent excuse not to do what he did not wish to do; and at the same time, he could not resort to the normal human impulse to run away from a difficult problem. Every one came to see him; he spent neither time nor energy moving from this conference to that.
>
> Many of the men who came in regular contact with him avow that they envied his even temper and clear head at the close of days which had worn them out. He impressed his close friends as having emerged from his illness less impetuous, more serene and judicially minded, though without loss of decisiveness.[40]

* From *Franklin D. Roosevelt: A Career in Progressive Democracy*, by Ernest K. Lindley, copyright 1931, used by special permission of the publishers, The Bobbs-Merrill Company, Inc.

Eleanor Roosevelt observed that the main effect of the polio upon her husband was to accentuate his already great power of self-control. The fact that he had to decide on a course of treatment, and then wait a year or two to see its effect, forced him to the attitude that "once you make a decision you must not worry about it." This greatly influenced his future life. Many public men, after they have made a decision over which they have no further control, worry for fear it is not the right one. Roosevelt learned to put out of his mind the things he could do nothing more about.* "He could pull a curtain down and go to sleep," Mrs. Roosevelt has said. During the Presidency, and especially during the war, this was "a salvation to him." Polio gave him that capacity.[41]

---

* Mrs. Roosevelt remembers that at the time of a banking crisis when FDR was Governor that he sent for Lieutenant Governor Herbert Lehman, himself a banker, to give him advice. Lehman made the necessary decisions, and FDR accepted them, but Lehman then paced the floor. FDR could not pace because he could not walk. He sat in his chair and remarked that if Lehman, once he had made up his mind, would stop worrying, he would be much more useful the next day.

Against the Isolationist Tide

> I am not wholly convinced that the country is quite ready
> for a definite stand on our part in favor of immediate en-
> try into the League of Nations. That will come in time,
> but I am convinced that we should stand firmly against
> the isolation policy of Harding's administration.
> — FDR TO JAMES COX, *December 8, 1922.*

THE SWEEPING Democratic gains from New Hampshire to Washington in the 1922 election seemed to Roosevelt a magnificent
opportunity to renew the fight for a Wilsonian foreign policy. He
wished immediately to harness his own augmented political prestige
and that of the party in a drive to turn public opinion against the
foreign policy of the Harding Administration.

For the time being, he did not dare make any outright demands
that the United States enter the League of Nations, since Secretary
of State Charles Evans Hughes had been able, without much public
protest, to bury proposals that the United States promote even a
feeble Association of Nations. But he did feel the Democratic party
could awaken people to the dangers in the Harding policies. "I am
basically convinced," he wrote Cox, his running mate of 1920, "that
the country is beginning to recognize that national isolation on our
part will not only allow further disintegration in the Near East,
Europe, etc. but from our own purely selfish point of view will
bring hard times, cut off exports, etc. etc." He realized that he and
Cox would have difficulty in assuming open leadership in battling
the Republican foreign policies, since people would howl that they
were merely seeking the 1924 Presidential nomination. What he
wished was to unite party leaders on general policies.[1]

In keeping with this, behind the scenes, Roosevelt tried repeatedly
during the 1920's to commit Democratic leaders in Congress to a
firm opposition stand. This was not easy, since many of the Democrats, like Jim Reed of Missouri, were if anything more isolationist

than their Republican colleagues. The split on foreign policy cut through party lines in a fashion that made unity difficult if not impossible. Nevertheless, a few men like Cordell Hull co-operated.

Roosevelt played an equally active part in sustaining public interest in the Wilsonian program. Already, in January, 1921, before President Wilson had left office, Roosevelt had agreed with a friend that something should be done to show Wilson "in some visible way that many thousands are glad to testify to their appreciation of him." But he feared a testimonial dinner would be too arduous. Besides, while it would enable a few people in New York and Washington to express their gratitude, "it would be far better if something could be done which would give the people of the whole country a chance of uniting in tribute." In March, a few days after Wilson had left the White House, this feeling, on the part of Roosevelt and many others, led to a campaign to raise $500,000 "to endow an award for services to humanity as a memorial to the work of Woodrow Wilson." Roosevelt had become chairman of a preliminary committee, and declared, "This movement is an American movement to recognize a great American, and in doing that we, as Americans would be proud to have the assistance of thinking men and women in every part of the world." [2]

In planning the Foundation, Roosevelt enlisted the aid of Wilson himself. Wilson declined to see him in March, 1921, but had talked to him in June when he came to Washington to attend a memorial service for Franklin K. Lane. Roosevelt told Wilson, and subsequently wrote him, that the purpose of the award would be to recognize distinguished public service. This, he realized, was a rather vague statement, and he inquired if Wilson could suggest something more concrete. "We cannot too closely emulate the Nobel Prize," Roosevelt pointed out, but expressed the wish that "we could get some language which would more clearly set forth the basic principles which underlie the future success of the democrat [sic] form of government throughout the world." [3]

Wilson replied:

> I have noticed that the fund is frequently referred to as a "memorial," which suggests a dead one; and inasmuch as I hope in the near future to give frequent evidences that I am not dead, I have ventured to formulate a title — not as a gratuitous attempt at self-appreciation — but with a desire to put into words the pur-

pose I have understood my generous friends entertain. I therefore suggest the following title and description:

WOODROW WILSON ENDOWMENT

Created in recognition of the public services of Woodrow Wilson, twice President of the United States, who was instrumental in pointing out an effective method for the co-operation of the liberal forces of mankind throughout the world who love liberty and who intend to promote peace by the means of justice.

. . . I suggest that the statement with regard to the award be that it will be made to —
"The person who has made the most practical contribution to the liberal thought of the world with regard to human rights or international relationships."
My own hope would be that it should not be confined to Americans, but open to citizens of all countries.[4]

To Wilson's suggestions, Roosevelt responded, "That is splendid! I like both the Description and the Statement." Roosevelt questioned only the use of the word "endowment," which, like "memorial," to which Wilson had earlier objected, might convey the idea that Wilson was dead. He again proposed "foundation," which suggested an institution not only permanent but upon which to build. Wilson continued to object to the word because Carnegie and Rockefeller had previously used it; he feared his enemies might claim he was allowing the false impression to circulate that he had furnished the funds for the enterprise. Nevertheless, the term "Foundation" stuck.[5]

Despite this interchange, in the summer of 1921, Wilson seemed a trifle cool toward Roosevelt. When Roosevelt sent him two copies of a special edition of Washington's Farewell Address published in Wilson's honor, Wilson, through his secretary, declined to autograph them in order not to break a rule. But when the convalescing Wilson heard of Roosevelt's illness, he sent his "heartfelt sympathy." In November, 1921, he wrote Mrs. Roosevelt that he was "greatly relieved" to hear of Roosevelt's improvement. Indeed, during the brief remaining period of his life, there seemed to exist a warmth of cordiality and a personal bond of sympathy between the two men in sharp contrast to their earlier, rather formal relationship. Suffering brought them together.[6]

When Roosevelt, still a very ill man, sent birthday congratulations to Wilson on behalf of the Foundation on December 28, 1921, Wilson replied, "I am exceedingly proud of the proofs of friendship and confidence which the progress of the Foundation affords me, and your own friendship and unselfish devotion to its objects give me, as I hope you know, peculiar gratification." They continued to send occasional messages of encouragement to each other. Wilson wrote at the end of April, 1922, when Roosevelt had achieved braces and crutches, "I am indeed delighted to hear you are getting well so fast and so confidently, and I shall try and be generous enough not to envy you." He added, "I hope that your generous labours in behalf of the Foundation have not overtaxed you, and you are certainly to be congratulated on your successful leadership in the complicated and difficult undertaking." [7]

There was pathos in this too, for while Roosevelt was more vigorous than ever in mind, Wilson, while improved, was far from being the presidential leader of old. A mutual friend visited Wilson in December, 1922, and reported to Roosevelt: "His indomitable spirit is stronger than his body — stronger, may I say to you confidentially, than his old-time judgment. He can never again endure the heat and strain of battle, but some of his fool friends are telling him so and it inspires him. It is pathetic and almost tragic. . . . And the newspapers are making matters worse." [8]

Roosevelt replied, "As you say, his spirit is stronger than his body and I only wish that the newspapers could stop saying anything about him at all. He would continue to grow with the nation." And Roosevelt commented on the contributions of the former President: "Certainly," he declared, "Woodrow Wilson's administration gave to the average citizen a greater opportunity to take part in his own government than ever before." At the beginning of February, 1924, when he received word that Wilson was dying, he declared, "Woodrow Wilson in his life gave mankind a new vision of pure democracy," and added that the people of all the world had lost their greatest friend. "It is not a large circle of men and women who really understood the true inwardness of Woodrow Wilson, — it will be a circle which will grow, perhaps slowly, but will ever keep on growing as time passes. . . . The world of thought outside of America gives him far greater recognition today than we do here." [9]

As for the Wilson Foundation, Roosevelt felt that its awards could stimulate interest in "greater service to democracy and liberal thought" in the same fashion that the Nobel Prize had in the fields of literature and international peace. It pleased him that by the spring of 1923 it had raised a sum of 700,000 dollars, but he was less happy when in 1927 the Foundation devoted much of its efforts to an essay contest with 50,000 dollars in prizes on the subject "What Woodrow Wilson Means to Me." The results were disappointing; the Foundation decided not to award the main prizes. "Frankly, I am a good deal fed up with these Essay Contests," Roosevelt commented; "they have outlived their usefulness and, failing some outstanding American to make the award to next year, I should personally prefer to see the income devoted to travelling fellowships for Americans studying international relations to use to go to Europe or the Far East." [10]

Roosevelt's interest in establishing university training in international relations grew steadily in the 1920's. When George L. Radcliffe, in November, 1923, suggested the establishment of a Walter Hines Page Memorial at Johns Hopkins University, possibly in the form of a lectureship or professorship in international law, he replied at once that it was "a very interesting idea," and suggested a conference about it at his home. Soon the idea grew to a plan for a graduate school of international relations. When some Harvard men protested to Roosevelt against the establishment of a school of this sort, and particularly its establishment away from Cambridge, Roosevelt was gratified to receive the approval of President Charles Eliot. "You are splendid," he wrote Eliot. "Naturally I should have liked to see this school at Harvard, and this was my first thought, but the more I have considered the more I believe that Johns Hopkins, partly for reasons of location, will be a better place to start it. It might be possible that some members of the Senate, including the senior Senator from your State, might be persuaded to take a course at the new school!" * And to a friend, Roosevelt joked, "I am offering a scholarship the first year to Henry Cabot Lodge!" [11]

By 1927, Roosevelt and some of his friends were hoping to expand their plans for the Walter Hines Page School to encompass nationwide, and even world-wide, sponsorship of college courses in international relations. He suggested to Raymond Fosdick, who was in-

* FDR was bitter toward Lodge in the 1920's. He wrote it made his "gorge rise" to hear that Lodge had delivered a funeral oration for Wilson in the Senate: "What a mean and despicable figure Lodge will show in future history — probably the most damning summary will be that of President Elliott [sic] who was said to have remarked, 'I have known Lodge since a boy, and I have never known him to have a single generous impulse.' "

terested in this with him, the "calling of a conference of all similar movements in the other countries and the formation at that conference of some central body which, in the future, would act as a clearing house . . . of the international work." This would encompass not only schools of international studies, but also a program which the senior Henry Morgenthau envisaged of "lectureships in the smaller colleges throughout the world where, under present conditions, facilities on international relations are sadly lacking." [12]

The Page School, through the generosity of Owen D. Young and other philanthropists, became a reality. The larger schemes indicated only the direction of Roosevelt's thinking. So too did schemes Roosevelt devised during these same years to bring the United States into more active world leadership.

Roosevelt demonstrated the continued direction of his thinking when, in 1922, he contributed an inscription for a monument to be erected in Geneva: "Mankind will ever be grateful to the heroes living and dead who taught the world that the teaching 'Thou shalt love thy neighbor as thyself' applies to nations as truly as to individuals." [13]

When, in 1923, Edward Bok, a famous magazine editor, offered an award for a plan to preserve world peace, Roosevelt drafted one. In it, he tried to remedy the defects already apparent in the League of Nations. He differed from a good many more doctrinaire internationalists in his firm feeling that the League was only a means to an end, the preservation of peace, and was not an end in itself that would automatically guarantee peace. To him it was far more important that the United States enter and participate in some sort of international organization for the prevention of war than that it enter the existing League. Thinking in terms of practical politics in the United States, he felt that any plan to reconstitute the League of Nations very much as it already existed was sure to fail. "My plan avoided this," he pointed out at the time, "by providing for an International Conference to establish a brand-new permanent International Organization, i.e., to kill the existing League and set up something in its place that would have allowed countless thousands, who for personal or other reasons, could not stand for going into the present League, an opportunity to help put the United States into a new Society of Nations, saving face, honor, and all other fool things they think have to be saved." [14]

The preamble of the plan was cautiously worded to make allowance for the national prejudices of many Americans: "We seek not to become involved as a nation in the purely regional affairs of groups of other nations, nor to give to the representatives of other peoples the right to compel us to enter upon undertakings calling for or leading up to the use of armed force without our full and free consent, given through our constitutional procedure." Nevertheless, it was essential for the United States to participate in a continuing effort to eliminate the causes of war. Consequently, Roosevelt suggested a scheme which embodied many of the reservations suggested by critics of the League Covenant at the same time that it took over "all that is best in the existing League, including the great humanitarian and economic enterprises of the League – all of this with the belief that the amelioration of international social and economic ills is a necessary part in the prevention of future war." But in revising the disputed Article X of the League Covenant, he would have eliminated the mild provision that members would undertake "to preserve as against external aggression" the territorial integrity and political independence of members in order to make the milder stipulation that they would "undertake to respect the territorial integrity" of member nations. The Assembly would *recommend* the means for fulfilling this obligation. These presumably would take the form of nonintercourse and economic boycotts. However, at one point, the plan differed sharply from either the existing League or the subsequent United Nations: "A two-thirds majority of all members would be able to take action at meetings of the Assembly or of the Executive Committee in place of the unanimous vote rule now in force in the League." [15]

Apparently Roosevelt did not submit the plan for the Bok competition, since Eleanor Roosevelt became a member of the Jury of Award. But he did show it to Mrs. Roosevelt's friend, Esther Lape, who managed the competition, and in years that followed on several occasions reminded her of it. It apparently remained the basis of his thinking on international organizations in later years. On January 19, 1944, he attached to a copy of the plan a memorandum in which he commented, "It is interesting to note . . . that I recommended an Executive Committee instead of the Council of the League." Again, during the Quebec Conference, September 15, 1944, he dictated a memorandum in which he compared his early plan with that for the United Nations: "The Plan sets up an Assembly as does the plan discussed at Dumbarton Oaks. It sets up an Executive Committee instead of a Council, to be [in] continuing session. This Executive

Committee would have been composed of eleven members — five so-called great powers and six small nations." [16]

In one other respect, the plan showed Roosevelt's continued realistic thinking. He did not personally believe that any of the some fifty-five nations that belonged to the League had "given up, or been threatened with the loss of, a single iota of its national or constitutional powers, nor the rights and liberties of any of its citizens." Yet he was quite willing to appease isolationist opinion in the United States. As he had since 1919, he felt that what was most important was for the United States to be represented; the strings that might be attached to American membership were relatively unimportant. "I don't care how many restrictions or qualifications are put upon our [participation]," he wrote in 1925. "In other words I seek an end and do not care a rap about the methods of procedure." Consequently he was disturbed by any development that might further set American opinion against entrance into the League. He deplored Lord Robert Cecil's lack of tact in suggesting a League air force to engage in international policing. "It seems to me a pity to speak at this time in any way of the use of warlike implements by the League," he commented. "We are going through such a period of national sensitivity that we must wait until people come back to a more normal perspective." Finally, in a public statement on the Bok peace award, Roosevelt warned that it must not delude people into thinking that some simple plan would make it possible for them painlessly to achieve a panacea for the world's ills. "The world patient cannot be cured over night, by a simple surgical operation. A systematic course of treatment extending through the years will prove the only means of saving his life." [17]

There was one other aspect to the American Peace Award. Roosevelt himself received so much favorable publicity from it that an enthusiastic Texas Farmer-Labor booster of his wrote he believed the Award was created "for the purpose of building a strong progressive independent platform on which to run Franklin D. Roosevelt for president over the top to victory." [18]

This, of course, was entirely untrue. Roosevelt was well aware by 1923 that the League cause was far from popular; he granted that in a referendum a majority would probably be opposed to it. Rather he was deeply concerned in working, either directly with the public, or behind the scenes, to influence people in favor of the League. After the election of 1924, he concluded that many of the foreign-born and hyphenated groups of voters opposed the League then as they had previously. He proposed to Irving Fisher that the Irish, Germans, and Italians in the United States might be won over to the League by persuading responsible leaders in the various home countries to call upon them to support the League as a means of helping the mother country. "For instance," he pointed out, "if a number of responsible leaders of the Irish Free State could call upon Irish-Americans to support the league on the ground that Ireland would thereby be benefited thousands of Irish-Americans would be greatly impressed." [19]

Two years later, Roosevelt saw his long-time friends, the Hamlins, shortly after their return from visiting the League headquarters. "He wanted to know everything we had seen and done in Geneva, and above all what different delegates said and talked about," Mrs. Hamlin wrote in her diary. "One morning he telephoned me that he had a dream that I had written something very light about the League of Nations — that all the publications were learned and heavy and he thought more people could be interested in it if they could understand more easily." Consequently, at Roosevelt's urging, Mrs. Hamlin prepared an article; he spent an entire afternoon going over it with her and suggesting various ways in which she could tell more about what the League had already achieved and how it could help the United States. [20]

From the general to the specific, Roosevelt unknowingly demonstrated in his own viewpoints how difficult it was to engage in clear and consistent thinking on involved world affairs. It was impossible for him to see the potential consequences of his stand on reparations and war debts payments. He wrote his hearty congratulations to George P. Auld, Accountaint General of the Reparation Commission, when Auld anonymously attacked the position of John M. Keynes and other British economists that since the German capacity to pay was quite limited, reparations and debts must be scaled down. Auld suggested that what the British feared most was the competition of German industry, which would have to expand to meet reparations payments. Commented Roosevelt, "I particularly love the way you hand things to Mr. Keynes," and he expressed his dissatisfaction with the "silly notions" England was espousing — her trend toward imperial tariffs "and a selfish attitude too much like that of the United States." As for America, Roosevelt predicted correctly that it would co-

In Hyde Park, 1922, presenting membership certificates in the
Woodrow Wilson Foundation to Franklin, Jr., and John

FDR and Al Smith in New York, June, 1924

operate in a broad solution — "we won't guarantee loans or put up a lot of cas[h], but we will soon be ready to discuss." [21]

Roosevelt was decidedly more successful when he took his ideas on foreign affairs directly to the public. But until he was again well enough to address large audiences, this involved writing. The difficulty with that was that he always jumped with enthusiasm from one large writing project to another, and seldom had the patience to see through any but the shortest piece. While he was still Assistant Secretary of the Navy he had contracted for two books on the Navy; something always interfered with his delivering them. During his illness, he thought of many schemes, but seldom got beyond the point of introductions. In September, 1922, when George Marvin, who had accompanied him to Haiti, invited him to collaborate on an article on international affairs, Roosevelt replied with humor, and considerable insight into himself:

> In regard to my own actual pen-to-paper possibilities I am always in the delightful frame of mind of wanting to say "Yes" to anything in the way of writing, be it a magazine article or a 12-volume history of the Navy — always provided that the writing is to be done next week, or the week after. (Miss LeHand who is taking this is nodding her head and saying "Too true — too true!")
>
> Then there is another complication — i.e., I am carefully trying to stay out of print on controversial subjects, and by all that is holy if I got started on any kind of article on international matters my remarks would most assuredly be controversial.

The surprising outcome was that, under the continued prodding of Marvin, Roosevelt overcame his tendency to procrastinate, and drafted a highly significant article for *Asia* on relations between the United States and Japan. It was a Boston *Transcript* editorial on a *Current History* article that irritated him into the project. The *Transcript* took the position that the agreement of the United States not to arm Guam and the Philippines helped establish Japanese supremacy in Asiatic waters. This indicated, Roosevelt declared, that "people are still thinking in terms of war rather than in terms of trying to remove the causes of war." [22] He reaffirmed his faith in the Washington treaties of earlier that year, and reversed the feeling he had held so long while in the Navy Department: that conflict with Japan was almost irrepressible.

In the ensuing months, Roosevelt's article slowly took shape. Marvin gathered factual material for him from the Navy Department; significantly, he reported that the Admirals felt that the Japanese were acting in good faith to carry out their end of the new treaty obligations. Sometime in the winter of 1922–1923, Roosevelt dictated a rough draft, to which Marvin added considerable factual information. However, Marvin did not alter the ideas that Roosevelt himself had expressed.[23]

The main reason for distrust between the Japanese and the United States, Roosevelt declared in his draft, was a habit of mind in both countries dating back to the American acquisition of the Philippines in 1898. This led Americans to discuss how they could defend the islands, and anti-imperialists to warn of the threat of Japanese aggression. "So too, the Japanese, finding a new Western power in their south yard, used the new developments as an argument for naval expansion." As both countries expanded their navies during the next decade, mutual distrust was inevitable. The United States worried about its Pacific defenses; the Japanese were exercised over the American "open door" policy in China because they thought "we were seeking to close any outlet for Japanese population and surplus energy on the mainland."

Mutual suspicion between the two countries after 1898, Roosevelt asserted, was the "perfectly logical outcome" of the new conditions. "The question therefore resolves itself at the present time to this: Have these causes been, or can they be, sufficiently removed, [so that] a new point of view can be substituted for the old [?] Can we base our mutual thought of each other on the assumption of peace [?]" He answered in the affirmative. The "splendid success of the Washington Conference in 1921" at least temporarily had ended the naval race between the two countries, and lifted a heavy financial burden, primarily for Japan.* This had already done much to allay war talk. In addition, Roosevelt felt that whereas before the First World War, with existing weapons, the Philippines had been indefensible, new developments of airplanes and submarines would lead to a strategical deadlock between the United States and Japan if they resorted to war:

Naval experts have said, as long as ten years ago, that a fleet crossing a wide ocean from its home base must of necessity lose

* FDR wrote privately, "President Harding's Washington Conference of 1921 has, without question, removed the greater part of the indefinable something which bred suspicion and competition first in the defense departments, then in Congress, and finally among a large body of people who followed the doings of the government."[24]

from a quarter to a third of its fighting value. If that was true then it must be even more true today, for the addition of 2 new dimensions, under water and in the air, to the fighting area, has made the protection of the battleship, the principal fighting unit, an even harder task. If experts ten years ago doubted whether we could hold the Philippines with a fleet twice as powerful as that of Japan, what would they say today, when we have a fleet less than twice as powerful as that of Japan, and the new instruments of warfare capable of use over a short radius have been tremendously multiplied [?] Even if Japan ten years ago had any false notion that she could threaten us either through Mexico or the Pacific Coast, it is safe to say that her strategists have now abandoned any such idea. The result is not the possible deadlock of the past, but an actual deadlock of the present. The sooner the populations of both countries recognize that no quick military decision could be obtained by either side, the less they will indulge in talk of war. Nobody, of course, after all the prophets of 1914 had been proved false, would dare to say what would happen at the end of a military deadlock. Economic causes would, without doubt, become the determining factor, after the first year or two of war. Japan and the United States would be sitting five or six thousand miles away from each other making faces and showing their teeth. Some brilliant genius might at that time arise and ask the simple question of what it was all about anyway, and what was the use of continuing that kind of a struggle; or, on the other hand, jingo councils might prevail in both nations until one or the other, or both, had succumbed by bleeding to death through the pocketbook.*

Roosevelt disposed of points of difficulty between the United States and Japan with facility. He emphasized that Japan had carried out her treaties with Western powers in a spirit of good faith. As for the conflict between the two countries over China:

"The United States has been the proverbial friend of China. Our sympathies have been pro-Chinese, and today the broad basis of the policy of the open door has been put into effect through the Treaty of 1921. Perhaps at the same time we appreciate now a little more readily the Japanese point of view. Although today the open door is the only definitely expressed foreign policy of the United States, we

* FDR's only comment in the article on a matter which later seemed very important, the agreement not to add to fortifications on Guam and the Philippines, was: "To say 'add' is perhaps a euphemism for no fortifications now existing there can be seriously considered."

can now recognize the greater necessity to Japan of the markets and the raw products of the Chinese mainland contiguous to her island shores. Here again is another reason for altering the old-fashioned habit of mind."

On questions of Japanese immigration and landowning in the United States, he wished to apply the Golden Rule — that since Americans do not move in large numbers to Japan, Japanese should not move to this country *en masse*. Nor did commercial rivalry raise an insuperable problem in his mind. It had existed and would exist with Japan — as it had so long with England — but the raw materials and the potentialities for trade in the Pacific area were so large that surely two nations could prosper. "If it is true that within one great nation co-operation rather than cut-throat competition best fosters an honorable trade, why is not the same formula true as between two nations operating in the same broad area?" And in the task of rehabilitating those parts of the world still hard hit by the war, the two nations should co-operate: "It would seem a matter of common sense that if we do undertake the task of putting out the conflagration which still sweeps across the world, we should call in all the available fire engines we can find." One of these should be the Japanese.[25]

An English military expert, Hector C. Bywater, who had recently published a book on *Sea Power in the Pacific* (1921), sharply challenged Roosevelt when the article appeared. Roosevelt felt that Bywater's attitude — that of the military critic — was exactly what he was seeking to combat. He admitted it was easy to slip into that frame of mind; he himself had shared it during his years as Assistant Secretary of the Navy when his task, like that of the naval officers, was to plan defense against possible foes. The self-weakening action of the United States in the Western Pacific — agreeing "with our eyes open to build no more fortifications" — was deliberate. It was in the "new spirit of international relations," * in which spirituality was seeking to supplant materialism, and in which, he implied, the United States was seeking to avoid the endless circle in which armaments led to counter-armaments.[27]

"The whole trend of the times is against wars for colonial expansion. The thought of the world leans the other way. Populations themselves have a say. Subjects of dispute are being worked out more and more

---

* FDR asserted, "England's new fortifications at Singapore, Holland's new fleet for the Dutch East Indies — these are gestures not in accord with the spirit of the day. Why this new arming? . . . It is for fear of Japan. It will result in the same old vicious circle." [26]

by amicable means. No, the millennium has not arrived, but the nations are using greater and greater efforts to prevent war. Japan and the United States have not a single valid reason, and won't have as far as we can look ahead, for fighting each other. Neither has Japan in her relations with European Nations." [28]

Roosevelt's attitude made him popular in Japan. The correspondent for the Tokyo *Nichi-Nichi* wrote enthusiastically that he was "broadminded and fair" in his "plea for a better understanding and good neighborhood between the two countries." [29]

Yet while Roosevelt had dropped dramatically his Navy way of thinking about Japan, he persisted for several years in feeling much as he had earlier about Caribbean relations. This is understandable enough, since he had never been an isolationist, and being an internationalist did not seem incompatible with being an imperialist. During the First World War, he continued to hope that the United States could expand further in the Caribbean, and engaged in a delightful but unsuccessful bit of intrigue to sound out the Dutch on the sale of Curaçao.*

Through the first half of the 1920's, Roosevelt continued to favor strong-arm methods for cleaning up and policing backward areas. In 1922, he objected strenuously to an article which denounced the Marine oppression of the "small independent farmers" of Haiti. Recalling his own experiences in helping direct the Marine intervention in Haiti, he asserted that the article confused Haiti with rural New

---

* In March, 1918, when Marley F. Hay, a submarine expert, was about to sail to Holland, FDR requested him to inquire of the Dutch Government (with which Hay was on very good terms) whether or not they would be willing to sell the island of Curaçao. Hay asked if he should inform the Dutch Minister in Washington. FDR replied, "No, that is just what we don't want to do. That immediately makes it official" — and added, "I want to be in a position to repudiate you." An hour later, Secretary Daniels asked Hay if FDR had asked him to speak to the Dutch. When Hay replied in the affirmative, Daniels declared, "Well, I want you to forget that. I have talked it over with the President. The President won't hear of it. We have enough trouble already with those South American countries without adding anything to the list, so please forget it." A little later, FDR stopped by Hay's room:

"I understand you had a conversation with the Secretary an hour ago."

"Yes, I did."

"Well, he asked you not to carry on this idea of the purchase of the island of Curaçao?"

"Yes, he did."

"Well, I would like you to carry on just the same."

So Hay did. He took the matter up with the Dutch Foreign Minister, but the Government was not interested in selling the island for fear Germany would consider it an unneutral act. [30]

England or the better parts of the South; no such farmers existed. Rather, he regarded the attacks upon the Marines and the fabrication of atrocity stories as the work of a disgruntled minority of politicians which the honest government, sponsored by the United States, had deprived of their graft. The basic reason for American intervention, he declared, was to eliminate a potential center of infection: "It was a sore spot not only of danger to itself, but a menace to the health and prosperity of the neighboring islands of the West Indies. No sanitation existed, and in addition to the danger of the spread of highly contagious diseases, this human volcano was a constant source of dissatisfaction and disaffection among . . . colored races in the other islands. . . . It may be said by some who do not understand what might be called the closeness of geography under modern conditions of transportation and communication that the Haytians had a right to kill each other, commit atrocities, lapse back into barbarism if they preferred to do so. From the point of view of such people, the course of the American government was, and continues to be, wrong! Unfortunately, those who take such a position take at the same time a tremendous responsibility in regard to the rest of the world. It would be physically impossible to draw an imaginary wall or blockade around Hayti and allow Haytians to go from bad to worse." [31]

As for the "amiable and respectable gentlemen" who were criticizing American policies, "If I were President I would put a Navy ship at their disposal, take the whole bunch down to Hayti as the guests of the government and turn them loose somewhere up country for about thirty days – those who came back would be in favor of sending down the whole of that bloodthirsty organization known as the Marine Corps." [32]

Roosevelt was equally caustic toward the critics of his friend Leonard Wood, Governor General of the Philippines, who in 1922 was highly unpopular both with Filipinos and anti-imperialists because he refused to allow the Filipinos more self-government: * "I only wish it were possible for me to jump on a destroyer and dash out to the Philippines to see you," he wrote Wood. "I have heard from a number of people of the great difficulties you found on your arrival, and also of the splendid way you have taken hold of the solving of them. It

---

* Wood informed Roosevelt, "I found things financially in wretched shape and the administrative machinery much tangled up and have a big, hard and unremitting task. I want to hold on here long enough to place the Government on a sound basis, then take up my work at home." [33]

does seem a pity that both of our parties at home cannot get together and state definitely the American policy towards the Philippine Islands, Porto Rico, Hayti, and Santo Domingo. The vast majority of people in this country, I have always been certain, understand that complete independence for all of these people is not to be thought of for many years to come." [34]

In the six years that followed, Roosevelt gradually came to see the error in his thinking on imperialism and strongly sponsored a different sort of program. In the realm of international co-operation, he remained a rather realistic Wilsonian. His early efforts to establish strong leadership in foreign policy through the Democratic party had little tangible result. Undoubtedly, from a long-range viewpoint, his greatest success was in helping to educate, through the 1920's, a new generation that grew up believing that the United States must assume a major role in world affairs. As Herman Kahn has pointed out, during these years a quiet but most significant shift was taking place through the teaching in schools and colleges.[35] There Roosevelt was one of the prime movers, and the generation thus growing up in large part was ready to accept his leadership in international affairs in the '30s and '40s.

CHAPTER IX

Businessman

> I can't help feeling that you are built a bit like me — that
> you need something physically . . . active, with constant
> contact with all sorts of people in many kinds of places.
> — FDR TO GEORGE MARVIN, *August 10, 1922.*

BUSINESS, like poker and politics, was for Roosevelt a delightful
form of adventure, and he had no stomach for it unless it was
exciting. Referring to his business activities, Mrs. Roosevelt has remarked, "In a curious way Franklin had so many contradictions." He
was, for example, both a penny-pincher and a plunging speculator. In
his personal life he was thrifty — especially in the 1920's, when he
worried over the heavy expenses put upon him by his illness and the
rearing of a large family in upper-class fashion. So financially embarrassed was he in January, 1925, that he was forced to auction off
some of his highly prized naval and marine prints — which netted less
than a thousand dollars — and he economized by wearing clothes purchased many years before. Yet in his business ventures he risked
money recklessly, again and again, though seldom very much at a
time.*

The main exception to this pattern was the careful fashion in which
he administered the New York office of the Fidelity and Deposit
Company of Maryland. There he functioned much as he had at the
Navy Department. Whether Van-Lear Black hired him because it was
a smart business move or merely to collect a celebrity is impossible
to determine. In 1926, at Roosevelt's suggestion, Black tried to hire
Richard E. Byrd, the explorer. The worst that Wall Streeters unfriendly to Roosevelt were able to charge was that the company
wasted the twenty-five thousand dollars per year it paid him in salary.
On the other hand, Roosevelt brought with him an alluring name,

* This is Mrs. Roosevelt's impression, but she is not entirely sure of this, since
FDR seldom talked about finances with her. She has commented, "I had no idea
how much personal income he had." He in turn had no knowledge of his
mother's.[1]

eight years of large-scale management experience, and a wide and influential acquaintance among political figures. This last was most important of all, since political know-how, which played a considerable part in obtaining bonding business, was one of Roosevelt's outstanding talents.[2]

Roosevelt took hold with a will at Fidelity and Deposit. As early as March, 1921, Black congratulated him on his February showing: "If you can hold expenses the results will be actually world beating." During Roosevelt's long illness that autumn, Black insisted that he retain his connection with the firm. He resumed work by the end of January, 1922, although he was still in considerable pain. At first he arranged to hold conferences at his home every Tuesday afternoon to discuss underwriting and policies in the New York office. When he had further recovered, he spent part of his time at the office. During the summer and autumn of 1923 he was at the office every other week, and from November until early February, 1924, when he went to Florida, he was at his desk four days a week and available the other two days at his home on 65th Street.

Some of the other executives in the New York office, objecting to these hours, signed papers in Roosevelt's name during his absence. Roosevelt protested that he was available, and complained that they did not take sufficient advantage of the political contacts he had to offer them.* He recommended acidly that his principal critic "get to know more of the big men in New York City." Roosevelt pointed out, "A good many of these men are personal friends of mine and come in to lunch with me at the office. On my part I take every opportunity to introduce . . . them, but, I frankly feel that he should let me know a great deal more than he does in regard to the relationships which could be cultivated to the profit of the Company." [4]

Roosevelt demonstrated often how his system worked. He and Howe kept up a correspondence with labor leaders who had been friendly in Washington, and with a bottle of Scotch as a joking inducement, tried to persuade them to send labor bonding-business to Fidelity and

---

* FDR was quite ready to make use of old associations. To an executive of a firm holding Navy contracts he wrote: "A casual reference in a letter from one of my old friends in the Navy Department to the award of some 8-inch gun forgings to your company, brought to my mind the very pleasant relations we held during my term as Assistant Secretary of the Navy, and I wondered if you would feel like letting my company write some of the contract bonds that you are obliged to give the government from time to time. I would like very much to have one of our representatives call." [3]

Deposit. As a result of this correspondence and three or four trips to Washington on the part of Howe, the American Federation of Labor agreed to give Fidelity and Deposit its large schedule bond. The anticlimax was that the home office rejected the bond because it could not meet the low rate the A. F. of L. had received elsewhere for the past fifteen years.[5]

Through his political connections, Roosevelt tried to work up even more important business. His old friend William Gibbs McAdoo, already known to have his eye on the 1924 Democratic nomination, was at this time attorney for the Mexican Petroleum Company owned by Edward L. Doheny. In April, 1922, Roosevelt sent a West Coast vice president of the firm to call upon McAdoo, and at the same time wrote a personal letter in which he mixed business talk and political gossip. He reminded McAdoo that Doheny (soon to be involved in the Teapot Dome oil scandal) "is a good friend of mine and I feel sure he will be very glad to have you place the business our way."[6]

Of course Roosevelt's position in the state Democratic party was of prime importance to Fidelity and Deposit. When Alfred E. Smith again became Governor of New York in 1923, he appointed George K. Shuler, formerly a Marine captain, to be state treasurer. Howe helped Shuler with his publicity releases — one of which announced the policy of depositing state funds in local banks which were financing farmers (Howe reminded Shuler of one bank in which FDR was especially interested).* Banks receiving state funds had to protect them with bonds. Not unexpectedly, Roosevelt was able in January, 1924, to report to his home office some "interesting figures relating to depository bonds running to the state of New York." The National Surety Company held fifteen million dollars' worth; American Surety Company, twelve million; and Fidelity and Deposit, ten millions. This represented a gain of over three million dollars for Fidelity and Deposit; National Surety had gained only six hundred and eighty-four thousand dollars, and other rivals had lost heavily.

Within New York City, the company followed similar tactics. There was rejoicing when Al Smith's candidate for Mayor of New York, Jimmy Walker, defeated Hearst's candidate, Mayor John F. Hylan. Roosevelt promised he would speak to Walker about obtaining

* Howe wrote to Shuler, "Mr. Roosevelt was immensely pleased at being able to tell them that he felt sure you would realize the justice of their request for additional funds. As I told you, this is a family affair with Mr. Roosevelt and on that account I hope you can see your way clear to make the increase a little more liberal than you might ordinarily."[7]

the business of the city, and promptly gave jobs in the company to the sons of two Tammany leaders.[8]

Such incidents demonstrated the extent to which Roosevelt was master of this means of building the company. "Things in the office are going exceedingly well and we are really getting a lot of new business through my political connections," he once boasted to Black. "Last night I spoke over the radio and already this morning a brand-new bond has come in as a result!"

In spite of these triumphs, discontent within the New York office and cutthroat rivalry with the National Surety Company continued. Suddenly, in February, 1928, the key man in the New York office, a long-term malcontent, together with the main agent in Brooklyn, jumped to the rival firm at what Roosevelt described as "fabulous salaries and commissions." The threatened disaster frightened Roosevelt into announcing to the press that he was resigning from a number of his other interests and would thereafter devote "a large part of his time" to Fidelity and Deposit. He pointed out that the firm's New York business in the past five years had grown from two million to four million dollars, and concluded with a flourish, "I have seen vindication of my belief that a high standard of business ethics, courteous treatment, prompt service, and sound business judgment, in this business more than any other, would be appreciated by the public."

In the months that followed, Roosevelt successfully withstood the shock of the defection. Business was better than it had been the year before.[9]

Roosevelt regarded his law practice as being complementary to his bonding business, and was dissatisfied during the early 1920's because the two activities bore little relation to each other. Rather than being complementary, the law practice was secondary: actually he did very little work upon it. As his partner, Langdon P. Marvin, recalls: "I think that he gave most of his time to cleaning up his political matters and writing letters that had to do with them. I don't remember that he was active in the practice of law at that time." [10]

In the only important legal matter that Roosevelt handled during this period, he demonstrated his impatience with drawn-out procedure. In 1928, Supreme Court Justice Joseph Morschauser of Poughkeepsie appointed him referee in tax litigation between the Village of Larchmont and the New Haven Railroad. Larchmont had jumped its assessment against the railroad property to over half a million dollars;

the railroad claimed it should only be about half that amount. According to Earl Looker, Roosevelt was disgusted when he learned from the railroad counsel that the company alone would submit some six thousand pages of written testimony. Sitting four days a week, it would have taken him a month to go through it. Instead, he arranged with both sides to cut oral testimony to a bare minimum, and supplemented it with a trip to Larchmont where he compared the railroad property with that of similar worth in the vicinity, and checked the relative assessment of each. As a result, he settled the case in ten days instead of seventy. He arrived at a figure of 316,000 dollars — far nearer to what the railroad wished than the village, but the village attorney wrote Roosevelt, "I was satisfied that, as referee, you gave both sides all that they could possibly expect in the certiorari case, on the evidence." Roosevelt received a fee of fifteen hundred dollars from each side; he would have received far more if he had dragged out the case as was customary. When he reported back to the Supreme Court, Justice Morschauser joked that he could never give Roosevelt another such case, because he would bankrupt the legal profession.[11]

Just as Roosevelt refused to endure the boredom of prolonging this case in order to get a larger fee, he also took scant interest in the safe-and-sound practice of his law partners, Langdon Marvin and Grenville T. Emmet. He had been something of a disappointment to them. "I had always thought that he would be a great business getter," Marvin recalls, "but he was too busy with other things to bother much about clients. So we got very little business out of him, but we had a deep affection and friendship for him."[12]

The arrangement was mutually unsatisfactory. In the fall of 1924, Roosevelt decided to sever his partnership with Marvin and Emmet. Part of the reason was his physical condition. He wrote Emmet:

"There is no question that I shall have to spend the greater part of the next four or five years in devoting my primary attention to my legs. That means absence from New York during at least two months in the winter, and also during a greater part of the summer. Further, there is the practical difficulty of locomotion, and even though 52 Wall Street has been remodelled, the question of even two steps is a very difficult one as I have to be actually lifted up and down them."

With disarming frankness, he added that he considered their sort of practice rather out of his line. "I have accomplished practical things along the lines of business administration," he explained — "my whole training in the Navy Department was just that and in the Fidelity &

Deposit Company also everything relates to the practical management of business of one kind and another." [13]

Emmet and Marvin took the letter in good grace. Emmet remarked that he was rather glad, since he did not want people to think that they were using Roosevelt's name for advertising purposes.*

To Van-Lear Black, Roosevelt explained the breakup in more blunt terms that threw much light on his own attitude toward the law.

"The other partners are dear delightful people, but their type of law business . . . is mostly estates, wills, etc. all of which bore me to death. . . . Also, I get not one red cent out of my connection with them, whereas, if I were with some live people working along other lines I could be of material assistance on reorganizations, receiverships, etc. pulling my own weight in the boat and incidentally making some money out of it."

He projected a new firm "with my name at the head instead of at the tail as it now is," which he thought would "do only good to the F & D, as our connections would be with the type of corporations and companies which would help in the bonding end of the game." [15]

Consequently, in December, 1924, Roosevelt entered into a partnership with a vigorous young lawyer of the sort he admired, D. Basil O'Connor, Secretary of the Dartmouth Alumni Association. O'Connor had already assisted Roosevelt with several corporate clients. The fact that he had his office in the same building was of practical importance because of Roosevelt's difficulty in getting around. Finally, he was ready to guarantee Roosevelt 10,000 dollars a year from the new firm of Roosevelt and O'Connor.† This sounded satisfactory to Roosevelt and proved to be a lasting arrangement. [17]

Despite the small proportion of his time that he gave to legal work, Roosevelt characterized himself as a lawyer during the 1920's. He gave

---

* The remarkable way in which FDR was able to end the partnership without destroying the personal friendships is shown in Marvin's estimate of him many years later: "I think he grew tremendously from the time that he was my law partner. He had not achieved greatness then, but he had the elements in him. He was always optimistic, enthusiastic, anxious to do the right thing, anxious to do it quickly. He didn't like to study too much — he liked to act and he was therefore sometimes rather impulsive in his acts. . . . He was a very devoted and real friend to many whom he had gotten to know during a long and unusual career." [14]

† The most notable of FDR's legal clients was Julian Goldman, President of the Julian Goldman Stores, Inc. which operated the Julian Goldman Stores, the People's Stores, the Union Stores, the A&B Stores, and the National Stores. FDR gave legal advice, and O'Connor carried out most of the routine legal matters. [16]

an interview for a boy's magazine on the advantages of becoming a lawyer. When he was appointed chairman of the committee on "Legal Education and Standards of Professional Conduct" of the National Crime Commission, he wrote Dean Roscoe Pound of Harvard Law School that he would serve on the committee only if Dean Pound would become head of it. This put him in the interesting position of writing to the learned Dean Pound on legal ethics. "I hope I am not an alarmist," Roosevelt suggested, "but if the present agitation regarding crime continues I think the psychological condition of the minds of the Editors in this country is such as to bring down upon the heads of our profession generally a torrent of abuse and unreasoned criticism which will inflame the popular mind and, perhaps, lead to most unfortunate legislation." Roosevelt wanted this public indignation guided to a useful end, and suggested that this was the principal job for the commission.[18]

Unquestionably, he was interested in a high standard of ethics both in business and in law, and was unalterably opposed in principle both to the shyster and the unprincipled speculator. The surety bond business attracted him because of the absence of "that element of speculation which enters into so many classes of business." In 1923, he strongly advised young men to put their first thousand dollars into a savings bank as a permanent nest egg; thereafter, if they wished to invest in stocks and bonds, they should use only a part of their savings.[19]

This kind of advice could be characterized as "Do as I say, don't do as I do." During the 1920's Roosevelt found the buying and selling of securities a delightful game, and engaged in it on a sizeable scale.

There was a time at the beginning of 1923 when he feared a general depression was not many months away, and during that period he admitted, "I haven't gone into anything of late because I have been scared." [20] But when the depression failed to materialize, Roosevelt returned to his custom of undertaking a wide variety of ventures.*

Years later Jesse Jones expressed some dismay at the way Roosevelt played poker; not on a straight five-card basis as in Texas, but with

---

* Although FDR's fears were groundless at that moment, his analysis indicated the care with which he was watching the market. He predicted depression, caused by "1. slowing down of building operations, 2. less buying of railroad equipment, 3. falling off in steel industry, 4. farmers all broke, 5. shipping business broke, 6. no foreigners to buy our surplus stuff. Maybe we'll have good, or even better prices on stocks and bonds for the next few months, but my own theory is that a whole lot of the big fellows are quietly dumping all they can." [21]

deuces wild and all sorts of tricky innovations. He played business the same way. He had ample opportunity to do so: he had some capital, a valuable name and a flair for speculation. These were enough to cause promoters to buzz around him like flies. He liked these hearty vigorous men who promised to turn so little into so much in the most exciting ways. There was nothing stuffy about them; they were not stodgy or boring or overwhelmed with red tape. Naturally they appealed to a similar element in his own nature.[22]

Most of the schemes never materialized, some failed, and a few were quite successful. A number grew out of Roosevelt's interest in financing. One of them had international implications.

In the difficult reconstruction period of the early 1920's, the new German Republic was unable to maintain a stable currency. As the value of the mark plummeted spectacularly in 1922, Roosevelt joined in an "interesting proposition" which he thought could "save from further losses the foolish Americans who bought German marks at much higher prices." This was United European Investors, a Canadian corporation which used these marks to purchase stocks in various German corporations. It would not use dollars to buy marks directly, but would take advantage of the stringency of money and credit in Germany to make the best possible investments. Marks were selling then at the rate of 1500 per dollar, but 1500 marks had far greater purchasing power in Germany than a dollar had in the United States. Consequently, the stock was in German mark denomination, with par 10,000 marks per share.

With the first one hundred million marks invested (only fifteen thousand dollars), the company purchased stock in some nineteen German corporations producing power, explosives, chemicals, dyes, ores, machinery, and the like. Altogether, it purchased German securities with about one hundred thousand dollars' worth of marks. Two years later, after inflation had run its course in Germany, the firm liquidated with a profit in excess of 200 per cent.

Nevertheless, later, when Roosevelt was running for re-election as Governor of New York in 1930, Republicans tried to arouse German-Americans against him by claiming he had capitalized upon financial distress in Germany. J. E. Ritter, a German-American leader, came to his defense with a statement that Roosevelt's company had helped Germany as well as the American owners of marks. It was Roosevelt's recollection that altogether he personally received about five thousand dollars over the three-year period of operation.[23]

Roosevelt's interest in investing German marks led Fred Britten, one of the most isolationist of Congressmen, to propose that he join in a somewhat similar scheme of Britten's, the Interocean Holding Company, which had contracts to market various types of German radios, equipment, and machinery in the United States. Perhaps because of his personal dislike for Britten, Roosevelt refused to have anything to do with this enterprise.[24]

However, in 1927 Roosevelt did agree to become one of the lesser backers of the International Germanic Trust Company, established to unite German and American capital and thus "serve the interests of those engaged in furthering the industrial development of Germany and in promoting international good-will through established channels." The company planned to invest in German securities and thus help finance German industry. Roosevelt purchased seventy-five shares of stock; the first meeting of the directors was held in his law office, and for about six months he served on the board. He later resigned, apparently because it was more profitable for his law firm to avoid any banking connections. Also the company, which had started auspiciously, was in financial difficulties by this time and ultimately went into receivership.[25]

Another venture — with strong, sound backing — was the Federal International Investment Trust, of which Roosevelt was one of the incorporators. Professor Edwin Kemmerer, a conservative Princeton economist and famous monetary consultant to small countries, was involved in the project. It was intended to act as a foreign trade clearing-house which would solve tariff inequalities through enabling American investors to accept securities guaranteed by foreign banks in payment of credit balances due for the export of American goods. Banks in the United States would be stockholders. The law firm of Roosevelt and O'Connor approved the legality of the stock issue. The company was to be chartered and supervised by the Federal Reserve Board, and the stock to be a legal investment for national banks. Nevertheless, legal obstacles prevented the company from even getting beyond the promotional stage.[26]

Other banking schemes in which Roosevelt was slightly involved were less impressive. There was the Compo Bond Corporation, a private enterprise which in 1922 tried to promote a scheme to sell through the banks thrift bonds similar to the savings stamps and bonds which the Treasury Department sold during the war. He was for a short while a director of both this company and of the Associated

Bankers Corporation, which handled the buying and selling of paper and other negotiable instruments for small banks. Soon after Roosevelt resigned as a director, the company went bankrupt. Nevertheless, in the summer of 1923 Roosevelt wrote an endorsement for the American Bank Depositors Association, a concern which advised clients on the worth of securities. "The mere enactment of Blue Sky Laws, and of so-called protective legislation, is not the proper way of stopping the tremendous waste of hard-earned savings of the public, which goes on from year to year," he declared. What was needed was sound education on the worth of securities.[27]

There was some reason to think, judging by Roosevelt's own fascination with risky investments, that he might have profited from a little of this education himself. There was, for example, the two thousand shares of stock he held in the Montacal Oil Company, which was wildcatting in the area around Baxter Basin in Wyoming. It struck gas rather than oil, and for gas at this time there was no market. As late as 1929, Roosevelt was hoping it could be piped into Salt Lake City so he could salvage his investment.[28]

Things like this began to happen too often. Finally, when Roosevelt's name appeared as a backer of a particularly shaky enterprise, the General Secretary of the Society for Promoting Financial Knowledge wrote him:

"I have noted with a great deal of concern the use of your name to further the sale of stocks of new promotions, that, while undoubtedly sincere in conception, are business risks of the more hazardous type and I am wondering if your attention has been called to the fact that these securities are being offered for public subscription as 'safe investments.' . . . It seems such a pity that a distinguished and honored name should be commercialized in such a manner, when there are so many opportunities for employing the prestige that it carries in activities designed to promote some public good." [29]

Roosevelt replied that in this case his name had been used without permission. "You know how difficult it is," he added, "for a man more or less in public life to keep his name from being used without authorization for all kinds of enterprises, but I try to be vigilant in this matter." [30]

In spite of this disclaimer, he could not resist the temptation to dabble incessantly in promotions of all sorts. Many centered around his old love — ships. In 1922 he co-operated with a group of shippers to try to bring about the merger of several small lines into a new strong shipping company, which would purchase ten surplus ships of the Hog Island type and run them through the Panama Canal on an intercoastal route. Claiming his physicians would not allow him to be vice president, Roosevelt became general counsel. "There is a lot of money to be made in the coast to coast shipping game," he asserted with characteristic ebullience, "and secondly, there is a cut-throat crowd out to 'hog' the whole business and eliminate competition." In the end the "cut-throat crowd" won out, not because they were making money but because they could afford to lose it longer than Roosevelt's associates. However, out of some stock purchases involved in the maneuvers, Roosevelt made several thousand dollars. When this affair evaporated, Roosevelt jumped to a scheme for reorganizing the Hudson Navigation Company in order to run freight service through the New York State Barge Canal and the Great Lakes from New York City to Chicago.[31]

This close association with shipping magnates led Roosevelt to deplore the wasteful policies of the Republican Administration in supporting a merchant fleet. In the spring of 1924 he wrote indignantly to the New York Times protesting the operation at a loss of the Emergency Fleet Corporation, established during the war. He was sure Wilson's Administration would never have allowed this enterprise to continue; it was costing the taxpayers over forty million a year net loss, plus millions more due to depreciation.[32] When Kermit Roosevelt inquired what policy he would advocate for shipping, he retorted:

"There is one thing very certain in my mind — we have tried since 1919 to foster an American Merchant Marine, and while it is true that government aid has kept a certain number of American flagships on the ocean, the cost has been something terrific. This annual net loss must be stopped someway. . . . I am fairly sure in my own mind that the dozens of ships which are now tied up in the Hudson, the Potomac, the Chesapeake, etc. and which have not been in commission for years ought to be sold for whatever they will bring." [33]

In spite of his righteous air, there is the distinct possibility that Roosevelt was less alarmed over the government giving a subsidy to shippers than over the fact that the subsidy was going to the big shippers who blocked him from breaking into the field.

Aviation seemed, in contrast, a virgin area. Unfortunately, he chose to back the wrong type of aviation. Although he had taken several short flights, he disliked airplanes and, in common with many people in the early '20s, thought that the future of air travel lay in dirigibles.

"I wish all my friends on the other side [of the Atlantic] would keep out of aeroplanes," he wrote in July, 1921. "I was horrified to get a cable from London the other day saying that my mother also had flown across from London to Paris. Wait until my dirigibles are running, and then you will be able to take a form of transportation which is absolutely safe." In 1923, together with Owen D. Young, Benedict Crowell (who had been Assistant Secretary of War under Wilson), and other notables, he organized the General Air Service to operate helium-filled dirigibles between New York and Chicago. But in a short time the superiority of the airplane became apparent, and this scheme too evaporated.[34]

Roosevelt's keen interest in conservation led him to propose, in November, 1922, the formation of a syndicate to purchase a tract of land within one hundred miles of New York, and operate on it a forest similar to the state or privately owned forests of western Europe. He estimated that with a working capital of a half-million dollars it would be possible to plant and operate ten to fifteen thousand acres of forest. Four years later he suggested a similar scheme to finance the purchase of Southern pine lands through bond sales. He argued that since pine was being cut faster than it could re-grow, the value should be up in twenty years. He found no takers for either plan.[35]

His prolific imagination conceived many stillborn schemes. Some were rather far-fetched and almost instantly forgotten, like his suggestion to sell advertising space in taxicabs, as in buses and streetcars. Some were feasible enough, but never gained the proper backing — for example, the plan to establish a resort chain from Warm Springs to Lake Placid, to be known as National Resorts, Inc. Others which led to nothing at the time occurred to him again during the New Deal. A prime example of this sort was his fascination with the possibility of developing tidal power at Passamaquoddy Bay. As early as May, 1921, he propounded an elaborate plan for such development to General Electric.[36]

Other schemes might better have died at birth. The most painful was his lobster business — one of an almost interminable number of promotions that that bluff super-salesman, Arthur P. Homer, kept bringing to Roosevelt. The lobster fiasco was the venture that finally ended Homer's influence over Roosevelt. Homer had persuaded him to become the majority stockholder in Witham Brothers, Inc., which purchased lobsters, held them in pounds until the prices were high, and then sold them throughout the country. It was a sound idea and apparently a thriving business, selling to big New York hotels. Roosevelt anticipated handsome profits. But the price of lobsters refused to rise, and Roosevelt was forced to keep pouring money into the company in order to bolster his weak investment. In the end, lobsters cost him almost 26,000 dollars. Although it was a sore subject, Howe did not hesitate to twit him about it. When a Texas clubwoman asked him to donate some white elephant for a "celebrity tea," Howe suggested, "Why not send them your stock in the lobster company — that comes under *this head!*" [37]

Another curious enterprise, which seemed to promise the greatest success at the time, in the end caused Roosevelt the most political embarrassment. This was Camco, the Consolidated Automatic Merchandising Corporation.

Camco was produced in 1928 by the merging of five vending-machine companies into one large corporation. Its plans to open a number of clerkless stores attracted much public attention. These machines were to be another achievement toward cultural progress, since they would release people from the drudgery of working in stores and free them for more satisfying pursuits. Camco opened three stores in New York City. The walls of these stores were banked with machines selling candy, cigarettes, razor blades, and other small articles. But problems arose: too often the machines accepted slugs, or failed to deliver the merchandise. Soon the depression hit, and amidst the hue-and-cry over "technological unemployment" it was smart politics for the Republicans to associate Roosevelt with an enterprise that supplanted men with machines. A suit was begun against the company during the 1932 campaign, and Senator Daniel O. Hastings of Delaware took advantage of the occasion to lambaste Roosevelt. [38]

Roosevelt protested then, as he had earlier, that his association with Camco was entirely nominal, and happened only because he (together with Henry Morgenthau, Sr.) was a director of the Sanitary Postal Service Company which merged into Camco. He had exchanged his old stock for the new at the time of the merger because he thought the new company could make a good profit, but a few months later when he was elected Governor of New York he had resigned his directorship.* "So much for a silly campaign yarn," he concluded. [40]

* As late as 1940, FDR was denouncing as "deliberately untrue" the story that he had backed a company to establish a chain of automatic department stores

His opponents did not allow him to slip away from the connection so easily. In 1934, the Chicago *Tribune* quoted from a Fireside Chat in which Roosevelt blamed the depression upon "that unfortunate decade characterized by a mad chase for unearned riches, and an unwillingness of leaders in almost every walk of life to look beyond their own schemes and speculations." Against this the *Tribune* juxtaposed a statement on Camco: "Extravagant estimates of earnings were put forward to attract innocent investors. The common stock rose as high as $18 a share. The other day you could buy two shares for a quarter and the company was petitioning for reorganization at the expense of its creditors. . . . The company in 1928 numbered among its directors Mr. Franklin D. Roosevelt." [41]

There is no indication that Roosevelt ever gave serious thought to the social implications of Camco, but then there is no indication that he ever gave much thought to Camco at all. It was simply one more venture.

He and the younger Morgenthau were directors of Photomaton, Inc., which was placing quarter-in-a-slot automatic cameras in stores and railroad stations. Photomaton, like Camco, was to go into a receivership early in the depression; but in December, 1928, its stock was rapidly increasing in value. Morgenthau purchased and resold five hundred shares of it for Roosevelt at a profit to him of three thousand dollars. Roosevelt wrote Morgenthau:

"It is thrilling about the Photomaton Stock. I had, as usual, entirely forgotten to give you, as I intended . . . , a check to cover the transaction and I really feel that as I did not do so, I am scarcely entitled to the profit. Why don't you and I split the profit in this transaction and each give one half of the total to the Patients Aid Fund at Warm Springs? This will cost us nothing and will enable us to deduct a fifteen hundred ($1,500) gift to charity from our income tax reports!" [42]

The only significance of these business experiences is the indication they give of Roosevelt's willingness to undertake risky ventures in the adventurous climate of the 1920's. Outwardly his presidency of the

---

from coast to coast. He understated: "In 1926, I took some stock in a company to sell postage stamps through a slot machine, and . . . later this company was bought up by another company which also sold weighing machines, etc. The President had some stock by exchange in the latter company for a few months but sold out as soon as he could." [39]

American Construction Council was more of the same. It did not provide any salary, it never functioned successfully, and its only purpose seemed to be to serve as another means of keeping his name before the public. Yet it forced him to grope towards solutions of business problems much like the problems that later confronted him during the New Deal. Thus, as John T. Flynn has pointed out, this enterprise was in several ways a forerunner of the National Recovery Administration.[43]

The concept behind the American Construction Council — and many similar trade associations of the time — was voluntary self-regulation under the auspices of a benevolent government. This apparently offered a solution to the problems of small businesses whose profits were dangerously cut by competition from big business. They could band together into trade associations, similar to the committees of the War Industries Board of the World War, but free from government compulsion. Through these organizations they could establish codes of ethics, standardize production, establish efficiency, and make substantial savings. Even more important, they could standardize prices at a level which would allow a good profit margin.

This plan was not without risk. Although trade associations came into existence with the paternal blessing of Commerce Secretary Herbert Hoover, the Supreme Court (which did not find U.S. Steel a conspiracy in restraint of trade) tended to crack down on them. So there was always a chance of prosecution under the Sherman Act. To some businessmen there seemed to be another risk: that ultimately such associations could lead to government regulation.*

However, they appeared to Roosevelt and many other small businessmen as the alternative to such regulation. In the '20s the construction industry, one of the largest in the country, was a stimulant to prosperity even greater than the automobile and other durable goods industries. Unfortunately, it suffered from almost anarchic seasonal variations, and also from the fact that occasionally contractors and labor leaders engaged in criminal connivance. A legislative investigation in New York in 1920 revealed shocking conditions. Obviously, one of Roosevelt's first tasks was to rebuild public confidence in the

* FDR's contractor friend, Elliott Brown, warned him against the "socialistic" tendencies of these associations and of Hoover specifically — "socialistic, because the moment a combination is formed, the Government will assert an interest and will express that interest through the medium of some clerk in the Department of Commerce, who will approve or disapprove many matters affecting the initiative and welfare of all peepul." [44]

industry in order to forestall a popular demand for government supervision.[45]

Just before he became president of the council, in June, 1922, he declared:

"The tendency lately has been toward regulation of industry. Something goes wrong somewhere in a given branch of work, immediately the public is aroused, immediately the press, the pulpit and public call for an investigation. That is fine. It is healthy. . . . But government regulation is not feasible. It is unwieldy; it is expensive. It means employment of men to carry on this phase of the work; it means higher taxes. The public doesn't want it: the industry doesn't want it. . . . When an industry begins to feel that the confidence of the public is slipping from it, then is the time to get on the job and find out what is wrong. . . . There has been no system, no co-operation, no intensive national planning. The time was ripe for an organization such as that being formed." [46]

Later, he pointed out that the condition in the industry which necessitated formation of the council was "complete lack of co-operation." The public tended to blame the entire industry for this evil when only a small part of it was at fault. His own role was twofold: to bring about co-operation, and to build better public relations. He received excellent publicity. Newspapers declared that his job, which affected 11,000,000 men, would do for construction what Judge Kenesaw Mountain Landis had done for baseball and what Will Hays was trying to do for the movies — only Roosevelt's job was bigger. It would have far-reaching effects upon national prosperity and probably lead to imitation in other countries. Roosevelt was far more modest.* To a magazine writer he declared, "Don't for heaven's sake, use the word 'dictator.' I am, rather, a combination of information dispenser, and referee of facts and conditions." [48]

Even before he became president of the council, Roosevelt announced that its purpose was to put the industry on a basis of efficiency and integrity, and to co-ordinate all its branches. Deploring the anarchism of seasonal employment, he also insisted the public had a definite re-

---

* FDR did point to the wide scope of the council: "All branches of the industry are represented in the new body and they have been divided into the following groups, each with equal voting power: Architects, engineers, general contractors, sub-contractors, construction labor, material and equipment dealers, financial, bond and real estate interests, public utility construction departments, and the construction divisions of Federal, state, and municipal governments." [47]

sponsibility to help solve the problem. They could do this by holding off building projects during the peak seasons, and instead ordering construction in the slack winter period. Wartime construction had proved that it was feasible to build through the bitterest winter weather; to do so under nonwar conditions would lead both to stabilization of employment and to economies for the public. In keeping with this, during the next few years Roosevelt repeatedly exhorted the public to build (in slow times) or not to build (in boom periods). He denounced the "flock of sheep method of building":

"Building fever comes in epidemics like the influenza or the grippe. There are times when every farmer wants a barn, every broker a house in the suburbs, every town a red-brick school house, every city a new prison, every state a new college and so on and on."

He proposed the solution: long-range planning to spread building over both seasons and years. In a sweeping manner prophetic of his later belief that the country should build its way out of a depression, he suggested periodic conferences among all those concerned with construction in various areas: "Let each produce their plans and contracts for a given period. . . . Then, when the question of building comes up, one can see at a glance how feasible or practicable from the labor or cost standpoint it would be to undertake new construction. If the men of one district are being drained to carry on construction in a second district, number one should hold off until the job is finished, then employ the men who are ready to undertake a new job. This is a patriotic duty as well as an economic one." [49]

Throughout the six years that Roosevelt headed the council, he continued to deplore the lack of adequate information on building to serve as a basis for rational planning. In May, 1923, at a meeting of the board of governors at his home, he proposed a resolution calling upon Secretary Hoover to provide a building index. At the same time, he warned that he did not think the Department of Commerce had the money to prepare one, or that Hoover really wanted to do that sort of thing, which Hoover and others considered a function of private business. [50]

As Roosevelt feared, when he wired Hoover for support he received a cold response. Hoover replied he hoped the council's work would be based entirely upon the construction industries, without government pressure, because business so feared government interference that it balked at volunteer efforts if anyone suggested they were government-inspired. [51]

If he could not get government aid, Roosevelt would manage without it. He announced the council would begin issuing a weekly forecast of building conditions all over the country, which would serve as a weathervane so that the industry could "hoist storm signals." He planned to establish a bureau of statistics and business information, but failed to obtain necessary funds. As late as 1928, the distinguished economist, Richard T. Ely, deplored to Roosevelt that he had not been able to carry on research as chairman of the council's Committee on the Economic Relationships of Construction because of lack of money.[52]

Indeed, the council remained little more than a paper organization, and Roosevelt's position involved little except the issuing of periodic manifestoes. He confessed, at the first annual meeting of the board of governors in May, 1923, that it "has not done one darned thing . . . except collect dues." And it had not done much of that.[53]

Peak construction in the early summer of 1923 caused shortages of labor and materials, and high prices. Therefore Roosevelt called upon the nation to delay nonurgent construction projects until September. This led him into a sharp controversy with the editor of the *Manufacturer's Record*, who expressed strong disapproval. "I fear that you deliberately insist that no organization of individuals, whether of capital or labor or both combined, should ever suggest a course of action to its individual members," Roosevelt wrote the editor. "Yours is a creed of 'Every man for himself and the devil take the hindmost.'" Roosevelt pointed out that the Secretary of Commerce, leading bankers, and manufacturers had approved, and that the only dissent had come from a few manufacturers or dealers in lumber, brick, and plumbing fixtures.[54]

In the autumn of 1923, in keeping with his advice early in the summer, Roosevelt urged the public to take advantage of the usual slackening of demand for materials and labor during winter in order to avoid a possible building crisis in the spring.[55]

The shortage that worried Roosevelt most was that of competent laborers. Repeatedly in the winter of 1923–1924 he urged young men to switch their aspirations from white collar work to the building trades. This entailed establishing a more active apprenticeship training system. Hoover co-operated through requesting a committee of his to designate the Construction Council as the proper leader for the apprenticeship movement, and by writing Roosevelt a letter which appeared in the newspapers, recommending that unions remove their limitations upon apprentices, and that contractors provide facilities for them.[56]

Roosevelt proposed to the chairman of the Apprenticeship Committee of the council a systematic approach to the problem: first, find out the types of trade in which labor shortages existed; second, establish the kind of training which would equip young men to become apprentices; third, assure these men of employment as steady as any in the building trade could be. Above all, Roosevelt concentrated upon the task of trying to persuade high-caliber young men to become skilled laborers. He tried to enlist the aid of Henry Ford to stem the "constantly growing tendency of our young men to avoid jobs that entail anything faintly resembling manual labor." He pointed out, "Our great Republic was founded by the work of the hands of our ancestors. If the Puritan fathers had sat down on the Plymouth shore and opened up real estate offices, city planning bureaus, and similar theoretical institutions instead of chopping wood and drawing water, I am afraid our progress towards being a nation would have been considerably retarded." [57]

To Roosevelt, the answer seemed to be to utilize modern science, but return to the medieval attitudes:

"I believe that we must do everything in our power to encourage what for lack of a better name I have described as the guild spirit. It is undoubtedly true that the wonderful craftsmanship of the period during which the guilds flourished was due to the general recognition that a skilled craftsman stood as high in the social scale as what we call today a professional man. How can we expect boys today with real ambition to enter trades so long as we insist on considering a ten dollar a week clerk as in some way higher up in the social scale than a sixty dollar a week mechanic[?] . . . I hope among other things we will be able to interest colleges in an effort to impress on a college youth that there are more real brains required to operate for instance a 2 ton drop hammer than is required to add with mechanical accuracy a column of figures in a book. . . . Just so long as we bring up our boys and girls to look up to white collars and down on overalls just so long will the white collar professions be so overcrowded as to earn only starvation wages while some of our most important trades, particularly in building, will be so deficient in members as to command unheard-of wages." [58]

He believed that when high-caliber young men entered building, construction would become more of a science and less of a trade.

Aside from the use of concrete, construction was little advanced from the Middle Ages; bright young men would "devote much of their spare time to devising means of eliminating manual drudgery from their job, and substituting improved mechanical processes." This, of course, was primarily an indication of how superficially Roosevelt examined the complexities of the building industry in America — how little attention he gave to strong resistance to change on the part of both contractors and unions. It appeared to him as simple a business as his own act of investing five hundred dollars with a man who had a process for turning out cheap poured-concrete bungalows and garages.* After doing this, Roosevelt assumed they would be produced. On the contrary, he never heard from the man again. But there is no indication that he gave further thought to the project, since his attention promptly veered elsewhere.[60]

Repeatedly he called upon the industry to eliminate construction "distinctly inferior in quality and unsound in financing." As early as 1923 he had warned that thousands of buildings were being so poorly built that they would deteriorate within ten years to a point almost of no value. "This rapid depreciation coupled with unsound methods of promotion must entail enormous loss of the principal investment," he pointed out. In addition to heavy expense for repairs and unnecessarily costly insurance, there was the serious effect of unsound financing. He singled out for special attention mortgage bonds of an improper sort:

"Mortgage bonds are issued on speculative buildings. Many such issues are based on improper security and fictitious statements of earnings at abnormal interest rates. They find buyers because of the general ignorance existing in many quarters as to the requirements for good real estate securities. Such purchasers are usually those who can least afford to be victimized." [61]

Nevertheless, when the boom period passed, and construction began to slip in 1926, it is the contention of Alva Johnston that Roosevelt advocated the continuing use of these same risky mortgage bonds in order to keep building at a high level. In his 1926 statement, Roosevelt described the slack in building as leading to more substantial construction. "This is by far the healthiest situation that has existed in the building industry for some years," he wrote, "as there has been

* A project to which FDR gave more thought was that of trying to enlist Rockefeller support to build garden apartments in Westchester County for people in the five to eight-thousand-dollar income bracket.[59]

a very noticeable recession in new speculative building not backed up by adequate values, and a better class of business is coming upon the market." [62]

In New York City, however, speculative building continued even though the housing shortage which required it had passed. The financial basis of it was mortgage bonds, being purchased by small investors. On January 19, 1926, the controller of the Metropolitan Life Insurance Company had urged a halt to this sort of building in New York City; on the same day, Roosevelt asserted his disbelief that "New York City is headed for a wave of extravagance or overbuilding as a general proposition." Following the collapse of a house handling mortgage bonds, the state attorney general's office began an investigation of them. Roosevelt headed a committee to recommend measures of self-regulation for the mortgage-bond houses. "The naming of Franklin D. Roosevelt as Chairman," declared the New York Times, "is in itself a guarantee that those behind the move mean business." However, the report suggested only new accounting practices and standard methods of appraisal; Attorney General Albert Ottinger denounced it as inadequate, and was proved right by the default of numerous mortgage bond issues during the depression. [63]

For Roosevelt himself, the presidency of the American Construction Council, far from making him a "czar" of the industry, left him with a feeling of frustration. The organization and regulation he had hoped would ensue did not take place, and funds continued scarce. Above all, new associations kept cropping up which were outside of the paper jurisdiction of the council. "I am frankly pretty skeptical about the Council accomplishing any great things in the next year or two," Roosevelt wrote in March, 1928. Nor did he think much could be done until the multiplying of associations stopped, and he felt the council could not put an end to this. "I feel very strongly," he concluded, "that the only practical result will be obtained by a good far-reaching period of depression throughout the construction industry. That will automatically eliminate the unnecessary organization." If there were other less drastic means, he was not the man to try for them. The year was 1928, and he was "all mixed up in politics." [64]

Obviously, voluntary self-regulation did not work. A few years later Roosevelt was to turn toward an alternate solution: to place behind self-regulation the force of the law.

In appraising her husband as a businessman, Mrs. Roosevelt has commented, "Franklin had a restless mind. It had to be busy with a number of things." Anything novel he undertook with great enthusiasm, but shortly his interest would waver. Fidelity and Deposit was a well-established firm, and he quickly learned its ways of doing business. Because it made him go downtown, do things, and see people, it was good for him. Not so much could be said for some of the other ventures, for, as Mrs. Roosevelt has said, in business he "was not experienced and not always wise." [65]

In its total effect upon his career, there is more than that to his business experiences. In the Navy Department he had already seen the interaction between business and government from the standpoint of the politician; on Wall Street, he saw it from the businessman's viewpoint. Undoubtedly his disappointments as a business leader had some bearing upon his triumphs as a political leader.

CHAPTER X

The Fight for the "Happy Warrior"

> He has a power to strike at error and wrongdoing that
> makes his adversaries quail before him. He has a person-
> ality that carries to every hearer not only the sincerity
> but the righteousness of what he says. He is the "Happy
> Warrior" of the political battlefield.
> — FDR, NOMINATING ALFRED E. SMITH, *June 26, 1924.*

"ISN'T it curious that everybody is after the Presidency?" Roosevelt commented to a friend in December, 1922. "Personal candi-
dacies so rarely develop into anything tangible. In our own Party
for the last 50 or 60 years the nomination for the Presidency has been
nearly every time a matter of luck, or some eleventh hour opportunity
boldly seized upon." * Consequently, Roosevelt felt it was important
to work not for individuals, but to try "to make the nation understand again that Republican rule means government by selfish interests or powerfully entrenched individuals." This he proposed to do
through an organization which would teach "fundamental truths,"
and possibly save the Democrats from "going after some will-of-the-
wisp and making it our beacon." [1]

To Roosevelt, one of the fundamentals was still government efficiency. In 1922 or 1923 he projected a book on "The Machinery of
Government," in which he proposed to write chapters on "The Crying Need of a National Budget," "A Revision of Departmental Functions," and "Make Government Service Attractive." In the preface
(which was all he ever wrote), he declared, "If American governments were private corporations they would go into the hands of a
receiver in about twenty-four hours." He sent an article along these

* FDR added: "In the Republican Party the nomination for the Presidency has
in nearly every instance been dictated by a comparatively small group who have
picked their man sometimes months beforehand and allowed all the rest of the
candidates to strive hopefully up to the last minute." As for the Democrats in
1923, "After all, no talk or effort on behalf of Underwood or Cox, or Pomerene
or McAdoo, or John Davis or Al Smith, or Copeland or Hylan, or Hearst or
Ford is going to do any good, either now or during the next twelve months."

lines to George Horace Lorimer, the editor of the *Saturday Evening Post;* Lorimer rejected it.[2]

In a similar vein, he came out in favor of a proposed constitutional amendment to eliminate "lame duck" sessions of Congress by making January the date for Congress and the new President to take office. "I can see no possible objection against it," he declared, "except by those people who cannot understand that our Constitution was written nearly a century and a half ago. The very provision in that Constitution providing for amendments made it clear that those who drafted it believed future generations capable of bettering it." But he was not so sure he would favor a preferential presidential primary for New York State, since he felt that the voters of the state had "never been educated up to the use of the Primaries in the western fashion." There had been very few primary contests in the state, and he still remembered how the machine had smashed him in the 1914 primary when he had sought the nomination for United States Senator. Nevertheless, he was ready to propose a national referendum to deal with Prohibition.[3]

From the outset, Roosevelt was wary over making too clear-cut a commitment on Prohibition, which was heartily supported in the country and thoroughly disliked in the big cities. In September, 1922, he recommended to a Dutchess County supporter that he favor 3 to 4 per cent beer as being nonintoxicating, and desirable if sold only through dispensaries. He warned the supporter to go slow in advocating light wines, since they contained 10 to 15 per cent alcohol, and were unquestionably intoxicating. In 1923, as feeling for and against Prohibition heightened, it threatened further to disrupt the rural and urban wings of the Democratic party. Roosevelt fell back upon a still safer straddle than to advocate nonintoxicating beer. In essence, he reverted to his position years earlier when he had served in the state senate: let the public decide. When he saw bone-Dry William Jennings Bryan in Florida, he proposed a national referendum to settle the question. Of course, he implied to Bryan that this would result in a landslide for the Drys. "New York State is not nearly as wet a State as some Democrats try to make out," he later wrote reassuringly to Bryan. "The City of New York and certain other cities, like Buffalo and Albany are undoubtedly in favor of light wines and beer, but the rural sections would, in my judgment, vote heavily against much or even any, modification of the Volstead Act." [4]

To a Wet friend, he wrote the same proposal a few weeks later, this time granting that the country was not nearly as bone-Dry as it had been three years earlier. He confessed he was not sure what national sentiment was, but felt the time almost ripe for a referendum: "The Wets are feeling so cocky that they believe they would carry it — the Drys are so sanctimoniously satisfied that they ought not to be afraid of the issue being put to popular vote. Let's go to it, take the vote and have both sides agree beforehand that they will abide by the result whatever it may be, if either side gets a ⅔ majority in the result." [5]

For all this fine display of faith in democracy, and this plea for principle, Prohibition inevitably involved Roosevelt in personalities — for the widening rift in the Democratic Party involved not only issues and areas, but also voters and their leaders. Within the same party, within Roosevelt's own political orbit, were the driest of Drys, like Bryan, and the wettest of Wets, like Smith. Through 1923, Roosevelt tried hard to stay in the good graces of both. He warned Bryan that a strong drive was being made to get the 1924 Democratic Convention for New York City — a move which Roosevelt labeled the work of "hopeful idiots who think the democratic platform will advocate repeal of the 18th amendment." These reactionary forces, he asserted, even if they could not write the platform or nominate one of their own men, hoped "to prevent the nomination of a real progressive democrat or an outspoken dry candidate." [6]

As an interesting counterpart, he was counseling caution to Al Smith, who, as Governor of New York, had to decide in May, 1923, whether or not to sign a bill repealing the state Prohibition law. He commiserated Smith over "the extremely difficult position in which you have been placed over this darned old liquor question," then went on to warn him that people who admired him greatly and were powerful in national affairs felt that it would hurt Smith throughout the country if he signed the repeal. On the other hand, Roosevelt granted that "the vote in all big cities of this state will shriek to heaven if you veto the Bill." Instead, Roosevelt suggested, Smith should first veto the bill on the grounds that New York was morally obligated to assist the Federal Government in the enforcement of Prohibition, and second, call a special session of the state legislature to prepare a new state Prohibition law going no further than to require law-enforcement authorities within the state to assist the federal officials when they were called upon to do so. This, he felt, would throw the onus back on President Harding, since the Federal Government was spending only a trifle on enforcement, and it would get around the objection to the existing state Prohibition law that it put a man in jeopardy twice for the same offense. It would have the additional delightful advantage, which Roosevelt did not point out, of thoroughly straddling a hot issue. Smith chose not to follow Roosevelt's advice. Instead, he signed the Act of Repeal, and confined himself to pointing out that this by no means nullified the Volstead Act in New York State. Of course, a howl went up from the Drys.[7]

Despite the signs of trouble ahead within the Democratic Party over Prohibition, and the vigorous application of the Federal enforcing statute, the Volstead Act, Roosevelt was fairly optimistic into the summer of 1923. He felt that the prospects for a Democratic victory in 1924 were good, although some party members were dangerously overconfident. The basis of his optimism was his expectation that the country would slip back into the depression from which it was just emerging:

"Much will depend on whether the Harding administration is able to bolster up general prosperity for another year. The general world conditions are almost hopelessly bad, due largely to the complete failure of the American government to help other nations to get back on their feet. The result is that our exports continue to dwindle and without these exports we face serious depression at home. I hear from Washington that the Administration will do everything possible to continue a false prosperity and to make the full dinner pail again a slogan." [8]

The country went into boom rather than depression: private loans to foreign countries bolstered American exports, while the high tariff kept out the imports that might have dulled the domestic market. At home, the building of automobiles and good highways, of radios and washing machines, and even more, the hectic pace of the construction industry over which Roosevelt theoretically presided, all stimulated a high degree of prosperity. This inevitably redounded to the credit of the Republicans. At the same time, the Republicans lost their greatest liability, President Harding, before the public came to realize that he was a weakling presiding over an Administration rotten at several points with scandal and corruption. Harding died suddenly on August 2, 1923, and was succeeded by the impeccable Calvin Coolidge. Roosevelt recognized the new President instantly for what he was:

"I cannot help feeling that Harding's unfortunate taking off has helped rather than hurt the Republican Party. Coolidge, as you know, is not a world beater, but in his past career he has been clever enough to take advantage of situations after the other fellow had done all the work — witness the Boston Police Strike, where Andrew Peters practically settled things before Coolidge made any move. It looks now to me as if he would be nominated next year. He will be considered, of course, a Conservative, and that means that we must nominate a Progressive without fail." [9]

Who that Progressive Democrat might be was not yet entirely clear in Roosevelt's mind. On one point he was certain: that the boom for two standpat Democratic Senators, Oscar Underwood of Alabama and Samuel Ralston of Indiana, was ridiculous. "If I did not still have these crutches," he remarked, "I should throw my own hat in the ring." Since this was obviously impossible, he cast about cautiously for a proper candidate to support at the convention. For some months he inclined toward William Gibbs McAdoo. When McAdoo's principal backer, Dan Roper, inquired if New York's delegates would support McAdoo, Roosevelt replied that the situation was too complex to put on paper, but invited Roper to come to see him for a long talk. To another McAdoo supporter, he commented that in New York he would "hear a lot about the impossibility of nominating McAdoo just as there is a lot of nonsense being talked about making the Democratic Party wet next year." As late as January, 1924, he was guardedly writing that he expected McAdoo to have "vastly more strength than Underwood," and was referring potential McAdoo backers to Roper.[10]

At the same time, there was no question in Roosevelt's mind that Al Smith would receive the vote of the entire New York delegation when the convention assembled. And he expected to see Smith gain additional strength in the East. However, he feared it would be sufficient only to deadlock the convention, between the city and country wings of the party, not sufficient to bring Smith the nomination. Consequently, he was anxious for Smith to make himself more widely known throughout the country, in order to build support outside of the East. "I have sent word to the Governor that I hope he will soon take occasion to speak on some national question," Roosevelt wrote in August, 1923. "The fact that he has never done so (except in the case of the Volstead Act) has made many people wonder if his knowledge was sufficiently broad to handle international affairs." To one of Smith's strongest partisans, Abram Elkus, Roosevelt wrote with equal frankness, "He is not yet regarded as a truly national figure. It goes without saying that I should, of course, be delighted if he could be nominated, but honestly I fear that the odds are against it at the present time." [11]

So the situation continued for many months. The country had entered an era of "Coolidge prosperity," but it was a prosperity ill-distributed among the American people: tax cuts and high tariff protection for American industry at the same time that the courts sternly disciplined organized labor, and that the farmers floundered under the burden of heavy mortgages and sinking produce prices. These were the conditions that caused Roosevelt to feel that the Democratic candidate, if he were to be successful, must be a progressive or perhaps even a radical. He must appeal to the farmers, workingmen, and small businessmen who were not sharing to any degree in the Republican prosperity. The man who seemed most nearly to make this appeal was McAdoo. He was a Dry and had the support of the Democratic farmers and their longtime darling, the aged Bryan. Since McAdoo as Railroad Administrator during the war had been generous to organized labor, he had the friendship of the unions. Into the winter of 1923–1924, he seemed the logical nominee. The Smith movement seemed no more than a Wet effort to block the nomination of McAdoo or some other Dry, and apparently had no conceivable chance of succeeding. [12]

At the beginning of 1924 came the exposure of the Harding scandals — most notably the Teapot Dome oil affair — and with it McAdoo's downfall. Edward L. Doheny, a California multimillionaire oil man and heavy contributor to the Democratic party, was one of the two main beneficiaries of Secretary of the Interior Albert Fall's dishonesty. Doheny had hired McAdoo as legal counsel at a retainer of 25,000 dollars per year. In accepting this money McAdoo, as he explained to a Senate committee, had been legally and perhaps even ethically correct. But he had the taint of oil upon him, at a time when it was politically fatal.* Consequently, a dramatic piece of wrongdoing in a Republican cabinet failed, because of the death of Harding, to

---

* In addition, McAdoo's law firm appeared in tax cases before the Treasury Department a short time after McAdoo resigned as Secretary. It was this which caused Senator Thomas J. Walsh, who was responsible for exposing the oil scandal, to withdraw his support from McAdoo. [13]

damage the Republican party, yet blasted the candidacy of a Democrat. At a time when the Republican party was in danger of popular repudiation because of the exposures of corruption high in its ranks, the exposures helped eliminate the one mildly progressive Democratic presidential candidate who might conceivably have threatened the Republicans.[14]

Roosevelt, wintering on the Florida keys, remained strategically silent while McAdoo's support dwindled and that of Smith grew. He explained that he was so far from a harbor that he had seen only an occasional paper and had read only fragmentary accounts of the exposures.* This was less than frank, since Howe from New York had kept him fully informed. "Everybody feels that McAdoo is out of the running," Howe had written, and had pointed out how impossible it was for McAdoo to convince the public that he had received the huge retainer from Doheny because of his ability as a constitutional lawyer, not because, at the time Doheny hired him, he was the son-in-law of President Wilson. Everyone was speculating where the votes would go, Howe reported, and in New York optimistic Democrats predicted Smith would get them. Considering how much of McAdoo's support had come from Drys and members of the Ku Klux Klan, Howe doubted if Smith would benefit.[16]

This was an astute political evaluation. While McAdoo failed to gain additional strength, he did hold onto his Klan and Dry support, since it could not possibly go to Smith, Wet and Catholic. However, Smith began to grow in strength among moderate and progressive Democrats throughout the country. He had a fine reputation as a progressive and efficient Governor of New York, and began to shift to a less wringing Wet stand against Prohibition. Howe reported to Roosevelt that Smith had called a conference of Prohibition officers and had urged them so emphatically to enforce the law that he created "quite a doubt in the minds of the public as to whether he was really as wet as reported." Further, "some of the Albany boys" told Howe that "in one way at least Smith is much drier than he used to be." Howe commented cynically, "How long he has sworn off for this time, God knows. Let us trust until after the national convention."[17]

This meant that by the spring of 1924 Smith was more appealing

---

* FDR commented: "There is no question that poor old Harding was perfectly honest himself, but was not the kind of man who could ever tell the difference between a real friend and a crooked one, and he allowed himself to be surrounded by a pretty rotten crowd."[15]

than any other Democrat to progressive intellectuals. Among them, there was little harm if he were theoretically opposed to Prohibition (as were most of them) providing he was not too heavy a drinker. Roosevelt made much of this a little later. He kept clear his own position as a moderate Dry by writing political correspondents that he differed from the Governor on Prohibition, but was sure that if Smith were President he would enforce to the best of his ability whatever laws Congress passed concerning liquor.[18]

In answer to an inquiry from Mrs. Henry Noble MacCracken, wife of the liberal President of Vassar College, Roosevelt wrote concerning Smith's drinking: "As to his personal habits, I can only tell you that he used to drink beer in the old days, that after 'prohibition' came in, he tried drinking whiskey, and found that it was poison to his system. Since last autumn, it happens to be a fact that he has been entirely on the water wagon, and you need have no fear that he has ever been or would ever be a drunkard." [19]

As for Roosevelt, while there is no sign that he had any expectation that Smith could win the nomination, as early as at the end of January, 1924, he was committed to support Smith's candidacy.* When the New York *Post* announced that he had switched from McAdoo to Smith, he retorted indignantly by reminding the *Post's* political writer that he had started the Smith-for-Governor movement in 1922. "I have always supposed that if I went to the next Convention I would, in common with the rest of the delegation, be for Al," he asserted. "Please don't accuse me again of shifts or changes of heart!" [21]

While he was formally committed, he was no more wholehearted in his support of Smith during the early months of 1924 than he had been for McAdoo during the spring of 1920. While Roosevelt himself remained aloof in Florida, Howe was working quietly and rather effectively on behalf of not Smith but Roosevelt. They had already sized up 1924 as another politically bad year for the Democrats. The previous November, Roosevelt (taking into account the normal inflation of political predictions) had been flatly pessimistic in appraising the chances for victory in the East. He saw the possibilities as only "fair to middling" because of the split over Prohibition and the lack of party organization in the country districts. What Howe was after for Roosevelt in 1924, therefore, because of both Roosevelt's poor

---

* At about the same time, Mrs. Roosevelt also announced her support of Smith, and later in the spring seconded a resolution supporting Smith, passed by the state Democratic committee.[20]

physical condition and the ailments of the Democratic party, was not the nomination, but merely a handful of complimentary votes at the convention. These could serve as a build-up for a serious effort in a more propitious year. There were quiet negotiations with delegates from Colorado, Wisconsin, West Virginia, the District of Columbia and elsewhere. Howe tried to make one such deal with Lewis Green Stevenson of Illinois (son of a vice president under Cleveland, and father of the Democratic candidate of 1952). He and Roosevelt had become acquainted with Stevenson during the war, while Stevenson was a special investigator for the Navy Department.

When Stevenson came East with Boss Brennan to consult Hearst on how the Illinois delegation should vote, they saw Howe.[22]

Howe wrote Roosevelt:

"The present plan is to give Hearst the first ballot and then distribute a few more complimentary votes until they see which way the cat is jumping. Mr. Stevenson arranged for me to meet Mr. Brennan in a perfectly natural way and when this programme was mentioned in the conversation, Stevenson rather cleverly remarked, 'Why would not Mr. Roosevelt be a good man for a complimentary vote?' to which Mr. Brennan replied, 'That's a good idea.' " [23]

This type of minor maneuvering had nothing to do with who ultimately received the Democratic nomination. By the beginning of April, the political lines were beginning to firm. Tammany had obtained the convention for New York City, and Howe learned that they hoped to make a real effort to stampede it for Smith, if they could keep it deadlocked long enough for the delegates to wonder how they were going to pay their hotel bills. "They are demanding thirty-five hundred seats," Howe declared, "and the plan is to pack the house when the psychological moment arrives with Smith rooters." Nevertheless, as Howe well knew, McAdoo would still have the largest and strongest block of delegates. The action of Underwood of Alabama in coming out against the Ku Klux Klan had thrown it solidly behind McAdoo. As for the McAdoo leaders, Howe pointed out:

"They have the good judgement to impress on their weak-kneed supporters the wisdom of standing by McAdoo even if he has no chance of being nominated, so that they will be a part of a block so large that no one can be nominated without their consent. It looks now as if the McAdoo people would absolutely control the nomination, provided always they do not get into a factional fight among themselves. A general guess is that the leading candidates will be trotted out one after another for enough ballots to make it evident that they cannot secure the nomination, and that after that they will hold a conference in a back room amongst the leaders of the largest blocks of votes at which some unguessable and perhaps unknown John Smith will be picked on as the man whom every Democrat has been really yearning to see as the standard bearer of his party. . . . Mr. Roosevelt is sitting perfectly tight and not even talking about any second choice in case Smith does not go through."[24]

Undoubtedly, Roosevelt agreed with Howe's remarkably accurate prediction that the convention would deadlock with McAdoo dominant and Smith almost certain to lose the nomination. Furthermore, Roosevelt was well aware that the strength Smith was gaining came not only from progressives, but in considerable part from conservatives opposed to McAdoo. Nevertheless, on May 1, Roosevelt assumed active leadership of Smith's campaign.

There was nothing mysterious about Smith's choice of Roosevelt. Boss Murphy had just died, leaving the Smith forces without a single leader of strong standing nationally within the party. In addition, Smith's supporters were almost entirely of the city-Wet-Catholic faction of the party; they badly needed someone who could serve as an emissary to the rural-Dry-Protestant wing. Roosevelt filled both of these essential requisites. Besides, Smith and the men around him underestimated Roosevelt — they still had a certain snobbery toward the well-born, kid-glove politician who had not come up through the Tammany hierarchy. Consequently they regarded their acquisition as no more than a showy but harmless piece of window dressing, not as an ambitious hardbitten political operator who might take over the campaign and lead it in new directions.[25]

As for Roosevelt, this was a repetition of his 1922 maneuver. He had boosted Smith then in order to gain his own ends, in order to re-establish himself as a leading political figure in the state. In 1924, Smith enabled him to do the same thing in the nation. This does not mean that Roosevelt engaged in any subtle undercutting of Smith. On the contrary, Smith could not have obtained a more warm, diligent, and shrewd campaign manager. Roosevelt built his own standing by devoting himself with complete loyalty to the Smith candidacy. If, when the fight was over, many Democratic leaders throughout the country regarded Roosevelt as more attractive than Smith, this casts no discredit on Roosevelt.

"What the campaign lost in practical political ability through the death of Murphy," commented the New York *Herald Tribune*, "it has now compensated for in prestige and principles." In point of fact, Roosevelt (and Howe) brought both to Smith. They took full advantage of the opportunity to correspond with the many Democratic leaders throughout the country with whom Roosevelt had become acquainted during the Wilson Administration and the 1920 campaign. These men were delighted to renew their political relations with him, and even when they were flatly and unequivocally opposed to Smith, wrote him in warm and friendly terms. Among many of them, Roosevelt was able to build much good will for Smith, and perhaps even a few votes.[26]

In taking over the leading role for Smith, Roosevelt assumed for the first time a position of prestige among those city, Catholic Democrats who had looked rather askance at him since he had led the fight in the state senate against "Blue-eyed" Billy Sheehan. He was able to expunge fully the suspicion that he might be anti-Catholic. To ambitious party workers, he became a man of importance. That indefatigable political letter writer, James A. Farley of the New York State Athletic Commission, hastily wrote his congratulations to Roosevelt, and to Smith upon obtaining Roosevelt. The names of Roosevelt's new correspondents in the Eastern cities were in contrast to those of his old acquaintances throughout the country; they read like a sampling from the Dublin telephone directory.[27]

"Governor Smith is the most wonderful vote getter that I have ever seen," Roosevelt wrote in his stock letter to delegates. "This state is roughly divided in its views between the City of New York and the rest of the state, and has given tremendous Republican majorities, particularly in presidential elections. Speaking in general, upstate is exceedingly dry, and until Governor Smith was nominated it was always considered impossible to elect a Catholic, owing to upstate prejudice on the religious issue, yet after he had served a term as Governor, he had so won the confidence of the people throughout the state generally as to receive one million one hundred thousand votes more than Governor Cox and myself, who were running on the national ticket." In addition, Roosevelt recapitulated the 1922 Smith victory, and pointed to the manner in which Smith had functioned as governor without the slightest favor to one religious sect over another.[28]

From the time Roosevelt took over the Smith chairmanship, he insisted that the Smith workers must not stir up animosities that would last beyond the convention.* Toward other candidates they must follow a policy of nonirritation, noninterference, and nonintrusiveness. He wrote a long letter to McAdoo on May 19, assuring him that Smith workers would not try to persuade delegates committed to McAdoo to vote for Smith. "To argue as persuasively as we may the merits of our own man because of the faith that is in us, that is eminently proper," Roosevelt wrote; "to decry the merits of others, to misrepresent, to attempt to keep full knowledge of their just claims for consideration from the delegates, and most of all to inject a spirit of partisan bitterness into this weighing of candidates, is wrong, and everything which would leave scars behind in our own party will be scrupulously avoided by the friends of Governor Smith." 30

Unfortunately, just this sort of bitterness began rapidly to develop. The McAdoo workers used no moderation in trying to undermine Smith because of his religion and his opposition to Prohibition. Roosevelt would not retort by accusing McAdoo of depending upon Klan support, but by June was warning delegates pledged to McAdoo that McAdoo would not be nearly as effective a vote-getter as Smith, and would have great difficulty in carrying Eastern or Middle Western states.31

Both the liquor and religious issues worried Roosevelt, as well they might. Sinclair Lewis wrote in the Nation in June that since voters were more interested in whiskey than in politics, Coolidge would be overwhelmingly elected. Walter Lippmann of the New York World expressed his concern to Roosevelt because a pamphlet on Smith that Roosevelt sent him was silent on the Governor's attitude toward prohibition. While Lippmann did not wish to see it dragged into the campaign, he pointed out that this was one of the first things people wanted to know about Smith. Roosevelt agreed that this must be corrected in subsequent editions, but was far more disturbed by reports he was receiving from "certain sections of the country." These were the quantities of letters, which Howe was summarizing and analyzing,

* FDR wrote his old chief, Daniels (a McAdoo delegate), who jokingly proposed a Daniels-Roosevelt ticket: "There is still, of course, a chance in this year of grace — if things come to the pass of keeping us all in New York until the 255th ballot on July 31st you and I can end the deadlock dramatically and effectively by putting your candidate and mine into a room together armed with a complete Navy outfit ranging from bean soup to 16″ guns with orders that only one man can come out alive. Probably neither will come out alive and a grateful Convention will give us the nomination by acclamation." 29

belaboring Smith for being a Catholic. These came to Roosevelt from persons of high social position and low: "You are being criticized by your old friends in your class for bring[ing] Smith out, a Romanist. . . . It is belittling a good Roosevelt name, and no one can understand it." Again: "Keep the Pope out of the U.S. He is bad enough where he is. Yours, KKK." [32]

Feeling against nominating a Catholic was very strong, Roosevelt confessed to A. Mitchell Palmer, who had been Wilson's Attorney General. He asked Palmer, "Should the party take the bull by the horns this time and make one of the campaign issues a return to the religious freedom guaranteed by the Constitution or should we pussy-foot and sidestep the whole issue?" Palmer replied that he thought Smith's Catholicism would hurt him more in the convention than in the campaign, since a national convention in the mass was always cowardly. But he did not see how, combining the Wet and religious issues, Smith could be nominated. Therefore, he urged Roosevelt to give careful thought to a second choice, agreeable to the Smith supporters. [33]

All this furor obscured the basic issues between Democrats and Republicans upon which Roosevelt would have liked to see the campaign fought. Neither Smith nor the Democrats could meet anything short of disaster in a prosperous year if they allowed attention to center on liquor and creed. Already the Democrats were suffering seriously from the inability of most voters to distinguish between their program and that of the Republicans. As Roosevelt knew, when the Baltimore *Sun* conducted a contest that spring to define the difference between a Democrat and a Republican, 77 per cent of those who replied declared that there was no difference. Roosevelt pointed out in periodicals and private letters how splendidly the governor had reorganized the state administration, and he assured League advocates (without having any real basis for doing so) that Smith would be liberal in foreign policy. [34]

Above all, Roosevelt wished to obtain Smith support among the Middle Western farmers, who were becoming actively hostile toward the Republican party because of its failure to provide a strong national farm relief program. "The Governor is especially weak on any appeal to the discontented and disgruntled agriculturists," a farm leader warned Roosevelt. "A real honest-to-God agricultural program will have to be mapped out for him before his candidacy would appeal to the farmers of this country in their present frame of mind."

Yet Smith would make no statement on the farm problem. Roosevelt at the time described this as "a very proper attitude" — that Smith should devote himself entirely to being governor and leave his candidacy completely to his friends.[35]

Afterwards, Roosevelt explained: "The trouble was, of course, that Governor Smith positively forbade anything being done for his candidacy prior to May 1st — that meant that anything done after that time in the way of statements by him on national questions would have looked too much like campaign propaganda rather than any strong personal views of his own. He, himself, vetoed many suggestions that were made in regard to statements by him on the farm question and other national issues." [36]

This left Roosevelt as Smith's manager in a weak position. He was well aware of the demand among Middle Western Democrats that Smith take a strong stand on farm relief if he wished to gain their votes. A Minnesota leader wired him that the delegation was twenty to twenty-four for Smith, and would be solidly for Smith when McAdoo was eliminated. He called upon Roosevelt to obtain Smith's firm support for the farm relief measure before Congress, the McNary-Haugen Bill, and promised, "Smith can carry Minnesota next November if his friends vote to save agriculture." The most Roosevelt could do was himself to wire Senator Copeland urging that Congress not adjourn until it passed a farm relief bill. He did not even go so far as to specify the McNary-Haugen bill, and a few days later declared himself not in favor of "the artificial price fixing scheme." The Republican majority in Congress did nothing; it voted adjournment so that it could attend the party convention to nominate Coolidge.[37]

With Coolidge at the head of the Republican ticket, Roosevelt knew that vast numbers of Middle Western farmers would revolt under the leadership of Senator Robert M. La Follette of Wisconsin. One of Roosevelt's Minnesota correspondents warned him that the leader of the La Follette movement was predicting that the third party would carry eleven states in the Middle West and Northwest. The Minnesotan reminded Roosevelt, "Don't overlook the fact that this third party outfit is desperately in earnest and that they may spill a lot of political beans." Almost immediately Roosevelt tried to get in touch with La Follette. At the beginning of June, he sent La Follette a copy of his telegram advocating farm relief, and on June 9 sent him a letter extolling Smith as a progressive. Roosevelt expressed his strong wish that he could have a talk with La Follette concerning the state of the nation.[38]

La Follette was not well, and in any event could not possibly have entered into an alliance with the Wet Tammany man toward whom such a large part of his rural following looked with suspicion. Smith did well in the Democratic primary in Wisconsin, but that merely indicated his strength among the Wet foreign-born minority there.

Unmistakably, issues other than liquor and religion had disappeared, and nothing Roosevelt could do would bring them back. Personal political maneuvering could be of some aid. In the South, he dealt with politicians who would not back Smith but did assert that the nomination of Smith would not throw their states to the Republican party. This was despite the fact that most well-to-do businessmen in cities like Atlanta preferred Coolidge and his economic program over any Democratic candidate. They would vote against Smith as a Catholic, or against McAdoo as a radical. In the North, Roosevelt was more successful. He was in constant negotiation with Joseph Guffey, who wrote him letters of advice on how to obtain the large Pennsylvania delegation. Roosevelt was cordial toward Guffey but did not entirely trust him, since he had heard rumors that Guffey was also negotiating with Albert Ritchie, the conservative Wet Governor of Maryland. Although Roosevelt feared that Guffey was "riding many horses," Guffey did swing a majority of the Pennsylvania delegation to Smith.[39]

Roosevelt was able to make some use of Smith's considerable personal following. The nature of much of it was well illustrated by a letter he received from Babe Ruth, whom he had invited to serve on a Smith committee. Ruth wrote:

> Sure, I'm for Al. Smith. There is one thing about your letter, Mr. Roosevelt, that went across with me good and strong, — that was the take about the humble beginning of Governor Smith.
> Maybe you know I wasn't fed with a gold spoon when I was a kid. No poor boy can go any too high in this world to suit me.
> You know, we Ball players travel around the country a good deal and I hear Lots of fellows talking about Al. Smith and his chances to be president and I'm telling you that most everybody I talk to is with him.[40]

Within New York City, where the convention met, there was no question about Smith's overwhelming popularity. One of the Tammany leaders arranged on behalf of Roosevelt to have Smith's picture exhibited in all the motion picture theaters of greater New York. The Rivoli advertised a novelty, "phonofilm or talking movies" of the Governor. At the Rialto, the orchestra played "East Side, West Side . . . " and a Smith song written by Irving Berlin. The George M. Cohan theater went still further by displaying Smith's photograph to advertise the Cecil B. DeMille production, "The Ten Commandments." The implication was that Smith could best carry them out. No delegate to the convention could mistake the temper of Manhattan.[41]

In contrast, the convention machinery was under the complete control of the McAdoo majority, which would extend no favors to Smith men. Howe complained that they were not playing "very sporty ball." With the scene set for the great contest, there seemed very little likelihood that either side would demonstrate noteworthy sportsmanship.[42]

As campaign managers must, on the eve of the convention Roosevelt issued a statement boasting that his man was the overwhelming public choice and the leading candidate. He declared, "I am afraid that the second roll call is going to disturb the beatific day dreams of some of the gentlemen who have been seeing triumphant majorities for the men of their choice." At first he predicted no more than a hundred votes for Smith at the beginning of the balloting, but two days before the convention opened, he upped his estimate to over two hundred. Both he and Smith displayed strong optimism before the reporters. Smith told them: "You can write the headline now, boys, 'Smith wins the nomination.'" Roosevelt added, "There is not the shadow of a doubt about it." On the opening day of the convention, Roosevelt told the Smith workers that McAdoo's strength was waning, and that this was the psychological moment to put Smith over. He advised them, "Get out and do missionary work."[43]

For Roosevelt, the task at the convention was twofold. He was floor leader, and he made the speech placing Smith in nomination. For one man to perform both tasks was unusual. Had Bourke Cockran, the most gifted of Tammany orators, lived, he would have spoken for Smith again, as he had in 1920. Cockran's death left a gap which Smith found hard to fill. He tried out several speakers and was dissatisfied with each of them. Finally he turned to Roosevelt,* who wisecracked

* Many years later, Smith told John T. Flynn that FDR had begged to be allowed to make the speech in order to make a political comeback, and that Smith

that he would be glad to nominate Smith provided he did not have to audition.[45]

Ordinarily, the ornate, windy nominating speeches are one of the most boring paraphernalia of a convention; Roosevelt prepared carefully to make his spot in the limelight notable. One June day, Moses Smith, who was a tenant farmer for Roosevelt, was cultivating corn when he saw Roosevelt sitting on a blanket on a hill near Val Kill Creek, dictating to Missy LeHand. "Moses, what do you think I'm doing?" Roosevelt called. "I am writing a nominating speech to nominate Al Smith for President." [46]

The speech was a high point in the convention. It was a personal triumph for Roosevelt in the face of the disaster the fourteen-day struggle dealt the Democratic party. The delegates cheered for three minutes as he swung on crutches to the speakers' stand — his first important public appearance since the polio attack. They listened enthusiastically to his nominating speech, far more intently than to the average one, and interrupted him frequently to applaud. He combined with his splendid voice and infectious charm the tremendous appeal of being a courageous man battling against a severe physical handicap. The speech was good. Mark Sullivan called it "a noble utterance," and Walter Lippmann thought it a "moving and distinguished thing." Lippmann wrote Roosevelt, "I am utterly hard-boiled about speeches, but yours seemed to me perfect in temper and manner and most eloquent in its effect." Beyond this, it was Roosevelt's dramatic delivery of it on crutches that inspired such warm admiration for him, and helped make him the most popular figure at the convention — far more popular than his candidate, Smith.[47]

Roosevelt's description of Smith was of standard nominating speech quality. He portrayed him as a man loved by "every class and every section of the community," who stood "first in the affections of the people of the State." He dwelt at length upon Smith's progressivism, his many excellent actions as Governor of New York, and his remarkable achievements as a campaigner — "the 'Happy Warrior' of the political battlefield." All this was, of course, the handiwork of several persons who had worked over Roosevelt's draft. It was Judge Joseph M. Proskauer, one of Smith's most trusted advisers, who inserted the

---

finally agreed because he felt sorry for Roosevelt. But this story smacks of the bitterness of a disappointed man and goes against contemporary evidence.[44]

catchwords "Happy Warrior," which went back to the poet William Wordsworth.[48]

Will Rogers felt that Roosevelt had missed the opportunity of a lifetime by not confining himself to the words, "Delegates, I put in nomination Alfred Smith; try and find out something against him." But he granted that when Roosevelt "did get to the end and named Al you would have thought somebody had thrown a wildcat in your face. The galleries went wild and about ten State delegations marched and hollered for an hour." [49]

In retrospect the most noteworthy passages of Roosevelt's speech, and those which most clearly bore his own thought, were those in which he pleaded with the delegates for unity. Fearing that a battle over the platform would arise between the two main factions, he urged them: "You equally who come from the great cities of the East and from the plains and hills of the West, from the slopes of the Pacific and from the homes and fields of the Southland, I ask you in all sincerity, in balloting on that platform tomorrow, to keep first in your hearts and minds the words of Abraham Lincoln: 'With malice toward none, with charity to all.' " [50]

At the time the delegates cheered loudly, but in the ensuing days of bitterness they paid no heed. Before the balloting even began, they split vehemently asunder over a resolution to condemn the Ku Klux Klan. Everything seemed to turn out badly. When an Underwood supporter from Georgia made an attack upon the Klan, many Northerners joined in a demonstration, and the organ began playing "Marching through Georgia." The aged, perspiring Bryan, in his last appearance before a Democratic convention, pleaded against mentioning the Klan by name, and his every sentence was punctuated with the cacaphony of the Tammany-packed galleries. Rural nativism and urban rowdyism clashed head on. The roll call on whether or not to mention the Klan in the resolution illustrated dramatically the evenness of the split: the anti-Klan forces lost, 542⁷⁄₂₀ to 543³⁄₂₀.

When Roosevelt was recognized by the chair, the clamor was so great that for some time he could not make himself heard. Finally he said, "It is now nearly two o'clock of the morning of the Sabbath Day," and he moved adjournment. Even this motion was opposed by many delegates, but the chairman ruled that it carried.[51]

"My motto of malice towards none and charity to all was not the mere rhetoric of a nominating speech, but was the keynote of our whole campaign," Roosevelt ruefully wrote not long after the convention. "I do not believe in a campaign for nomination which leaves scars in our party." Thus through the long, hot, sordid proceedings, he had worked indefatigably to try to prevent schisms. Without success, he had tried to persuade the Smith faction not to fight out the Klan issue, but to accept a compromise plank denouncing all secret organizations. He was consistently ingratiating in his quest for Smith delegates, and performed the remarkable feat of winning considerable support and making relatively few enemies. Unfortunately, the vociferous rudeness of the galleries* undid much of his work.[53]

From the outset of the voting, it was obvious that the deadlock Roosevelt and Howe had so long feared had become a reality. For ballot after ballot the basic vote of the main candidates held firm, with McAdoo receiving at the most 530, and Smith, 368. Neither was able to pull from the other; the shifts were toward or away from various favorite son or dark-horse candidates. For the most part, Roosevelt (like any good manager) worked behind the scenes, spending more of his time at the Smith headquarters in the Prudential Building, at 43rd Street and Madison Avenue, than in his special seat on the center aisle at Madison Square Garden. Twice more he addressed the convention. After the sixty-sixth ballot, he moved that the delegates suspend the rules to allow Smith to address them for a half hour at the opening of the next session. He was wildly cheered when he appeared at the rostrum, but shouts of "No, no," were mingled with the applause when he stated his request. The vote was 604½ for, and 473 against the resolution; since it required two-thirds approval, it lost. Roosevelt was well satisfied, since the strategy of the Smith managers was to give all candidates an opportunity to address the convention. They felt that the refusal of the McAdoo forces to agree placed McAdoo on the defensive.[54]

The balloting went on and on, until the proceedings began to re-

---

* An Oregon delegate later wrote FDR a bitter description of how one of his friends had been excluded from the gallery, although he had a pass, because supposedly all available space was taken. Soon he noticed the emblems of those being admitted: a Smith button and a piece of ribbon of the proper color. When he secured them, he was admitted. "It was an evident fact," the Oregonian wrote, "that any one wearing a Smith button, or their collar on backwards, experienced no trouble in gaining admittance. . . . This, of course, didn't leave the best of taste with real Americans, to know that their foreign born brothers were preferable in their own native land." Nevertheless, this delegate concluded by assuring FDR, "I have the utmost confidence in you, and want to say that I supported you four years ago and would be glad to support you again, if you will get right." [52]

semble a farce. On July 8, after the ninety-third ballot (upon which Smith had received 355½ votes and McAdoo, 314, compared with 731 necessary to nominate), Roosevelt again addressed the convention:

"Mr. Chairman and fellow delegates: You have been far too good to me, much better than I deserve [cries of "No!" "No!" Applause].
. . . The candidate for whom I speak now leads the poll in this Convention. We have advocated his nomination as the representative of great Democratic principles, but the future of the Democratic Party rises far above the success of any candidate. [Cries of "Attaboy." Applause.] After nearly one hundred ballots it is quite apparent to him and to me that the forces in this Convention behind Governor Smith, the leader in the race, and those behind Mr. McAdoo, a close second, cannot be amalgamated. For the sake of the party, therefore, Governor Smith authorizes me to say that immediately upon the withdrawal by Mr. McAdoo of his name, Governor Smith will withdraw his name also from the consideration of the Convention. [Loud applause.] And as one of the representatives of Governor Smith I would add only this, that until such withdrawal has been made by Mr. McAdoo, I can say that Governor Smith's supporters will continue to vote for Governor Smith. [Loud Applause. Cries of "Attaboy!" "Attaboy!"]" 55

McAdoo refused to withdraw. Finally, after it no longer made much difference, on the one hundred and third ballot, the convention nominated a compromise candidate, John W. Davis.

Roosevelt received only one or two complimentary votes on sixteen of the ballots, most of them from a Wisconsin admirer. If this was a disappointment, he showed no sign of it, since it was more than compensated for by the many suggestions that he would be the most desirable of compromise candidates, if only he had his health back. The Chicago Tribune predicted as early as July 6 that because of the general admiration for him he "might be the nominee if it were not for his loyalty to Smith," and that if Smith were to withdraw, he "might easily be the legatee." * His embarrassed protests whenever

---

* A Florida delegate later wrote FDR that at the time he offered to withdraw Smith's name, the Florida and North Carolina delegations were conferring on whether to throw their votes to FDR, but were so angered because FDR announced Smith would not withdraw until McAdoo did, that they decided not to do so.

The Lieutenant Governor of Ohio wrote that he would have liked to see Ohio switch to FDR. An Arkansas delegate informed FDR, "Like the overwhelming majority of the delegates who attended the convention, I became a very

he was approached by delegates, that "it was impossible for me even to think of any support in view of my position as the manager for somebody else," only added to his attractiveness.[57]

Smith's followers were delighted with Roosevelt's dogged work on behalf of their hero. "An electric fixture minus the bulb would be Smith without Roosevelt," one of them wired. James J. Hoey declared, "You gave the Governor the best ride he could have had under any circumstances and I know he is thoroughly satisfied." Hoey and many others would have liked to see Roosevelt run for governor, had his health permitted, since they thought he could "win in a walk." After Roosevelt firmly refused to run for any office until he could walk again, Davis persuaded Smith to run for a third term in order to strengthen the ticket in New York.[58]

Throughout the country, among all groups, Roosevelt had strengthened himself. Lippmann wired him, "There never was a better political battle nor one in which the spirit of a gentleman and a good sport rose so clearly above faction and hatred. Your own personal service to New York has been incalculable." * Tom Pendergast, the Democratic boss of Kansas City, told one of his supporters, Ike Dunlap (so Dunlap reported): "I met your friend Franklin Roosevelt in New York and had just a few words with him. I want to say this, Dunlap, you know I am seldom carried away or become overly enthused in meeting men in all stations of life, but I want to tell you that had Mr. Roosevelt . . . been physically able to have withstood the campaign, he would have been named by acclamation the first few days of the Convention. He has the most magnetic personality of any individual I have ever met, and I predict he will be the candidate on the Democratic ticket in 1928." [60]

Aside from the personal triumph for Roosevelt, little that could have pleased him had come out of the convention. It had been conducted in a fashion that lowered the party in public esteem; it had been the sort of a wake in which, as Gavin McNab pointed out to

---

ardent admirer of yours, and had your physical condition permitted, you would have been nominated." [56]

* The New York *World* declared, "The popularity of Franklin D. Roosevelt in the convention stood the test of all its bitterness. He was a gallant and generous figure at all times, and by sheer force of his personality did more to offset the unsportsmanlike and often brutal behavior of some of those in the galleries than any other man." [59]

Roosevelt, "you and I acted as pallbearers for the Party, and where the crepe was hung on the door before the election instead of after the election as is the custom." Another delegate pointed out to him, "While it may be true that most of the crooks are to be found in the Republican ranks one must admit that we have most of the d—— fools." [61]

This was only part of the trouble. Even if the convention had been short and harmonious, the Democrats would have taken a sound drubbing in November because of their candidate. He was a conservative, low-tariff, League of Nations Democrat, one of the finest constitutional lawyers the nation had ever produced, and a gentleman of wealth and polish, who lived in Locust Valley, Long Island. His law firm was counsel for J. P. Morgan and Company. There was little to indicate that he would alter drastically the status quo of the Republicans if he were elected President. For those happy with Republican prosperity, there seemed little reason to take a chance and shift to a Democrat, even if he were as distinguished a conservative as Davis. They preferred to "Keep Cool with Coolidge." As for the disgruntled farmers, embittered union men, and others who were discontent, there seemed little likelihood that Davis would listen to their demands. They had looked with little enough favor upon the more progressive McAdoo. Representative Henry T. Rainey of Illinois reflected the feeling of many Middle Western farmers when he wrote Roosevelt that the convention had offered a choice only "between Doheny's attorney and Morgan's attorney." The La Follette third ticket quickly took shape, and received the endorsement of the unions and many farmers. During the campaign, Davis competed with Coolidge only in his denunciation of La Follette as a radical menace. The people he frightened away from La Follette went not toward himself but toward Coolidge.[62]

Roosevelt remained almost completely aloof from the campaign and devoted himself to improving his physical condition. There was some talk of making him Davis's Eastern manager, but the Smith followers were so angry over the failure of their idol to receive the nomination that Davis and Smith agreed that an Irish Catholic should receive the appointment. Roosevelt was not sure that even that would be consolation enough, since "bunches of our Irish Catholic friends are awfully sore." Roosevelt was also well aware of the disaffection of the farmers. He miscalculated, accordingly, that the La Follette vote would be quite large, perhaps large enough so that none of the three candidates would get a majority of the electoral votes, and the election would be thrown into the House of Representatives.[63]

On the other hand, Roosevelt personally admired Davis, whom he hoped to see emerge during the autumn as a dynamic campaigner. Glenn Frank, editor of Century Magazine, after meeting Davis at Roosevelt's home at Hyde Park, wrote Roosevelt his hope that Roosevelt would "sidetrack everything in the interest of the one thing of 'getting your legs back' by June 1928, for I want to be able to vote for a President with greater enthusiasm than I am able to muster this year." [64]

Roosevelt replied: "I am glad you had the chance to see Davis. I honestly believe he will grow as the campaign goes on. His little speeches . . . are always charming and beautifully expressed, but during the campaign he will have to be more dramatic. To rise superior to Coolidge will be a hard thing, as Coolidge is inarticulate to the extent of being thought a mystery. To stick the knife into ghosts is always hard, but I trust that the voters as a whole will come to realize that there is nothing behind Coolidge's silence and mystery except a spectr[e]." [65]

But Davis, for all his splendid ability, lacked that remarkable degree of political showmanship which Roosevelt had long since developed. When Roosevelt spoke over the radio on behalf of Davis on September 24, he emphasized Davis's sound qualifications to be President.* The balance of power in the new Congress as in the old one, he pointed out, would lie with the Democrats and those insurgent Republicans who were "in thought and deed much more in sympathy with Democratic policies than they are with the old line Republican policies." The country, he asserted, could be run more smoothly and effectively, if the executive and Congress were in harmony with each other rather than at loggerheads. Finally, with an eye to La Follette supporters, he warned that while a vote for La Follette was perfectly understandable, it was no more than a protest since he could not possibly be elected. "Don't waste your vote!" Roosevelt concluded.[67]

It was a vain plea, and although Roosevelt was far from optimistic, the results were more devastatingly against the Democrats than even four years previously. Only slightly more than half of those eligible

---

* Radio was still an unfamiliar medium for FDR. At the conclusion of the talk, not realizing that he was still on the air, he turned to the announcer and inquired, to the amusement of listeners, "How did it sound?" [66]

to vote even bothered to go to the polls, and of those who did, 54 per cent voted for Coolidge, 16.5 per cent for La Follette, and only 28.8 per cent for Davis. "La Follette's candidacy certainly cut both ways," Roosevelt concluded. "He polled more Democratic votes than he should have, and an extraordinary number of Democrats voted the straight Republican ticket for the sole purpose of eliminating La Follette hopelessly." [68]

To Roosevelt, the future seemed difficult but by no means impossible. He wrote, in December, 1924:

"In 1920 after the poke we got that year, I remarked to a number of my friends that I did not think the nation would elect a Democrat again until the Republicans had led us into a serious period of depression and unemployment. I still [think] that forecast holds true, for much as we Democrats may be the party of honesty and progress the people will not turn out the Republicans while wages are good and the markets are booming. Every war brings after it a period of materialism and conservatism; people tire quickly of ideals and we are now but repeating history. Nevertheless the Republican leaders are not through with dishonesty nor will the present prosperity continue unabated. I only wish that the Democrats throughout the country would unite more closely, get rid of their factionalism and their localisms, get better hearing from the press and put their national organization on a sound financial basis. If we can do that and stop talking about candidates for 3 years we may win in 1928!" [69]

The Struggle to Walk

> Why not look at the cheerful side of all kinds of luck,
> good or bad? The older I grow the more I realize that we
> cannot tell at the time which is the good and which is the
> bad luck.
>
> — FDR TO THOMAS HALLY, *August 14, 1924.*

DURING the early 1920's, Roosevelt enjoyed political activity as fascinating recreation which did much for his morale. "The convention was great fun," he wrote in the summer of 1924 — "did me no harm and has actually put more pep into my legs than I ever had before!" [1] In the end, his interest in politics was dominant, but for several years it was subordinate to his ceaseless struggle to walk again. Until he could walk or give the illusion of walking, people might not take his political aspirations seriously. Despite his splendid appearance at Madison Square Garden, the consensus was that he was through. Thomas Wolfe, visiting on an estate a few miles above Hyde Park that summer, caught these overtones with his ear as sensitive as a tape recorder, and reproduced them in *Of Time and the River:**

"By the way, Ida," Mr. Joel growled, tugging at his short and grizzled mustache, "how is Frank? Have you been over to see them, lately?"

"Yes, Father," she answered, "we drove over last Tuesday and spent the evening with them. . . . He looks very well," she added, in answer to his question, "but, of *course*," she said decisively, "he's *never* going to be any better — they all say as much — "

"Hm," old Mr. Joel growled, tugging reflectively at his short and grizzled mustache for a moment longer, and then said: "Has he been taking any part in the campaign this summer?"

"Very little," she answered — "of course, the man has gone through hell these last few years — he's suffered agonies! He seems

* Reprinted from *Of Time and the River* by Thomas Wolfe (Garden City, N.Y., Sundial Press edition, 1944), 563-564; copyright 1935 by Charles Scribner's Sons; used by permission of the publishers.

THE STRUGGLE TO WALK

a little better now, but," her voice rose again on its tone of booming finality as she shook her head — "he'll never get back the use
of his legs again — the man is a *permanent* cripple," she said positively — "there's no getting around it — and he himself is reconciled to it."

"Hm," growled old Mr. Joel again, as he tugged at his short
mustache — "Pity! Nice fellow, Frank! Always liked him! . . .
A little on the flashy order, maybe — like all his family . . . too
easy-going, too agreeable . . . but great ability! . . . Pity!"

"Yes, isn't it!" Joel whispered with soft eager sympathy. "And,
Grandfather," he went on with an eager enthusiasm, " — his
charm is *simply* stupendous! . . . I've never known anything like
it! . . . The moment that he speaks to you he makes you his friend
forever — and he *knows* so much — he has such interesting things
to say — really the amount he knows is *simply* stupendous!"

"Hm, yes," old Mr. Joel agreed with a consenting growl, as he
tugged thoughtfully at his grizzled gray mustache, " — but a little
superficial, too. . . . The whole lot is like that . . . go hell-for-
leather at everything for three weeks at a time — and then forget
it. . . . Still," he muttered, " . . . an able fellow — very able. . . .
Pity this thing had to happen to him just at the start of his career."

"Still, Father," Mrs. Pierce put in, " — don't you think he'd
gone about as far as he was going when this thing hit him? . . .
I mean, of course, he *is* a charming person — every one agrees on
that. I never knew a man with more native charm than Frank —
But for all his charm, don't you think there's something rather
weak in his character? . . . Do you think he would have had the
stamina and determination to go much further if this disease
hadn't forced him to retire?"

"Um," Mr. Joel growled, as he tugged thoughtfully at his short
cropped mustache. " . . . Hard to say. . . . Hard to tell what
would have happened to him. . . . A little soft, perhaps, but great
ability . . . great charm . . . and great opportunists, every one
of them. . . . Have instinctive genius for seizing on the moment
when it comes. . . . Never know what's going to happen to a man
like that — "

"Well," said Mrs. Pierce, politely, but with an accent of conviction — "he might have kept on going — but I think he was
through — that he'd gone as far as he could — I don't think
he could have stood the gaff — I don't believe he had it in
him."

"Um," Mr. Joel growled, "perhaps you're right. . . . But great
pity just the same. . . . Always liked Frank. . . . Very able fellow — "

Of course, Roosevelt never seems to have thought of himself as politically through or a permanent cripple. He faced up only with difficulty to the realization that the task of regaining the use of his legs would be a long one. It was not until December, 1923, more than two years after the polio attack, that he wrote the officials of the Dutchess Golf & Country Club, requesting that he be transferred from active to nonresident membership because he was still on crutches and "cannot possibly play golf myself for a year or two." And a full year later he was still dreaming of the time when he could walk without crutches or leg braces. "Just as soon as that day comes I shall try my hand at golf again," he wrote General Richmond P. Davis. "As I remember it I could always outdrive you in the palmy old days." Quite obviously, that day was far off, but he would not reconcile himself to thinking it would never come.[2]

In his public appearances, Roosevelt tried to give the semblance of an entirely well man. It was a point of pride with him that on these occasions he seemed his old self. "Franklin stood at the desk at the platform as if nothing was wrong with him — his fine height and superb head showing in silhouette from where we sat," Mrs. Hamlin wrote after attending the 1924 convention. At less important occasions when he spoke before gatherings, he arrived early, and by the time the audience arrived, was implanted in an armchair on the stage. Only once did Roosevelt give vent to his feelings on this touchy matter. This was when in January, 1925, someone wrote him upbraiding him because at a mass meeting at Madison Square Garden, he had not risen to his feet when tribute was paid to President Coolidge.* He answered:

"As I wear steel braces on both legs and use crutches it is impossible for me to rise or sit down without the help of two people. After presiding at the opening of the meeting and turning it over to Bishop Manning I returned to my seat, sat down and remained seated during the rest of the evening. It is, of course, not exactly pleasant

---

* The occasion was the climax of the drive to raise funds for the Cathedral of St. John the Divine. FDR reported to his half-brother: "I was scared to death when I stumped forward to call the meeting to order, as everybody had long faces and [the] prayer only made the atmosphere more churchlike. I had to do something as my own short address was exceedingly solemn, so I started off by grinning at the audience and remarking that it seemed natural to be back in Madison Square Garden again. That broke the ice and from then on all was smooth sailing." [3]

for me to have to remain seated during the playing of the National Anthem and on other occasions when the audiences rise, but I am presented with the alternative of doing that or of not taking part in any community enterprises whatsoever." [4]

No one was better aware than Roosevelt that braces were no more than a device to help him in getting around. "A leg in a brace does not have a chance for muscle development," he wrote in the fall of 1924. "This muscle development must come through exercise when the brace is not on — such as swimming, etc." Constantly he sought suitable means of exercise to restore the strength in his muscles. [5]

No matter how ridiculous the proffered cure, Roosevelt was ready at least to give it a thought. One of his friends spoke to Professor Emile Coué about him, for Coué at the end of 1923 was the rage in America, effecting cures through having his patients chant endlessly, "Day by day in every way I am getting better and better." But Coué admitted to Roosevelt's friend that he could do very little for polio victims. One of the most notorious of American political bosses recommended that he buy a widely advertised electric belt. Another friend, an English noblewoman, suggested some new elixir. [6] This last was too much for Roosevelt, who with common-sense amusement wrote in February, 1923, to Dr. Draper about this "latest quack medicine":

"It may be monkey glands or perhaps it is made out of the dried eyes of the extinct three-toed rhinoceros. You doctors have sure got imaginations! Have any of your people thought of distilling the remains of King Tut-Ankh-Amen? The serum might put new life into some of our mutual friends. In the meantime, I am going to Florida to let nature take its course — nothing like Old Mother Nature anyway!" [7]

And so he did. He rented a houseboat, the *Weona II*, and spent several happy weeks cruising along the Florida Keys. He enjoyed the fishing, and the carefree companionship of old and treasured friends who wandered around aboard "in pyjamas, nighties and bathing suits." In his log, "Admiral" Roosevelt recorded the adventures of the party:

Tuesday, Feb. 27
Under way at seven bells, crossing Bay of Florida, rounding Cape Sable 12–1 casting anchor Little Sharp River at 1:30. The Admiral continued boat building operations during the voyage assisted by a little sawing on the part of Mr. Cas & Mrs. Grubaround.

Lunch 4 bells

3 o'clock all start out trolling up the fascinating winding river, stared at curiously by bold pelicans & shy herons. The Admiral made the first haul — 10 lb. Red Grouper. Then the great battle came when Mr. Cas after a valiant fight of 30 minutes finally landed a 42 lb. "Jew Fish"! . . . Two more black groupers about 8 lbs each, by Ruth & Fisherman deRham II ended the day's sport.

The Admiral had his first bath in two weeks — Dropping gracefully overboard by means of davits was met in ocean by his friends in a festive swimming party.

Grog, grub & writing of the log —

March 4 Sunday

. . . Heaved, on a rising swell, in about lunch time to find the Admiral all beautifully gotten up for Sunday — white flannel trousers, pure white tennis shirt with violet monogramed hanky sticking sportily out of pocket. (looking very doggy-dog, having used Glovers' m.c. the night before.)

Typical after Sunday lunch feeling — sit and sit and talk and talk. Finally, about 1 bell p.m. (having steamed out nearer the Gulf) F.D.R. & F[rances] D. deR[ham] went swimming in Florida water, while the others went up the crick and saw one skinned 'gater. . . .

Official measuring of the Admiral's sidechops, the longest hair measures ⅜ inches. . . .

Roosevelt also contributed to the log of the *Weona II* some doggerel of value only as an indication of his holiday mood:

—COMMUNITY LIFE—

You can slack off peak halyards — and eat with your knife,
You can dine in your shirtsleeves, and so can your wife —
These are some of the joys of Community Life!

* * * * *

When they first come on board they think it's so nice —
With staterooms and bathtubs and comforts sans price —
Till they suddenly realize that every partition
Sounds intimate echoes of each guest's condition
Of mind and of body — For whispers of details
The wall in its wisdom with great gusto retails.

* * * * *

No secrets or thoughts between husband and wife
Can safely be had in Community Life. . . .

F.D.R.[8]

All this was highly expensive — the charter of the boat for three weeks cost Roosevelt fifteen hundred dollars — but worked wonders for his health as well as for his spirits. He basked in the sun until he was burned, and went swimming repeatedly. By the end of March his legs had improved so markedly that he was thinking again of the time when he could rid his legs of straight braces so that he would be able to go up and down stairs. "Except for the braces," he wrote Carter Glass, "I have never been in better health in my life." [9]

Roosevelt was so delighted with the Florida experiment that he decided to buy a houseboat in partnership with his friend John S. Lawrence, who like him did not enjoy the full use of his legs. Lawrence has referred to it as their "floating tenement," with an engine that sometimes worked and sometimes did not: "She was comfortable and she made it possible to work over our legs." This Roosevelt christened (in a contraction of "Lawrence, Roosevelt and Company") the *Larooco*. For three successive years, in the early months of 1924, 1925, and 1926, he went on long, outwardly happy trips on the vessel. His share of the expenses placed a financial drain upon him, and he had to worry constantly over one or another difficulty in keeping the *Larooco* in good repair. Nevertheless, it was the sort of detail he relished, and reported in high spirits to his partner.[10]

A few days after he first went aboard, on February 11, 1924, he wrote Lawrence from Daytona, Florida:

> *Larooco's* a great little packet, but has lots of bad luck! I put her in commission at Jacksonville the 3rd. We bought sundry supplies, left the 4th to come through with fine weather to St. Augustine. Left there the 6th, ran aground at Matanzas Inlet that day — high and dry — got off during the night, and the 7th were stopped in company with a dozen other boats by a slide in the canal. Stayed there three days: The water in these channels and canals is very low. Today just before getting here we hit a long log (sunken) and burst the port shaft. So tomorrow I must be hauled out — Held up for 10 hours by a busted drawbridge:
> I am starting to paint — light blue furniture and green decks — begins to look very flossy.[11]

Along the Florida Keys, Roosevelt lived a thoroughly relaxed existence on the *Larooco*. Mrs. Roosevelt was too tied to her private-school teaching and other activities in New York to spend more than a few days with him. But Howe, Missy LeHand, and various of the children were there much of the time. Lawrence spent only a few weeks aboard in the third winter, but there was a constant stream of congenial visitors.* These included the Morgenthaus, Henry de Rhams, and Livingston Davis, and occasionally a short call from some dignitary such as President William Green of the American Federation of Labor. Among the guests were Sir Oswald E. and Lady Cynthia Mosley, "a most delightful couple." Needless to say, Mosley was not yet the leader of the British Fascists. Roosevelt's gaiety kept the guests in a state of high merriment.[13]

Roosevelt disliked the resorts. At Palm Beach, "I found the growth of mushroom millionaires' houses luxuriant," he wrote in the log. "The women we saw went well with the place — and we desired to meet them no more than we wished to remain in the harbor even an hour more than necessary." He infinitely preferred poking along the swamps and inlets in quiet waters south of Miami.[14]

While he was planning his 1925 visit, he wrote:

> I propose to go on board at Miami about February 1st and cruise thence by slow stages south through the bays and inland water ways all the way to Key West, a distance of about 200 miles. Practically all the way we follow the Florida East Coast Railway on the famous viaduct that runs from key to key. Often we stay for 3 or 4 days in the same place if the swimming or fishing are good. Supplies, laundry etc. are sent down to us once a week from Miami. It practically never rains and we use the big top deck which is covered with an awning during the greater part of the day when we are not off fishing. . . . Last year I caught 41 different varieties of fish, and aside from the sport they are nearly all delicious eating. Down there I average 10 hours sleep every night — you simply can't keep awake after 9 or 9:30 P.M.
>
> The top deck is plenty big enough to exercise on. While one can swim directly off the boat (being lowered into the water in a sling) we do not do much of that on account of sharks, but prefer to go [to] the occasional sandy beaches and splash around in shallow water. In this shallow water I have been able to do many of Mrs. Lake's special exercises for the legs.[15]

There was time for rest and contemplation too. He spent much of his time on the top deck working on his stamp collection, and part of it at writing projects. He made a start on a history of the United States. Had he finished it, the result would have been even more diffuse than Woodrow Wilson's. But it held his interest for only fourteen pages, and he never got past the explorers. He did rather better with a biography of John Paul Jones, but this too he failed to complete.[16]

Withal there were serious drawbacks to the *Larooco*. Because of Lawrence's failure to use it more, the expenses fell on Roosevelt more heavily than he could afford, and he feared that because of his illness he was an unfair burden to his family. Because the weather was not always warm enough, he was not able to swim as much as he would have liked, and because of quantities of sharks in deep water, he dared swim only in a few shallow spots. Sand beaches were rare, and on them he had more sunning than swimming. In addition, he had difficulty moving about from the deck of the houseboat to the launch and to the beach. It was far from ideal for a man in his condition, and on one occasion led to a painful mishap. The first week he was in Florida, in the winter of 1925, during a storm he had a bad fall in the launch, tearing the muscles below his right knee so seriously that it undid much of the improvement he had made up to that time. It was a month before they healed sufficiently for him to get much exercise. At times he was able to achieve the appearance of gaiety only through determined effort. Missy LeHand once told Frances Perkins that there were days on the *Larooco* when it was noon before he could pull himself out of depression and greet his guests wearing his lighthearted façade. Because the venture was disappointing, by the spring of 1925, he had decided to charter or sell the *Larooco*. He was unsuccessful in doing so, and cruised on her again in the spring of 1926. That September, a violent hurricane snapped her from her moorings and drove her several miles inland. When the waters receded, she was permanently beached in a pine forest.[17]

During these same years, Roosevelt sought other means of improving his muscles. In the summer of 1924, he experimented briefly with a tricycle which his mother brought him from Europe. He declared that it was "a great success" — but almost immediately abandoned it. He tried riding horseback too, but could do no more than sit on the horse and be led around. This was rather precarious because of the lack of grip in his legs, and he complained jocularly that what he needed was "a horse which is constitutionally unable to trot, and which is also guaranteed against any sidewise motions." He spent little time on horseback.[18]

Again and again, he came back to the water as the way to improvement. In the spring of 1924 when he was in Boston having new braces fitted, he talked with Dr. Lovett about his experimental work with polio. Dr. Lovett commented to him that most of his patients were New Englanders, and many from the seashore; he urged them all to swim as much as possible. But the patients who were able to swim in the warm waters of Buzzards Bay or Long Island Sound improved much more than those who went to the North Shore or the coast of Maine, where the water was so cold that they could stay in for only a few minutes. As a result, he told Roosevelt, he had constructed a shallow tank at the Children's Hospital of Boston in order to try exercising muscles in water instead of on tables. If Roosevelt were to exercise more in water, one of his needs was a good swimming pool at Hyde Park. He made tentative plans to have his friend Elliott Brown construct one for him close to the house, but Mrs. Roosevelt persuaded him to undertake a different sort of project about a mile and a half east of the house. She and her friends Nancy Cook and Marion Dickerman wished to build a permanent cottage, and to locate the pool there.[19]

Roosevelt reported:

"My Missus and some of her female political friends want to build a shack on a stream in the back woods and want, instead of a beautiful marble bath, to have the stream dug out so as to form an old fashioned swimmin' hole. Apparently the girls think that this will get them more closely back to nature and I foresee that I shall have to put a substantial board fence around the swimmin' hole to keep interested neighbors from seeing how close they get back to nature when they take their morning plunge!"[20]

The following summer, Roosevelt himself arranged the building of the pool and cottage. Later, Mrs. Roosevelt built the Val-Kill Furniture Factory there.*

By the end of the summer of 1924, Roosevelt was able to stand up without support in water just below his shoulders. At this point,

* In 1936, Mrs. Roosevelt remodeled the factory into a house; it became her home after FDR's death.[21]

his old friend and supporter, George Foster Peabody, the philanthropist and banker, wrote him about a pool in which Peabody owned a half-interest where he might do even better. He enclosed a testimonial from a polio sufferer, Louis Joseph, who had gone there almost a complete cripple except for his arms, and after three years was able to get about the streets with only a cane. In addition, Tom Loyless, a former newspaperman, who was one of the part owners, came to New York to talk to Roosevelt about it.[22]

Roosevelt was immediately interested. He wrote a doctor:

"I am planning to go to Warm Springs, Georgia on October 3d to try out a remarkable swimming pool of natural highly mineralized water which comes out of the hillside at a temperature of 90 degrees. I have had such success with sunlight and swimming that I believe that in such a pool I could actually walk around at the shallow end with the water up to my shoulders, an[d] thereby get the normal walking motion better than any other way." [23]

When Roosevelt arrived there, the decaying old Southern resort was a pathetic sight. The old hotel and the auditorium were deserted; the grounds were overgrown with weeds. There was no doctor or anything medical. "It was," Roosevelt once declared, "a perfectly good down-at-the-heel summer resort and nothing else. It was in awful condition." But the pool was everything he could have expected. The water came out of the ground from under nearby Pine Mountain at the rate of eighteen hundred gallons a minute, heated to a temperature of about 88 degrees. It was so laden with mineral salts that it was highly buoyant, yet so remarkably refreshing that Roosevelt could stay in it for as much as two hours without becoming enervated as he would in other water of this temperature. It was exactly what he needed in order to move his damaged muscles. He began to improve immediately, and for the first time since August, 1921, felt life in his toes. At the end of October he was able to boast, "I walk around in water 4' deep without braces or crutches almost as well as if I had nothing the matter with my legs." [24]

Cleburne E. Gregory, political writer for the Atlanta *Journal*, came to Warm Springs to visit Roosevelt. For five days he went swimming with him, two or three times a day, between times buying hot dogs from a small stand near the pool, and washing them down with an occasional bottle of beer. Gregory wrote an article for the *Journal* entitled "Franklin Roosevelt Will Swim to Health," in which he described how Roosevelt "has the large swimming pool all to himself for two hours or more each day. He swims, dives, using the swinging rings and horizontal bar over the water, and finally crawls out on the concrete pier for a sun bath that lasts another hour." This brought publicity to Warm Springs as well as to Roosevelt, and numerous sufferers from infantile paralysis became interested in the remarkable pool. While Roosevelt was away for the winter, Loyless, who was ill, was unable even to keep up with inquiries. Yet already Loyless and Roosevelt were hoping that Warm Springs could become a curative center. Patients began to arrive before there were any facilities for treating them.[25]

The following spring, Roosevelt returned and faced this problem:

> One day Mr. Loyless . . . and some of us . . . were sitting around when a messenger came up the hill to Mr. Loyless and said, "Two people have been carried off the train down at the station. What shall we do with them? Neither of them can walk."
>
> Well, we held a consultation. It was long before anything was done here in the way of a hotel or cottages. We decided that we could take care of them in the village overnight, and then, in a couple of days we could fix up what is now "The Wreck," and put them in it. Well, before we could put that cottage in order, eight others had arrived. They came like Topsy and got here before we knew it.
>
> We did not know what to do with them so I sent for Dr. [James] Johnson. He came and looked them over and guaranteed that they did not have heart trouble or something from which they would suddenly die, and he recommended cream and fattening diets for some and he recommended very little food for some of the others.
>
> And then I undertook to be doctor and physio-therapist, all rolled into one. I taught Fred Botts to swim. I taught them all at least to play around in the water. I remember there were two quite large ladies; and when I was trying to teach them an exercise which I had really invented, which was the elevating exercise in the medium of water, one of these ladies found great difficulty in getting both feet down to the bottom of the pool. Well, I would take one large knee and I would force this large knee then I would say, "Have you got it?" and she would say, "Yes," and I would say, "Hold it, hold it." Then I would reach up and get hold of the other knee very quickly and start to put it down and then number one knee would pop up. This used to go on for half an hour at a time; but before I left in the spring, I could get both those knees down at the same time.[26]

With John W. Davis and Al Smith at Hyde Park, August 7, 1924

On the houseboat *Larooco* in Florida in 1926, with jewfish
caught by Elliott

Together with the local doctors, Roosevelt established a clinic, prepared charts for the muscles, and directed the exercises of various patients. "You would howl with glee," Roosevelt wrote "Livy" Davis at the time, "if you could see the clinic in operation at the side of the pool, and the patients doing various exercises in the water under my leadership — they are male and female of all ages and weights."

It was a magnificent outlet for Roosevelt's energy and enthusiasm. Not only did he supervise the treatment of the patients, but he undertook the physical rehabilitation of the area:

"In addition to all this I am consulting architect and landscape engineer for the Warm Springs Co. — am giving free advice on the moving of buildings, the buildings of roads, setting out of trees and remodelling the hotel. We, i.e., the Company plus F. D. R., are working out a new water system, new sewage plan, fishing pond, and tomorrow we hold an organization meeting to start the Pine Mountain Club which will run the dance hall, tea room, picnic grounds, golf course and other forms of indoor and outdoor sports. I sometimes wish I could find some spot on the globe where it was not essential and necessary for me to start something new — a sand bar in the ocean might answer, but I would probably start building a sea wall around it and digging for pirate treasure in the middle." [27]

Roosevelt's boundless energy was an index to his soaring morale. At the end of April he reported that Warm Springs was doing his legs more good than any other spot. In only three weeks he had improved so much that he was able to put ten or fifteen pounds more weight on his legs than previously.[28]

He was impatient to improve still more rapidly, so in the summer of 1925 he sought a rather different type of treatment. This was with Dr. William McDonald of Marion, Massachusetts, an excellent neurologist, who had devised a set of exercises, both in and out of water, so successful that he devoted himself entirely to working with polio patients. McDonald took only four patients at a time, but he soon accepted Roosevelt. In August, Roosevelt left New York by automobile to visit with Howe at Westport Point, and to begin treatments.* Roosevelt found that the treatment would be very strenuous; so much

---

* "The car will as usual be crowded," FDR wrote his mother. "Louis and I on the back seat with various packages tucked around and under us . . . several score suitcases, braces, crutches, canes, sandwiches thrown in for good measure. However it saves $11 for each person to travel thus to the Beach!" [29]

the better. With determination, he gave his full energies to it. He went swimming much as at Warm Springs, but because the water was colder, could not stay in as long. In addition, without his braces, he spent two or three hours a day going round and round a rectangle of wood, hauling himself along the railing hand over hand, dragging his legs after him. Once more his optimism bubbled over. "This time I think I have hit it," he wrote after a week. "Dr. McDonald has gone one step further than the others and his exercises are doing such wonders that I expect in the course of another 10 days to be able to stand up without braces. What I did before in the way of swimming at Warm Springs all to the good, but now I begin to see actual daylight ahead." At the end of October, he still felt the treatment so valuable that he voted by mail rather than lose three days by going home. By the beginning of December, when he was preparing to leave for the winter, he was able to walk a considerable distance — from the house to the wharf — with only one brace, and hoped to get rid of that in the course of the winter.[30]

The following summer, Roosevelt again worked valiantly with Dr. McDonald. He never ceased trying. One evening, he and Mrs. Roosevelt went to the Hamlins' nearby for dinner. Mrs. Hamlin remembers:

"He was carried in to a seat at the dining room table. He told the men not to return until 9:30. We wondered how he would spend the evening — probably staying in the dining room. But when dinner was over — Franklin pushed back his chair and said — "See me get into the next room." He dropped down on the floor and went in on his hands and knees and got up into another chair by himself. My husband was so overcome at such courage and seeing that superb young fellow so pleased by being able to do this — that on the plea of hearing the telephone — he went into his den for a while. It seems that Dr. McDonald taught his patients this way of helping themselves so that they would have a feeling of freedom to move if necessary — or for reasons of safety." [31]

But Roosevelt did not improve as much as he had hoped; he did not succeed in walking without braces. Consequently, he ended his treatments with Dr. McDonald, and turned his entire attention to his main love, Warm Springs.

During the winter of 1925–1926, the ailing Loyless was having increasing difficulties in running the resort, and financially was losing heavily. He was the lessee of Peabody, who also was taking a considerable loss. But Roosevelt, who was working so hard already for the rehabilitation of Warm Springs as a therapeutic center, dreamed of taking it over. At the end of February, 1926, he began negotiations for its purchase, feeling that it could do a great deal of good and be made to pay.[32]

Mrs. Roosevelt worried about his assuming such an exceedingly heavy financial obligation — about two hundred thousand dollars ultimately, and more than two thirds of his fortune. It was the first and only time in his life that he took such a serious risk with his money. If anything went wrong, she was afraid they would not be able to put their boys through college.* Consequently, she discussed it with him, and asked him if it were fair to the children. He replied, "Ma will always see the children through." Besides, he was certain Warm Springs would succeed.[34]

First, he felt he must enlist the support of medical men. He went to Atlanta to the national convention of the American Orthopedic Association, in order to suggest to the doctors that they begin experiments at Warm Springs. They were reluctant to accept a suggestion from a layman, but Roosevelt was equal to the task of winning them over. They established an investigating committee consisting of three of their eminent members, to receive reports from a physician in charge. Roosevelt chose, as this physician, Dr. LeRoy W. Hubbard, an orthopedic surgeon attached to the New York State Department of Health, who had nine years of experience in polio after-care. He and a nurse who was a trained physiotherapist observed twenty-three patients during the summer and autumn of 1926, and reported improvement in every case. The committee approved, and recommended establishment of a hydrotherapeutic center.[35]

On the basis of this report, Roosevelt at the beginning of 1927 formed the Georgia Warm Springs Foundation, a nonstock, nonprofit institution, which on February 1 took over the property. Later in the spring it acquired an additional twelve hundred acres of surrounding land. Roosevelt persuaded Dr. Hubbard to become chief physio-

* Mrs. Roosevelt demonstrated her reservations over Warm Springs in a letter she wrote FDR, May 4, 1926: "I know you love creative work, my only feeling is that Georgia is somewhat distant for you to keep in touch with what is really a big undertaking. One cannot, it seems to me, have *vital* interests in widely divided places, but that may be because I'm old and rather overwhelmed by what there is to do in one place and it wearies me to think of even undertaking to make new ties. Don't be discouraged by me; I have great confidence in your extraordinary interest and enthusiasm. It is just that I couldn't do it." [33]

therapist, and rapidly expanded the plant and the staff. Before the end of the year, they had treated one hundred and fifty patients.[36]

To Roosevelt, Warm Springs was not only the spot where he could continue his efforts to walk and teach others to walk, but also a second home. He at once built a cottage for himself there, "really very good in every way." * And to Georgia he carried his zest for farming and the growing of trees. He purchased a farm of 1750 acres on the summit of nearby Pine Mountain, which he used primarily for raising cattle. It also enabled him to construct a magnificent drive on his own property. In February, 1927, he wrote in high good spirits to his mother, "This morning I have driven . . . over the 'Pine Mountain Scenic Highway' — five miles long, out to the Knob, marvellous views all the way and cost me only $1050! I've been in the pool each day and done all the exercises and stretching and am feeling finely. The weather is warm and bright, the peach blossoms coming out." [38]

Warm Springs was wonderful for his spirits — better even than for his legs. It brought him happiness, but it did not make him able to walk again. That will-o'-the-wisp remained always ahead, tantalizingly just out of reach.

* This was not the "Little White House," in which he died, which was not constructed until 1932.[37]

CHAPTER XII

The Search for a New Jefferson

Hamiltons we have to-day. Is a Jefferson on the horizon?
— FDR IN NEW YORK WORLD, *December 3, 1925.*

AFTER Al Smith failed to win the Democratic nomination for President at the 1924 convention, newspapers carried the persistent rumor that he would refuse to run for re-election as Governor of New York. This inspired Abram I. Elkus,* who for many years successfully had combined loyalty to Tammany and interest in clean government, to write Roosevelt urging him to accept the nomination for governor.

Roosevelt replied with candor:

"First: as to the Governor himself, for the sake of the party I hope he will run. His candidacy would do more to carry the state for the whole Democratic ticket than anything else. Nevertheless, I fully appreciate his desire to return to private life. . . . Secondly: as to the possibility of running myself, I think it is true that I would unite all factions of the party, and unless it is a Republican landslide, I should probably be elected over any Republican now in sight. Nevertheless, I honestly cannot consider it for one moment, and you will understand why better than anybody else. You and I have been hit by germs so similar that our cases are in many ways parallel, and I am perfectly convinced that if you and I devote another two or three years to overcoming our disability, we will be in much better shape to render service than if we were at this time to enter actively into a campaign." [1]

This set the theme for Roosevelt's political activities during the next four years. He was well appreciative of his own strong political potentialities, but was insistent that he remain somewhat in the background and not himself run for office. His own determination to regain the use of his legs was only part of the reason why he refused to run and repeatedly backed Smith. The Democratic Party was also suffering serious disability, and parallel to his personal fight, he engaged in a constant political struggle to put it too back on its feet.

* Elkus was Ambassador to Turkey in the Wilson Administration.

Al Smith did run again for Governor in 1924, and against a Roosevelt — Theodore Roosevelt, Jr., the Assistant Secretary of the Navy. Franklin Roosevelt, who had not forgotten nor forgiven his unkind remarks during the 1920 campaign, had never reconciled himself to this Roosevelt's being Assistant Secretary.* He declined to write to the Assistant Secretary on behalf of a friend because "judging by some of his utterances, I doubt whether his affection for me is overwhelming." And when a letter arrived addressed to Franklin Roosevelt as Assistant Secretary, he commented, "Poor little T. R. Jr. would have more fits than he is having now if he knew that I am still believed to be Assistant Secretary of the Navy by anybody in the world." Roosevelt did not himself campaign against T. R., Jr., but Eleanor Roosevelt, the candidate's first cousin, who was active as a leader of Democratic women in the state, did so with a vengeance. There was still much excitement over the Teapot Dome oil scandal, and Theodore Roosevelt, Jr., as Assistant Secretary of the Navy, had done nothing to prevent the transfer of the naval oil reserves out from under his nose. He was negligent only in that he might have made political capital out of blocking the machinations.† Consequently, Howe and Mrs. Roosevelt constructed a large teapot, spouting steam, on the top of a car, and with it trailed the Republican candidate around the state. Later, Mrs. Roosevelt felt rather ruefully that this had been a "rough stunt." But it pointed out how ineffectual an administrator T. R., Jr., had been. Even the Coolidge landslide could not pull him through against Smith with his excellent record as Governor and skill as a campaigner.[3]

Smith's new triumph was, of course, a political asset for Roosevelt, who was more closely than ever identified with Smith, because of his vigorous support of Smith before and during the 1924 convention. Nevertheless, after the national debacle for the Democrats in November, he deliberately dissociated himself from Smith, as he began once more to try to close the dangerous schism between the city and country wings of the party.

* In 1923 Livingston Davis sent FDR a parody:
   In that dear old navy office where I used to rule the sea
   There's another Roosevelt sitting, — and I know he thinks of me;
   For my boss is back at Raleigh, and I hear the middies mourn
   Come back you gallant seaman, come you back to Washington.[2]
† The efforts of oil men to get the reserves transferred to the Interior Department so that they could then lease them had long been fought in the Navy Department. FDR had helped Daniels prevent the transfer during the Wilson administration.

The device that Roosevelt employed was an excellent one — probably another of Howe's ideas. It was to write to the men who formed the effective backbone of the Democratic party, those who had been sufficiently loyal and experienced workers to be delegates to the convention. Of these he inquired what could be done "to make the Democracy a stronger and more militant organization nationally." He pointed out that while Democrats frequently won on the state level they often failed to carry these same states for presidential candidates. Hence he reasoned that the party was weaker nationally than locally. But at the same time that he was asking for suggestions from the delegates, he suggested to them a concrete program:

I take it that we are all agreed on certain fundamental truths:

1. That the National Committee, or its Executive machinery, should function every day in every year and not merely in Presidential election years.

2. That the National Committee should be brought into far closer touch with the State organizations.

3. That the executive machinery for year in and year out work should be put on a continuing and businesslike financial basis.

4. That publicity for fundamental party policy and for the dissemination of current information should be greatly extended.

5. That party leaders from all sections should meet more frequently in order to exchange views and plan for united party action.

This applied to machinery; it did not touch on the fundamental weakness, the rift. This he referred to more cautiously:

"The Republican leadership has stood and still stands for conservatism, for the control of the social and economic structure of the nation by a small minority of hand-picked associates. The Democratic Party organization is made more difficult by the fact that it is made up in chief part by men and women who are unwilling to stand still but who often differ as to the methods and lines of progress. Yet we are unequivocally the party of progress and liberal thought. Only by uniting can we win." [4]

What Roosevelt hoped to achieve was to discover some liberal position upon which all party factions could agree. He wished to analyze the replies in order to find "what seems to be the common meeting points of Democratic minds from the North, South, East and West."

When he had these clearly in mind, he felt he would be better able to make concrete suggestions.[5]

Quantities of answers came to Roosevelt from all over the country, many from the most distinguished members of the Democratic Party. They were invaluable to Roosevelt in two ways. They again put him directly in touch with quantities of Democratic leaders, helping to establish him even more firmly as a politician's politician. In them, more than one Democrat speculated that perhaps the leader the party so badly needed was none other than Roosevelt. An Indiana patent medicine manufacturer queried, "Can we find a Moses? . . . Can we find a Joan of Arc?" In addition, they provided Roosevelt with detailed information as to how deep the split was in the party. From the rank and file, there were many rancorous letters for or against the Ku Klux Klan and Prohibition; but from important leaders came equally strong statements on even more basic matters. From ultraconservative Easterners came letters like the one from Senator William Cabell Bruce of Maryland, who recommended that the Democrats return to the policies of Grover Cleveland. He declared that the conflict between the Eastern and Western wings of the party was nothing less than one between two conflicting systems of government. "John W. Davis wrote to me shortly after his nomination asking me what course the Party in Maryland should pursue," Bruce informed Roosevelt. "I told him that it should draw down an iron curtain between the East and the Bryan West." Westerners were just as bitter toward the East. Governor William E. Sweet of Colorado pointed out to Roosevelt that progressivism had never made much of an impress on the East for any length of time. He commented on the statement of the conservative Governor Albert C. Ritchie of Maryland that the party must return to the principles of Jeffersonian Democracy: "The Governor forgot that Thomas Jefferson was a radical of the radicals in his day. It seems to me that what we need is a different spirit among the Democratic leaders of the East and Middle West. The leadership in these sections is far too conservative." Former Governor Samuel V. Stewart of Montana told Roosevelt much the same — that the South and West were progressive. The West, he felt, had been forced by circumstances to vote for Coolidge and the Republican ticket. "They would not go to the extreme limit of radicalism for a La Follette and Wheeler, and as between conservatives they selected the conservative who had conservative party backing behind him." To Governor Stewart the answer was simple. The Democratic party must "get away from the notion that it can become conservative by nominating conservative candidates and thereby succeed. Every time it nominates conservative candidates it loses the progressives and fails to get the conservatives." [6]

It was readily apparent from these letters that the bitterness of feeling among the lesser Democrats over the Prohibition and Catholic issues would be difficult to overcome. At the same time, the great body of Western Democrats, and a good many Southern Democrats, like Josephus Daniels of North Carolina (representatives of middle-class small-business and professional men and farmers) were still adhering to the progressive doctrines which had been so appealing to these classes before the World War. Much of the social welfare legislation they favored also appealed to the Catholic, immigrant, labor groups which formed the backbone of the city Democratic organizations. Governor Stewart of Montana granted that Al Smith was the one great Eastern progressive. What all these groups had in common was their failure to share very substantially in the Coolidge prosperity. They were in a minority in the country, but a majority in the party. Senator Bruce and Governor Ritchie were spokesmen for a powerful minority of the Democrats, dominant in the South, but nevertheless a minority. Through an emphasis upon fairly vague progressive aims, it might be possible to bring together the rural and urban wings of the party, to stop the Ku Klux Klan sniping on the city machines, and to persuade the city organizations not to dump the state and national tickets in order to guarantee victory in local contests. Finally, many a correspondent, like Representative Henry T. Rainey of Illinois, felt the Democrats could not win until the Republican policies led to economic disaster.[7]

Upon letters like these, Roosevelt based his course of action. He was certain that the Democrats could not win with any leader until they had formulated a set of principles upon which they could agree, distinctly different from those of the Republicans: "In the present state of the country neither Mr. McAdoo nor Governor Smith, nor, for that matter, any other Democrat who is in sight, could be elected President for the very good reason that the Democratic Party at the present moment makes no sufficiently clear issue on which to appeal to the average voter to stop voting for Republican national candidates." This issue must be an appeal to idealistic progressivism.[8]

Idealism persisted despite the outward materialism of the 1920's, Roosevelt thought; it simply was not so open. It was like the man who a few years earlier had read the Bible on the subway and now read it only in his room. What was important, Roosevelt pointed out, was that the man still read his Bible. "Our Public men are, at this moment, politically afraid of idealism, but it doesn't change the fact that the country still is willing to listen to things other than materialism, he asserted." [9] This was the framework for party unity.* "This talk of combination between South and East or between South and West [is] wicked as well as destructive in the long run," he commented to Edwin T. Meredith of Iowa, a powerful leader of the farm faction. "There is one common ground — Progressive Democracy — on which we can all agree." [11]

Again and again, Roosevelt expanded on the necessity for a progressive program which must be neither conservative nor radical. When a former Populist inquired if a union of La Follette progressives and Democrats could be brought about, he replied that the only place for the progressives was in the Democratic party. Consequently, there should be no overtures. "The Democratic Party is *the* Progressive party of the country," he emphasized, "but it is not and I hope never will be the radical party of the country which is a very different thing." In explicit terms he spelled out his mistrust of radicalism:

"We cannot surely progress unless each advancing footstep is placed on firm and tried ground. To rush blindly along the paths proclaimed as highways to Utopia by some of our radical friends would be to find ourselves hopelessly mired in the quicksands of unsound political theories and unworkable doctrines of Government. This would not be progression, it would be only demoralization and the only result would be such suffering and unhappiness to our country as we have witnessed in some of those countries abroad which have tried purely theoretical schemes of Government before they have tested their soundness or practicability." [12]

From an idealistic standpoint, Roosevelt was ready to proclaim a return to Jeffersonian principles. No stand could be more inclusive among the Democrats, since it aligned him even with the thoroughly

* FDR wrote: "History . . . shows that the conservatives find it nearly always easy to control government at least two-thirds of the time because they are united on the perfectly simple proposition of 'doing nothing' and of 'letting well enough alone.' Progressives and liberals on the other hand have necessarily a constructive program, and on the details of this program they insist on dividing among themselves. I am convinced that a majority of the voters in this country are really progressives but are generally unable to control the government because of their subdivisions and unwillingness to agree as to method and machinery." [10]

conservative Governor Ritchie. His enthusiasm was contagious when he reviewed Claude Bowers's *Jefferson and Hamilton* for the New York *World* in December, 1925. It was a revelation to him, since apparently he had never heard of Charles Beard's books on the fathers of the Constitution and on Jeffersonian democracy, which had appeared a decade and more earlier. "I felt like saying 'At last' as I read Mr. . . . Bowers's thrilling" book, Roosevelt declared. He expressed the wish that the simple historic facts in it be learned in newspaper editorial rooms as well as homes and schools. Still smarting from the sneers of editorial writers who had laughed at his suggestions in the letter to Democratic leaders that Jeffersonianism could apply in 1925, he reiterated anew his belief that the differences between the principles of the two parties were much the same as they had been: "I have a breathless feeling as I lay down this book — a picture of escape after escape which this nation passed through in those first ten years; a picture of what might have been if the Republic had been finally organized as Alexander Hamilton sought. But I have a breathless feeling, too, as I wonder if, a century and a quarter later, the same contending forces are not again mobilizing." [13]

Generalities like these were politically valuable; Roosevelt was quite willing in private correspondence, and in his stand on specific issues, to move from them to the concrete economic realities of the era of Coolidge prosperity. He continued to advocate state rights — "less governing from Washington with a decrease in the existing functions of the national government, and a decrease in the amount of legislation ground out by Congress each year." Nevertheless, he was ready to return to an economic program similar to that of the progressive era, one which would benefit the farmers, small businessmen, and other middle-class groups who were not sharing in the fruits of the boom. [14]

This, in a private letter, he compared to the Jeffersonian program: "It will be hard for us to make inroads in the Republican ranks so long as material prosperity continues. They are putting all their bets on a continuation of industrial prosperity, but this prosperity does not come from their efforts, but rather from the world economic situation following the war. We are approaching a period similar to that from 1790–1800 when Alexander Hamilton ran the federal government for the primary good of the chambers of commerce, the speculators and the inside ring of the national government. He was a fundamental believer in an aristocracy of wealth and power — Jefferson brought the government back to the hands of the average voter, through insistence on fundamental principles and the education of the average voter. We need a similar campaign of education today, and perhaps we shall find another Jefferson." [15]

In his own public actions, Roosevelt tried to function like another Jefferson.* First, he tried to assemble from everywhere ideas for his progressive program. The polio had not only given him the opportunity to think and express himself in writing, but also the time to read many books and talk to persons of all sorts. With his delight in people, he found this a pleasure as well as a significant means of education. Mrs. Roosevelt, whose own social horizons were broadening so rapidly during the 1920's, established a habit which she continued until his death. She would give him one or another book to read on some social or economic problem. If he expressed interest in it, she would then bring around the author to talk to him. It was from conversation that he learned the most, and with incredible rapidity. Others, with completely different backgrounds from his, talked to him also, and as he listened with sympathy to their ideas, he began reorienting himself toward the underprivileged. Attitudes he had acquired years earlier at home, at Groton, and in the New York legislature, again came to the forefront. [17]

In November, 1925, Mrs. Hamlin recorded in her diary an instance of this. She had tea with Roosevelt at Marion, Massachusetts, and caught a glimpse of a young man who was leaving to catch the Fall River night boat for New York:

"After he had gone — Franklin told me that he was an east side Jew — a tailor — from New York. He had come over on the boat the previous night and had been over once before to spend the day. Franklin said he had a chance in this way to learn a great deal about conditions in [the young man's] life — his clubs and other organizations — at first hand. He felt he got to the bottom of situations that could and should be remedied — the scandalous housing conditions — labour — schools — churches and the family life. He said the patience of people under unbearable tenement living — the lack of decent provisions for sanitary purposes — sometimes one water faucet for a whole house — and that in some cases the properties were owned by wealthy people who left the care to agents who had no interest but to extract the rent." [18]

On other occasions, Roosevelt sounded out people by letter. To

---

* Curiously enough, in 1921, when Arthur H. Vandenberg, who was writing a book on Hamilton, inquired of FDR whom he considered the "Greatest American," FDR replied "George Washington." [16]

Winter Russell, a proponent of public ownership of public utilities, he wrote that despite his distrust of big government, he thought that "the complexities of modern civilization and the breaking down of state boundaries in such agencies as public utilities, interstate commerce and the kind of selling of commodities through country-wide large corporations, seem in many cases to demand some form of government requisition to prevent abuses or extortion." He declared he had been talking to a good many people from all parts of the country about the pros and cons of public ownership or operation of public utilities. While there was less demand for it than ten years previously, he was not opposed to it in principle and indeed was interested in a compromise scheme. This he inquired about:

"The other day a man high up in electric power developments told me that within the next 10 years the federal government would have to regulate interstate power transmission just as the interstate commerce commission now regulates the railroads. He went one step further and admitted that the federal government could, with the state government, properly own, finance and build all the new hydro-electric developments and produce power on a 4% investment basis where private capital now has to raise the money on 8% or 9% basis. Such ownership, construction and operation of the production of power would not involve a large force of federal employees, whereas the actual delivery of power to the individual user should, in his judgment be left to private companies as this part of the work required little cash, but the employment of a large force of workers. This presents a possibility for a step forward which might obtain wide-spread approval throughout the country. Write me what you think." [19]

The proposal, Russell replied, was similar to that by which the subway companies got the City of New York "to provide them with a wonderful business at the expenditure of comparatively little capital in which all the profit goes to the private companies and practically all the expenditure is on the part of the city." That was sufficient for Roosevelt; he said no more about the scheme. But he continued to talk and think about the relationship of the federal government to power production, and by 1927 had reached the point in his thinking where he was ready to espouse the advanced stand of men like Senator George Norris in favor of what in the New Deal became the TVA.

This involved another problem: how best to spread propaganda in favor of a progressive program. "Jefferson organized by disseminating facts," Roosevelt pointed out to Claude Bowers – "how can the good work be reincarnated today when the Republicans own all the campaign chests and most of the newspapers?" Roosevelt found no ready answer. He was intrigued with the possibility that the Democratic National Committee, after it was reorganized, might sponsor a string of newspapers. The rapid growth in power of illustrated tabloid dailies, such as the New York News, impressed him; and the rapid growth in circulation of the new tabloids that Cornelius Vanderbilt, Jr., established in Miami and Los Angeles misled him into thinking that here was an opportunity to make money as well as converts for the Democratic party. Vanderbilt's papers became spectacular money losers; in addition, Roosevelt's small earlier excursion into financial backing of a liberal newspaper, the New York Post, had ended badly. Nothing came of these proposals.[20]

As an alternative, Roosevelt hoped Democratic ideas could be spread more widely through liberal columnists. He was on cordial terms with the most influential of these, Walter Lippmann. Frank Kent of the Baltimore Sun impressed him so deeply that for some time he urged Van-Lear Black to arrange for the Sun to syndicate his column. In February, 1925, he and Senator Walsh talked to Kent while they were on a Florida-bound train. Both of them were "enthusiastic over the idea of getting Kent's ability and fairness of statement and honesty across to the country." Roosevelt wished him to be free from partisanship, but a Democratic counterpart of Mark Sullivan. Of course, his column must be syndicated without the official sponsorship in any way of the Democratic National Committee. This scheme worked. Ultimately Kent's column appeared in a hundred papers – and Kent himself became one of Roosevelt's sharpest critics.[21]

Roosevelt toyed with the idea of himself manipulating public opinion through a syndicated column. In the spring of 1925, while he was at Warm Springs, for several weeks he took over the Macon Telegraph column of his friend, Tom Loyless. With studied artlessness, he began his first column by asserting that he had been double-crossed as always by newspapermen, that Loyless was "out picking wild flowers and I have returned to my former profession – I used to edit the college paper in the old days." Then almost immediately he swung into a diatribe against the almost complete Republican monopoly over the press in the North. In succeeding columns he touched upon familiar themes: conservation, tolerance toward immigrants, civil service reform, government efficiency, and the need for a new foreign policy. His intention was not just to amuse himself while his friend rested, nor was it merely to reach the readers of one newspaper. He tried to interest a syndicate in the columns, and failed.* His name was not yet big enough to carry them. In addition, they lacked the snap and sparkle of his better speeches; they were a bit too much like the editorials he had once turned out for the *Crimson*.[22]

In practice, Roosevelt, in order to spread Democratic doctrine, had to resort mainly to public statements and speeches, which either he or other prominent Democrats could voice. These usually received some attention in the Republican press. For example, in the realm of government promotion of power, in 1927 he urged Al Smith to be spokesman:

"I talked to Fred Green in regard to your saying something later on in regard to flood prevention in the Mississippi Valley. It is a long distance job, but eventually we as a nation will undertake the storing of the waters on the higher reaches of the tributary rivers and in conjunction with these, will develop hydroelectric power for the benefit of the people of the United States. This is sound doctrine and it is time it was said by somebody in authority." [23]

For his own part, Roosevelt was ready in speeches to label the Republican talk of Coolidge prosperity as "dishonest drivel" to cover up their lavish expenditures to buy up elections:

As a simple matter of fact, our so-called prosperity since the World War has come in spite of and not because of politicians and political measures. Our possession of the larger part of all the gold in the world has given us easy credit — too easy in all probability. Construction, building, improved transportation, increased production of all sorts were made necessary by the wear and tear and the temporary expedients of the war years. Add to this the development of new popular needs such as the cheaper automobile, the radio, electrical devices of all kinds, the spread of electric power and good roads, and last but not least, the great increase of purchasing by the instalment method, and it becomes clearer that the Republican party in Washington is guilty of the statutory offence of seeking to obtain under false pretences, a thing of value belonging to somebody else — in this case, the people of the United States.

But unfortunately the prosperity they talk of is not country-

* Only the Atlanta *Constitution* showed any interest in taking them.

wide by any means. Large sections of the nation, especially those great areas which raise our food supply from the soil have felt the hand of debt and a depreciated purchasing power.

To these groups, Roosevelt appealed by attacking monopolies and the high tariff. The tariff on aluminum had recently gone up substantially. Paying his respects to Secretary of the Treasury Andrew Mellon, who had headed the aluminum trust, he wisecracked that the Republican party had laid a large aluminum cuckoo egg in the home of American industry. This, he declared at the New York State Democratic Convention in 1926, was but one of the industries enriched through the Republican tariff by every housewife.* The exorbitant sugar tariff was costing housewives 250,000,000 dollars per year.[25]

Thus Roosevelt assumed leadership in trying to establish a Democratic program while he was waiting for the drivers of the high-powered Republican automobile "to run into a ditch and to make some stupendous blunder." Whether this would be as a result of their "political insanity" in helping to maintain outrageous profits for Eastern manufacturers who contributed heavily to their campaign funds, or "some soothing formula of empty words that will keep the impoverished and neglected agriculturists of the West and South from open revolt," or "some new glaring mistake in a totally different direction," Roosevelt was not sure. He was certain that the national organization of the Democratic party, on the progressive ideological basis he was outlining, must move swiftly and smoothly to heal over its schisms so that, when disaster hit the Republicans, the Democrats would be in a position to take over. Just what the organization should be was of little importance to him, compared with his strong feeling that there should be an effective one. He and Howe developed a lengthy proposal (doubtless in consultation with other Democrats) to harness state-rights feeling within the party, and build a strong national committee on the foundation of state committees. The national committee would channel patronage through the state committees, and in return assess them on a pro rata basis for funds with which to carry on party work. An incidental advantage of this would be to relieve the party of its

* However, FDR warned a magazine writer on the tariff that he must emphasize that the Democratic party was not a free-trade party, but rather believed in a tariff high enough to maintain legitimate American industries without giving them "the exclusive right to overcharge the American public for their wares."[24]

financial dependence upon a few millionaires by spreading broadly the base from which it obtained contributions. Whatever was done, Roosevelt believed the starting point must be the calling of a conference of Democratic leaders. He and Howe labored long and hard through the early months of 1925 to try to persuade the leaders of the conflicting factions within the party that they must confer.[26]

To William A. Oldfield of Arkansas, Chairman of the Democratic National Congressional Committee, Roosevelt bluntly stated his objectives:

1. In the minds of the average voter the Democratic Party has today no definite constructive aims. The average voter believes rightly that it has no national organization and that in Congress the minority in both houses is seeking merely to make trouble for the Republicans — to seize on some new scandal or to take advantage of some mis-step on the part of the majority. I submit that that is not a program for a great national party.

2. It is absolutely necessary that some Democrats get together and establish a constructive policy — not one voter in 100,000 has read last year's Democratic platform. That document was a grab-bag — the only thing it did not contain was a paragraph of welcome to the new Irish Envoy and Minister Plenipotentiary to the "Court" at Washington. . . . The voters don't quite understand what the Democratic minority is striving to attain.

3. One reason for this lack of information is the fact that the National Committee organization work consists, as I understand it, of two ladies occupying one room in a Washington office building. We have no money, no publicity, "no nothing"! — not even any *plans* for having an organization.

4. As to the sordid matter of finances we owe large sums and the National Chairman is visiting, from time to time, multi-millionaires and getting them to endorse notes for him. Could anything be much more of a farce? [27]

Toward the end of February, 1925, while Roosevelt was in Florida, Louis Howe, aided by Fred Essary, a Washington newspaperman, entered into long and involved negotiations to try to win the support of key Democrats for Roosevelt's plan. John W. Davis, titular head of the party, invited Howe to his apartment for dinner, and at first heartily agreed to the proposals, and promised to try to get the support of the man he had appointed as Chairman of the Democratic National Committee, Clem Shaver. Senator Thomas J. Walsh of Montana and Colonel Edward M. House not only approved, but pushed hard for a conference. In order to gain public attention for the plan Roosevelt, on February 28, 1925, sent a letter to Senator Walsh in his official position as Permanent Chairman of the 1924 Democratic Convention, requesting that a conference be called. Democratic papers throughout the country warmly approved of the idea. But National Chairman Shaver and other conservative Democratic leaders held back because, ostensibly, they feared that any sort of meeting would renew the factional spirit which had wrecked the 1924 convention.[28]

The Republican papers took advantage of the situation, as Roosevelt wryly pointed out, "to shriek once more from the housetops that the Democratic Party is so hopelessly split up into factions that even its leaders are afraid to meet together." He himself demonstrated how groundless this was by conferring with Bryan in Miami in April. Although Roosevelt had been the Smith leader at the 1924 Convention, Bryan was cordial: "He was, at first, fearful that a conference, especially a large one, would result in more trouble than good. After we had talked for over an hour he agreed that if the conference were kept small, as I outlined, it would accomplish very great things. . . . Mr. Bryan is, of course, fearful of the domination of the Party by the big cities of the East and Middle West, but, as I pointed out to him, there are millions of really progressive Democratic voters in these localities who cannot be read out of the Party by making Democracy a mere combination of the South and West, and he agreed that the Party policies and Party effort must be made national instead of sectional." [29]

In the long run, it was not Bryan and the rural progressive wing of the party that wrecked Roosevelt's plans for a conference; it was the conservatives around John W. Davis. They had no reason to help build the political reputation of Roosevelt; he would have presided over the conference. They certainly did not want to commit the Democratic party to Roosevelt's progressive program. One of the main purposes of the conference would have been to outline a set of issues upon which the Democrats could seek to win control of Congress in 1926. Various ostensibly Democratic newspapers, Roosevelt and Howe charged, particularly did not want a conference until after 1926 because they did not want a Democratic Congress. Howe, after further negotiations with Adolph S. Ochs of the New York Times — who was at first favorable, then later discouraging — concluded that the real interest of Ochs was to keep the Democratic party a minority party large enough and active enough to prevent the establishment of a dangerous radical party, but not powerful enough to interfere with the Republican control of the government. Perhaps this was true of some of the conservative Democratic politicians, too. They were willing enough to talk broadly about the need for a return to Jefferson, but they were opposed to translating Jeffersonian principles into terms that applied concretely to the American economy of the 1920's. That task continued to a considerable extent to be peculiarly and personally Roosevelt's.[30]

At the Gridiron Dinner in Washington that spring, the newspapermen sang of the rift in the Democratic Party to the tune of the "Lost Chord":

> It may be that some bright leader
> Will bring us to peace again;
> It may be that we shall not find it
> 'Till we raise up a brand-new man.
> It may be that Franklin Roosevelt
> Will bring us to our reward;
> It may be that only hereafter
> We shall find that lost accord.[31]

CHAPTER XIII

The Young Elder Statesman

The Governor is obviously our State leader. In national affairs I am seeking no leadership but have been doing everything possible to help the Party nationally to get back on its feet.

— FDR TO W. T. DOTY, *February 15, 1926.*

THROUGHOUT the Coolidge Administration, Roosevelt continued to develop his broad strategy to advance the fortunes of the Democratic party — and Franklin D. Roosevelt. In terms of principles, progressivism continued to be his rallying cry; in terms of persons, Al Smith. His inability to use his legs and his strong personal loyalty to Smith helped draw attention away from the fact that above all he was working quietly and steadily toward the time, obviously still years away, when he himself could become the Democratic candidate for President of the United States, and win.

From the perspective of 1925 to 1927, if he could best serve that objective when the next election year came by helping nominate Smith, he was eager to do so. For several years he was not entirely sure that this would be most expedient, for it appeared that the 1928 convention would be much like that of 1924, another deadlock between Smith and McAdoo, with another search for an available man. Consequently, during these years, Howe was quietly pushing Roosevelt's own claims as the man who could best bridge the gap between the two factions. But the candidacy must not under any circumstances develop until Smith had been eliminated.

Beginning in the summer of 1924, there had been an occasional straw blowing by. Some District of Columbia enthusiasts almost immediately after Davis's nomination formed a Franklin D. Roosevelt club. The following winter, a Hearst reporter charged that the purpose of Roosevelt's efforts to rebuild the Democratic organization was primarily to build Roosevelt as a presidential candidate. What was more, he asserted that what Roosevelt was fishing for in Florida was nothing less than delegates to the next convention. This was so displeasing to Roosevelt that he personally wrote a tart denial to the reporter. "I suppose you are such a hopeless cynic," he asserted, "that it would be useless for me to tell you that I have no desire to run for the Presidency in 1928, so we will let it go at that!" Obviously it might disturb his long-range plans if newspapers printed rumors that he was a presidential aspirant.[1]

For them to float nebulously about was different. When various Democratic leaders began to speculate in private conversation that perhaps the way out in 1928 would be to turn to Roosevelt, he was, of course, pleased. What was most surprising was that peppery, conservative Senator Carter Glass of Virginia, who both earlier and later displayed marked distaste for the flamboyance of Roosevelt, as early as 1926 seemed to consider Roosevelt the best possible compromise candidate. When Louis B. Wehle, who had tried to promote a Hoover-Roosevelt ticket in 1920, broached Roosevelt's name to Glass, he expressed his affection for Roosevelt and admiration for his qualities. Glass told Wehle he had frequently thought of Roosevelt as the possible solution to the difficulties of the Democrats. While Roosevelt proclaimed that the Democrats must not talk about any candidate, least of all himself, he was quite willing to have a "little chat" with Wehle about Glass. This was as far as he would go.[2]

There was only the faintest likelihood that presidential lightning would strike Roosevelt in 1928, and if he did receive the nomination, barring a sudden freeze in economic conditions, even less chance that he could be elected. Therefore, it was far more to his advantage to continue the aloof, elder statesman role that his physical handicap imposed upon him, a role which kept him above factions within the party, helped create friendliness and sympathy for him, and kept him from being the target of jealousy. At the same time, his constant cheerful talk of what he would do when he could walk without braces gave warning that sometime, in the still remote future, he would return to a more active status. He badly wanted the nomination, but only if it would mean something. Glass's friendly interest in Roosevelt as a presidential nominee probably indicated no more than the feeling on the part of some Southern conservatives that they could use him to kill off the Smith candidacy, or at best use him as an attractive but impotent trustee of the party in a black election year.

Howe made perfectly clear what the game was in a letter to Roosevelt when the Hearst newspapers again printed a Roosevelt-for-President rumor early in 1926:

"Its purpose to split up the Smith backing was obvious. It seemed fatal to let it stand at this time. You as an active candidate just now would wreck the excellent chance you have of being at least one of — if not *the* one — among the leaders who all turn to. So I saw to it that the next day one of 'Mr. Roosevelt's close friends' was quoted as follows. 'You can state positively that Frank is not and will not be under any circumstances a candidate for the Presidency. He sees no political contingency in which he could be drafted to make the run.' " [3]

This unquestionably met with Roosevelt's full approval. He demonstrated in another way how valuable he felt the Elder Statesman role to be, by shying away from the nomination for United States Senator in 1926 — although, as in 1922, he would surely have been elected. In the Senate he would have been forced to commit himself on many of the issues over which Democrats were divided; he would have appeared openly as another ambitious politician, and would thus discard the glamor and immunity from attack with which his illness was cloaking him. It was far too high a price for him to pay to enter what was for men of lesser ambition the most exclusive club in the United States; for presidential aspirants, almost invariably a burying ground. Pressure came from within the state and without — Senators Thomas J. Walsh and Burton K. Wheeler of Montana hoped he would run — but to everyone Roosevelt gave a pat answer:

"There are two good reasons why I can't run for the Senate next year. The first is that my legs are coming back in such fine shape that if I devote another two years to them I shall be on my feet again without my braces. The 2nd is that I am temperamentally unfitted to be a member of the uninteresting body known as the United States Senate. I like administrative or executive work, but do not want to have my hands and feet tied and my wings clipped for 6 long years." [4]

To a close friend, Roosevelt, master already of political timing, confided, "My explosions would come at too frequent intervals to be effective." [5]

Nevertheless, as the 1926 New York State Democratic Convention prepared to meet, politicians continued to look to Roosevelt as the best vote getter. This worried Howe, who obviously feared Roosevelt might be susceptible to a draft:

"I have been warned of a plan to get you up to make a speech and then demand you to accept the nomination by a stampeded convention with everybody yelling 'We want Franklin!' This is, of course, a possibility, but I hope your spine is still sufficiently strong to assure them that you are still nigh to death's door for the next two years. Please try and look pallid and worn and weary when you address the convention so it will not be too exceedingly difficult to get by with the statement that you[r] health will not permit you to run for anything for 2 years more." [6]

Smith telephoned Roosevelt to ask him to act as temporary chairman of the state convention on September 27, and make the keynote address. Roosevelt, delighted, proclaimed privately, "Look out for the fire works!" He worked long and carefully on it, drawing from Owen D. Young of General Electric and Walter Lippmann some suggestions for an attack upon "Coolidge prosperity." The result was in part an elaborate defense of the Smith program as Governor of New York, but to a larger extent an onslaught against the Republicans nationally. He charged the President with favoring the privileged multimillionaires ("Calvin Coolidge would like to have God on his side, but he must have Andrew Mellon") and with inaction to bring relief to farmers, or end a coal strike. "The people of the East have well learned, through months of struggle to get coal for their furnaces and stoves, the hard meaning of the slogan 'Keep cool with Coolidge.'" [7]

The convention audience enthusiastically cheered Roosevelt both before and after; he was in fine form. But there was no danger of a stampede, for Tammany had agreed upon a slate several weeks in advance. "Thank the Lord I am not the candidate for senator!" Roosevelt had commented. The day before the nominations, the posters had already gone up announcing the choice of the delegates: Al Smith for Governor, and Robert F. Wagner for Senator. What was perhaps even more important than Roosevelt's smiling appearance before the Democratic politicians was the fact that he broadcast his speech to a wide radio audience, and it commanded large headlines in the newspapers. He was maintaining, perhaps even increasing, his following among the voters. As for the movement to force the senatorial nomination upon him, that had been as good for him as the senatorship itself would have been bad.[8]

Quite possibly, too, Roosevelt's refusal to seek the nomination was the key to his outwardly cordial relations with Smith during these years. Roosevelt took Smith exceedingly seriously, and despite awareness of his shortcomings as a national leader, respected and admired

him. There was affection as well as political expediency in his consistent support. This Smith did not altogether reciprocate. It was hard
for a self-made man, always acutely aware of his beginnings near
the Fulton Fish Market, to appreciate an associate born on a Hudson
River estate. To Smith, who never read books but had a firm grasp
of every detail of the state government, Roosevelt with his glittering, sweeping discourses seemed a hopelessly impractical intellectual.
Roosevelt was not much of a reader, either, but picked the brains
of every reader around him, and was fascinated with the sort of
ideas that were well beyond Smith's horizons. Money symbolized
power to Smith, and already by 1927 (as Henry Pringle pointed out
in a remarkably penetrating campaign biography), Smith preferred
the society of moneyed people. Already, he tended to be a bit cen-
sorious of those humble people who had not like himself worked
their way to high position. One day as he drove in an open car
through a factory town, his bodyguard was startled to hear him
mutter under his breath at the workers crowded at the windows to
see him, "Get back to work! Get back to work!" [9]

The Roosevelts at Hyde Park were not the sort of moneyed people
with whom Smith felt at ease. They represented social position more
than opulence, and were firm in their faith in *noblesse oblige*. Certainly they were outwardly gracious toward him, although they may
have lacked any real inward warmth. Sara Delano Roosevelt, according to one person close to her, in many little ways made things unpleasant, but according to another, out of a desire to further her son's
political career, she was unhesitatingly cordial to all of his friends,
Smith included. A strong indication that both she and Eleanor Roosevelt succeeded in being pleasant is the fact that Smith held them
in high regard. Probably more of a factor in his uneasiness was their
failure to provide him with the steady supply of liquor which in
other surroundings relaxed tensions for him. He was by no means as
heavy a drinker as Winston Churchill, for whom Eleanor Roosevelt
had to stock the White House at the end of 1941, but he liked to
have a glass in his hand. In the 1920's Mrs. Roosevelt, who had much
faith in Prohibition, failed to keep one there and keep it filled.[10]

It was easy, therefore, for Smith to feel mildly contemptuous of
Roosevelt's airy plans, his many hobbies, and his country squire way
of life. Smith took him at face value as a crippled millionaire playboy
permanently out of politics, a genial and rather useful patron of the
party, irritating at times and never to be taken very seriously. More

than once Jim Farley heard Smith pungently refer to Roosevelt as a visionary with little practical knowledge of politics.[11]

Roosevelt was fortunate, since had Smith guessed that this man in time would eclipse him politically, he could have made things extremely difficult. Roosevelt studiedly stayed out of his path and that of Tammany. He spiked David Lawrence's rumor that he was about to assume Democratic leadership in New York State. He killed off a Roosevelt for Mayor Club in New York City at the beginning of 1925, and sent a copy of the letter doing so (he was never a resident of New York City and thus never a member of Tammany) to Boss Olvany: "I am and always will be an upstate hayseed farmer! Stick these in your files to prove to his Honor the Mayor that I don't want his job!" [12] When the jaunty playboy of Tammany, James J. Walker, won the election, he sent his hearty congratulations; and when, as Howe reported, "wine, women and song" began to play "the very devil with Jimmy Walker" it was Mrs. Roosevelt, not Roosevelt, who was asked to reason with Walker.[13]

On state matters, Roosevelt and Smith conferred once in a while. "It was great to see you last night," Roosevelt wrote Smith on one such occasion in 1925, "and I wish that you and I could have more long talks, more often!" But they were not frequent. Smith threw a few insignificant bits his way; in 1925 he appointed Roosevelt to a State Assembly campaign committee, and to a committee to consider a 100,000,000-dollar bond issue proposal.[14]

The one appointment of some slight significance was to make Roosevelt chairman of the Taconic State Park Commission, which was authorized to lay out the Taconic Parkway, to run northward from New York City through Roosevelt's Dutchess County. Roosevelt took the project seriously, and threw his energies behind it. Immediately he came into conflict with an equally vigorous and determined politician, Robert Moses, who was President of the New York State Council of Parks. The story was long current that the struggle between the two arose because Moses blocked Roosevelt from putting Howe on the payroll of the Taconic Commission. This had something to do with it; Roosevelt protested to Smith late in 1926, "It is an absurd and humiliating position to be put in, to be informed that we could have no money because, through lack of an Executive, we have not been able to properly expend the money we had and then to be informed that we cannot have an Executive because we have not been given more money."

This was not the crux of the matter, since at about this time Howe was already on the payroll of the Fidelity and Deposit Company, and worked part-time for the National Crime Commission. Rather, Roosevelt was determined to make his own position more than honorary — to get a parkway built through Dutchess County as speedily as possible; while Moses was channeling almost all the available money into a magnificent park and parkway system for Long Island. Smith sided with Moses on the ground that the Long Island system would benefit more people in the immediate future; Roosevelt's program looked "away into the future." [15]

When, at the end of 1927, Roosevelt learned that Smith and the Budget Commission planned to abandon plans to build the parkway from Westchester County northward, he sent Smith a vehement telegram and letter. Either the Commission should create a parkway to relieve dangerous congestion on existing highways, or plans should be abandoned, Roosevelt asserted. "It is a case of fish, cut bait, or swim ashore." The two men conferred at the Biltmore Hotel in New York City, but came no closer to an agreement. Smith, ordinarily laconic in his correspondence, reiterated his views in a five-page letter. He declared he had never thought of the parkway as extending through Dutchess County; the Commission should be willing to wait for funds. Roosevelt retorted even more heatedly, "I wasn't born yesterday!" — and accused Moses of having played a skin game. Smith responded by citing figures to prove that the legislature was making cuts as deep as this one in Moses's projects also.[16]

Some of Smith's comments are of far more interest than the minor squabble to which they relate, since they indicate the attitude he could assume when Roosevelt irritated him:

I know of no man I have met in my whole public career who I have any stronger affection for than for yourself. Therefore, you can find as much fault with me as you like. I will not get into a fight with you for anything or for anybody. But that does not stop me from giving you a little tip and the tip is don't be so sure about things that you have not the personal handling of yourself. I have lived, ate, and slept with this park question for three and one-half years. I know all about it and I know the attitude of the legislative leaders to the whole thing. I fought and battled with them in the regular session and in fact called an extraordinary session of the legislature to deal with this whole question of supporting the parks. When

I told you at the Hotel Biltmore that the legislative leaders would not stand for these appropriations, I was telling you what I knew to be a fact and you were guessing at it. . . . I am satisfied with all of the park plans and I expect to see them all carried out but at the same time I have sense enough not to be crashing my head up against a stone wall. What happened to the appropriation bill after I sent it up is abundant proof that I knew exactly what I was talking about.[17]

While this dispute reveals some of the underlying tensions between Smith and Roosevelt, it is by no means typical of their relations at that time. On the whole they functioned in non-competing areas. Roosevelt continued to concentrate upon trying to reform the Democratic National Committee; Smith paid little or no atention to what Roosevelt was doing.

Roosevelt particularly wished to change the methods of financing the Democratic Party. The idea of soliciting small contributions from millions of people continued to appeal to him.* Previous efforts to solicit dollar or five-dollar contributions directly for the national committee had failed, he knew, because the cost of collecting them was too high, but he was sure local organizations could thus easily raise 200,000 dollars per year for the national headquarters. In private conversations, Roosevelt was quite critical of Jesse Jones of Houston, Texas, the Director of Finance of the Democratic National Committee, because, he charged, Jones was raising funds to pay off the 1924 campaign debt "from a mere handful of very rich or moderately rich gentlemen."

Actually, Jones recalls that he was engaged in a maneuver to prevent the Democratic National Committee from falling into the hands of either the McAdoo or the Smith faction. It had wound up the campaign of 1924 owing a "substantial amount of money, as I remember, between $300,000 and $400,000 . . . a lot of money in those days . . . "

I proceeded to get more pledges, payable when called for by me, but because of the fight between the Smith and McAdoo

* FDR wrote, "Just as the idea of the professional Republican politicians is an endless chain of obtaining public office so as to grant favors to wealthy corporations so that wealthy corporations will give them large sums to enable them to elect their candidates so as to grant them more favors and so on indefinitely, the fundamental Democratic idea that a political party is a piece of machinery by which the ideals of its principles can be put into actual practice in government should be carried into the financial side by refusing to permit large contributions and make instead almost every Democratic voter an equal partner through his subscription in our enterprize. If we believe in granting special favors to none, should we not be equally firm in refusing to accept special favors from none?" [18]

forces, I decided it would be better for the party for the National Committee to remain in debt, in the belief that neither side would make too much effort to get control of the committee and carry on the fight, with it owing a lot of money. So, instead of calling for payment of the pledges, I borrowed from a bank to pay the bills and for operating expenses during the next four years.

The Smith forces, which included Roosevelt, knew that I had gotten pledges, but they did not know how many or how much. Some time after coming home, I had a long telegram from the New York World, asking me questions, intended to smoke me out as to the committee's finances and my pledges. I didn't smoke! but answered in such a way that the publication of my wire would not hurt the party.

It did give offense to Roosevelt, who felt Jones was unfair to him in the telegram. The result was an interchange of chilly letters in which Roosevelt admitted his criticisms of Jones, but emphasized that he had never, on principle, aired them in the press. Jones assured Roosevelt he was "one of the best assets of our party," but, in explaining his policy of obtaining pledges from large contributors in this instance, indirectly granted Roosevelt's main premise — that ordinarily such contributors donated with an expectation of return:[19]

"I can see no possible harm to come from patriotic democrats giving substantial amounts to pay for stale water long since over the dam, and I cannot see any advantage to come from a widespread campaign to pay such a deficit as we wound up with in 1924. People are usually willing to give money for a live issue but few of them are willing to contribute where there is no hope of reward or possibility of the enjoyment of success to the enterprise contributed to." [20]

In practice, of course, the Democratic party continued to raise money by old sure-fire methods, primarily by soliciting contributors. Although he could have paid at any time, Jones continued deliberately to keep the committee in debt and finance its operating expenses until the 1928 National Convention. The members of the committee were quite willing to let him do this, since it relieved them from the task of raising money. After the convention, Jones paid all the debts and gave his successor a check for 151,000 dollars with which to start the campaign.

Roosevelt's proposals were the more idealistic; Jones's program the more realistic. It was prophetic of the way the two men differed over financial matters during the New Deal.

Since Roosevelt was not able at any point to influence what he and Howe considered a moribund Democratic National Committee, he turned to the Democrats in Congress as official spokesmen for Democratic issues. On his way to Florida, in February, 1926, he stopped in Washington and attended a dinner at which Senator Walsh had gathered a group of Democratic congressional leaders. Roosevelt exhorted them to advocate definite policies and form a militant force in the congressional election that fall. Roosevelt was encouraged by favorable newspaper accounts, and from Florida tried by correspondence to continue the work. He urged the Democratic minority floor leader of the House, Finis J. Garrett, to co-operate with Western progressive Republicans in promoting legislation to remedy the economic plight of the farmers. Roosevelt favored, as "the most acceptable and the least unsound," a rather mild program being advocated by former Governor Frank Lowden of Illinois. The end would be political capital for the Democrats, since Roosevelt did not think the White House would accept it. This, Roosevelt pointed out to Senator Walsh, would help strengthen the Democratic friendship with the progressive Republicans and bring nearer the "day of definite cleavage" within the Republican party.[21]

One of the topics of discussion at the Walsh dinner was the attitude Democratic Congressmen should take toward ratifying an agreement settling the Italian war debt. The question itself was minor, but it well illustrates both Roosevelt's technique and the energetic and imaginative way in which Howe worked for him. The agreement, negotiated in November, 1925, on a basis of capacity to pay, cut the interest to four tenths of one per cent and consequently reduced the debt about four fifths. At the same time, J. P. Morgan and Company arranged the sale of Italian bonds to private investors within the United States in order to provide capital for Italy. Economists argued that Italy would never be able to pay more than the amount negotiated, if indeed that. Financiers pointed out that the private loan would help rehabilitate Italian industry and enable conservative Italian capitalists to dominate Mussolini. But some experts on foreign policy feared the money would, instead, help finance Mussolini in a small war, and a large part of the public, thinking in terms of their own personal borrowing, saw no reason why the debts or interest should be scaled down. It was potentially a political hot potato; Roosevelt and Walsh were not sure whether the Democratic party could make capital out of it by taking some firm stand. Roosevelt at the dinner apparently gave the impression that he opposed the settlement and loan, for the New York *Times* editorially attacked the negative attitude of the "travelling statesman." * This was not fair, for in writing to Walsh he demonstrated his wariness:

"The ratification of the Italian Debt Settlement worries me considerably. As a general proposition the Party should encourage every effort to work out the old war problems, and to oppose, without clear and sound reasons, would be an act of folly. We cannot, for instance, contend against the settlement on the mere ground that we do not like Mussolini the Dictator, or that the proposed Morgan Loan may be used by the Dictator to finance another war. It occurs to me that if the Democrats in Congress decide to oppose they must base their action on the broader democratic policy. Since 1919 we have sought a general, and not a piecemeal, settlement of all the international debts; the Republican policy has been to seek piecemeal settlements. Further, it should be the Democratic policy, in the case of nations financially weak, to effect temporary arrangements and not to tie our hands by giving drastic concessions over a period of 60 years." [23]

Senator Walsh agreed with Roosevelt that perhaps the Democrats should "argue for a temporary adjustment of the Italian Debt, keeping Mussolini on his good behavior," but Howe in New York, sensing political dynamite, on his own initiative made a searching inquiry into what Roosevelt's policy should be. He countered the derogatory remark in the New York *Times* by assuring Ochs that Roosevelt would come to no conclusions until he knew all the facts. Howe proceeded to ferret out the facts by interviewing and corresponding with Owen D. Young, the expert on the debt question, Walter Lippmann, Newton D. Baker, George W. Wickersham, and the acting head of the House of Morgan, Thomas Cochran. From these men he learned of the immense complexities of the question, and the strong political support for each side. Consequently, he concluded the Democrats should be very cautious about making an issue of it. Acting for Roosevelt, he wrote a nine-page report summarizing the opinions of these men and his own conclusions. This he sent to Senators Walsh and Pat Harrison, and to Representative Cordell Hull.[24]

* The *Times* declared, "The policy was supposed to have been determined upon in haphazard fashion at a recent dinner in Washington attended by several Senators and one or two travelling statesmen. They agreed that the party must have an 'issue.' If one did not exist, it must be invented." [22]

The outcome was the easy ratification of the debt agreement, but added prestige for Roosevelt among the Democratic Senators. That was what much of the skirmishing was about. While many of the prominent Democrats had been pleased by Roosevelt's dinner conference — Harrison and Hull especially — according to Howe, "Baruch who evidently has it in for us — rushed down to Washington and 'poo pooed' the whole thing. He is of course backing Ritchie and whether he feels you stand in Ritchie's way or whether his sensitive . . . soul has taken offense at something — Lord knows what — I don't know yet." * But Howe "handed him a neat one" in the Italian loan report, by stating on the first page that he had not consulted Baruch because he understood Baruch was in complete agreement with the Morgans. This the acting head of Morgan and Company had told him. Howe gloated that when the anti-Wall Street Senators "Joe Robinson and Walsh read that it will more than even up accounts!" [25]

Again, at the beginning of 1927, Roosevelt met with the Democratic leaders in Washington, this time to exhort them to issue a Jefferson's Birthday manifesto stating the fundamentals upon which they agreed and dodging controversial issues like Prohibition. Most of the Democratic Senators agreed. "Mr. Roosevelt has the right idea," Tom Walsh declared. "There is something more important to us than who shall be the candidate in 1928, namely, what shall our principles and policies be, or shall we have any?" But a few diehards like Senator Bruce of Maryland dissented, and the party remained as divided as ever.[26]

Since it was next to impossible for Democratic leaders to agree sufficiently to issue joint declarations, Roosevelt had some justification in seeking to initiate policies by himself. His greatest motive was obviously (as his critics claimed) self-advertisement, but what benefited him was of still more value to the party. Such was the nature of Roosevelt's agitation for the calling of a special session of Congress to enact flood relief and flood control legislation, in the summer of 1927 when the Mississippi River was on the most disastrous rampage in the history of the United States. The river inundated several thousands of acres, causing hundreds of millions of dollars' loss, and making thousands of people homeless. Both the Red Cross and the Federal Government were active in providing relief; Secretary of Commerce

* According to Alvin Johnson, President Coolidge had summoned Baruch to the White House and persuaded him to line up Democratic votes in Congress in favor of ratification.

Hoover, who supervised the aid, again appeared as a humanitarian hero. But Howe, feeling the Coolidge Administration was being lax, urged Roosevelt to issue "a ringing demand in the name of humanity etc" for a special session of Congress, and to "raise Hell generally." He remarked, "Wouldn't such a move go grand in the South and make you the fair-haired boy?" [27]

Roosevelt not only complied, but followed up the suggestion with a systematic campaign. He queried the Senators in the affected states on their needs; on the whole they responded enthusiastically in favor of a special session to appropriate funds for levees. Senator Kenneth McKellar of Tennessee remarked acidly that the most Hoover had done in Memphis was to advertise himself, and that the country favored the Federal Government taking over the rebuilding of levees immediately. Roosevelt proclaimed these ideas as widely as possible, but received scant notice in the press compared with Hoover, who was announcing similar plans. Moreover, when President Coolidge announced at the beginning of August that he did not choose to run for President in 1928, Hoover immediately was regarded as the leading Republican candidate. This made Roosevelt's agitation appear unmistakably as politicking against Hoover.* Roosevelt's vigor alarmed Senator Harrison of Mississippi, who urged him to go easy until the Administration framed an appropriation bill. "Knowing Hoover's character as I do, I feel that he is highly sensitive of criticism or any expression that takes issue with him," Harrison explained. "He feels that he has rendered great service in the flooded regions, and I am sure feels further that the people in that section should be grateful for it. I am grateful for what Hoover has done." As Harrison had hoped, the Republicans were ready to vote large sums for the building and strengthening of levees in the Democratic South, from Cape Girardeau, Missouri, to the Gulf. Although Roosevelt still ventured some criticism, the sum voted in May, 1928, was for the time a staggering one: $325,000,000. Roosevelt had failed to wrest the issue from the Republicans. To Southern flood victims, not Roosevelt but Hoover was "the fair-haired boy." [29]

---

* FDR still considered Hoover a personal friend, and ordinarily was careful not to criticize him publicly. When he differed with one of Hoover's policies early in 1926, he felt a banker or merchant should answer Hoover "as an attack by me might be considered to be actuated primarily from political motives. This last would, incidentally, be about 99% true." When Hoover was about to be nominated in 1928, FDR refused to write an article against him because he was "an old personal friend." [28]

Moreover, while Hoover was easily, with the possible exception of President Coolidge, the most popular man in the United States, Roosevelt was comparatively unknown to the public. In May, 1926, Roosevelt delivered a felicitous commencement address at Milton Academy. Entitled "Whither Bound?" it was a thoughtful exhortation to liberalism. He contrasted the cohesiveness among the conservatives with the chaotic disagreement among liberals which kept them out of power most of the time. When they did get in, they "translate the constantly working leaven of progress into law or custom or use, but rarely obtain enough time in control to make further economic or social experiments." The menace to the nation would not come from four or eight years of liberal or even radical control of government, but from too many years of conservative government which would fail to keep up with the new and startling developments of the future. The address was so challenging that Houghton Mifflin Company published it as a small book. Lippmann, who read it with "great admiration," considered it "a charming thing." Yet Roosevelt had as yet attracted so little attention that, some months after it appeared, it had sold only 340 copies.[30]

If Roosevelt thought he was well known enough to run successfully for President without first having held some additional important office, he was mistaken. Nevertheless, in 1927, there was more Roosevelt-for-President talk. Several Georgia leaders and the powerful Atlanta *Constitution* boomed him.

Bone-Dry Josephus Daniels wrote his former assistant, "I'd come out for you if it wouldn't queer you." And queer Roosevelt was exactly what enough Southern Dry support would do — queer him with the urban, Wet, Catholic wing of the party, which was growing steadily more enthusiastic over Smith. When Carter Glass came to New York in April, 1927, and confided in a number of political leaders that when the proper time came the Southern Drys would demand that Smith withdraw in Roosevelt's favor, Howe was almost in a panic. "I threw enough cold water on the idea to extinguish the Woolworth Building," Howe reported.[31]

As for Roosevelt, he was quite ready to grant in private letters that Smith could make a better run in 1928 than could he:

Of course, it goes without saying that I am not a candidate myself, publicly or privately, but, if for the sake of argument I were to run in 1928, I should find the greatest possible difficulty in carrying any of the eastern states, including New York, with their very large electoral votes. Furthermore, there is no reason why I should expect to carry any of the middle western states. I could without doubt, carry most or all of the southern and, possibly, a number of the mountain states, but if you will figure out the vote, it would not bring me within 100 of the necessary 266 votes in the electoral college.

On the other hand, Governor Smith, if nominated, would stand more than any other Democrat a chance of carrying Massachusetts, Rhode Island, Connecticut, New York, New Jersey and Delaware . . . I think he would also carry just as many, if not more, of the western states than I would — I mean Missouri, Oklahoma, Oregon. Add up these votes and you will see that on the assumption that he can carry most of the south, he would have a total very close to the necessary majority.

Can any other Democrat make such a good November showing? I doubt it.[32]

CHAPTER XIV

Smith for President

The political pot boils and it certainly looks to me as if
the Governor has an increasingly good chance for the
nomination. Quite aside from my loyalty to him, I honestly have no desire either to run for the Presidency or
to be President. I have seen much of Presidents and administrations. Even though it may sound selfish, I would
rather do my bit as a private in the ranks.
— FDR TO STANLEY W. PRENOSIL, *May 24, 1927.*

FOR ROOSEVELT to write that he had no interest in being President was political applesauce; for him to assert that Smith could
come closer than he to winning in 1928 was considerably more than
this. Although Roosevelt promoted his own political fortunes to the
utmost from 1924 through 1928, at no time did he display the slightest
disloyalty toward Smith. If Smith had been eliminated as a candidate,
he would have been quite ready to take advantage of the opportunity;
in the meanwhile he worked diligently to promote Smith throughout
the South and West. In his personal dealings with Smith, again and
again he offered sound advice aimed at remedying some of Smith's
weaknesses as a national political figure.

Roosevelt worried because Smith continued to concentrate on the
State of New York and its problems almost to the exclusion of everything else. At the close of the 1924 convention, Smith had not improved
the bad impression his claque made upon many delegates from distant
states when he appeared before them and talked on and on about his
magnificent achievements as Governor of New York. Roosevelt felt
Smith should counter this by speaking throughout the country on
broad noncontroversial subjects. Immediately after the 1924 election,
and into the early part of 1926, he pressed Smith to do this. Smith
refused on the grounds that he was not a candidate for the Presidency;
the nomination must seek him, not he the nomination.* In September,

* William Allen White, a Republican who admired Smith, tried through FDR
to persuade Smith to address Kansas editors in April, 1928. "Smith is supposed to
have horns and a tail out West," White asserted. He thought it would help both
Smith and Kansas to learn about each other. FDR tried to persuade Smith to
accept the engagement, but failed.[1]

1926, Roosevelt was even more alarmed when some Tammanyites tried to persuade Smith not to run for governor again, but instead to devote the next two years to going around the country making nonpolitical speeches. This, Roosevelt warned Smith, would make him appear "an open out and out candidate" far too soon. "You can do this as Governor without being called a candidate," he replied, "especially if you cut out political meetings like the one George Brennan gave you in Chicago and go instead to nonpolitical gatherings, where you can speak on nonpolitical subjects such as child welfare, prison reform, state organization, etc. etc." [2]

Smith ran for Governor again in 1926, and his re-election by the largest margin in the history of New York projected him into a leading position among the aspirants for the Democratic nomination. Despite Roosevelt's intermittent prodding, he scarcely budged from the state. Al Smith the name became increasingly widely known throughout the nation, but not Al Smith the person. This, both Roosevelt and Howe felt, was exceedingly unfortunate because a bad impression of Smith persisted in the Protestant, Dry sections of the country. It was increased by the overzealousness of some of Smith's supporters. Since the death of Boss Murphy, Tammany had operated chaotically under the leadership of George Olvany, who lacked Murphy's firm grip on the organization and common-sense realization of the national antipathy to Tammany. Roosevelt was on friendly terms with Olvany, solicited a few minor patronage favors from him, and managed to hold him in line. But lesser Tammany men created the havoc. They wanted to set up Smith organizations in state after state where McAdoo had received the convention votes in 1924. Had they done so they would have won almost no fights and brought down on Smith the wrath of the existing organizations. Roosevelt and Howe fought this tooth and nail, since they were sure that by mentioning the names of no candidates for several years, they could, in a drive shortly before the convention, win many of these organizations for Smith. By the spring of 1927, as Howe commented, McAdoo was "an admittedly dead cock in the fight." The main danger was that the Tammanyites might bring him back to life. They came closest to success one day while Olvany and the other cooler heads were away, when they proposed that Tammany as a fraternal order extend itself nationally. Aside from Prohibition and religion, the strongest objection to Smith throughout the nation was fear that Tammany wished to run the country from the White House. Republican newspapers almost immediately ran cartoons depicting voracious tiger cubs streaking across the nation.[3]

As early as September, 1926, Roosevelt had firmly warned Smith against the misplaced enthusiasm of his Tammany supporters:

> I am convinced that some of your friends are, without your knowledge or consent, giving you *aggressive* publicity in the south and west, where such publicity is at the present time harmful. You will have noticed from the papers that these people, who are pushing you to the front as individuals, are stirring up the opposition and giving the old McAdoo crowd and the Know Nothings a reason for organizing against you.
>
> In every letter I have written I have taken the stand that no one can tell at this early date who the right man will be and that we should devote ourselves to building up a strong National Organization. More work along this line would have resulted in all the little booms for little candidates picking up courage . . . In other words, it is much better to encourage local candidates who would have delegates not unfriendly to you as second choice than to build up any strong Anti-Smith feeling at this time.[4]

Smith followed this policy of silence, and by May, 1927, Roosevelt reported that it was leading to "a very remarkable trend towards your candidacy . . . among the southern leaders." Roosevelt rather worried that it had developed so soon, and again urged Smith to muzzle his supporters. Smith agreed that the swing was a bit too early, and assured Roosevelt, "I am, as you notice, keeping very quiet and doing what I can to keep everybody else quiet." [5]

An almost equally serious problem for Roosevelt in building Smith support was the religious issue. The Ku Klux Klan was on the wane as an organization, but the anti-Catholic sentiment upon which it had capitalized was still at a high pitch. In the face of this, Smith and his family proudly placed emphasis upon their Catholicism. Howe fretted because when they came back from Rome and an audience with the Pope, in the spring of 1925, Mrs. Smith described everywhere in detail and with gusto how the Pope had turned to a Tammany man with them and had urged him to work even harder for Smith at the next election. In the spring of 1928, Smith's daughter insisted upon being married by a cardinal with his retinue. Howe fussed, "Won't the News Reels . . . look nice in the happy Southland?" To top this, the Pope stirred up a hornet's nest in Rhode Island by excommunicating a publisher for suing a bishop. As a result, Howe felt he detected "a great determination" among Protestant Democrats and Independents in the area "to say nothing & 'vote agin the Pope.'" [6]

Among Southern political leaders, Roosevelt argued constantly against these prejudices, pointing out that in no instance had Smith functioned as a Catholic during his many years as Governor of New York. Among intellectuals, Roosevelt was partly instrumental in persuading Smith to state his position for the *Atlantic Monthly*. As late as January, 1927, Roosevelt felt that there was no need for Smith to give an interview on his religion. Ellery Sedgwick, the editor of the *Atlantic*, changed this by publishing in the April number an "Open Letter," charging that Smith's religion would bind him to do the bidding of the Catholic Church. He sent Roosevelt a copy in advance, with a strong invitation to obtain a reply. Roosevelt protested to Sedgwick that it would stir up Ku Klux Klan animosities that were only just dying down, and that it was ridiculously legalistic — as good a case could be made against electing a Unitarian, Baptist, or Episcopalian.[7]

Since he knew Sedgwick intended to publish "the fool article" anyway, Roosevelt recommended to Smith:

"When all is said and done, the boldest, and therefore, the most effective way of dealing with this whole situation would be for you to answer it yourself. You can do it in such a way that people all over the United States will respect you even more than they do now." [8]

Smith accepted the challenge. He wrote a ringing reply that he by no means considered the Church a higher authority than the state. Intellectuals applauded. Roosevelt declared, "It seems to me that . . . [it] is a real answer to people who have had honest doubts about this question in the past. The only remaining dissenters will be a handful of people like Tom Heflin and probably a few professional preachers." Roosevelt miscalculated badly. The Tom Heflins many times outnumbered the "people who have had honest doubts," and the constant sniping against Smith continued.[9]

Nevertheless, the bewildered rural, Dry element in the party, since McAdoo had become a dead gamecock, could find no strong candidate with which to oppose Smith. As early as the summer of 1927, Daniels expressed to Roosevelt the qualms this group felt increasingly as the convention approached:

"This is the first time in my life that I have felt so perfectly at sea as to what we ought to do and what we can do. The liquor question is much more acute tha[n] it appears on the surface; and the religious question, which ought not to exist but which does on both sides; and the hero-worship of Smith to which you refer; and the lack of any other leader with commanding support, all combine to muddy the water so that it will take a keener eye tha[n] I possess to see to clear water." [10]

What prevented the anti-Smith Democrats from combining upon some desperate strategy, to command the one-third-plus-one of the delegates necessary to block his nomination, was the growing realization that (as Roosevelt emphasized to them) Smith's chances were better than those of any compromise choice. The source of Roosevelt's optimism was his faith that, once Smith was nominated, aside from the possible defection of Tennessee and Kentucky — which had previously gone Republican — the South would "hold its nose and vote for him." What also restrained some anti-Smith Democrats was the undeniable fact that the Coolidge prosperity was continuing; no Democrat stood much of a chance.[11]

Roosevelt pointed out to Daniels in the summer of 1927:

"Strictly between ourselves, I am very doubtful whether any Democrat can win in 1928. It will depend somewhat on whether the present undoubted general prosperity of the country continues. You and I may recognize the serious hardships which the farmers in the south and west are laboring under, but the farmers in the south will vote the Democratic ticket anyway and I do not believe that the farmers of the west will vote the Democratic ticket in sufficient numbers even if they are starving." [12]

A few months before the convention, the anti-Smith forces collapsed so completely that Howe was predicting that Smith would have the necessary two-thirds vote at the convention on the second or third ballot. He repeated the gossip (emphatically denied by Baruch) that Baruch was recommending that Smith be allowed to run and be beaten at the polls. Roosevelt agreed that this seemed to be the strategy, but hoped national enthusiasm for the Democratic ticket would burst forth before election day. He was even more active on behalf of Smith than four years previously, conferring with political leaders in both the South and the Middle West.[13]

The nomination of Smith seemed so certain that Roosevelt gave much of his thought to subsidiary matters. He was not, as in 1924, Smith's pre-convention manager; that task fell to Smith's former personal secretary, George R. Van Namee, a member of the state public service commission. Roosevelt peppered both Van Namee and the members of the Democratic National Committee with ample advice. Beginning in January, 1928, he besieged National Chairman Shaver and Finance Director Jesse Jones with demands that they put the party machinery into high gear even before the convention — and he provided quantities of specific detailed suggestions. By sending copies of his requests to a number of Democratic leaders, he was able to nudge Shaver and Jones into action. Jones retorted, "Your suggestions are very sound: in fact, they are exactly what I have been working to for the last three years." [14]

To Van Namee, Roosevelt sent the same suggestions and more. He felt that during the campaign there should not be one national headquarters, but four regional ones. The question of who should be Vice President concerned him; he felt it should be a Southerner, and concluded that Cordell Hull would be an excellent choice.* Unfortunately for Hull's chances, his friends began a movement to nominate him for the Presidency, and Smith ultimately turned to Senator Joseph Robinson of Arkansas. [16]

Issues continued to concern Roosevelt deeply. "As to the platform," he wrote in April, "I hope we shall have a simple and short one and if the Governor does not like it he will change it or modify it in his own good terms." † His hope was that the party would avoid taking

---

* FDR wrote:
I have been convinced for several months that the Vice Presidential Candidate should come from the South. In that field the choice is not large — Governor Byrd of Virginia, Senator George of Georgia, Governor Moody of Texas and Cordell Hull of Tennessee. I may change my mind many times in the next two months but I am inclined to think that Byrd comes from too close to New York, that George has made some bad mistakes in the past few months, that Moody is very young and untried and that Cordell Hull would make an excellent choice.

He has a splendid record, great experience, is universally liked and would be very helpful to the ticket in Tennessee and to a certain extent in Kentucky and Missouri. He is not a fanatic. Furthermore, I am old fashioned enough to believe that the nominee for Vice President should be chosen with the thought that the Almighty might call on him to succeed to the presidency, and Hull would make a fine President. [15]

† FDR in effect wrote his own platform in a letter to be read at a Portland, Oregon, Jefferson Day banquet:
My own feeling is that the following are the most vital of the many arguments for changing the party in control of the Federal Government:
First, place agriculture on a parity with industry in making and carrying out our laws.
Second, restore the tariff to an honest basis, so as to eliminate the present favoritism.
Third, honest and effective enforcement of all laws, equally including

any radical stand on either Prohibition or farm relief; if the party displayed common sense at the convention, he thought it would be safe. Of all the issues, as for years, foreign policy gave him the most concern.[18]

Since 1924, Roosevelt had continued to advocate a Wilsonian foreign policy. While he tempered this with expediency, and advocated merely "the ridiculously small first step of joining the World Court," rather than immediate entrance into the League, international co-operation was his ultimate goal. He asserted in "Whither Bound?": "Isolation of individual nations will be as difficult in [the] future as would be the isolation of New England or the South today." [19]

Applied to Coolidge foreign policy, Roosevelt's principles had led him to question the Italian debt settlement, partly for political expediency, partly because he shared the liberals' fear that Mussolini might use his improved financial position to start a war. On the larger question of overall settlement of the debts of America's former allies, he was scornful because President Coolidge in the face of their financial distress was supposed to have inquired, "Well, they hired the money, didn't they?" He declared:

"Let it be well remembered that quite apart from moral justice, the ill will of other nations will cost us in the end in practical dollars more billions than we will gain in interest under the debt settlements. We loaned to our associates in the war less than 10,000,000,000. . . . And piecemeal, time-serving, we have with grudging contempt condescended to accept 22,000,000,000 in payment of the 10 we loaned. Shall we place along side the old words 'With malice towards none, with charity to all' the newer saying, 'Well, you hired the money, didn't you[?]' " [20]

---

whatever law the people decide on as a means of carrying out the eighteenth amendment.

Fourth, honesty in conducting the public affairs of the United States together with a reorganization of Governmental machinery so as to prevent duplication, waste and favoritism.

Fifth, a definite policy of noninterference in the internal affairs of other nations and co-operation with other nations for the elimination of war and for the settlement of international problems and disputes, and a definite effort to end the hate and dislike of America, now shared by every other civilized nation in the world.

Sixth, preservation of national resources, particularly water power in the ultimate ownership of the people.

Seventh, the substitution of a Democratic Government of practical idealism in the place of an Oligarchy of gross materialism.[17]

At the same time, Roosevelt was ready to accuse Coolidge of the opposite of thrift in his failure to deal adequately with questions of international security. The President had failed to follow up the limitation of battleships provided by the Treaty of Washington (which Roosevelt still praised) with an effective limitation of cruisers at the Geneva Conference. After the failure, he had presented to Congress proposals for a large-scale naval building program. Roosevelt, by the spring of 1928, had so far outgrown his earlier beliefs as Assistant Secretary of the Navy that he advised the Democrats in Congress to support only the immediate construction of a few of the ships, and oppose the authorization of future ships. The long-range program was "indefensible and is merely handing a cudgel to the State Department to use over the heads of other nations," he asserted. "We can get much further in the limitation of Naval Armaments by [sitting over] a table with them instead of brandishing a stick." When Rear Admiral R. E. Coontz urged him to put a preparedness plank into the Democratic platform in order to help restore public confidence in the Navy, he retorted he would do everything possible to put in the right kind of plank to restore that confidence — "unfortunately shaken at the present time not only by the belief that it is badly administered, but also by the foolish efforts last winter to get appropriations running into the billions." The only conceivable naval foe of the United States was Japan, and Roosevelt continued to feel that "there is no fundamental reason why our relations with Japan should not be on a permanent and cordial basis." [21]

Roosevelt's antipathy for Coolidge foreign policy carried over even into the Latin American area. He so strongly opposed the armed intervention by the Marine Corps in Nicaragua that he came to feel that even those previous occupations in which he had played some part had not been wise.* "This present Nicaraguan mess," he complained in 1927, was "a further reason for dislike of the United States by every Central and South American nation." He inquired of Senator Glass in January, 1928, if it was not reason to revive the doctrine of President Wilson's Mobile Speech of 1913: that the United States should invite

---

* FDR demonstrated how he was torn between his old feelings and new in what he wrote in 1928 to the commander of the Second Marine Brigade in Nicaragua: "I am very sure that the Marines are doing a splendid piece of work, though frankly from the point of view of sound government, I do not like this expedition which has been sent down to carry out an agreement which has never had the sanction of Congress. It must be interesting but very difficult work and I hope that the health of the Brigade is holding up well." [22]

the other American republics to join with it where intervention might be necessary. Conversations and correspondence with Norman H. Davis, Hamilton Fish Armstrong and, above all, with a longtime friend, Sumner Welles, did much to influence Roosevelt in the direction of a Latin American policy based more on co-operation than force.[23]

It was with these views in mind that Roosevelt undertook in the spring of 1928 to write an article on Democratic foreign policy for *Foreign Affairs*. Armstrong, the editor, requested him to obtain Senator Glass to write the article, but although Glass pungently opposed the Coolidge policies, he was too busy to comply. Roosevelt drafted the article with unusual care, for he was sure that, if it was any good at all, it would become the blueprint for the Democratic party. He obtained quantities of materials from Armstrong, Welles, and others. To Norman H. Davis he sent a hurried request for a statement, "a large rough hewn Democratic platform plank, out of which a highly finished carving can be made!"[24]

One of the reasons for Roosevelt's vigorous undertaking was his fear that deficient as Smith was in statements on some domestic issues such as farm relief, he was even more deficient in foreign policy. There were signs that this might react against him seriously among well-educated liberals. Colonel House wrote Roosevelt in January, 1928, that he was often asked about Smith's views on foreign affairs by people who hoped Smith would define them. House recommended to Roosevelt that instead Smith should state that if elected he would consult with the best informed persons and devote his every energy to the proper solution of each problem as it arose. Without using House's name, Roosevelt forwarded this advice to Smith, and he himself followed it. He wrote Welles that he felt if Smith became President, "he will make up for his lack of experience in foreign affairs by bringing to the White House a mind of the most extraordinary and simple clarity which enables him to get at the fundamentals and at the same time formulate humanitarian policies which the average citizen could understand and approve."[25]

At the same time, Roosevelt persistently sent foreign policy data to Smith: a memorandum he himself wrote denouncing the occupation in Nicaragua, letters and memoranda from Welles recommending a "good neighbor" type policy for Latin America, and the like. He was so afraid that Judge Proskauer, one of Smith's closest advisers, would influence Smith against the World Court that he arranged for Welles to have an interview with Proskauer. There is no evidence that any of this particularly swayed Smith, although he did at one point reply to Roosevelt, "I have your note of the 19th, also letter from Mr. Welles. Am keeping it in front of me to digest it." [26]

As for the article in Foreign Affairs, in some respects it was like Roosevelt's subsequent productions as governor and as President, the work of many men. He embodied in it many of the ideas he had obtained through conversations, correspondence, books and articles,* and he sent the draft to Armstrong and Davis for criticism. Both of them replied with lengthy comments, quite critical (although they did not say so outright) because of its superficialities. Roosevelt made some repairs, and returned it to Armstrong. It appeared in the July number of Foreign Affairs, paired with an article on Republican foreign policy by Ogden Mills, Undersecretary of the Treasury.[28]

Because Roosevelt hoped to make his article the standard statement of Democratic aims, and wished to reach a far wider group of readers than the usual writer for Foreign Affairs, he deliberately wrote it in a simple, direct style, "almost in words of one syllable." He conceived of it as covering three main topics: "First, a review of our international history to prove our broad leadership in progressive international thought most of the time up to 1919; secondly, a review of the past nine years to prove that this leadership has fallen by the way-side; third, to point out wherein we may resume that leadership along certain broad, but at the same time fairly concrete lines." In it he stated his views on war debts, naval disarmament, co-operation with other nations, and the need for a new Latin American policy.[29]

Concerning Latin America he especially emphasized that, as a result of the series of American interventions culminating in the expedition

---

* For instance, Manley O. Hudson, subsequently a Justice on the World Court, wrote for FDR in a memorandum concerning the Kellogg–Briand pact outlawing war: "I hope . . . that Mr. Roosevelt will emphasize the impossibility of effectuating world peace by a fiat. For hundreds of years, nations have made treaties of 'perpetual peace,' Secretary Kellogg proposes little more than that. Without institutions, the fiat is worse than worthless because it begets misplaced alliance." FDR wrote in his article: "It is of the utmost importance that this nation realize that war cannot be outlawed by resolution alone. That has failed for two thousand years. Since earliest history nations have entered into treaties of 'eternal peace and friendship.' . . . The primary cause of failure in the past has been the lack of machinery for the elimination of the causes of disputes before they reach grave proportions. Practical machinery must be erected and kept in good working order. Secretary Kellogg's plan, even if approved by the leading nations, still fails in two points. It leads to a false belief in America that we have taken a great step forward. It does not contribute in any way to settling matters of international controversy." [27]

to Nicaragua, "never before in our history have we had fewer friends in the Western Hemisphere than we have today." The answer: "Single-handed intervention by us in the internal affairs of other nations must end; with the co-operation of others we shall have more order in this hemisphere and less dislike." On the highly controversial questions of American entrance into the League and the World Court, he somewhat equivocated. After several paragraphs praising the League, he concluded, "We should co-operate with the League as the first great agency for the maintenance of peace and for the solution of common problems ever known to civilization, and without entering into European politics, we should take an active, hearty and official part in all those proceedings which bear on the general good of mankind." Concerning the World Court, he concluded that, if the President had wished, with the Senate he could have found some way "by which this nation without loss of any real or even contingent sovereign right" could participate. "Perhaps the country will find in the Democratic Party . . . the national leader who, by the application of common sense and the ordinary principles of fairness and good business dealing, will enable the United States to help — instead of clinging tightly to the top rail of the fence." [30]

As was correct in a sound political manifesto, Roosevelt was dealing with the general, not the specific, and appealing to the heart as much as to the head. For those who believed in international co-operation, there was much attraction in his conclusion:

> If the leadership is right — or, more truly, if the spirit behind it is great — the United States can regain the world's trust and friendship and become again of service. We can point the way once more to the reducing of armaments; we can co-operate officially and whole-heartedly with every agency that studies and works to relieve the common ills of mankind; and we can for all time renounce the practice of arbitrary intervention in the home affairs of our neighbors.
> It is the spirit, sir, which matters. [31]

This call for Wilsonian idealists to support the Democratic party was strong, and perhaps even effective, but it disappointed zealous backers of American entrance into the League and World Court. Roosevelt had consciously written the article with the thought that Smith would be the candidate and that it would serve "more or less as a guidance in the treatment of foreign affairs in the campaign." Neither in it nor in the Democratic platform was he willing to place emphasis upon America's joining international organizations. In June, he withstood the pressure of Mrs. Roosevelt's friend, Esther Lape, and other strong proponents of a plank advocating the resumption of negotiations looking toward the entrance of the United States into the World Court. It would be too difficult to obtain, he explained. Walter Lippmann granted that Roosevelt was correct, but felt that Roosevelt, Newton D. Baker, and John W. Davis could get it, if they set their minds to it. Consequently, Lippmann wrote an editorial for the New York *World* in order to prod them.[32]

These tactics accomplished nothing more than to force Roosevelt to admit the real reason for his reluctance, which was political expediency. "What people don't realize," he protested to Miss Lape, "is that it is more important to elect friends of the World Court than it is to make platform declarations." He granted to former Supreme Court Justice John H. Clarke that he felt "rather ashamed" of the treatment he had given the World Court and League in his article, but felt it more important to get Smith "the largest possible number of votes rather than to stir up any of the old prejudices." On the same grounds he was ready to justify the equivocal foreign policy plank in the platform. "Frankly, I cannot blame you for being upset," he wrote Clark M. Eichelberger, Executive Secretary of the League of Nations Non-Partisan Association. "You are not the only one who is disappointed." Smith's advisers, he explained (not admitting his own dominant role in formulating a foreign policy stand), "felt that glittering generalities would, on the whole, lose fewer votes." Obviously Roosevelt hoped that, unsatisfactory as the generalities might be, the internationalists would find them preferable to the Republican foreign policy. They were aimed to win the internationalists without alienating those opposed to direct American participation in the League or the World Court.[33]

Roosevelt arranged to have reprints of his *Foreign Affairs* article distributed among the delegates at the National Democratic Convention, but they arrived too late, so he mailed a copy to each delegate and alternate. In the final analysis, neither they nor the foreign policy plank were of much effect. Some liberals may have supported Smith in part because they felt he would develop a preferable foreign policy, but other issues were almost completely to overshadow that platform plank in the campaign. The main significance of the article was that it had led Roosevelt to make a systematic study of foreign affairs, and in at least one area, relations with Latin America, to advocate a new policy, which he helped implement as President five years later.[34]

At the National Democratic Convention, held in Houston, Texas, at the end of June, Roosevelt was concerned less with the platform than with making sure that there was no slip-up in the nomination of Smith. Senator Wagner served as Smith's representative on the Platform Committee, while Roosevelt was again floor manager. At first Boss Frank Hague of Jersey City was scheduled for the post. There could not have been a more unfortunate choice from the standpoint of bringing Smith rural support; when he was eliminated Howe exclaimed, "Thank God." Roosevelt as floor manager was sure Smith had the votes and to spare, but took no chances. He even made use of a photostatic seating plan of the auditorium, with the location of each delegation penciled in, and arranged to use the mansion of former Governor Will Hogg, about two miles outside of Houston, for the holding of conferences.

Compared with four years previously, Roosevelt gave the appearance to a remarkable extent of having regained the use of his legs. The crutches were gone; in their place he used a cane and leaned on the arm of his sturdy son Elliott. He worried only about getting up the steps to the speaker's stand in the auditorium, and handled that inconspicuously. To the vast assemblage of delegates he seemed not crippled, but lame.[35]

The only critical moment at the convention came early during discussion of the platform. Roosevelt had to throw his weight behind the Smith forces in order to prevent Governor Ritchie and the wringing Wets from upsetting the preliminary planning and writing in a forthright Wet plank.* As Roosevelt had wished, it was finally a platform designed as far as possible to conciliate all the diverse elements within the Democratic Party. Newton D. Baker lamented to him afterwards, "McKinley could have run on the tariff plank and Lodge on the one on international relations." Roosevelt replied with more charm than candor, "You are not alone in having unhappy sessions with yourself over the platform. If you or I had been the candidate, we would have ordered it otherwise — and thereby insured our defeat in November." [37]

---

* Otherwise, the only slip-up to which FDR had to attend was a minor one. On the last night of the convention, Herbert Lehman had Henry Morgenthau, Jr., call FDR's attention to the fact that clergymen of every religious faith but

The high point for Roosevelt at the Convention was when he delivered his speech nominating Smith. He had prepared it carefully. Howe had seen to it that it would receive the utmost publicity, by sending advance copies to newspaper editors all over the country. In writing the speech, Roosevelt kept in the forefront of his mind the enormous political potentialities of the relatively new medium — radio. Four years earlier his speech at Madison Square Garden had been broadcast, but radio had still seemed rather a novelty. By 1928, thanks to improved broadcasting techniques and national networks, it provided a remarkable opportunity to bring Roosevelt's political ideas and personal charm directly to millions of people. In addition, it served to circumvent hostile newspapers and magazines.[38]

Even more than other politicians, Roosevelt grasped the potentialities of this. Smith, a talented extemporaneous speaker, had earlier found it disconcerting to stand before a microphone — a "pie plate," Smith had called it — and had disliked the tinny quality he felt amplifiers gave his voice. And Smith's suspicions were well justified, for his East Side accent grated harshly on the ears of suspicious outlanders. It would have been better for Smith if radio had not been developed. For Roosevelt it was a new challenge to write carefully for the new medium, and to project his personality over the air. At the beginning of 1928, sensing how important radio would become during the campaign, he urged National Chairman Shaver immediately to arrange radio time through Owen D. Young. Roosevelt had heard a rumor that the Republicans would try to monopolize all the time of all the stations. Finance Director Jesse Jones obtained assurances that the companies with which Young was influential would give the Democrats an equal apportionment of time.[39]

Radio had become so popular that Roosevelt wondered if anyone

Jewish had delivered invocations. FDR presided the next morning over the closing session of the convention. He later wrote Morgenthau:

"Yes, we have no rabbi today!" . . . when I got to the platform, I found that four policemen and several firemen were searching Houston to try to find either of the rabbis. No report had been received from these sleuths and they had dashed out and acquired a willing baptist to meet the emergency. There was the baptist brother on the stand, and just as I was about to introduce him to the assembled mob your good rabbi was led in handcuffed, delivered over to me and day was saved.

Apparently, the rabbis in Houston, like the Catholic priests, were backward about coming forward. The other sky pilots were so anxious to pray for our souls (or rather make political speeches to us) that the authorities had to draw lots! [36]

would bother to read his campaign speech rather than merely listen to it:* "Sometimes I think that we are driving so wholly into a radio future that we shall get even our detective stories over the air instead of through the printed page." He planned his speech "convinced that the old-fashioned type of oratory would serve no useful purpose," so he directed it toward "the 15,000,000 radio listeners rather than the 15,000 in the Convention Hall." † He was spectacularly successful.[42]

Houston was steaming hot and jammed with Democrats. Afterwards Roosevelt wrote, "The only remark of the Convention which will live was that of Will Rogers, who said that in trying to mop his brow in the Rice Hotel mob, he mopped three others before he reached his own." But Roosevelt was in top form. The delegates cheered wildly when he was introduced, and again, when he took the few steps forward to the microphones. Most of the cheering was for Smith, but some of it for Roosevelt himself, who, with his healthy appearance and radiant high spirits, belied their preconception of him as a cripple. In a firm, clear voice he praised Smith's constructive work as Governor of New York and set forth his qualifications for the Presidency.[43]

Even the arch-Republican Chicago *Tribune* fell under its spell, and in an editorial entitled "The Twilight of the Silver Tongues," praised Roosevelt as "the only Republican in the Democratic party." [44]

The New York *Times* called it "A High-Bred Speech":

"There was nothing strained or fantastic or extravagant in what he said. It was the address of a fair minded and cultivated man, avoiding the usual perils of national convention oratory, and discussing in an intelligent way the qualifications which should be sought for in the President of the United States and the ability of ALFRED SMITH to meet every fair test of capacity. . . . It is seldom that a political

---

* Not only was it published as a campaign document by the Democratic National Committee, but Houghton Mifflin published it together with a sketch of Smith by FDR as a small book, *The Happy Warrior*. It sold in boards at seventy-five cents. Houghton Mifflin offered a pamphlet edition of 20,000 to the Democratic National Committee at twenty cents each, but Smith's close adviser, Belle Moskowitz, only took "about half a minute" to refuse it.[40]

† FDR wrote that great authority on public opinion, Lippmann: "I tried the definite experiment this year of writing and delivering my speech wholly for the benefit of the radio audience and press rather than for any forensic effect it might have on the delegates and audience in the convention hall. Smith had the votes anyway and it seemed to me more important to reach out for the republicans and independents throughout the country." [41]

speech attains this kind of eloquence. Indeed, the entire address of Mr. FRANKLIN ROOSEVELT is a model of its kind — limpid and unaffected in style and without a single trace of fustian." [45]

Smith tore the editorial out of the *Times*, circled it with a blue pencil, and sent it to Roosevelt with the notation in the margin:

> DEAR FRANK:
> This must be right because it brought tears in the Mansion when you spoke it
>
> AL

Smith was nominated on the first ballot; it was his hour of triumph, and Roosevelt had to some extent helped bring it about. At the same time, Roosevelt had gone far to prepare the way for future triumphs of his own.

CHAPTER XV

Roosevelt for Governor

> I accept the nomination for Governor because I am a
> disciple in a great cause. I have been enlisted as a private
> in the ranks for many years and I cannot fail to heed a
> call to more active service in a time when so much is at
> stake.
>
> — FDR, Acceptance Address, *October 16, 1928.*

"**H**ISTORY shows that true leaders come forward only at rather rare intervals," Roosevelt wrote a friend in June, 1928. "For instance, this nation had no real leader between the death of Lincoln in 1865 to the rise of Theodore Roosevelt in 1901. Wilson, the last leader, has only been gone for eight or nine years, and the present gray period may last another ten years. But there is just the possibility that if Smith is elected, he will prove equal to the task of new leadership; in my judgment, it is at least a gamble worth taking!" [1]

While Roosevelt considered Hoover a great man, he thought Smith a greater one, and predicted that the campaign of 1928 would "be a horse race." But in the weeks after Roosevelt left the Houston convention with high hopes, Smith failed to provide militant national leadership of the sort Roosevelt felt essential. Smith tried to make prosperity the main issue — to outdo the Republicans in his conservative appeal. He endorsed heartily the farm relief program for which Middle Western farmers were agitating, but his New York City background nullified much of his appeal to them. Unwilling or unable to strike out along sufficiently bold progressive lines in contrast to the Republicans, he could not prevent the campaign from degenerating into a discussion, at times low and scurrilous, of those two destructive issues, Prohibition and religion. Not much else appeared really to distinguish the Democrats from the Republicans. Before the end of the summer, the gamble to which Roosevelt had referred seemed to have been lost.[2]

Before the nomination, Roosevelt had expected that he would be one of Smith's key organizers and advisers, "needed every second of the day and night," especially through July and August. Had he been so, he would have insisted that Smith concentrate upon a progressive attack against the Coolidge-Hoover economic program. From Houston, Roosevelt went to Warm Springs for a brief rest; then, in response to a telegraphic summons, returned to New York for a meeting of the Democratic National Committee early in July. Even before his return, he felt that "the Governor will be a law unto himself," a prediction that was more than justified. Roosevelt himself declined the chairmanship of the Democratic National Committee (so he wrote his mother), but hoped to influence the selection. He was opposed to the man he thought to be Smith's choice, Peter Gerry of Rhode Island. Instead, Smith turned to a man against whom Roosevelt had far more serious objections. At a dinner for his closest campaign associates, Smith asserted that the Democratic party could not expect to win until it obtained the support of big business. Consequently, he was choosing John J. Raskob, chairman of the Finance Committee of General Motors, an associate of the Du Ponts, and reputedly one of the country's wealthiest men. What was more, he was listed in *Who's Who* as a Republican. Smith asked his supporters what they thought of the choice. All of them approved, except Joe Robinson and Roosevelt.[3]

Smith and his advisers felt that since Smith himself was a Wet and a Catholic, it would not hurt for the National Chairman to be so too. Among the Catholic Wet Democrats of the cities, undoubtedly Raskob's appointment did no harm. Certain it was that, throughout the campaign, Smith's popularity soared in the cities. Women of immigrant background for the first time went to the polls in large numbers, and voted the Democratic ticket. As Samuel Lubell has pointed out, Smith for the first time won a preponderance of the large cities for the Democratic Party.[4]

But as Roosevelt told Smith at the time, he did inestimable damage to himself and the party throughout the South and the West:

> The appointment was a bold stroke to try to end the 99% of business (big and little) preference for the Republican Party. I told Smith quite plainly that it would make the whole situation far more difficult for the Democracy of the south, but Smith felt that we should take our chance on this as we would lose any way if we did not carry the big industrial states.
>
> Furthermore, I told the Governor that if he decided on Raskob, he should make it clear that it was a purely personal appointment

of an old friend and that Raskob would be merely a business manager and have nothing to say about issues. Smith would not agree to this last as he thought it would be disloyal to Raskob to tie his hands. The result has been that Raskob has talked too much and now Smith has had to make it clear that he (Smith) is responsible for the issues and policies, and not Raskob or any one else.

I am still doing my best to line up the campaign issues on something other than this Wet and Dry question. Frankly, I am disturbed, but as you know, the campaign is very young yet and past history shows that the true issues are apt to come out during September, and the false issues be relegated to the background. I pray this may be so this year.[5]

The howls of protest to Roosevelt from the South and West more than bore out his foreboding, but he could not communicate the seriousness of these to Smith. To a startling extent, Smith had cut himself off from the Southern and liberal leaders of the party. Daniels was able to get to him, to protest the damage Smith's Wetness was doing in North Carolina, but Roosevelt had trouble trying to arrange a conference for Newton D. Baker. Roosevelt found his own way to Smith so effectively blocked by Mrs. Belle Moskowitz, Judge Proskauer, and Raskob that he confessed to Harry Byrd, "I rarely get a chance to see the Governor himself and can communicate only by way of other people." Roosevelt and Baruch carried on complicated negotiations with the sulking McAdoo, to try to get McAdoo to come out for Smith. But Roosevelt was not able to see Smith personally about it, and the triumvirate through indifference or hostility bungled the matter. McAdoo did not come out for Smith until November 4, far too late to be of any value.[6]

Smith and Raskob continued to put emphasis upon Prohibition, which Roosevelt strongly felt should be soft-pedaled. He apparently impressed the serious need of this upon his Dry wife, for he wrote a friend, "Thanks for sending me that awful picture of my Missus. She is apparently looking at a fly on the ceiling with the hope of finding out how to be wet and dry at the same time." He made no impression upon the Wet Smith, although Scott Ferris, the National Committeeman from Oklahoma, warned Roosevelt that thanks to Raskob's pronouncements on Prohibition, the party must do a lot of work in the great plains and border states. An Oklahoma Methodist minister, who said he had planned to vote for Smith as a rebuke to religious intolerance, wrote Roosevelt he would not do so if the election were to be turned into a referendum on Prohibition. When Byrd predicted to Roosevelt early in August that, if the election were held the next day, Virginia would go Republican, Roosevelt could only reply, "You are not the only person who has been frankly worried by the trend of things in Albany." [7]

Added to this was steady attrition from the anti-Catholic smears against Smith, which, of course, were not his fault. As a Protestant, Roosevelt said it made his blood boil the way a number of ministers and bishops, not just as individuals, but in their official capacities, were warning against the danger of electing a Roman Catholic President. They were doing, Roosevelt felt, exactly what they accused the Roman Catholic Church of wanting to do. With strong indignation, Roosevelt complained in a letter that "the Governor is faced with the meanest and dirtiest kind of attacks, some in the open but most of the whispering variety." On the whispering level, the accusations were partly vile, occasionally ludicrous. Later in the campaign, in New York State, Roosevelt told an audience that in Georgia handbills were being distributed asserting that if Smith were elected, the marriages of Protestants would be void and their children illegitimate. [8]

Despite his forebodings, Roosevelt worked energetically in the campaign. He wrote optimistic letters to his many casual political acquaintances and scheduled campaign speeches in Georgia and Cleveland, Ohio. His most important work was to organize the Division of Commerce, Industry and Professional Activities for the Smith campaign. This involved, ironically enough, enlisting the support of prominent business leaders for Smith. It was good politics for Roosevelt personally, since it brought his name to the attention of thousands of substantial citizens: one appeal over his signature and on his personal stationery went to pharmacists all over the United States; others went to other groups. Although the appeals to businessmen were somewhat at variance with Roosevelt's protest against the appointment of Raskob, they were less so than Roosevelt's own planning during the summer of 1928 to accept the presidency of a proposed multimillion-dollar Wall Street bank. He sent the promoters to try to raise part of the capital from Raskob, a clear indication of how successfully Roosevelt could compartmentalize his varied activities. [9]

At the beginning of September, 1928, the future seemed to hold for

Roosevelt a combination of conservative financial activities and progressive political work. Aside from speeches in the last few weeks of the campaign, he was expecting to devote himself again to working on his legs at Warm Springs. He had almost completed his contribution to the campaign.

During the summer, politicians and newspaper editorial writers had repeatedly urged him to run for Governor of New York as a means of aiding Smith's presidential race. In answer to all of these, he wrote firm refusals. His legs had improved to the point where he was able to get about with leg braces and canes. Thanks in large part to a 25,000-dollar gift from Edsel Ford, a new enclosed pool was being constructed at Warm Springs where he would be able to work on his legs through the winter. He was only forty-six years old, and he hoped by persistent effort in another two or three years to be able to discard one of the braces and one of the canes. This, consistently, was his story, and undoubtedly he firmly believed it.

Yet the progress he was making toward walking was painfully slow. It was seven years since the infantile paralysis attack at Campobello, and he still in no real sense was able to walk. He did take a few hesitant steps unaided toward the end of September, 1928, but he was wearing braces, so this was more an achievement in balance and the swinging of hips than in the return of leg muscles. Enormous though his faith in himself was, his hope that he could ultimately get rid of one brace and one cane indicates that realistically he knew in the future he could make only small gains from long and tedious effort. Mrs. Roosevelt, looking back at 1928, feels that he had progressed about as far as he was capable.[10]

There were other excuses for staying out of the governorship race: "I have got so much tied up in the development of the Georgia Warm Springs Foundation that I have to devote a lot of time to that. . . . Also, I feel that I can help Smith more in the national field than if I were to run in the state campaign." [11]

Valid though these were, beyond and behind them was the all-important fact that Roosevelt and Howe did not think it would be politically expedient for him to run in 1928. Ernest Lindley, writing before Roosevelt became President, speculated that his position had been so secure that he did not have to become governor in order to be a serious contender for the presidential nomination: "His reputation was made; he did not particularly need another office to enhance it. In a sense he was stepping out of a broad arena into a smaller one

— one in which he would be sure to meet embarrassing problems and perhaps contract political liabilities." Roosevelt and Howe may very well have felt this, for it is hinted in some of their correspondence. However, any rapid scanning of newspapers and magazines of the period makes obvious how far Roosevelt was, in 1928, from being a commanding political personality. He was still in serious need of the governorship, for all its liabilities, as a steppingstone to the White House.[12]

Undoubtedly the most important factor was that both Roosevelt and Howe manifestly regarded 1928 as a bad political year. For Roosevelt to have gone down to defeat with Smith would have been a disastrous setback. For him to serve as Governor during continuing years of Republican prosperity might bring him to a presidential nomination in a year when he could not possibly win. Roosevelt, as his negotiations for the presidency of a trust company indicate, thought a financial crash was still no immediate likelihood. Howe once told Warren Moscow that the plan was for Roosevelt to run for governor in 1932, and for President in 1936.[13]

Whatever the combination of factors and the reasoning, Howe, Mrs. Roosevelt, and Roosevelt himself were all firmly agreed that he should resist any pressure to force him to run for governor. He stayed in Warm Springs when the state convention met in Rochester at the end of September. There followed a week-long drama of conferences, telegrams, and telephone calls.

New York Democratic leaders emphatically believed that Roosevelt would greatly strengthen the ticket, for he was that remarkable combination: an upstate Protestant with a name that still had all the glamor among Republicans with which Theodore Roosevelt had endowed it; co-operative with Tammany, but not a member of the organization — hence free from its stigma; on Prohibition an adept fence-sitter. With the campaign centering, in New York State as elsewhere, on a "rum, Romanism and Tammany" debate, Roosevelt could obviously lure more upstate votes than any other candidate Tammany would accept.[14]

At the same time, upstate and Tammany Democrats refused to compromise upon any other candidate for governor. The upstate possibilities seemed too weak or too Dry; the most likely New York City contender, Herbert Lehman, was unacceptable to the Syracuse leader. They claimed that without Roosevelt, it would be impossible for Smith to carry New York, and without its forty-five electoral

Mr. and Mrs. Roosevelt on the south porch at Hyde Park, on the occasion of the Dutchess County Historical Society Pilgrimage, September 16, 1927

FDR and V. Warwick Halsey at Warm Springs, November, 1928

votes he could not win the election, that therefore the election of Smith depended upon running Roosevelt for Governor. They negotiated with Howe, who had to concede that they should not try to agree on a best substitute until Roosevelt declared himself because of his health — definitely, finally, and irrevocably out. Howe wired all this to Roosevelt, adding that his own conviction Roosevelt should not run was stronger than ever, and that Mrs. Roosevelt agreed with him. He warned further: THERE IS NO ANSWER TO THE HEALTH PLEA BUT ANY OTHER REASON WILL BE OVERRULED BY THE GOVERNOR HIMSELF.[15]

It was significant that with Roosevelt being pressured in Warm Springs, Howe was in New York City where he could attempt to put iron in Roosevelt's refusals only by frequent and frantic telegraphing. Roosevelt did not send the definite, final, and irrevocable refusal; Howe dared only issue weaker statements in New York. He warned Roosevelt the next day that Olvany was planning to send a man to Warm Springs; that unless Roosevelt got a definite wire to New York immediately he would have no peace. At the same time, the Democratic leaders started on a new tack: if Roosevelt's health was preventing him from running, they would nominate a lieutenant governor who would take over for Roosevelt during the legislative sessions. Howe retorted that Roosevelt was "not the kind of man who would take a job and leave it to an understudy." And to Roosevelt, who still had not issued the statement, he wired, "I do not believe your running will really induce anyone to vote for Al but on contrary some of your friends now voting for Al for your sake will vote for you and not for Al." If there were to be a goat, Howe added, why should it not be Senator Wagner? Two days later on September 28, Howe warned Roosevelt that a direct statement was the only way to stop the persistent belief that he was jockeying for the nomination. He recommended Roosevelt give it to the New York *Sun*. Roosevelt did so, and, for the time being, his refusal was generally accepted.[16]

Nevertheless, the pressure upon Roosevelt continued. Al Smith, before he headed west on a September campaign trip, instructed Boss Ed Flynn of the Bronx, who was particularly friendly with Roosevelt, to work on him over the telephone. Flynn made a series of calls, during which he first received a frosty negative, later less emphatic ones. After each of them, he telephoned Smith to report on the progress; Smith each time egged him on. Soon Flynn felt he detected a weakness in Roosevelt's fortifications. Roosevelt did not, as Howe had recommended, stick solely to the health reason for not running; he told Flynn of his financial worry. When Flynn told Smith that this seemed to be the crucial factor, Smith said to tell Roosevelt that could be straightened out somehow. On September 29, from Milwaukee, Smith telephoned Mrs. Roosevelt. She was reluctant to intervene, feeling as always that basically her husband must make his own political decisions, and recommended to Smith that he call her husband. Roosevelt was firm with Smith, and parried all of his arguments until Smith concluded, "Well, you're the doctor," and hung up.[17]

Roosevelt was still so strongly opposed to running that, in what for him was a most unusual move, he wired Smith a confirmation of his telephone message. There were two compelling reasons why he could not run, he declared — his health and the fact that he was not really needed. "Your own record in New York State is so clear to the voters," he told Smith, "that you will carry the State regardless of who is nominated and my nomination would make no difference to your success on the national ticket." [18]

This telegram awaited Smith when he arrived at the Hotel Seneca in Rochester on the morning of October 1. Smith was ready at this point to take Roosevelt's "No" as final, but the dejected Tammany and upstate leaders refused to agree on any other candidate. They felt, as Will Rogers reported, that Roosevelt was about two hundred thousand votes stronger than any other candidate. They were desperately in need of those votes, because the Republicans had just nominated the short, aggressive, and spectacular attorney general of the state, Albert Ottinger, who could run on a splendid record of fighting loan sharks, fraudulent dealers in stocks, food profiteers, and dealers in impure food products. In addition, he was the first Jew to be nominated for the governorship, an important asset in New York City. He had the air of a practical man, and thus in some respects the same sort of appeal as Smith. At once there was much talk of ticket-splitting — of voting for "Al and Al." [19]

After a morning conference on the fifth floor of the Seneca Hotel, Smith again tried to get Roosevelt on the telephone. Roosevelt, fearing perhaps that he would capitulate to the renewed pleading, refused to take the call.* He was exercising in the pool at Warm Springs,

---

* For the moment, Howe had FDR's ear. He had wired FDR the day before that "the real pressure comes from leaders and jobholders who feel you will be elected Governor and patronage made secure . . . Governor [Smith] does not really consider your nomination vital to his personal success." [20]

but had word sent back that he was on a picnic; from that was going to a meeting somewhere unspecified, and would not be back all day. When he came back from the picnic there were more telephone messages and wires, including one from his daughter Anna, "Go ahead and take it." The next day he replied, "You ought to be spanked." He dressed and left for Manchester, Georgia, ten miles away, to make an address.

At a second conference in the afternoon, the Democratic leaders again balked at settling on a substitute nominee. When James A. Farley moved that they choose Roosevelt and that Smith telephone him again, the resolution was unanimously adopted. By this time, too, Smith had new bait for his hook. He had conferred with Lehman, an administrator of proved excellence, who agreed to run for lieutenant governor and to take over state affairs during whatever periods Roosevelt needed to be in Warm Springs; and with Raskob, who promised if necessary to underwrite Roosevelt's investment in Warm Springs.[21]

Next, Smith saw Mrs. Roosevelt, to persuade her to get her husband on the phone, since he would not answer Smith's calls. "I feel that this is Mr. Roosevelt's own problem," she calmly told Smith and the leaders. "I am not trying to influence him either way." Her own position was embarrassing; she had come to the convention with some reluctance, since, as she wrote her husband in advance, "They feel so strongly about your running and even good explanations can be made to sound foolish." Finally she agreed to get him on the phone, but firmly refused to try to influence him.[22]

By this time, Roosevelt was on the platform of the school auditorium in Manchester, Georgia — three flights up, with the aisles jammed to the door in the rear. A messenger came with the word that Mrs. Roosevelt was on the telephone at the corner drugstore. He could not have gone then if he had wished to do so, and when further messages came later while he was speaking, he perversely extended his remarks for an extra half-hour. They were in praise of Smith.

Finally Roosevelt came to the drugstore telephone. He gleefully told his wife that he had been purposely staying away from it all day, and would not have answered then except that she was calling. She was late for the midnight train to New York (she had to begin teaching at Todhunter School the following morning), so she handed the telephone to Smith, left hastily, and did not know her husband's decision until the next day.[23]

According to Ernest K. Lindley, this is what happened:*

Raskob came on the telephone. Something went wrong with the connection.

"It's no use, John," Roosevelt at last shouted, "I can't hear you." Then came a roar — Alfred E. Smith.

He could not be understood. The operator broke in with the message that as soon as Mr. Roosevelt could get back to Warm Springs he should go to the telephone in the hotel. Often the connection to Warm Springs is bad, but when he got there a half-hour later, Raskob's quiet voice came through clear as a bell. He pleaded with him to take the nomination as a service to the party nationally. Roosevelt presented other objections — he had to see the Warm Springs Foundation through, for example.

"Damn the Foundation," replied Raskob. "We'll take care of it."

Smith took over the job and in his own graphic manner described the predicament of the party and the unanimous demand of the leaders for his nomination.

"You take the nomination, Frank," he continued in substance. "You can make a couple of radio speeches and you'll be elected. Then you can go back to Warm Springs. After you have made your inaugural speech and sent your message to the Legislature you can go back there again for a couple of months. You know the Legislature doesn't do very much during the first two months. Then you can come back and get your thirty days' bills out and go back for the rest of the summer."

Roosevelt's response to this was a leaf from Al Smith: "Don't hand me that boloney."

Lehman came on to say that he would take the nomination for Lieutenant-Governor and spell him whenever he asked. Then Smith came back: "Frank, I told you I wasn't going to put this on a personal basis, but I've got to." He asked him as a personal favor to let him present his name to the convention. Roosevelt tried to reassure Smith that the political outlook was not as gloomy as he made it appear.

"I just want to ask you one more question," said Smith finally. "If those fellows nominate you to-morrow and adjourn, will you refuse to run?"

Roosevelt hesitated. They all knew why he did not want to re-enter public life yet, he said, and he could not sanction the pre-

* From *Franklin D. Roosevelt: A Career in Progressive Democracy*, by Ernest K. Lindley, copyright 1931, used by special permission of the publishers, The Bobbs-Merrill Company, Inc.

sentation of his name. What he would do if he were actually nominated, he didn't know.

"All right," said Smith, "I won't ask you any more questions."

Colonel Lehman came back on the telephone, and in another minute the whole matter was arranged.[24]

The following afternoon, Mayor Jimmy Walker of New York City put up Roosevelt's name at the convention. It was almost an anticlimax. The delegates cheered for only two minutes, and there was none of the usual noise-making and parading. But they nominated him by acclamation, and returned home delighted with their handiwork. Reporters showed Smith dispatches from Atlanta stating that Roosevelt did not intend to run. Smith answered, "The convention has the consent of Mr. Roosevelt to do what it did. It nominated him and he will run." And so Roosevelt did.[25]

Mrs. Roosevelt telegraphed, REGRET THAT YOU HAD TO ACCEPT BUT KNOW THAT YOU FELT IT OBLIGATORY. To the newspapermen she explained, "In the end you have to do what your friends want you to. There comes to every man, if he is wanted, the feeling that there is almost an obligation to return the confidence shown [in] him." For the moment, Howe could not be so philosophical, for he feared that Roosevelt was heading into a political disaster comparable to the 1914 senatorial debacle. MESS IS NO NAME FOR IT, he wired tartly, and: FOR ONCE I HAVE NO ADVICE TO GIVE.[26]

At this, perhaps the most critical point in his career, Roosevelt had discarded Howe's counsel and taken a bold move entirely on his own. Whether, as Ed Flynn and others have speculated, it was because of Raskob's promise of financial aid, it is impossible to say. Roosevelt had two hundred thousand dollars invested in Warm Springs, secured by a promissory note. The amount was a financial worry to him, and he knew he would have to face a serious drop in income if he became governor. Over the telephone he had told Raskob the sum he was worrying about amounted to 250,000 dollars; Raskob not only offered to loan it to him for a year, but promptly afterward sent him a check for the amount. After Roosevelt returned to New York, he handed the check back to Raskob with his thanks, explaining that it was sufficient to know that Raskob was willing to underwrite him. He did not at any time borrow from Raskob. However, during the next three years Raskob was one of the largest benefactors of Warm Springs, giving a total of over 100,000 dollars.[27]

During approximately the same period, the Warm Springs Foundation repaid about 70,000 dollars on Roosevelt's loan.* It would be hard to establish any significant relationship between Raskob's gifts and Roosevelt's personal finances. Raskob gave an initial 25,000 dollars in October, 1928; Roosevelt did not receive the first installment on his note — approximately 14,000 dollars — until January 31, 1930. He had long since planned the fund raising drive for Warm Springs which took place in 1929; Raskob could be considered no more than an especially generous contributor. While Raskob had a keen political interest in Roosevelt during the campaign of 1928, thereafter, while Raskob was still making gifts, politically they began rapidly to drift poles apart. Yet as late as the campaign of 1950, Republicans in New York cited these contributions as justification for some highly intricate financial transactions involving their own leaders.[28]

There is every probability that neither Raskob's generous offer of money, nor Lehman's of time, had half as much to do with Roosevelt's decision as the lure of political adventure.

---

* FDR, incidentally, between 1928 and 1933 made deductions in the loan totaling 18,500 dollars, which, considering the size of his estate, was a very substantial contribution.

CHAPTER XVI

Victory by a Hair's Breadth

> If I could keep on campaigning twelve months longer,
> I'd throw away my canes.
> — FDR, speech at Yonkers, *November 1, 1928.*

THE CAMPAIGN for the governorship was an exciting and happy four weeks for Roosevelt. It put him fully and completely back into the game he loved best.

The news of his nomination shifted the betting odds that Smith would carry New York from even money to six to five; Ottinger, who had been an overwhelming favorite to win the governorship, was given no more than an even chance. Democratic newspapers carried jubilant editorials, and at the outset even Republican newspapers complimented Roosevelt on his idealism and high personal stature. Two papers which were supporting Hoover for President, the New York *Sun* and the *Telegraph*, endorsed Roosevelt for governor. Letters of congratulations began to arrive in numbers at the Democratic headquarters — strangely enough, in a ratio of five from Republicans to each one from a Democrat.[1]

Obviously, Roosevelt was a serious menace to the Republican chances of sweeping the state. Although Republican papers spoke well of him as a person, almost immediately they devised a tactic to try to prevent a switch to him. They portrayed him as a dangerously ill man, warned by his physicians not to run, forced by Smith's ambition to risk perhaps even his life. "There is something both pathetic and pitiless in the 'drafting' of Franklin D. Roosevelt by Alfred E. Smith," the New York *Post* asserted. "Stung by the Presidential bee, driven by the necessity of getting New York's electoral vote, the Governor made this most loyal of friends agree to serve his ambition at a price that is beyond all reason. . . . But even [Roosevelt's] own friends, out of love for him, will hesitate to vote for him now."[2] To top this, rumors spread rapidly that for his health's sake Roosevelt, if elected, would have to resign and permit Lehman to become Governor. Others suggested, since Roosevelt had been so active an advocate of a Democratic foreign policy, that if Smith were elected, he would resign the governorship to become Secretary of State.[3]

These stories were so persistent that Roosevelt had to issue flat denials. On October 5, he declared:

> I am amazed to hear that efforts are being made to make it appear that I have been "sacrificed" by Governor Smith to further his own election and that my friends should vote against me to prevent such "sacrifice." . . .
>
> I do not believe that appeals to personal friendship should form any part of a plea to the electorate. But if I did, my own appeal would be: "Not only do I want my friends to vote for me, but if they are my real friends I ask them to get as many other people to vote for me as possible."
>
> I trust this statement will eliminate this particular bit of nonsense from the campaign from the very beginning.[4]

As for Roosevelt's supposed physical inability to serve as Governor, Al Smith had already laughed it out of the way at a press conference on the train from Rochester to Albany. He pointed out that Roosevelt was mentally as competent as ever in his life, that he lacked muscular control in his legs: "But the answer to that is that a Governor does not have to be an acrobat. We do not elect him for his ability to do a double back-flip or a handspring." [5]

Imaginative Republican editorials soon dropped the subject because the leaders of their party feared it might backfire. Roosevelt would be difficult enough to try to defeat on questions of state policies without stirring up sympathy over his physical condition. Since he was alluring to well-educated Republicans, it was safer to undercut him as too intellectual, too impractical an idealist for the rough-and-tough mundane political world. "Mr. Roosevelt's campaign portrait needs to be 'roughened up,' " the New York *Post* declared patronizingly. "He is, as we say, an extremely nice man. He has the habit and diction of a reformer. The practical political worker would shy off him." Throughout the campaign, Republican newspapers tried to make the stereotype stick. The *Post* referred to one of his speeches as breathing "that loftiness of inspiration which makes so much of Mr. Roosevelt's campaigning almost too exalted for human nature's daily food." His listeners, it reported on another occasion, had to struggle with his "$80 words." And it wound up sarcastically at the end of the campaign, "We must . . . plunk our ballots for Roosevelt because he has a sort of halo as a nonpractical politician in politics." [6]

The one effective way in which Roosevelt could combat these stereo-
types — that he was an invalid, and that he was hopelessly intellectual —
was to display himself frequently and vigorously to the electorate of
New York. He rose to the challenge flamboyantly, and was the more
spectacular because newspapers had predicted he could do so little.
They had reported on the day of his nomination that, because of his
frail physique, party leaders promised that he need make only four or
five speeches. Mrs. Roosevelt, they predicted, would stump the state
for him. She replied when they queried her, "You don't have to cross
bridges until you come to them." She did not have to cross this particular bridge at all. She was already carrying the main office burden
under Mrs. Moskowitz for the women's division of the party. Her
husband felt she was obligated to remain there, although it absorbed
almost all of her time and attention. Consequently she took almost no
part in his race for the governorship.[7]

"I had planned beforehand to spend three weeks preceding November 6 in a speaking campaign in New York State in behalf of the
national ticket," Roosevelt told reporters on October 3, "and the
nomination at Rochester does not mean change in this plan. At
the same time I shall say a few kind words in behalf of the state
ticket." [8]

In New York City, Howe worked immediately to help set up an
effective campaign organization. An ardent Smith man, Van Namee,
became campaign manager. Two wealthy industrialists helped serve
as money raisers: William Woodin of the American Car and Foundry
Company and Arthur Curtiss James, a railroad and copper magnate,
who like Raskob was a Republican. State Athletic Commissioner Jim
Farley, who had recently become secretary of the state committee,
threw his time and energy magnificently into the state campaign in
an effort to bring moribund upstate Democratic organizations back to
life. A gifted, versatile, and exceedingly hard-working young lawyer
who had helped gather speech material for Smith, Samuel I. Rosenman, was delegated to perform the same function for Roosevelt on his
campaign trips. The plan of campaign was simple. While Tammany
took care of New York City, Roosevelt would concentrate upon upstate New York where he must pick up large quantities of Republican
and independent votes if he were to win. Among the registered voters
in the state, the Republicans outnumbered the Democrats by more
than 200,000. Roosevelt drew up an itinerary parallel to that he had
followed in the state during the campaign of 1920. It would take him

to twice as many towns as his opponent Ottinger, and to more than Smith had visited in any state campaign since his first in 1918.[9]

On his way to New York to begin his campaign, Roosevelt warmed up with several speeches in Georgia, and one in Cleveland, in which he made forthright attacks upon bigotry. Upon his arrival at Hyde Park on October 7, he received the folksy sort of homecoming he so keenly relished. The Dutchess County Democratic Committee was by no means as co-operative as Howe wished,* but they had assembled about 200 neighbors to meet Roosevelt at the station and accompany him to his home in an automobile parade. Poughkeepsie the next day was bedecked with flags when he drove through — escorted by the mayor, a band, and twenty automobiles. Recognizing that most of the celebrants were honoring a Dutchess County man, not hailing their choice for Governor, he told them that he would try to be a "good Governor for all and not only a good Governor for the Democrats." [11]

When he arrived at his headquarters at the Biltmore Hotel in New York City later that day, his physical condition was of keen interest to the newspapermen. He entered, one of them wrote:

> . . . supporting himself on the left side with a crutch and on the right side with a cane, and leaning forward on these supports so that he could draw his feet after him in a sliding gait.
>
> "How's the state of your optimism?" he was asked.
>
> "Fine," he said. "I told them in Poughkeepsie this afternoon that most people who are nominated for the Governorship have to run, but obviously I am not in condition to run, and therefore I am counting on my friends all over the state to make it possible for me to walk in." [12]

In talking to the press, he referred to his physical condition in joking terms like these. When he was asked if he would go South after each session of the legislature, he made a laughing reference to the fact that the acting governor would be a banker: "I can leave the combination of my safe to Colonel Lehman, knowing that it will be in safe hands." He

---

* While Tom Lynch and John E. Mack loyally worked for FDR, several of the Dutchess County Democratic supporters, jealous because of the way FDR had long overshadowed them, supposedly were caught wearing Hoover buttons. Howe wrote FDR: "My own remedy for the lackadaisical attitude of your own county committee would be to invite them to a picnic on the banks of Wappingers Creek. By offering them free food or free anything, they would all come and then I would invite them, one by one, to a private conference behind the bushes and drop them into the creek with a weight about their neck like so many sick kittens. This would do a world of good for the Democratic party in your county — think it over." [10]

shifted to a more serious vein when he talked about his campaign plans. "I have been a critic of people who ran for State office on national issues," he said, explaining that he would not expect the people to elect him on that basis. Nevertheless, he said he would let nothing stand in the way of his support of Smith in all of his speeches. Consequently he expected to divide most of them into two sections, one on state and the other on national problems.[13]

From the outset, Roosevelt focused attention upon the issues, and kept it there. The audience hardly noticed his legs when he rose to deliver his acceptance address in New York City on October 16; the only evidence of his difficulty was the cane upon which he slightly leaned. His clear succinct talk, in which he outlined four main state issues, held their attention and admiration. The State of New York, he told them, was "committed to the principle of progressive government. Under magnificent leadership we have first aroused public interest, and then have obtained public approval for a program of governmental improvement which has few parallels in any similar period of time." To continue the work of Governor Smith, he pledged reforms in court procedure, and in state and local administration, aid to farmers, and power development. The only really controversial point was that concerning power, where he was pledging himself to continue the Smith policy of state control and development of waterpower sites. These issues set the basic tone of the campaign, but Roosevelt was in no hurry to elaborate upon them.[14]

The following morning, October 17, Roosevelt crossed on the ferry to Hoboken, and took an Erie Railroad train for Binghamton. Rosenman, loaded down with red Manila envelopes containing campaign material, sorted out according to subject matter, met him for the first time. A zealous Al Smith liberal, Rosenman expected to find working for Roosevelt a letdown:

> This man was different — different in bearing, in speech, in personality. He was cordial, but not gruffly so. He spoke impeccable English with a cultured accent and inflection. He was obviously not the self-made man risen from city streets; he was the country squire, dressed carelessly — soft collar, loose-fitting tweed suit, well-used felt hat. He was friendly, but there was about his bearing an unspoken dignity which held off any undue familiarity.
>
> I had heard stories of his being something of a playboy and idler, of his weakness and ineffectiveness. That was the kind of

man I had expected to meet. But the broad jaw and upthrust chin, the piercing, flashing eyes, the firm hands — they did not fit the description.[15]

For the first three days, Roosevelt ignored Rosenman's Manila envelopes and the issues of the acceptance address. Instead, as he traveled through the southern tier of New York counties — a stronghold of both Republicanism and Ku Klux Klan sentiment — he concentrated upon lambasting bigots. Ottinger had opened his campaign at Binghamton the day before by calling upon the voters to "Hooverize" the election; Roosevelt, making his first major address there, attacked the anti-Catholic sentiment, and predicted the day would come when education would eliminate "this vile thing that is hanging over our heads in this Presidential election." [16]

As he traveled westward through the Republican territory, Roosevelt developed a routine. He was unperturbed by the pictures of Hoover in almost every window and the correspondingly lukewarm attitude of the small crowds that greeted him, as he stopped at Bath, Corning, Hornell, Wellsville, Olean, Salamanca and other towns. At each stop, he pulled himself to his feet in the back of his automobile, snapped his braces to hold himself upright, and in an ingratiating manner launched into a short speech. The formula, according to the New York *Herald Tribune*, was "a few words of fulsome praise for Alfred E. Smith, a reference to his last call in the town . . . an allusion to himself as 'an upstate farmer too,' a description of the campaign as one of reactionaryism versus progressivism and an invitation to the crowd to take a look and judge for itself the state of his health." Whenever he asked the crowd if he looked like a sick man, everyone would laugh. Then he would sit down again, greet local Democrats with a warm smile and handshake, and, nodding enthusiastic appreciation, listen to their reports of progress.* Thence to the next town.[17]

Roosevelt's energetic stumping was serving at least to convince newspapermen as well as his audiences that he was in magnificent health. After four days, one of the reporters wrote that Roosevelt was in better condition than anyone else in his party. His advisers were none too

---

* Frances Perkins, watching him pour his charm on a rather dreary group of Utica Democratic leaders, contrasted it with the way in which he would turn his back on bores when he was in the state senate in 1911. He was no longer physically capable of walking away, but, more than that, he had learned the politicians' knack of winning the loyalty of these nondescript people by making them feel important. The technique was so fascinating to him that the practice of it undoubtedly kept him from being bored.

happy, however, for obviously he was not setting the voters on fire. He seemed to be engaged in a rather quixotic campaign for Al Smith, to the neglect of himself and state matters. Rosenman, who was beginning to wonder if he were excess baggage, received a wire from one of the state leaders, TELL THE CANDIDATE THAT HE IS NOT RUNNING FOR PRESIDENT BUT FOR GOVERNOR, AND TELL HIM TO STICK TO STATE ISSUES.[18]

It was not necessary for Rosenman to show the telegram to the candidate, for at that point Roosevelt abruptly shifted his type of campaign. He returned to the theme of his acceptance talk, and in address after address developed pungently and lengthily one or another of the state issues. He not only set Rosenman to digging into the red Manila folders, but had him draft speeches as well — something new for Rosenman, since Smith spoke from topics jotted on the back of envelopes. Roosevelt himself carefully worked over these drafts, adding dramatic and colorful touches. The result was a series of major addresses which not only brought a strong response from the audience, but gave the newspapermen an interesting, clearcut story every day.[19]

At Buffalo, Roosevelt talked on labor. He described how the Republican leaders had, in a pigeonhole somewhere, "a large envelope, soiled, worn, bearing a date that goes back twenty-five or thirty years," bearing the words "Promises to labor," but nowhere did they have "a single page bearing the title 'Promises kept.'" In contrast, he underscored the Democratic pledges: an eight-hour day and forty-eight hour week for women and children, study of the problem of old-age pensions, establishment of an advisory minimum wage board for women and children, extension of the Workmen's Compensation Act, liberalization of laws relating to the welfare of mothers and children, and passage of a law declaring that labor of human beings was not a commodity. Thus, he succeeded in calling attention dramatically to a program far more attractive to New York labor than what the Republicans were offering them.[20]

At Rochester on October 22, he talked in similar vivid fashion about the Democratic humanitarian program — education, child welfare, and aid to crippled children and widowed mothers. He admitted that he himself was intensely interested in the care of crippled children: "I suppose that people readily will recognize that I myself furnish a perfectly good example of what can be done by the right kind of care. I dislike to use this personal example, but it happens to fit. . . . By personal good fortune I was able to get the very best kind of care, and the result of having the right kind of care is that today I am on my feet." * What private means had done for Roosevelt, state aid could do for countless others, and in terms of the usefulness to society of restoring these cripples to active life, the cost would be relatively small.[21]

While Rosenman watched with admiration, Roosevelt dictated onto the beginning of an intricate and rather dull draft of a speech on public power policy, which he delivered at Syracuse: "This is history and a sermon on the subject of water power, and I preach from the Old Testament. The text is 'Thou shalt not steal.' " He did not make very clear in his speech where he would draw the line between public and private development of power, but he did leave the strong implication that his opponent, Ottinger, as state attorney general had been conniving with the big utilities in a power grab.† Ottinger was stung to reply, "One could refer to the good book also and remind [Roosevelt]: 'Thou shalt not bear false witness against thy neighbor.' " But Ottinger's involved explanations were feeble compared with Roosevelt's blunt attack.[22]

This technique in Roosevelt's speeches brought him such fine headlines in comparison with Ottinger's that a few days later he mocked his opponent by telling an audience that he chose to speak on only one subject at a time, "instead of making the forty-three promises that Mr. Ottinger made, which include everything from abolition of taxes to the abolition of flat tires." Roosevelt laughed when, after he left this meeting, he found that his own automobile had a flat tire.[23]

As Roosevelt moved eastward through the Mohawk Valley, his campaign rapidly picked up momentum. Both his personality and his issues were beginning to attract support, while Ottinger showed signs of floundering. The crowds were so large in Republican Fonda, Gloversville, and Amsterdam, which he had been scheduled to speed through, that he had to speak in each, and barely reached Schenectady in time for his major address there. The next day, when he returned to Hyde Park, he pointed out that in many places on his tour the audiences were twice as large as the total number of registered Democrats in the town — proof that he was at least being heard by quantities of Republicans and independents.[24]

---

* FDR added: "And while I shall not vouch for the mental side of it, I am quite certain that from the physical point of view I am quite capable of going to Albany and staying there two years."

† This charge incensed Owen D. Young of General Electric, but fortunately for FDR, he confined himself to a private protest while he continued his public support.

At the same time, Roosevelt's campaign headquarters in New York City functioned highly effectively. Howe wrote Roosevelt on October 22 that although they had been operating for only a week, they had already raised a hundred thousand dollars, which was two thirds of the amount Smith had obtained during his entire campaign two years previously. The portents were all so favorable that Howe abandoned his early gloom. "I am horribly afraid you are going to be elected," he declared. Gamblers in New York City shared the same feeling. Before Roosevelt's nomination the betting odds were two to one on Ottinger; by the end of October they were almost two to one in Roosevelt's favor, and the consensus was that Roosevelt had a better chance than Smith to carry the state.[25]

By the close of the campaign, Roosevelt had countered Ottinger's stand as a foe of corruption by establishing himself as the heir to Smith's record as the proponent of efficient government. On welfare legislation, aid to agriculture and labor, and power policy, he appealed to many voters who preferred his position to Ottinger's more conservative one. On Prohibition, he had sufficiently endorsed Al Smith's Wet stand to retain city support, yet had acted Dry enough not to alienate upstate voters. Since Ottinger engaged in similar fence-sitting, between the two of them they fairly well eliminated Prohibition as an important campaign issue.

The religious issue remained. It served as an excellent excuse for political dirty work on a local level. Many upstate Protestant voters were ready to vote for Hoover and Roosevelt to avoid voting for a Catholic and a Jew. At the same time, in the cities the "Al and Al" movement continued, complicated by considerable sentiment in favor of voting for Ottinger for governor and Lehman for lieutenant governor. A former Corporation Counsel for New York City addressed a letter to Roosevelt attacking both groups of bigots. Roosevelt replied, for publication, "I am very certain from what I know of the Jewish citizens of this State that they will in casting their ballots consider first the fitness of the candidates and the great issues involved." [26]

Much of the skulduggery involved nothing more or less than old political quarrels. Ottinger had made himself unpopular with many of the Republican leaders; Hamilton Ward of Buffalo, who was running for attorney general on the Republican ticket, detested him, and was ready to swap Roosevelt votes for Ward votes. Altogether, the switching and counter-switching became too complex for accurate analysis, but the overall pattern was clear. After a survey, John Godfrey Saxe predicted to Roosevelt on November 2 that he would run many thousands of votes ahead of the ticket upstate, and behind in New York City.[27]

On one point Roosevelt could be sure. He had proved almost beyond question his physical vigor, and had re-established himself with the public as an exciting campaigner. When he joined Smith for a final campaign tour of New York City on November 2, he received tremendous acclaim. As he entered a hall in Brooklyn that evening, despite a half-dozen protecting policemen the crowd surged around him as he began the difficult descent down an emergency ramp to the stage. Between the problem of clearing a path for him and his painful means of walking, it took him five minutes to get to his place on the platform; for the entire time the crowd stood waving flags and cheering. In Yorkville, he had to submit to the indignity (which he hated above all else) of being carried up the fire escape and in a back window into the hall, but he entered unruffled and smiling. He was able to laugh at the "chain of gossip" still circulating that if elected he would resign in favor of Lehman. From October 17 to the end of the campaign, he traveled 1300 miles and made nearly fifty speeches, a schedule so arduous that it had worn out most of those with him. His health was obviously so radiant that at the beginning of November he joked to an audience, "I am getting many letters . . . asking me to confirm whether or not it is expected that I would not live after January 1." He commented repeatedly that he was "feeling much fitter and walking much better than when the campaign began."[28]

This spectacular display of physical endurance helped endow him with glamor. Even his battered brown campaign hat became of public interest. At the end of the campaign, when he was seated in an armchair in front of a woodfire in his library at Hyde Park, one of those who had accompanied him on the campaign inquired about its health.

"Don't you make fun of that old hat of mine," Roosevelt replied. "I have a peculiar superstition about hats. Back in 1910, when I was running for the State Senate I tried to catch a Lexington Avenue street car one day. I missed my grip and my head hit the pavement. The old brown felt hat saved me from serious injury and I got off with a slight cut. Since that time I have had a feeling that old brown felt hats bring me good luck."

Someone interjected, "You don't mean to say that is the same hat you wore in 1910?"

"My family says it is," Roosevelt replied, "but I say that the hat I'm wearing in this campaign dates back only to 1920. When I began this campaign, my family began a campaign to make me buy a new hat, but I told them nothing doing until after the 6th of November. Even then it will take a struggle to make me abandon the hat I have now." [29]

Shortly before eleven o'clock on the morning of November 6, Roosevelt arrived at the Hyde Park Town Hall to cast his ballot. A group of newspaper and newsreel photographers prepared to take his picture as he left the car. "No movies of me getting out of the machine, boys," he requested, and they turned away until he had alighted, adjusted his braces, and taken a pose. Then they went to work. [30]

That evening, Roosevelt went to the campaign headquarters at the Biltmore Hotel in New York City to listen to the election returns. It was another black night for the Democrats, for from the outset it was obvious that Smith was being defeated, and as the hours passed the dimensions of the avalanche grew. Even in New York State, he was losing by about a hundred thousand votes. Roosevelt seemed certain to be buried in the landslide. Howe was brokenhearted, but Roosevelt remained in good spirits with his jaw firm.

At one point, Roosevelt handed over to Sam Rosenman some bad returns from some upstate districts, and remarked that he thought the politicians there were up to their old tricks — delaying the returns until they saw how many votes they would have to stuff into the boxes to overcome Roosevelt's New York City lead. The same thought occurred to Ed Flynn. Enough good returns began to come in from scattered districts so that when Flynn drew up a projection of votes at one o'clock, it gave Roosevelt a narrow victory. It was all-important to speed up the slow returns from upstate in order to prevent the election from being stolen. Roosevelt, according to Rosenman, picked up the telephone and called sheriff after sheriff in the slow counties demanding that they see the ballots were not tampered with. Flynn issued a statement to the press at two in the morning, charging the Republicans with perpetrating fraud by delaying the ballot, and announcing that the Democrats were immediately sending a hundred lawyers into these counties. Roosevelt took advantage of his position as vice president of Fidelity and Deposit to wire the agents in every county to call the county clerk in their districts and wire Roosevelt a verification of the returns. To a large extent this was bluff, as Rosenman and Flynn have labeled it, but it did speed up the returns. In the ensuing days, a number of Democratic lawyers were sent into the doubtful counties to prevent frauds.* Jim Farley did not dare go to bed for three days, he was so afraid there would be an upset. The result was a hairline finish for Roosevelt: he received 2,130,193 votes to Ottinger's 2,104,629. He was elected by a margin of twenty-five thousand votes out of a total of four and a quarter million.[32]

By the day after the election, Roosevelt was certain that he had pulled through, but expressed keen disappointment over the defeat of Smith. It was more than a week before Ottinger conceded. "I have just heard from my *late* opponent," Roosevelt wrote Archie Roosevelt on November 19, "and since he is going to permit me to go to Albany, it looks like I will have a man sized job on my hands for the next two years." By the time Roosevelt wrote the letter, he was already at Warm Springs with state Democratic leaders, making plans for the governorship.[33]

And in New York City, Howe was already looking still further ahead. He was preparing form letters to go out over Roosevelt's signature to Democratic leaders all over the country, to county chairmen, convention delegates, and Congressmen, asking their opinion as to how the party could be reorganized and strengthened, and inviting them to attend his inaugural in Albany. In familiar terms, Roosevelt himself wrote the top leaders, "Certainly we must not talk candidates, but must concentrate on publicity of the right kind." [34]

Democrats all over the country were already discussing candidates. Despite Roosevelt's narrow margin of victory (during the next two years among friends he called himself the "one-half of one per cent governor"), the man who had become the most talked-about possibility was the Governor Elect of New York. On his trip to Georgia, he was hailed everywhere as the 1932 standard-bearer.[35]

Sumner Welles summed up the sentiment:

"The one bright spot on this extremely dark horizon is the fact that you have been elected Governor of New York. . . . Newspapers, politicians, and private citizens, many of whom do not know you and

* Ed Flynn in his reminiscences described this maneuver as completely bluff, forgetting that lawyers were actually sent. They investigated the returns in a number of counties. Although they found no serious errors (the gain for FDR was only 640 votes in 14 counties), Van Namee felt that the four thousand dollars they cost was an excellent investment against frauds in the next election.[31]

have not heard you, are all saying that if there is one man who can hold the Democratic party together and prevent schism which now exists from becoming permanent, that man is yourself. More power to you!" [36]

Will Rogers, sending a check for Warm Springs, put it more simply: "I don't know how the Party can ever get through paying you, You pulled them out of a tough hole." [37]

Roosevelt's ordeal was over. He had not regained the use of his legs, but what was far more important he had mastered his physical handicap and made a spectacular political comeback. Within a year, the nation was to be crippled with the paralysis of depression. Within four, a majority of its voters would turn to Roosevelt to lead the nation out of its ordeal.

Bibliographical Note

Like its predecessor, this volume is primarily based on the large quantities of manuscripts in the Franklin D. Roosevelt Library at Hyde Park. These are described in the bibliographical note in *Franklin D. Roosevelt: The Apprenticeship*, and in the annual reports of the Library. Almost all of them for the period 1918–1928 are open for research, except those relating to Roosevelt's personal finances. A most useful publication of the Library, Robert L. Jacoby, compiler, *Calendar of the Speeches and Other Published Statements of Franklin D. Roosevelt 1910–1920* (Hyde Park, N.Y., 1952) covers speech manuscripts and many clippings in scrapbooks.

Additional manuscript materials are in the Secretary of the Navy files in the National Archives (referred to by file number in the notes), and in the Josephus Daniels, Woodrow Wilson, and Thomas J. Walsh papers at the Library of Congress.

Again I have made use of the tape-recorded reminiscences of Hyde Park persons who knew Roosevelt, gathered by the National Park Service under the supervision of George A. Palmer. Interviews obtained by the Oral History Project at Columbia University, under the direction of Allan Nevins, contain much significant information. I have quoted from those with Arthur Krock, Langdon P. Marvin, and Marley F. Hay with their permission and that of the directors of the Project. In addition, several people have generously helped me directly through interviews and correspondence. Among them were: Renah H. Camalier, Josephus Daniels, John M. Hancock, Herbert Hoover, Jesse H. Jones, Charles McCarthy, John E. Mack, Frances Perkins, Helene Phillibert, Eleanor Roosevelt, Harold R. Stark, Lela Stiles, Joseph K. Taussig, Archibald D. Turnbull, and Henry Braid Wilson.

Roosevelt's family letters and the logbook of the *Larooco* are in *F.D.R., His Personal Letters,* Elliott Roosevelt, editor. (3 vols., New York, 1947–1950.) I am grateful to Duell, Sloan and Pearce for permission to quote from them. Some of Roosevelt's reminiscences and a selection of his more important addresses in the campaign of 1928 are in *The Public Papers and Addresses of Franklin D. Roosevelt,* Samuel I. Rosenman, editor. (13 vols., New York, 1938–1950.)

In addition to the general works on Roosevelt and those applying to his work as Assistant Secretary of the Navy, which are described in *The Apprenticeship,* the following have been especially useful:

On the campaign of 1920: James M. Cox, *Journey Through My Years* (New York, 1946), and Thomas A. Bailey, *Woodrow Wilson and the Great Betrayal* (New York, 1945). On the campaign of 1924: Kenneth C. McKay, *The Progressive Movement of 1924* (New York, 1947). On the campaign of 1928: Samuel I. Rosenman's brilliant *Working With Roosevelt* (New York, 1952) and Roy V. Peel and Thomas C. Donnelly, *The 1928 Campaign. An Analysis* (New York, 1931).

On politics in the 1920's: Ernest K. Lindley's almost contemporary but very perceptive *Franklin D. Roosevelt, A Career in Progressive Democracy* (Indianapolis, 1931); Harold F. Gosnell, *Champion Campaigner, Franklin D. Roosevelt* (New York, 1952); James A. Farley, *Behind the Ballots* (New York, 1939); Edward J. Flynn, *You're the Boss* (New York, 1947); Warren Moscow, *Politics in the Empire State* (New York, 1948); and Karl Schriftgiesser, *This Was Normalcy* (Boston, 1948).

On Roosevelt's illness and struggle to recover: Turnley Walker, *Roosevelt and the Warm Springs Story* (New York, 1953) is the definitive account, written with remarkable insight by a former patient at Warm Springs. There is also much of interest in Earle Looker, *This Man Roosevelt* (New York, 1932). John Gunther, *Roosevelt in Retrospect, A Profile in History* (New York, 1950) contains important medical details.

On Roosevelt's personal life: Eleanor Roosevelt's *This Is My Story* (New York, 1937) and *This I Remember* (New York, 1949) are indispensable. There are additional insights and anecdotes in Anna Roosevelt's reminiscences of her father in *Woman,* vol. 23, July, August, 1949. Roosevelt's columns and the story behind them are in Donald Scott Carmichael, editor, *F.D.R. Columnist, The Uncollected Columns of Franklin D. Roosevelt* (Chicago, 1947).

On Roosevelt as a businessman, Alva Johnston, "Mr. Roosevelt as a Businessman," *Saturday Evening Post,* vol. 209 (October 31, 1936) and John T. Flynn, *Country Squire in the White House* (New York, 1940) are critical. On foreign policy, William L. Neumann, "Franklin D. Roosevelt and Japan, 1913–1933," *Pacific Historical Review,* May, 1953, 22: 143–153, is a detailed analysis.

Other books and articles are cited in the footnotes.

Acknowledgments

I am deeply indebted to a number of persons who have generously contributed their time and thought. Those who have aided me with interviews or by answering queries I have already mentioned. Richard N. Current labored long and hard over the manuscript, making valuable suggestions which have improved both the style and contents. Others who greatly to my benefit have read all or part of the manuscript or proofs are: Spencer Brodney, Jonathan Daniels, Charles C. Griffin, Oscar Handlin, Richard Hofstadter, Arthur Schlesinger, Jr., George and Roberta Scouffas, and Gertrude Almy Slichter. Among those who have given me significant aid are: Bernard Bellush, Arthur E. Bestor, Jr., Frederick C. Dietz, John Garraty, Horace Samuel Merrill, and Kenneth M. Stampp. With characteristic generosity, the late Charles A. Beard gave me his notes on Roosevelt's speeches in the 1920 campaign. At every stage I have benefited from the suggestions and skillful editing of Ned Bradford and the staff of Little, Brown and Company.

The staffs of numerous libraries have helped me immeasurably. My debt to that at the Roosevelt Library has grown still larger, especially to Herman Kahn, the Director, Edgar Nixon, George Roach, Margaret Suckley, William J. Nichols, Carl Spicer, Robert Jacoby, Raymond Corry, and Betty Hirscher. I also wish to thank George A. Palmer of the National Park Service, Wendell H. Link of the Oral History Project, Katherine Brand of the Library of Congress, Carl Lokke of the National Archives, and Icko Iben and Nelle M. Signor of the University of Illinois Library.

I wish to express my appreciation to the Roosevelt Library for permission to quote from manuscripts and to reproduce the photographs in this volume, and to the Daniels family, Lodge family, and Jesse H. Jones for permission to quote from manuscripts.

The Research Board of the University of Illinois has generously provided me with grants which have materially aided in the preparation of this book. For research assistance, I am grateful to Gertrude Almy Slichter, George Lobdell, William R. Thompson, and Ian C. C. Graham; for typing, to Margaret Mulligan, Kathleen M. Schaub, and Joan and Dale Henning. Finally, for aid and encouragement of every sort, I owe much to my wife, Elisabeth Margo Freidel.

Notes

Abbreviations

FDR: Franklin D. Roosevelt
ER: Eleanor Roosevelt
DNC: Democratic National Committee manuscripts, Roosevelt Library, Hyde Park, New York
FDR mss: Franklin D. Roosevelt manuscripts, Roosevelt Library. Unless otherwise attributed, all manuscripts cited are from this collection.
GO: Governor's Official file, New York State archives, Albany, New York
GP: Governor's Personal file, Roosevelt Library
Howe mss.: Louis McHenry Howe papers, Roosevelt Library
OHP: Oral History Project, Columbia University
PL: Elliott Roosevelt, editor, *F.D.R., His Personal Letters* (3 vols., New York, 1947–1950)
PPA: Samuel I. Rosenman, editor, *The Public Papers and Addresses of Franklin D. Roosevelt* (13 vols., New York, 1938–1950). These are cited by year covered by volume; i.e., PPA, 1936, etc.
PPF: President's Personal File, Roosevelt Library

CHAPTER I

Spectator at Paris

1. ER, *This Is My Story* (New York, 1937), 275; Jeremiah A. Walsh, "My Eleventh Trip on a Transport, U.S.S. *George Washington*," January 3, 5, 6, 1919; PL, 2:445. The copy of *The Education of Henry Adams* is in the Roosevelt Library.
2. PL, 2:445; ER, *This Is My Story*, 275; FDR to Josephus Daniels, January 9, 1919, Daniels mss.
3. FDR, penciled note, November 12, 1918.
4. FDR to Daniels, November 14, 1918, Daniels mss.
5. Daniels to FDR, December 4, 1918.
6. Daniels to FDR, December 7, 1918; FDR to Daniels, copy in FDR's hand, December 7, 1918.
7. Daniels to William S. Sims and William S. Benson, penciled draft in

FDR's hand, Daniels mss.; Opnav to Benson, cablegram received December 18, 1918; ER, *op. cit.*, 273; Daniels to FDR, December 24, 1918, travel orders; Navy News Bureau, press statement, December 30, 1918.

8. Walsh, "My Eleventh Trip," January 1, 1919; ER, *op. cit.*, 274.

9. Walsh, "My Eleventh Trip," January 10, 1919.

10. FDR to Daniels, January 13, 1919; PL, 2:448-449.

11. Daniels to FDR, January 13, 1919; Daniels, Diary, January 13, 1919; Daniels, autobiography, draft, Daniels mss.; Daniels, *Wilson Era* (Chapel Hill, N.C., 1946), 2:256-257.

12. PL, 2:454-455, *et passim*.

13. Eva A. Frank to FDR, March 7, 1919; PL, 2:454-455; Thomas A. Bailey, *Woodrow Wilson and the Lost Peace* (New York, 1944), 119, 308-309.

14. Benson to Daniels, January 23, 1919, Daniel mss.; interview with John M. Hancock, April 14, 1948.

15. Interview with Hancock, April 14, 1948; Hancock to FDR, February 14, 1919; FDR to Daniels, January 28, 1919.

16. FDR to Daniels, February 21, 1919; notes in Daniels mss.; FDR to Daniels, April 10, 1919, compiled by Hancock; George P. Auld to FDR, January 27, 1919, in FDR to Daniels, April 10, 1919.

17. Frederick Hobbes Allen to FDR, August 16, 1932, Box 692, Democratic National Committee mss.

18. PL, 2:453; FDR to Daniels, January 15, 28, 1919; FDR to André Tardieu, January 25, February 14, 1919; agreement of February 13, 1919, all in FDR to Daniels, April 10, 1919; FDR to David W. Todd, January 17, 1919; Interview with Hancock, April 14, 1948.

19. Interview with Hancock, April 14, 1948.

20. FDR to S. Orsini, January 21, 1919, in FDR to Daniels, April 10, 1919.

21. FDR to Daniels, January 20, two cablegrams, and subsequent correspondence in FDR to Daniels, April 10, 1919; PL, 2:456-457, places the dates of the conferences as January 16 and 17, 1919; interview with Hancock, April 14, 1948.

22. ER, *op. cit.*, 280-283; FDR to A. T. Long, January 21, 1919; FDR, "Transcript of Rough Notes Made on Automobile Trip from Paris to Boulogne, January 19, 1919"; PL, 2:460-462.

23. Two confidential sources.

24. FDR to Daniels, January 28, April 10, 1919.

25. PL, 2:464-465.

26. London *Mail*, January 23, 1919; London *Telegraph*, January 30, 1919.

27. ER, *op. cit.*, 285; FDR, unfinished letter to Sara Delano Roosevelt and Anna Roosevelt, February 10, 1919; FDR to George H. Thornton, March 24, 1943, PPF 2160.

28. W. W. Hoffman to FDR, February 2, 1919; FDR to Hoffman, March 5, 1919; Albert of Belgium to FDR, February 2, 1919.

29. Elmira *Herald*, March 4, 1919; interview with ER, May 1, 1948; Ernest K. Lindley, *Franklin D. Roosevelt* (Indianapolis, 1931), 182; PL, 3:1323-1325.

30. FDR to Sims, February 10, 1919; PL, 2:456.

31. William D. Leahy, *I was There* (New York, 1950), 301.
32. ER, *op. cit.*, 288; interview with ER, May 1, 1948; FDR to Collector of the Port of New York, February 23, 1918.
33. ER, *op. cit.*, 289; interview with ER, May 1, 1948.
34. Boston *Traveler*, February 24, 1919; Ray Stannard Baker, *American Chronicle* (New York, 1945), 470; Daniels, *Wilson Era*, 2:256.
35. ER, *op. cit.*, 292–293.

CHAPTER II

Toward More Efficient Government

1. FDR, address at Harvard Union, February 26, 1920.
2. Clipping, FDR scrapbook; FDR, address before New York Bar Association, March 8, 1919, transcript.
3. *Loc. cit.*, Washington *Star*, March 2, 1919; Rochester *Post Express*, December 27, 1919; FDR to Warren Delano Robbins, October 17, 1919; Mrs. Charles Hamlin, "Some Memories of Franklin D. Roosevelt," ms. in FDR Library.
4. New York *Tribune*, March 2, 1919.
5. Eva A. Frank wrote FDR, March 7, 1919: "At the League of Nations luncheon last Saturday, you spoke with contempt of those who refused to believe that Russian soviets had nationalized women. If it is true, let us speak of it sorrowfully not exultantly – as we would speak of our own average lynchings."
6. Syracuse *Herald*, July 4, 1919; FDR, address at Worcester Polytechnical Institute, June 25, 1919.
7. FDR, address at New York Bar Association, March 8, 1919; Newburgh *Journal*, January 14, 1920; FDR, address at Worcester Polytechnical Institute, June 25, 1919. See also Philadelphia *Inquirer*, March 29, 1919; Philadelphia *North American*, March 29, 1919; Baltimore *Star*, June 10, 1919; FDR, address before State Convention of American Legion, Rochester, N. Y., October 11, 1919; FDR to Herbert O. Dunn, January 24, 1920; FDR to Langdon Marvin, April 19, 1919; Washington *Post*, May 28, 1919.
8. Newburgh *Journal*, January 14, 1920.
9. FDR to State Department, April 26, 1919. This letter was prepared by OP 56.
10. William V. Pratt to FDR, March 31, 1919.
11. W. B. Caperton to Chief of Naval Operations, May 12, 1919; FDR to R. E. Coontz, undated; Coontz to FDR, November 10, 1919. FDR also publicly commended Admiral Caperton's visits to South American Republics. *Army and Navy Register*, April 19, 1919; Robert Lansing to FDR, August 22, 1919.
12. Navy News Bureau Release, March 7, 1919; Daniels, *Wilson Era*, 2:389–429, 575–581.
13. Daniels to FDR, March 13, 14, 23, 1919.
14. FDR to Daniels, April 3, 1919; *Army and Navy Register*, March 29, 1919.

15. FDR to Walter Camp, March 24, 1919; Boston *Transcript*, April 4, 1919; FDR to John McIlhenny, May 23, 1919.

16. FDR to Livingston Davis, January 23, 1920.

17. FDR to Davis, April 26, 1919.

18. FDR to Herbert Bayard Swope, September 30, 1919.

19. Boston *Transcript*, May 5, 1919. FDR backed water on part of his proposal when protests came in from areas where the ships were moored at the time. See M. H. Gulesian and others to FDR, May 6, 1919; and several similar interchanges of correspondence. New York *Mail*, April 3, 1919; Washington *Star*, April 25, 1919; Washington *Post*, August 13, 1919; FDR to Richard Derby, August 15, 1919.

20. New York *Times*, May 15, 1919; PL, 2:472.

21. Benjamin F. Hutchinson to Louis McHenry Howe, September 27, 1920. FDR to Harry Garfield, March 24, 1919, Navy News Bureau Release.

22. New York *Times*, March 26, 1919; FDR to A. Lawrence Lowell, April 12, 1919.

23. New York *Tribune*, March 28, 1919.

24. FDR, address before Democratic Women's Club, Syracuse, N. Y., clipping in FDR scrapbook; FDR address at Knights of Columbus dinner, Philadelphia, November 11, 1919, clippings in FDR scrapbook. See also Philadelphia *Record*, November 12, 1919; Boston *Traveler*, April 12, 1920.

25. Ms. article on Roosevelt and labor, possibly by Howe, 1920; FDR, address before Democratic Women's Club, Syracuse, N. Y., summer, 1919; FDR, address at Knights of Columbus dinner, Philadelphia, November 11, 1919.

26. New York *Sun*, May 13, 1919.

27. FDR, Memorandum for Thomas G. Frothingham, "Jellicoe's American Visit," c. 1925–1926. Among books in the FDR Library is an inscribed copy of Jellicoe, *The Grand Fleet 1914–1916* (New York, 1919), with FDR's notation, "Autographed for me by Lord Jellicoe on the occasion of his coming to our house in Washington, Jan. 5, 1920, on his Tour around the World." See also Hamlin, "Memories."

28. FDR, address at New York Aeronautical Exposition, March 8, 1919; John M. Hancock to FDR, February 15, 1919; New York *Times*, April 14, 1919; New York *World*, April 14, 1919.

29. New York *Times*, June 29, 1919.

30. U. S. 71st Congress, 2nd Sess., Senate Committee on Interstate Commerce, *Hearings . . . on S6* (Washington, 1930), 1089. For a corroborating statement by Cary T. Grayson, see *ibid.*, 1175.

31. W. G. H. Bullard, "Some Facts Connected with the Past and Present Radio Situation in the United States," United States Naval Institute, *Proceedings*, October, 1923, 49:1629–1631; New York *Times*, July 24, 1919.

32. FDR to Owen D. Young, April 4, 1919, in *Hearings on S6*, 1108; FDR to Daniels, December 5, 1929.

33. FDR to Daniels, December 5, 1929. FDR described the proposal in a press conference, October 1, 1919 – transcript in Daniels mss.; New York *Times*, July 25, 1919; Bullard, "Radio Situation," 1632–1633.

34. FDR to Kermit Roosevelt, May 9, 1924.

35. Clippings, FDR scrapbook, June 3, 1919.
36. PL, 2:479–480; FDR to Joseph R. Hamlem, July 26, 1919.
37. FDR address before Knights of Columbus Peace Convention, August 6, 1919.
38. New York *Commercial*, July 19, 1919. See also D. D. Glassford to FDR, July 3, 15, 1919.
39. Clipping, FDR scrapbook.
40. FDR to Samuel S. Robison, December 30, 1919; Robison to FDR, December 27, 1919.
41. New York *Times*, September 12, 1919; Paul Tuckerman to FDR, November 19, 1919; A. Lawrence Lowell to Tuckerman, October 27, 1919; "Boston Police Strike and Harvard Teachers: Utterances of Harold J. Laski," *School and Society*, November 1, 1919, 10:524–525; FDR to Paul Tuckerman, November 20, 1919.
42. U. S. 66th Congress, 1st Sess., House of Representatives, Select Committee on Budget, *Hearings* . . . (Washington, 1919), 620; Daniels to FDR, March 29, 1938, Daniels mss.
43. FDR, Budget Statement, October 1, 1919, FDR mss.; also in *Hearings*, 649–677. See also FDR, "Is the Federal Government Necessarily Inefficient?" [1924], FDR mss.
44. Clipping, Poughkeepsie newspaper, July, 1919, FDR scrapbook; Rochester *Post Express*, December 27, 1919.
45. Carter Glass to FDR, September 3, 1919.
46. FDR, address at Harvard Union, February 26, 1920, transcript; FDR, "Is the Federal Government Necessarily Inefficient?" [1924], FDR mss.; Rochester *Post Express*, December 27, 1919.

CHAPTER III

A Search for Scapegoats

1. FDR to Daniels, March 1, 1921, Daniels mss.
2. Interview with Daniels, May 29, 1947; confidential interviews and correspondence.
3. Joseph E. Pogue, *The Economics of Petroleum* (New York, 1921), 3, 4, 10, 11, 59, cited in Searle Franklin Charles, "American Oil Companies and Mexican Relations 1919–1921," unpublished Master's Thesis, University of Wisconsin, 1947; David Potter to Chief of Naval Operations, June 27, 1921, Naval Archives, 13668-744:18; Samuel McGowan, Paymaster General of the Navy, to all Suppliers of Navy Fuel Oil, February 27, 1920, copy in contract No. 2853, Naval Archives, 26801-1222; FDR, Address at New Bedford, Mass., September 16, 1920.
4. U. S. 66th Congress, 3rd Sess., House of Representatives, Subcommittee . . . in charge of Naval Appropriations Bill for 1922, *Hearing* . . . (Washington, 1921), 915–919, 940–941; Daniels, diary, April 3, 1920, Daniels mss.; contract with Cochrane, Harper, and Company for furnishing Petroleum, Fuel Oil and Gasoline, May 4, 1920, Contract No. 2853, Naval

Archives, 26801-1222; Memorandum for Assistant Secretary Woodbury, December 10, 1920.

5. Interview with Josephus Daniels, May 29, 1947; L. Howland to Elliot C. Brown, May 13, 1920, copy, enclosed in Brown to FDR, May 19, 1920; J. P. Morgan to FDR, February 6, 1920; PL, 2:485.

6. Cochrane, Harper and Company contract with Regiones Petroliferas Mexicanas, Sociedad Anonima, February 14, 1919, Naval Archives, 26801-1222; Henry Morgenthau, Jr., to FDR, January 28, 1920.

7. Daniels, diary, April 3, 10, 15, 27, 1920, Daniels mss; Herman Kahn to the present writer, October 8, 1951.

8. FDR, address at New Bedford, Mass., September 16, 1920.

9. Letter to the present writer, confidential source.

10. FDR to Daniels, March 14, 1919; FDR to Mrs. William S. Sims, December 24, 1919; Sims to FDR, August 26, 1919.

11. U. S. 66th Congress, 2nd Sess., Senate, Subcommittee of the Committee on Naval Affairs, Hearings . . . Naval Investigation (Washington, 1921), 1–9; Ralph D. Paine to FDR, January 21, 1920; FDR to Livingston Davis, January 23, 1920.

12. FDR address at Brooklyn Academy of Music, February 1, 1920; clipping of AP dispatch, FDR scrapbook.

13. See for example Daniels, diary, February 21, 1920, Daniels mss.

14. FDR to Daniels, February 24, 1922.

15. Ladies' Home Journal, June 1917, 34:25; New York Sun, June 14, 1919.

16. San Diego Union, April 14, 1914; Daniels, diary, March 17, 1919, Daniels mss.; interview with Daniels, May 29, 1947; T. M. Osborne to FDR, March 9, 14, July 17, 23, August 17, 1917; FDR to Osborne, July 19, 1917.

17. Osborne to FDR, March 4, 1918; Frank Tannenbaum, Osborne of Sing Sing (Chapel Hill, N. C., 1933), 278–279.

18. Interview with Daniels, May 29, 1947; see also Daniels, Wilson Era, 1:317–318.

19. New York Times, October 30, 1947.

20. Joseph K. Taussig to the present writer, November 18, 1946. There is a letter from a prisoner to this purport in the Naval Archives, 26288-944; Army and Navy Journal, January 3, 10, 1920.

21. FDR to the Editor, Army and Navy Journal, January 21, 1920, originally drafted January 17, and subsequently revised at the suggestion of the Judge Advocate General to leave out more explicit statements concerning offenses; Judge Advocate General to FDR, January 22, 1920; all in Naval Archives, 26288-944. See also Army and Navy Journal, January 24, 1920.

22. Taussig to Secretary of the Navy, February 4, 1920, enclosing Chief of Bureau of Navigation (written by Taussig) to Secretary of the Navy, May 26, 1919.

23. Daniels, diary, February 14, 1920. See also entries for February 11, 13, 1920, Daniels mss.; FDR to Taussig, February 28, 1920; Taussig to FDR, March 1, 1920, Naval Archives, 26288-944; FDR to Taussig, February 17, 1920; Taussig to FDR, February 18, 1920; interview with Taussig, June 7, 1947.

24. Taussig to FDR, March 1, 1920, Naval Archives, 26288-944; Taussig to Daniels, February 4, 1920.

25. FDR to Osborne, January 2, 12, 1920; Osborne to FDR, January 3, 10, 1920; Daniels to FDR, January 2, 1920; Daniels to Thomas S. Butler, January 9, 1920, Daniels mss.; Butler to Daniels, January 7, 1920; Daniels to FDR, January 9, 1920, Naval Archives, 26288-944; H. O. Dunn to FDR, January 16, 29, 1920; FDR to Dunn, January 19, 24, 1920; FDR to Dunn, January 19, 1920; Osborne to FDR, February 9, 1920, Naval Archives, 26288-944; Chamberlain, *Osborne*, 379–380; transcript of press conference, January 17, 1920; Charles Magnus Charlton to FDR, January 16, 1920; L. S. Adams to FDR, January 20, 1920, Naval Archives, 26288-944; Board Appointed to Report on General Conditions at the Portsmouth Naval Prison to Secretary of the Navy, February 26, 1920, Naval Archives, 26288-944; Osborne to Daniels, November 26, 1919, enclosing "Assistant Secretary Roosevelt's Memorandum Regarding Future Policy of Naval Prison, Navy Yard, Portsmouth, N. H."

26. Osborne to Daniels, March 2, 1920, Naval Archives, 26288-944; Daniels, diary, March 3, 1920, Daniels mss.; Albion W. Wadhams to FDR, March 20, 1920; New York *Herald*, July 21, 1921.

27. Daniels, *Wilson Era*, 2:187; there are extensive files on prevention and elimination of vice in the Daniels mss.; Boston *Traveler*, June 22, 1917.

28. R. H. Leigh to Daniels, May 7, 1920; FDR to Daniels, March 1, 1921, Daniels mss.; FDR, statement of July 18, 1921; FDR to Thomas Washington, February 3, 1921; U. S. 67th Congress, 1st Sess., Senate, Committee on Naval Affairs, *Alleged Immoral Conditions at Newport (R.I.) Naval Training Station* (Washington, 1921); Senator William H. King, "Statement and Preliminary Minority Report," typewritten copy in FDR mss. There are quantities of detailed material on this, some of it in FDR's own hand, in the FDR mss., and Naval Archives, 26288-944. For FDR's public statement, see PL, 2:514–522.

29. Anne H. Sims to ER, December 7, 1919; interview with Taussig, June 7, 1947; John R. Rathom to FDR, January 22, 1920; FDR to Rathom, undated, in Navy News Bureau Release, January 26, 1920, Naval Archives, 26288-944.

30. W. H. Bagley to Daniels, February 10, 1920; FDR to Carroll S. Page, February 16, 1920, Naval Archives, 26288-944; FDR to Page, February 16, 1920; see also FDR to Frank Foxcroft, February 28, 1920.

31. FDR to Robert L. O'Brien, February 12, 1920, Naval Archives, 26288-944.

32. Dunn to FDR, March 3, 1920; FDR to Langdon P. Marvin, May 13, 1920; FDR to Dunn, May 28, 1920, Naval Archives, 26288-944.

33. New York *Times*, March 27, 1920; see also Philadelphia *Public Ledger*, March 12, 1920.

34. Clipping of editorial on Boston address in FDR scrapbook; Brooklyn *Standard Union*, April 25, 1920; Daniels, diary, April 21, 1920, Daniels mss.; FDR to Livingston Davis, May 15, 1920.

35. FDR to Davis, May 15, 1920.

36. FDR to Frederick Hale, June 4, 1920, Navy Press Release; New

York *Times*, June 5, 1920; *Hearings*, 3391-3393; Daniels, diary, June 5, 1920, Daniels mss.; PL, 3:723.

37. See, for example, a long and rather favorable editorial in the New York *Times*, June 7, 1920; New York *Tribune*, June 27, 1920.

38. PL, 2:xvii-xviii.

CHAPTER IV

Candidate for Vice President

1. New York *Sun*, May 22, 1919.

2. FDR to William Wallace Witherspoon, May 23, 1919; New York *Times*, June 25, 1920.

3. John F. King to FDR, June 10, 1919; FDR to King, June 20, 1919.

4. FDR to H. Morton Merriman, March 5, 1919; FDR to Sidney Gunn, December 29, 1925.

5. Chicago *Tribune*, May 30, 1919.

6. FDR, address at Banquet of Democratic National Committee, Chicago, May 29, 1919.

7. Grand Rapids, Michigan, *Herald*, June 1, 1919.

8. George E. Miller to William K. Kelsey, May 31, 1919. See also New York *World*, May 31, 1919; Fort Plain, New York, *Standard*, July 3, 1919.

9. Rush Jones in Boston newspaper clipping, FDR scrapbook; New York *Herald*, November 26, 1919; FDR to Henry M. Heymann, December 2, November 26, 1919; Heymann to FDR, November 29, 1919.

10. FDR to Chester C. Platt, December 15, 1919.

11. Hamlin, "Memories."

12. FDR to Stephen Beach Cooke, March 5, 1920.

13. FDR to John K. Sague, March 1, 1920; yet on March 5, 1920, FDR wrote McAdoo suggesting they have a talk.

14. FDR to Hugh Gibson, January 2, 1920. See also Fancher M. Hopkins to FDR, March 10, 1920, and FDR to Hoover, March 12, 1920.

15. New York *Times*, January 25, 1920, February 9, 18, 24, 26, 29, 1920, March 19, 1920.

16. Herbert Hoover to the present writer, October 11, 1951.

17. PL, 3:193-194.

18. Hoover to the present writer, September 24, 1951.

19. Milton McKaye, "The Governor," *New Yorker*, August 22, 1931, 7:28-29; interview with ER, May 1, 1948.

20. *Republican Campaign Textbook*, 1920, 83.

21. Daniels, diary, February 22, 1920, Daniels mss.

22. New York *Telegraph*, May 3, 1920; Homer Cummings to Joseph Tumulty, February 12, 1920; A. Mitchell Palmer to Wilson, March 1, 1920; FDR to Tumulty, April 20, 1920; John J. McMullen to Wilson, May 4, 1920, Wilson mss.

23. FDR to Sague, March 1, 1920; FDR to William Gorham Rice, May 6, 1920; FDR to A. M. Scriber, May 6, 1920.

24. FDR to William W. Farley, May 3, 1920; mimeographed copies sent

to all delegates with covering letter dated May 4, 1920; New York *Times*, May 6, 1920; Albany *Knickerbocker Press*, May 6, 1920.

25. FDR to Lathrop Brown, May 18, 1920; FDR to Hiram R. Wood, May 13, 1920.

26. New York *Times*, May 9, 1920; New York *Tribune*, May 9, 1920.

27. FDR to A. V. Wadhams, May 13, 1920.

28. Poughkeepsie *Star*, June 5, 7, 1920; FDR to ——, May 17, 1920 (form letter to county committeemen of Columbia, Dutchess, Orange, and Putnam Counties).

29. Louis B. Wehle, *Hidden Threads of History* (New York, 1953), 81–86; Wehle to FDR, July 9, 1920; A. J. Berres to FDR, June 23, 1920; Langdon P. Marvin to FDR, June 16, 1920; FDR to Marvin, June 17, 1920.

30. Daniels, diary, June 8, 1920, Daniels mss.; FDR to John E. Mack, June 10, 1920; H. T. Livingston[?] to James Gee, June 4, 1920, carbon copy in FDR mss. He suggested that the Mare Island workers arrange a luncheon in FDR's honor while he was at the convention.

31. For accounts of the convention and candidates, see Thomas A. Bailey, *Woodrow Wilson and the Great Betrayal* (New York, 1945), 315–319; James M. Cox, *Journey Through My Years* (New York, 1946), 225–233.

32. New York *Tribune*, June 27, 1920; New York *World*, July 1, 1920.

33. New York *Tribune*, June 29, 1920; Brooklyn *Eagle*, June 29, 1920.

34. H. L. Mencken, *Heathen Days, 1890–1936* (New York, 1947), 186; *Official Proceedings of the Democratic National Convention . . .* (Indianapolis, 1920), 140–141. FDR had jotted notes, but digressed from them considerably when he made the speech. They are on the back of Berres to FDR, June 23, 1920.

35. New York *Tribune*, July 3, 1920; Schenectady *Union Star*, July 2, 1920; Grenville Emmet to Marvin, July 8, 1920.

36. Albany *Times-Union*, July 7, 1920.

37. Sara Delano Roosevelt to FDR, July 8, 1920.

38. FDR to John W. Davis, July 24, 1920.

39. San Francisco *Chronicle*, July 6, 1920; Brooklyn *Standard-Union*, July 7, 1920.

40. Albany *Times-Union*, July 7, 1920.

41. Interview with John J. Fitzgerald, June 17, 1948; Palmer interview with John E. Mack, February 1, 1949; Mack in Poughkeepsie *Eagle*, July 14, 1920, and numerous newspaper accounts.

42. New York *Sun & Herald*, July 12, 1920.

43. San Francisco *Chronicle*, July 7, 1920; Cox, *Journey Through My Years*, 232.

44. Mack in Poughkeepsie *Eagle*, July 14, 1920.

45. New York *Times*, July 7, 25, 1920; Middletown *Herald*, July 6, 1920; David Lawrence in Binghamton *Sun*, July 8, 1920.

46. Interview with Fitzgerald, June 17, 1948; David Lawrence in Binghamton *Sun*, July 8, 1920; New York *Sun & Herald*, July 20, 1920.

47. FDR to Jewett P. Cain, July 28, 1920; New York *Tribune*, July 14, 1920; New York *Post*, July 14, 1920; Washington *Star*, July 7, 1920.

48. Ansberry's account in New York *Sun & Herald*, July 12, 1920; Miss Helene Phillibert told the present writer about the telephone call to the Navy Department.

49. *Proceedings of the Democratic National Convention,* 1920, 420–450.

50. Daniels to FDR, July 7, 1920; Walter Lippmann to FDR, July 8, 1920; Herbert Hoover to FDR, July 13, 1920; New York *Times*, July 7, 1920.

51. New York *Times*, July 7, 1920.

52. *Ibid.;* Brooklyn *Standard-Union*, July 7, 1920.

CHAPTER V

The First Presidential Campaign

1. FDR to Daniels, September 12, 1932, Daniels mss.

2. *Literary Digest*, July 17, 1920, 66:14; New York *Tribune*, July 8, 1920; Frank E. Gannett to FDR, July 15, 1920, enclosing long editorial; New York *Sun & Herald*, July 18, 1920; Chicago *Tribune*, August 13, 1920.

3. L. Heisler Ball to Henry Cabot Lodge, July 12, 1920; Lodge to Ball, July 15, 1920, Lodge mss.

4. For example of Rathom attacks, see the Chicago *Tribune*, August 13, 1920, which printed one as its "Editorial of the Day." New York *Times*, October 25, 26, 29, 1920; Arthur Krock interview, April, 1950, OHP.

5. Lodge to Charles S. Groves, July 26, 1920, Lodge mss.

6. Sara Delano Roosevelt to FDR, July 8, 1920; clipping, FDR scrapbook.

7. Richmond *News-Leader* cited in *Literary Digest*, July 31, 1920, 66:42; Howe to ER; ER to Howe, July 7, 1920; clippings, FDR scrapbook; ER to Charles McCarthy, August 25, 1920; ER, *This Is My Story*, 313.

8. Howe to FDR, July 7, 1920; New York *Times*, July 13, 1920; William W. Farley to FDR, July 16, 1920.

9. Cox, *Journey Through My Years*, 238; New York *Times*, July 13, 1920.

10. *Literary Digest*, July 24, 1920, 66:9.

11. New York *Times*, July 14, 15, 1920; *Journey Through My Years*, 243.

12. Claude Bowers to Cox, *Journey Through My Years*, 241–242.

13. New York *Times*, July 17, 1920; PL, 2:495; Charles S. Groves to Lodge, July 24, 1920, Lodge mss.

14. New York *Times*, July 17, 1920.

15. Wilson to FDR, July 26, 1920, Wilson mss.

16. Boston *Globe*, July 26, 1920; New York *Journal*, July 30, 1920; William Allen White to FDR, December 22, 1939.

17. Washington *Herald*, August 7, 1920; FDR to Wilson, July 23, 1920, Wilson mss; Wilson to FDR, July 26, 1920, Wilson mss.; Daniels to Wilson, August 27, 1920, enclosing draft of Wilson to FDR, Wilson mss.

18. FDR to Daniels, August 6, 1920, Daniels mss. For the full letter and Daniels reply, see PL, 2:489–491.

19. Daniels, diary, August 4, 6, 1920, Daniels mss.; New York *Times*, July 21, 1920; FDR to Ray Baker Harris, September 5, 1933; FDR to Frederick A. Delano, March 7, 1944, PPF 769.

20. Cincinnati *Enquirer*, July 17, 1920; Louisville *Times*, July 15, 1920.

21. New York *Times*, July 21, 1920; Charles Willis Thompson in New York *Times*, July 11, 1920.

22. FDR to W. Appleton Lawrence, July 24, 1920; *Literary Digest*, July 17, 1920, 66:13.

23. FDR to Ellery Sedgwick, July 31, 1920.

24. FDR to Franklin K. Lane, July 28, 1920.

25. For the entire speech, and a description of the occasion, see PL, 2:499-508.

26. Daniels, diary, August 9, 1920, Daniels mss.; New York *Post*, August 10, 1920; F. W. Taussig to FDR, August 12, 1920.

27. Edwin F. Gay to FDR, August 20, 1920.

28. Stephen Early's telegrams and letters are in the FDR mss.

29. Early to FDR, August 9, 1920.

30. Early to Howe, August 11, 1920.

31. FDR address at Chicago, August 11, 1920; PL, 2:509; FDR, address at Waukegan, Ill., press release, August 12, 1920.

32. FDR, address at St. Paul, Minn., press release, August 13, 1920; Early to Howe, August 14, 1920.

33. Early to FDR, August 16, 1920.

34. John G. Brown to FDR, August 29, 1931; FDR, address at Helena or Butte, Montana, press release, August 18, 1920. FDR gave almost the same talk at both places.

35. New York *Times*, August 19, 29, 1920.

36. New York *Herald*, October 18, 1920. See, for example, the Republican (Helena) *Montana Record-Herald*, August 18, 1920 and the Democratic Helena *Independent*, August 19, 1920; Newburgh *Journal*, January 14, 1920; *Nation*, May 23, 1928, 126:596; FDR to Oswald Garrison Villard, May 24, 1928. See also Cleveland *Press*, January 8, 1930; [Guernsey Cross?] to Editor, Cleveland *Press*, January 27, 1930, GP.

37. FDR, address at San Francisco, stenographic transcript, August 23, 1920. See also FDR, address at Portland, August 21, 1920; New York *Times*, August 23, 1920. A comparison of transcripts, of speeches, and of press releases with newspaper reports indicates that FDR's subsequent charge — that Republican newspapers in the West and the Associated Press were chronically misquoting him — does not hold water.

38. New York *Tribune*, August 20, 1920; New York *Telegraph*, August 28, 1920; Chicago *Tribune*, August 26, 1920; New York *Times*, September 3, 1920.

39. New York *Times*, September 18, 1920.

40. New York *Times*, September 18, 1920; Villard to FDR, July 7, 1920; Howe to FDR, July 13, 1920; *Literary Digest*, October 30, 1920, 67:16; Daniels, diary, September 4, 1920, Daniels mss.; FDR to Daniels, October 16, 1920. See, for example, "The Democratic Party and the Liberal Vote," *New Republic*, September 22, 1920, 24:82-83.

41. Riggs to FDR, August 16, 1920; FDR to Howe, August 16, 1920; FDR, address at Billings, Montana, press release, August 17, 1920; FDR, address at Spokane, Washington, August 21, 1920; FDR, address at Tacoma, Washington, August 21, 1920; *Nation*, July 17, 1920, 61:57; FDR, address at Centralia, Washington, August 21, 1920; FDR, address at Tacoma, Washington, August 21, 1920.

42. FDR, address at Cumberland, W. Va., October 27, 1920.

43. McCarthy to FDR, August 19, 1920; New York *Times*, September 18, 1920.

44. FDR, statement [September 6, 1920?]; FDR to Victor Blue, September 10, 1920; L. C. Probert to Daniels, August 13, 1920; Early to Howe, September 8, 1920.

45. McCarthy to FDR, October 18, 1920; McCarthy to FDR, August 27, 1920; FDR to George White, September 6, 1920; McCarthy to FDR, October 8, 1920.

46. Early reported New Hampshire lost — Early to Howe, September 12, 1920; and John Sague declared New York hopeless — Sague to Howe, September 22, 1920. See also Marvin McIntyre to McCarthy, September 21, 1920; FDR, address at Manchester, New Hampshire, September 13, 1920.

47. Interview with ER, September 3, 1952; FDR to Daniels, October 11, 1920, Daniels mss.; FDR to McCarthy, October 9, 1920; interview with Renah H. Camalier, May 28, 1948.

48. FDR, address at Cincinnati, October 16, 1920.

49. *Literary Digest*, October 30, 1920, 67:10–11; New York *Times*, October 21, 1920.

50. New York *Times*, October 12, 1920.

51. FDR, address at San Francisco, August 23, 1920.

52. *Literary Digest*, Setember 18, 1920; FDR, address at Syracuse, N. Y., September 22, 1920.

53. FDR to McCarthy, October 9, 1920.

54. Lindley, *Roosevelt*, 198.

55. FDR to James J. Montague, September 18, 1920; FDR to Joseph Tumulty, October 17, 1920; Early to Howe, August 12, 1920; Harry S. New, to Republican Speakers, mimeographed form.

56. *Literary Digest*, October 23, 1920, 67:14; McCarthy to FDR, October 8, 1920: New York *Times*, October 28, 1920.

57. FDR to Cox, October 23, 1920; Cox to FDR, October 20, 1920. See also Langdon P. Marvin interview, October, 1949, OHP.

58. FDR to Cox, October 23, 1920; FDR, final pre-election statement, October 31, 1920.

59. FDR to Calvin Coolidge, November 3, 1920; FDR statement, November 3, 1920.

60. FDR to Mathew Hale, November 6, 1920; FDR to Wehle, November 6, 1920. See also FDR to Martin Archer-Shee, November 9, 1920.

61. FDR to Ralph Hayes, November 16, 1920; Robert S. Doubleday to FDR, November 5, 1920.

62. See, for example, FDR to John P. Hume, Chairman Democratic

State Central Committee of Wisconsin, November 8, 1920; FDR to Osborne, November 17, 1920; PL, 2:514.

CHAPTER VI

Infantile Paralysis

1. PL, 2:511–513.
2. Van-Lear Black to FDR, November 10, 1920; Looker, *This Man Roosevelt*, 109; New York *Times*, August 20, 1930.
3. *National Underwriter*, March 24, 1921.
4. Newspaper clipping, 1920, FDR scrapbook.
5. New York *Times*, January 8, 1921.
6. New York *Tribune*, New York *World*, January 8, 1921.
7. FDR to Ralph Hayes, January 7, 1921; Emmet, Marvin, and Roosevelt, announcement, March 1, 1920; FDR to Gustavus A. Rogers, March 8, 1920; FDR to Felix Frankfurter, January 7, 1921.
8. George C. Gibbs to FDR, February 8, 1921; J. Fredrick Talbott to FDR, November 9, 1920; Winifred Holt to FDR, May 5, 1921; New York *Mail*, March 17, 1921; FDR to Charles V. Vickrey, January 12, 1921; FDR to Isaiah Bowman, February 3, 1921.
9. FDR to Ralph M. Easley, February 24, 1921.
10. FDR to Alfred E. Smith, November 9, 1920; FDR to Forest Luther, January 17, 1921; FDR to Osborne, January 27, 1921; James W. Gerard to FDR, March 31, 1921; FDR scrapbook, undated clipping, *c.* April, 1921; FDR to W. C. Osborn, June 20, 1921; Albany *Knickerbocker Press*, June 10, 1921; New York *Sun*, June 8, 1921.
11. FDR to E. J. Coleman, March 30, 1921.
12. FDR to A. Lawrence Lowell, April 19, 1921; FDR to Frank Gannett, May 13, 1921; FDR to Robert Goldsmith, June 30, 1921.
13. For instance, see Samuel Eliot Morison and Henry Steele Commager, *The Growth of the American Republic* (4th ed., New York, 1950), 2:500.
14. FDR to F. Della Torre, July 6, 1925.
15. PL, 2:511; Daniels, diary, December 11, 1920, Daniels mss.; E. A. Cobey, "Memorandum of Conference, November 18, 1920"; Graham Egerton to Woodbury, February 21, 1921, Naval Archives, 26801-1222; Woodbury to W. S. Benson, November 12, 1920, enclosing telegram from FDR, Naval Archives, 13668:774:9; also confidential sources.
16. New York *Times*, July 20, 1921.
17. U. S., 67th Congress, 1st Sess., Senate, Committee on Naval Affairs, *Alleged Immoral Conditions at Newport (R. I.) Naval Training Station, Report. . . .* (Washington, 1921).
18. PL, 2:517; "For the Press, Statement by Franklin D. Roosevelt . . . ," July 18, 1921, in PL, 2:519–522; FDR, statement to Senate Naval Affairs Committee, July 18, 1921, 27 longhand pages. See also Looker, *Roosevelt*, 93–100.
19. FDR to McCarthy, July 26, 1921.

20. Clipping, July 28, 1921, FDR scrapbook.
21. Ross T. McIntire, *White House Physician* (New York, 1946), 31; Marguerite A. LeHand to ER, August 23, 1921.
22. Lindley, *Roosevelt*, 201; Looker, *Roosevelt*, 110.
23. Looker, *op. cit.*, 111.
24. *Ibid.*; Anna Roosevelt, "How Polio Helped Father," *Woman*, July, 1949, 23:54.
25. Looker, *Roosevelt*, 111.
26. Looker, 111–112; Anna Roosevelt, *op. cit.*, 54; McIntire, *op. cit.*, 31, citing FDR to Dr. William Eggleston, October 11, 1924, in *Journal of the South Carolina Medical Association*, January, 1945.
27. Anna Roosevelt, *op. cit.*, 54; McIntire, *op. cit.*, 31; PL, 2:524.
28. ER, *This Is My Story*, 331–332; PL, 2:524; McIntire, *op. cit.*, 32.
29. PL, 2:525.
30. Interview with Frances Perkins, May, 1953; FDR to Bessie G. Norwalk, August 17, 1921.
31. Frederic A. Delano to ER, August 20, 1921; PL, 2:527–528; Gunther, *Roosevelt*, 225.
32. SDR to Frederic Delano, September 2 [1921].
33. PL, 2:526; Henry Noble MacCracken to FDR, August 13, 1921, with FDR notation; [Howe?] to Herbert Pell, September 12, 1921; interviews with ER, May 1, 1948, September 3, 1952.
34. New York *Times*, August 27, 1921; Lindley, *op. cit.*, 202.
35. Interview with ER, May 1, 1948; Gunther, *op. cit.*, 223; ER, *op. cit.*, 333; New York *World*, September 14, 1921, cited in Lindley, Roosevelt, 203.
36. FDR to Adolph S. Ochs, September 16, 1921.
37. Pell to FDR, October 2, 1921; FDR to Robert Goldsmith, September 22, 1921.
38. Gunther, 226.
39. Lindley, 205.
40. Gunther, 226; Daniels, *Wilson Era*, 1:131; interview with Daniels, May 29, 1947.
41. FDR to G. S. Barrow, December 8, 1921.
42. Gunther, 227; McIntire, 32.
43. Gunther, 228–229; McIntire, 32.
44. ER, 336, 338; Anna Roosevelt, 112.
45. ER, 338.
46. *Ibid.*, 339–340.
47. Lindley, 213–214.

CHAPTER VII

The Comeback Begins

1. Lindley, *Roosevelt*, 202.
2. Howe to McCarthy, January 7, 1924; McCarthy to FDR, December 29, 1920, January 19, 1921.
3. FDR to A. J. Wall, June 20, 1923; FDR to A. C. Flick, November 12,

1923, and related correspondence in Group 14. *Minutes of the Council of Appointment of New York April 4, 1778–May 3, 1779* (Hyde Park, N. Y., 1925); FDR, editor, *Records of the Town of Hyde Park, Dutchess County* (Hyde Park, 1928).

4. FDR, "Preserve the Pictures of Old Landmarks," *De Halve Maen,* April, 1923; Holland Society correspondence in Group 14.

5. Helen Wilkinson Reynolds, *Dutch Houses in the Hudson River Valley before 1776* (New York, 1929), introductory pages not numbered.

6. Lindley, *Roosevelt,* 204–205; FDR to Dr. A. L. Boyce, March 8, 1922.

7. FDR letter, June 15, 1925.

8. FDR, statement for press, [December 18, 1923]; cathedral correspondence in Group 14.

9. FDR to A. M. Fraser, December 17, 1925.

10. ER, *This Is My Story,* 323–324, 340–342, 346–347, 352; ER, *This I Remember,* 30–32; New York *Times,* April 20, 1924; interview with ER, September 3, 1952.

11. FDR to Caroline O'Day, January 28, 1922.

12. Marguerite A. LeHand to FDR, November 21, 1920. For a biographical sketch, see Grace Tully, *F. D. R. My Boss* (New York, 1949), 338–340.

13. FDR to E. Thomas Killmer, September 28, 1921; FDR to Jesse J. Graham, October 19, 1921; FDR to Hull, November 4, 1921; Charles B. Forbes to FDR, November 3, 1921; Hull to FDR, November 12, December 31, 1921.

14. FDR to Harvey G. Starkweather, December 27, 1921.

15. New York *World,* January 23, 1922; New York *Times,* May 25, 1922, quoting Chicago *Tribune;* Watertown *Times,* May 27, 1922.

16. FDR to George Albert, July 20, 1922.

17. Anna Roosevelt, "My Life with F. D. R.," *Woman,* May, 1949, 22:9.

18. Mrs. Charles Hamlin diary, after June 10, 1922.

19. FDR to Cogswell Bentley, July 12, 1924; McIntire, *White House Physician,* 32; George A. Palmer, interview with Louis Depew, January 5, 1948, transcript.

20. Gunther, *Roosevelt,* 229; interview with ER, September 3, 1952.

21. New York *Post,* June 14, 1921; Poughkeepsie *Courier,* June 19, 1921.

22. FDR to Henry A. Wallace, July 30, 1942, PPF 446; FDR to S. T. Millard, October 8, 1929, GP.

23. FDR to John W. Kean, December 8, 1923.

24. See Dutchess County files in FDR mss.; John E. Mack and J. E. Townsend to FDR, June 14, 1915; FDR to Mack, June 23, 1915; FDR to Henry Morgenthau, Jr., June 8, 1915.

25. Alfred E. Smith, *Up to Now* (New York, 1929), 228–230; Edward J. Flynn, *You're the Boss* (New York, 1947), 34–35.

26. FDR to Neal Brewster and others, June 30, 1922; New York *Times,* July 8, 1921.

27. FDR to Smith, July 28, 1922; Smith to FDR, July 24, 1922.

28. Lindley, *Roosevelt*, 219–220.
29. FDR to Smith, August 13, 1922.
30. New York *Herald*, New York *World*, August 13, 1922; Smith to FDR, August 15, 1922.
31. New York *Post*, August 16, 1922; George Foster Peabody to FDR, August 17, 1922; New York *World*, August 16, 1922; New York *Times*, August 19, 1922; FDR to Charles Jerome Edwards, August 22, 1922.
32. See Dutchess County files in FDR mss.; FDR to Democratic County Committee of Dutchess County, September 23, 1922.
33. Smith to FDR, October 9, 1922.
34. Lindley, 220; Howe to FDR, telegram, September 29, 1922; Flynn, *You're the Boss*, 35–36.
35. Royal S. Copeland to FDR, October 11, 1922; FDR to Copeland, February 23, 1931.
36. FDR to Smith, October 25, 1922; Smith, *Up to Now*, 245; FDR to George Lunn, November 9, 1922; FDR to Smith, November 9, 1922. See Roosevelt-Smith correspondence, December, 1922, and early in 1923.
37. FDR to Joseph E. Davies, November 18, 1922; Smith, *Up to Now*, 230–232.
38. FDR to Cox, December 8, 1922.
39. Turnley Walker, *Roosevelt and the Warm Springs Story* (New York, 1953), 8–9; Looker, *Roosevelt*, 113; Lindley, 207; Langdon P. Marvin interview, October, 1949, OHP.
40. Lindley, 207.
41. Interview with ER, September 3, 1952; see also ER, *This I Remember*, 68.

CHAPTER VIII

Against the Isolationist Tide

1. FDR to Cox, December 8, 1922.
2. FDR to Stansbury Hagar, January 27, 1921; Hagar to FDR, January 24, 1921; New York *Times*, March 16, 1921.
3. FDR to Woodrow Wilson, and Wilson to FDR, March 23, 1921, telegrams, Wilson mss.; FDR to Wilson, June 2, 1921, Wilson mss.; FDR to Wilson, June 29, 1921.
4. Wilson to FDR, July 4, 1921.
5. FDR to Wilson, July 7, 1921; FDR to Hamilton Holt, July 7, 1921; John R. Bolling to FDR, July 9, 1921.
6. FDR to Wilson, July 28, 1921; Bolling to FDR, August 2, 1921, Wilson mss.; Wilson to FDR, September 16, 1921, Wilson mss.; Wilson to ER, November 9, 1921, Wilson mss.
7. Wilson to FDR, January 5, April 30, 1922, Wilson mss. See also, Wilson to FDR, December 30, 1923, FDR mss.; Wilson to FDR, January 29, 1923; FDR to Wilson, April 4, 27, 1923; Bolling to FDR, April 6, 1923, Wilson mss.
8. Byron R. Newton to FDR, December 14, 1922.

9. FDR to Newton, December 20, 1922; FDR, note, February 1, 1924; FDR to John Spargo, March 17, 1924.

10. FDR to Violet M. Leroy, January 11, 1922; FDR to Edwin A. Alderman, April 25, 1923; FDR to W. G. Rice, January 5, 1928; Francis R. Bellamy to FDR, February 8, 1927.

11. George L. Radcliffe to FDR, November 17, 1923; FDR to Radcliffe, November 20, 1923; FDR to George Wickersham, April 18, 1924; Archibald Cary Coolidge to FDR, April 29, 1924; FDR to Charles W. Eliot, May 26, 1924; FDR to Livingston Davis, April 29, 1924.

12. FDR to Raymond B. Fosdick, February 10, 1927.

13. FDR to Theodore Bret, January 17, 1922.

14. FDR to George Marvin, January 29, 1924.

15. FDR, "A Plan to Preserve World Peace." The plan is reprinted in full in ER, *This I Remember*, 353–356.

16. FDR, typed initialed memorandum, January 19, 1944; ER, *op. cit.*, 24; FDR, unsigned memorandum, Quebec, September 15, 1944.

17. FDR to Thomas Amory Lee [after May 29, 1925]; FDR to George Rich, February 7, 1923; FDR, Statement on American Peace Award, [1923].

18. A. E. Jury to [American Peace Award], December 31, 1923.

19. FDR to Alfred Lucking, April 30, 1923; FDR to Irving Fisher, November 18, 1924.

20. Hamlin, "Memories," October 1, 1925.

21. FDR to S. C. G. Watkins, May 21, 1923; "Alpha," "Reparations and the Policy of Repudiation: An American View," *Foreign Affairs*, September 15, 1923, 2:55–83; FDR to George P. Auld, October 13, 1923.

22. FDR to George Marvin, September 12, October 10, 1922; Marvin to FDR, September 3, 21, 1922.

23. George Marvin to FDR, October 19, 1922; March 22, 1923.

24. FDR to George Foster Peabody, September 26, 1923.

25. FDR, "The Japs — A Habit of Mind," draft in FDR mss. See FDR, "Shall We Trust Japan?" *Asia*, July, 1923, 23:475–478, 526, 528. Also see Donald S. Carmichael, *F. D. R. Columnist* (Chicago, 1947), 56–60, for a column on the same subject written for the Macon, Ga., *Telegraph*, April 30, 1925.

26. FDR to Editor, Baltimore *Sun*, August 13, 1923.

27. FDR to J. H. Adams, August 13, 1923; FDR to George Foster Peabody, September 26, 1923.

28. FDR to Editor, Baltimore *Sun*, August 13, 1923.

29. K. K. Kawakami in Tokyo *Nichi-Nichi* (English Daily Edition) June 28, 1924, clipping enclosed in George Marvin to FDR, June 30, 1924.

30. Interview with Marley F. Hay, April, 1950, OHP.

31. FDR, Memorandum in regard to Haiti [1922].

32. *Ibid.*

33. Leonard Wood to FDR, March 30, 1922.

34. FDR to Wood, May 2, 1922.

35. Herman Kahn, at Mississippi Valley Historical Association meeting, spring, 1952.

CHAPTER IX

Businessman

1. FDR, folder penciled: "Sale of my Navy & Marine Prints & Paintings 1925"; ER, *This I Remember,* 25; interview with ER, September 3, 1952.
2. Richard E. Byrd to FDR, October 2, 1926; interview with John M. Hancock, April 14, 1948.
3. FDR to A. C. Dinkey, June 21, 1922.
4. Black to FDR, March 2, 1921; FDR, memo, January 26, 1922; FDR to Edgar A. Hamilton, March 17, 1924.
5. See FDR correspondence with Berres, 1921–1922; Berres to Howe, November 26, 1921; Howe to Berres, December 20, 1921; FDR memo to Robert S. Hart, December 2, 1924.
6. FDR to William Gibbs McAdoo, April 13, 1922.
7. Howe to George Kent Shuler, May 22, 1923.
8. FDR to Edgar A. Hamilton, January 15, 1924; John A. Griffin to FDR, September 23, 1925; FDR to Griffin, October 6, 1925, and subsequent correspondence.
9. FDR to Black, September 24, 1924; February 25 and July 25, 1928; FDR press statement, February 23, 1928.
10. Langdon P. Marvin interview, April, 1949, OHP.
11. Looker, *Roosevelt,* 114–115; Clarence DeWitt Rogers to FDR, October 30, 1925; People of the State of N. Y. Ex. Rel. N. Y., N. H. & H. Railroad Co. vs. the Village of Larchmont, box of mss. in Group 14, FDR mss.
12. Marvin interview, October, 1949, OHP.
13. FDR to Emmet, September 24, 1924.
14. Marvin interview, April, 1949, OHP.
15. FDR to Black, September 24, 1924.
16. See especially Julian Goldman to FDR, February 16, 1925, and FDR to Goldman, January 15, 1925.
17. D. Basil O'Connor to FDR, December 8, 1924.
18. FDR to Roscoe Pound, December 19, 1925.
19. *National Underwriter,* March 24, 1921; FDR to John C. Klein, July 19, 1923.
20. FDR to G. Hall Roosevelt, January 15, 1923.
21. *Ibid.*
22. Jesse H. Jones, *Fifty Billion Dollars* (New York, 1951), 263.
23. FDR to Almet Jenks, May 20, 1941, PPF 7553.
24. Fred A. Britten to Howe, September 7, 1922; Britten to FDR, September 19, 1922; Howe to Britten, July 2, 1923.
25. M. S. Martin to FDR, May 24, 1927; Harold G. Aaron to FDR, July 9, 1927; Julian Gerard to FDR, September 12, 1927; FDR to Gerard, January 27, 1928; Alva Johnston, "Mr. Roosevelt as a Businessman," *Saturday Evening Post* (October 31, 1936), 209: 64.

26. See correspondence in FDR mss., Group 14; Johnston, *op. cit.*, 64.

27. FDR to Board of Directors, Compo Bond Corporation, April 24, 1923; Boston *Financial News*, July 26, 1922; Clarence M. Sherwood to FDR, August 28, 1922; FDR to Robert Woolley, January 4, 1923; FDR to Chairman, Board of Directors, Associated Bankers Corporation, January 25, 1923; FDR to Kimball, August 23, 1923.

28. FDR to Marvin, May 30, 1923; related correspondence in FDR mss. Group 14.

29. Fred R. Andree to FDR, July 20, 1923.

30. FDR to Andree, July 31, 1923.

31. FDR to Barron G. Collier, December 11, 1922; Inter-Coastal Shipping Company file, Group 14, FDR mss.; Hudson Navigation Company file, Group 14, FDR mss.

32. New York *Times*, May 5, 1924, cited in Johnston, "Mr. Roosevelt as a Businessman," 12.

33. FDR to Kermit Roosevelt, May 9, 1924.

34. FDR to Emmet, July 26, 1921; Johnston, *op. cit.*, 64.

35. FDR to George D. Pratt, November 25, 1922; FDR to Charles Hill, January 6, 1926.

36. J. B. Shearer to FDR, January 14, 1924; Dwight L. Hoopingarner to Frederick J. Faulks, April 7, 1927; FDR to G. Hall Roosevelt, May 20, 1921.

37. Arthur P. Homer to FDR, February 10, 1922; Howe to Homer, February 23, 1922; Harold Payson to Mr. Chapin, April 30, 1923; FDR to Ensign Otis, May 1, 1924; FDR to E. H. Griswold, May 9, 1924; Leslie Clancy to FDR, April 7, 1925; Johnston, *op. cit.*, 64.

38. George Gercke to FDR, October 22, 1932, New York City file, DNC 1932; New York *World*, September 12, 1930; "Camco" Prospectus, July 23, 1928.

39. FDR to Stephen T. Early, July 31, 1940, PPF; Johnston, *op. cit.*, 12–13.

40. Gercke to FDR, October 22, 1932.

41. Chicago *Tribune*, July 7, 1934; PPA, 1934, 313.

42. FDR to Henry Morgenthau, Jr., December 6, 1928, GO; Morgenthau to FDR, December 4, 1928, GO; Johnston, *op. cit.*, 13.

43. John T. Flynn, *Country Squire in the White House* (New York, 1940), 34–35.

44. Elliott Brown to FDR, May 15, 1922.

45. George Soule, *Prosperity Decade* (New York, 1947), 170–171; Flynn, *op. cit.*, 33–34.

46. New York *Times*, June 4, 1922.

47. New York *Tribune*, May 5, 1922.

48. Buffalo *News*, June 22, 1922; FDR to Johnson Heywood, October 29, 1923.

49. New York *Times*, June 4, 1922.

50. Meeting of the Board of Governors of the American Construction Council, May 16, 1923, shorthand report.

51. Herbert Hoover to FDR, June 12, 1923.

52. New York *Times,* May 27, 1923; Richard T. Ely to FDR, May 9, 1928.

53. Meeting of the Board of Governors of the American Construction Council, May 16, 1923, shorthand report.

54. New York *Times,* June 9, 1923; Richard H. Edmonds to FDR, June 15, 1923; FDR's letter appeared in *Manufacturer's Record,* June 21, 1923, p. 63; see also New York *Times,* July 1, 1923.

55. New York *Times,* October 22, December 2, 1923.

56. FDR to D. Knickerbacker Boyd, November 20, 1923; Hoover to FDR, December 3, 1923.

57. FDR to F. W. Walker, December 4, 1923; FDR to Henry Ford, January 23, 1924; New York *Times,* December 6, 1923.

58. FDR to Ellis F. Lawrence, January 9, 1924.

59. FDR to Raymond B. Fosdick, June 17, 1926; Fosdick to FDR, June 18, 1926.

60. FDR to Albert Henderson, January 7, 1924; FDR to J. Arthur Holly, December 10, 1923; FDR to William Parmelee of the Raymond Syndicate, October 16, 1923.

61. New York *Times,* May 12, 1923; see also FDR, Semiannual statement, October 13, 1924; FDR statement, May 8–9 [1925?].

62. FDR, Semiannual statement, 1926.

63. New York *Times,* December 4, 1926; Johnston, *op. cit.,* 66.

64. FDR to Hoopingarner, March 26, 1928.

65. Interview with ER, September 3, 1952.

CHAPTER X

The Fight for the "Happy Warrior"

1. FDR to Byron R. Newton, December 20, 1922.

2. FDR, Preface to a projected book on *The Machinery of Government* [1922 or 1923?].

3. FDR to New York *World,* February 15, 1923; FDR to George Henry Payne, February 3, 1923.

4. FDR to Thomas Pendell, September 4, 1922; FDR to William Jennings Bryan, June 20, 1923.

5. FDR to McCarthy, July 24, 1923.

6. FDR to Bryan, June 20, 1923.

7. W. C. Osborn to FDR, May 14, 1923; FDR to Osborn, May, 1923; FDR to Smith, May 21, 1923; Smith to FDR, June 5, 1923, enclosing memo of June 1, 1923.

8. FDR to Edward S. Moore, June 18, 1923.

9. FDR to Abram I. Elkus, August 20, 1923.

10. FDR to John Wilber Jenkins, August 20, 1923; FDR to Daniel C. Roper, September 7, 1923; Roper to FDR, August 22, 1923; FDR to William Morton, January 17, 1924.

11. FDR to Morton, September 26, 1923; FDR to Irving Washburn, August 13, 1923; FDR to Elkus, August 20, 1923.

12. Kenneth C. MacKay, *The Progressive Movement of 1924* (New York, 1947), 102 *et passim;* FDR to John Wilber Jenkins, August 20, 1923.

13. Thomas J. Walsh to William Gibbs McAdoo, April 3, 1924, Walsh mss.

14. See, for example, Thomas J. Walsh to Mark Sullivan, July 25, 1927, Walsh mss.

15. FDR to David S. Hawkins, March 22, 1924.

16. Howe to FDR, February 6, 1924.

17. Howe to FDR, February 25, 1924.

18. FDR to John F. McLaughlin, April 22, 1924.

19. FDR to Marjorie D. MacCracken, May 13, 1924.

20. Lindley, *Roosevelt,* 221.

21. New York *Post,* January 23, 1924; FDR to H. J. Adamson, January 28, 1924.

22. FDR to L. W. Arnett, November 27, 1923; see correspondence with Charles McCarthy and R. H. Camalier; Camalier to Howe, May 12, 1924.

23. Howe to FDR, February 14, 1924.

24. Howe to Thomas Mott Osborne, April 1, 1924.

25. Lindley, *op. cit.,* 221.

26. *Ibid.,* 222.

27. James A. Farley to Al Smith, May 2, 1924; Farley to FDR, May 1, 1924.

28. FDR to James A. Farley, May 28, 1924.

29. FDR to Daniels, May 26, 1924.

30. FDR to McAdoo, May 19, 1924.

31. FDR to Monta C. Burt, June 3, 1924.

32. Lippmann to FDR, May 9, 1924; FDR to Lippmann, May 26, 1924; Edna T. Rockey to FDR, May 14, 1924; anonymous letter to FDR, May 26, 1924.

33. FDR to A. Mitchell Palmer, May 29, 1924; Palmer to FDR, June 11, 1924.

34. Baltimore *Sun,* May 5, 1924, clipping in FDR mss.; FDR, "Smith — Public Servant," *Outlook,* June 25, 1924, 137:309–311; FDR to Marjorie D. MacCracken, May 13, 1924; FDR to Henry R. Micks, May 9, 1924.

35. FDR to Joseph C. Drum, May 17, 1924.

36. FDR to Marc W. Cole, August 5, 1924.

37. Thomas E. Cashman to FDR, June 2, 1924; FDR to Royal S. Copeland, June 3, 1924; FDR to James Norris, June 10, 1924.

38. Sloane Gordon to FDR, May 26, 1924; FDR to La Follette, June 3, 9, 1924.

39. Joseph Johnson to FDR, May 21, 1924; Howe to FDR, May 13, 1924; FDR to Montgomery Hare, May 13, 1924, and quantities of similar letters; Joseph Guffey to FDR, May 8, 10, 1924; FDR to Guffey, May 15, 1924.

40. George Herman Ruth to FDR, June 13, 1924.

41. James J. Hoey to FDR, June 19, 1924.

42. Howe to McCarthy, June 18, 1924.

43. FDR statement, filed under "H" in mss. on 1924 campaign; New York *Times,* June 22, 24, 1924.

44. Flynn, *Roosevelt Myth*, 266.
45. Lindley, *Roosevelt*, 222.
46. George M. Palmer, interview with Moses Smith, January 15, 1948.
47. New York *Times*, June 27, 1924; Lindley, *op. cit.*, 223–224.
48. Lindley, *op. cit.*, 223.
49. New York *Times*, June 27, 1924.
50. Democratic National Convention, 1924, *Proceedings* (Indianapolis, 1924), 122–130.
51. *Proceedings*, 310, 334; MacKay, *op. cit.*, 101.
52. G. O. Marshall to FDR, January 7, 1925.
53. FDR to George J. Christie, July 22, 1924; Lindley, *op. cit.*, 228.
54. New York *Times*, July 5, 1924; *Proceedings*, 686–696.
55. *Proceedings*, 888.
56. Bryan Mack to FDR, February 10, 1928; Earl D. Bloom to FDR, December, 26, 1924; Charles H. Brough to FDR, February 7, 1925.
57. Chicago *Tribune*, July 6, 1924; Fred A. Russell to FDR, April 10, 1928; FDR to Russell, April 17, 1928.
58. Cronin to FDR, July 9, 1924; James J. Hoey to FDR, August 1, 1924; Lindley, 224.
59. New York *World*, July 11, 1924.
60. Lippmann to FDR, July 9, 1924; Ike B. Dunlap to FDR, July 10, 1924.
61. Gavin McNab to FDR, January 16, 1925; Oswald West to FDR, December 23, 1924.
62. Henry T. Rainey to FDR, December 30, 1924.
63. FDR to Norman E. Mack, August 5, 1924; FDR to James A. Edgerton, November 6, 1924; FDR to John S. Lawrence, September 4, 1924.
64. Glenn Frank to FDR, August 11, 1924.
65. FDR to Frank, August 12, 1924.
66. FDR to Joseph C. Reehill, September 30, 1924.
67. FDR, radio speech, September 24, 1924.
68. FDR to Alva B. Adams, November 12, 1924.
69. FDR to Willard Saulsbury, December 9, 1924.

CHAPTER XI

The Struggle to Walk

1. FDR to Elliott Brown, August 5, 1924.
2. FDR to John P. Adriance, December 15, 1923; FDR to Richmond P. Davis, October 27, 1924.
3. FDR to James Roosevelt Roosevelt, January 22, 1925; Hamlin, "Memories," July, 1924, and summer, 1926.
4. FDR to D. L. Corbett, January 22, 1925.
5. McIntire, *White House Physician*, 34.
6. Frederick Lewis Allen, *Only Yesterday* (New York, 1931), 83; FDR to S. R. Bertron, September 4, 1924.
7. FDR to Dr. George Draper, February 13, 1923.

8. PL, 2:535–536; FDR to Henry Noble MacCracken, March 27, 1923; *Weona II* log, FDR mss.

9. FDR to Carter Glass, March 27, 1923.

10. The logbooks of the *Larooco* are in PL, 2:537–560, 570–577, 593–610; FDR's correspondence with Lawrence forms part of an excellent account, Donald S. Carmichael, "An Introduction to The Log of the Larooco," *The Franklin D. Roosevelt Collector* (November, 1948), 1:1–37.

11. Carmichael, *op. cit.*, 25.

12. FDR to John S. Lawrence, April 30, 1925.

13. PL, 2:596 *et passim;* Oswald Mosley to FDR, undated [1926].

14. PL, 2:541–542.

15. FDR to Abram I. Elkus, October 24, 1924.

16. The fragment of the history is in PL, 2:546–552; FDR to Russell Doubleday, February 27, 1924.

17. FDR to Howe, March 5, 1924; interview with ER, September 3, 1952; FDR to Helen Wilkinson Reynolds, March 2, 1925; FDR to Livingston Davis, April 25, 1925; Carmichael, *op. cit.*, 32; PL, 2:609; interview with Frances Perkins, May, 1953.

18. FDR to Byron Stookey, August 12, 1924; Gunther, *Roosevelt*, 229; FDR to Arthur M. Van Rensselaer, December 21, 1923.

19. PPA, 1934:486.

20. FDR to Elliott Brown, August 5, 1924.

21. PL, 2:582–583.

22. Looker, *Roosevelt*, 118–119; Donald S. Carmichael, *FDR Columnist* (Chicago, 1947), 9.

23. FDR to Stookey, September 4, 1924.

24. Donald Day, *Franklin D. Roosevelt's Own Story* (Boston, 1951), 82; FDR to Elkus, October 24, 1924; Looker, *op. cit.*, 121–122; Gunther, *op. cit.*, 232–233. For a pleasant anecdotal history of Warm Springs, see Ella Godwin Hill, *The History of Warm Springs, Georgia* (Chastain, Arkansas, 1934); for a definitive, indispensable account, see Turnley Walker, *Roosevelt and the Warm Springs Story* (New York, 1953).

25. Carmichael, *FDR Columnist*, 11–12.

26. PPF, 1934: 487–488.

27. FDR to Livingston Davis, April 25, 1925.

28. FDR to Black, April 22, 1925.

29. PL, 2:586–587.

30. FDR to Black, August 31, 1925; PL, 2:588–589; FDR to Ferdinand Hoyt, October 29, 1925; Hamlin, "Memories."

31. Hamlin, *op. cit.*

32. Looker, 127; PL, 2:597, 600.

33. PL, 2:611.

34. Interview with ER, September 3, 1952.

35. PL, 2:609–610.

36. Looker, 130; PL, 2:618.

37. PL, 2:618.

38. PL, 2:621.

CHAPTER XII

The Search for a New Jefferson

1. FDR to Abram I. Elkus, July 18, 1924; Elkus to FDR, July 14, 1924.
2. Livingston Davis to FDR, October 13, 1923.
3. FDR to Mrs. Duncan Harris, September 11, 1922; FDR to Henry Hollis, January 17, 1922; ER, *This I Remember*, 31–32.
4. FDR to Charles F. Murphy (not sent), December 5, 1924.
5. FDR to James A. Edgerton, December 12, 1924.
6. S. F. Spohn to FDR, December 27, 1924; William Cabell Bruce to FDR, December 18, 1924; William E. Sweet to FDR, January 12, 1925; Samuel V. Stewart to FDR, December 20, 1924.
7. Henry T. Rainey to FDR, December 30, 1924, and numerous other replies to FDR's circular letter.
8. FDR to Thaddeus A. Adams, November 4, 1925.
9. FDR to James W. Remick, January 23, 1925.
10. FDR to J. A. H. Hopkins, April 8, 1925.
11. FDR to E. T. Meredith, March 17, 1925.
12. FDR to James A. Edgerton, December 12, 1924; Edgerton to FDR, November 11, 1924.
13. FDR, penciled draft of review. See also New York *World*, December 3, 1925.
14. FDR to Winter Russell, April 16, 1925.
15. FDR to Dr. W. C. Martin, December 9, 1925.
16. FDR to A. H. Vandenberg, January 20, 1921; Vandenberg to FDR, January 13, 1921.
17. Interview with ER, September 3, 1952.
18. Hamlin, "Memories."
19. FDR to Winter Russell, April 16, 1925.
20. Russell to FDR, May 19, 1925; FDR to Claude Bowers, December 17, 1925; FDR to Black, February 13, 1925. FDR had owned less than 1 per cent of the *Post* stock. FDR to Adrien Herzog, October 11, November 1, 1922; E. F. Gay to FDR, December 31, 1923; FDR to Gay, January 4, 1924.
21. FDR to Black, February 9, 1925.
22. For these columns (and ones FDR wrote for the Beacon, N. Y., *Standard*, in 1928) together with an excellent account of their background, see Donald Scott Carmichael, *FDR Columnist* (Chicago, 1947); Robert G. Paterson to FDR, June 29, July 22, 27, 1925.
23. FDR to Alfred E. Smith, May 20, 1927.
24. FDR to Holston Bartelson, May 21, 1925.
25. FDR speech, 1926; FDR press statement, Bureau of Publicity of the Democratic National Committee, 1926.
26. FDR to S. Grover Morrow, July 28, 1926; memorandum in FDR mss.
27. FDR to William A. Oldfield, April 11, 1925.
28. FDR to Thomas J. Walsh, February 28, 1925.

29. FDR to William A. Oldfield, April 11, 1925.

30. FDR to Charles Hammond, July 20, 1925; Howe to FDR, February 20, 24, 27, April 15, 1925; FDR to Clem Shaver, February 28, March 10, 1925; FDR to Oldfield, April 22, 1925; and numerous other letters in FDR mss. Walsh to FDR, March 7, 1925; Howe to Walsh, March 11, April 3, 1925; Walsh to Howe, April 8, 1925, T. J. Walsh mss.

31. New York *Times*, April 24, 1925.

CHAPTER XIII

The Young Elder Statesman

1. Joseph T. Croke to FDR, August 18, 1924; FDR to Louis J. Lang, February 21, 1925; New York *American*, February 10, 1925.

2. Louis B. Wehle to FDR, June 22, 1926; FDR to Wehle, July 8, 1926; Howe to FDR, April 26, 1927; Wehle, *Hidden Threads of History*, 92-93.

3. Howe to FDR, March 7, 1926.

4. FDR to Adolphus Ragan, December 9, 1925; Ragan to FDR, December 7, 1925.

5. FDR to George Foster Peabody, December 11, 1925.

6. Howe to FDR, undated, *c.* August or September, 1926.

7. FDR to McCarthy, August 24, 1926; FDR to Smith, September 15, 1926; FDR to Young, September 30, 1926; Young to FDR, October 7, 1926; Walter Lippmann to FDR, September 17, 1926; FDR speech before Democratic State Convention, September 27, 1926.

8. FDR to Abram I. Elkus, September 21, 1926; New York *Times*, September 15, 26, 28, 1926; New York *Herald Tribune*, September 28, 1926.

9. Pringle, *Smith*, 382; confidential source.

10. Two confidential sources.

11. James A. Farley, *Behind the Ballots* (New York, 1938), 78-79.

12. FDR to W. T. Doty, February 15, 1926; FDR to Lewis B. Emmerman, January 8, 1925; FDR to Olvany, January 8, 1925.

13. FDR to James J. Walker, November 8, 1925; Howe to FDR, April 1, 1927.

14. FDR to Smith, July 29, 1925; see also FDR to Smith, April 8, 1925; Smith to FDR, June 12, 25, 1925.

15. FDR to Smith, December 3, 1926; Smith to FDR, January 10, 1927.

16. FDR to Smith, December 14, 1927, telegram and letter; Smith to FDR, January 23, 1928; FDR to Smith, January 30, 1928.

17. Smith to FDR, February 3, 1928.

18. FDR to Myron D. Kings, June 15, 1925.

19. Jesse H. Jones to the present writer, May 29, 1953; FDR to Mrs. Burton W. Musser, March 5, 1926.

20. Jones to FDR, July 14, 1926; FDR to Jones, July 7, 1926.

21. Howe to Daniel C. Roper, March 26, 1926; FDR to Finis J. Garrett, February 23, 1926; FDR to Thomas J. Walsh, February 22, 1926.

22. New York *Times*, February 22, 1926.

23. FDR to Walsh, February 22, 1926.

24. Walsh to FDR, March 2, 1926; Howe to FDR, March, 1926; Howe, "Report of the Italian Debt Settlement."

25. Howe to FDR, March, 1926; New York *Times*, April 22, 1926; Alvin Johnson, "B. M. B., Prince of Israel," *Yale Review*, Spring, 1945, 34: 543–545.

26. Walsh to Hollins Randolph, March 8, 1927; Key Pittman to Randolph, March 9, 1927, copies in FDR mss.

27. Howe to FDR, undated, *c.* 1927.

28. FDR to Frederick Osborn, January 5, 1926; FDR to Walter M. Mahony, May 22, 1928.

29. Kenneth McKellar to FDR, July 14, 1927, and letters from other Southern senators; FDR to Editor, New York *Times*, August 22, 1927; Pat Harrison to FDR, September 17, 1927; FDR to Henry Ford, September 8, 1927 (form letter sent to numerous wealthy businessmen); New York *Times*, August 28, 1927; *National Business Review*, July 15, 1927; FDR to Hubert D. Stephens, January 27, 1928.

30. Lippmann to FDR, September 17, 1926; Roger L. Scaife to FDR, December 10, 1926; FDR, *Whither Bound?* (Boston, 1926).

31. FDR to Daniels, April 27, 1927; Daniels to FDR, April 30, 1927; Howe to FDR, April 26, 1927.

32. FDR to H. H. Gouchenour, May 24, 1927.

CHAPTER XIV

Smith for President

1. William Allen White to FDR, February 11, 1928; FDR to White, February 18, 28, 1928.

2. FDR to Smith, September 17, 1926; FDR to Berres, November 28, 1927; Pringle, *Smith*, 311–314.

3. Howe to FDR, March 14, April 18, 22, 1927; FDR to Bruce Rogers, January 31, 1927; FDR to Stephen F. Bayne, October 13, 1927.

4. FDR to Smith, September 17, 1926.

5. FDR to Smith, sometime before May 10, 1927; Smith to FDR, May 10, 1927.

6. Howe to FDR, April 15, 1925; Howe to FDR, spring, 1928; Howe to FDR, undated, about April, 1928.

7. FDR to Lithgow Osborne, February 2, 1927; FDR to Smith, March 10, 20, 1927; FDR to Ellery Sedgwick, March 19, 1927.

8. FDR to Smith, March 20, 1927.

9. FDR to Hollins N. Randolph, April 20, 1927.

10. Daniels to FDR, July 19, 1927.

11. FDR to Carter Field, May 12, 1927; FDR to George W. Wilson, May 12, 1927; FDR to Berres, November 28, 1927.

12. FDR to Daniels, June 23, 1927.

13. FDR to Howe, April 19, 1928; Howe to FDR, undated, *c.* April, 1928; FDR to George R. Van Namee, February 10, 1928; FDR to Will R. King, May 21, 1928.

14. FDR to Clem Shaver, January 17, 1928 (draft); Cordell Hull to FDR, March 22, 1928; Jesse H. Jones to FDR, March 26, 1928, and a number of similar letters.

15. FDR to Van Namee, March 26, 1928.

16. New York *Times*, April 3, 13, 15, 1928.

17. FDR to Carl C. Donaugh, March 27, 1928.

18. FDR to Richard Crane, April 26, 1928; FDR to Swagar Sherley, June 8, 1928.

19. FDR to Samuel Colcord, November 5, 1924; FDR, "Whither Bound?" — Commencement speech at Milton Academy, May 18, 1926.

20. FDR, speech draft, 1926.

21. FDR to Meyer Jacobstein, March 5, 1928; FDR to Coontz, May 23, 1928; Coontz to FDR, May 15, 1928; FDR to Arthur T. Flavin, January 19, 1926.

22. FDR to Logan Feland, September 1, 1928.

23. FDR to C. H. Kimball, January 10, 1927; FDR to Glass, January 25, 1928.

24. Hamilton Fish Armstrong to FDR, January 23, March 16, 1928; FDR to Armstrong, March 22, 1928; FDR to Glass, January 23, 1928; Glass to FDR, January 25, 1928; FDR to Norman H. Davis, March 30, 1928.

25. House to FDR, January 11, 1928; FDR to Sumner Welles, March 7, 1928.

26. Smith to FDR, March 23, 1928; see FDR, letter and memorandum to Colonel Frederick Stuart Greene, January 13, 1928; Sumner Welles to FDR, January 20, 1928; FDR to Welles, February 24, 1928; George B. Graves to FDR, March 3, 1928; FDR to Welles, May 28, 1928; Welles to FDR, June 1, 2, 1928.

27. FDR, "Our Foreign Policy, A Democratic View," *Foreign Affairs* (July, 1928), 6:585.

28. Davis to FDR, April 24, 1928; Armstrong to FDR, April 25, 1928.

29. FDR to Armstrong, March 22, April 17, 1928; FDR to Armstrong, April 17, 1928.

30. FDR, "Our Foreign Policy," 584, 585, 581, 581, 582.

31. FDR, *op. cit.*, 586.

32. FDR to Mrs. J. Malcolm Forbes, August 20, 1928; Lippmann to Esther Everett Lape, June 7, 1928.

33. FDR to Lape, June 14, 1928; FDR to John H. Clarke, August 10, 1928; FDR to Clarke M. Eichelberger, July 20, 1928.

34. FDR to J. B. A. Robertson, June 18, 1928; FDR to Louisa K. Fast, August 13, 1928.

35. Howe to FDR, undated, c. April or May, 1928; FDR to Clem Shaver, June 6, 18, 1928; seating plan in FDR mss.

36. FDR to Henry Morgenthau, Jr., July 7, 1928; Herbert H. Lehman to FDR, July 5, 1928; Morgenthau to FDR, July 5, 1928.

37. FDR to Newton D. Baker, July 12, 1928; Baker to FDR, July 6, 1928; FDR to Daniels, July 3, 1928.

38. FDR form letter, June 20, 1928.

39. Alfred E. Smith, *Up to Now — An Autobiography* (New York,

1929), 391; FDR to Shaver, January 17, 1928; Jones to FDR, March 26, 1928.

40. FDR to Milton Colvin, July 20, 1928; Scaife to FDR, June 28, July 19, August 27, September 11, 13, 15, 1928; Ferris Greenslet to FDR, July 6, 1928; FDR to Scaife, August 28, 1928; Frank M. Bruce to FDR, September 14, 1928.

41. FDR to Lippmann, August 6, 1928.

42. FDR to Milton Colvin, July 20, 1928; FDR to Zephaniah W. Pease, July 23, 1928; FDR to H. Walker, August 22, 1928.

43. FDR to Baker, July 12, 1928; New York *Times*, June 28, 1928.

44. Chicago *Tribune*, July 1, 1928.

45. New York *Times*, June 28, 1928.

CHAPTER XV

Roosevelt for Governor

1. FDR to J. W. Atwood, June 6, 1928.

2. FDR to John S. Lawrence, June 15, 1928.

3. FDR to Black, March 27, 1928; Howe to FDR, July 6, 1928; FDR to Radcliffe, July 6, 1928; PL, 2:640; Lindley, *Roosevelt*, 228–229.

4. Samuel Lubell, *The Future of American Politics* (New York, 1952), 35.

5. FDR to Daniels, July 20, 1928.

6. FDR to Harry F. Byrd, August 20, 1928; FDR to George Foster Peabody, September 17, 1928; S. R. Bertron to FDR, July 24, 28, August 27, 1928; FDR to Bertron, August 29, 1928; FDR to McAdoo, November 28, 1928.

7. FDR to Stanley W. Prenosil, August 23, 1928; Scott Ferris to FDR, July 23, 1928; Willmoore Kendall to FDR, August 9, 1928; Byrd to FDR, August 9, 1928; FDR to Byrd, August 20, 1928.

8. FDR to Daniels, July 26, 1928; FDR to Clark Howell, July 25, 1928; FDR to Samuel B. Adams, August 15, 1928; PPA, 1928–1932:20.

9. Form letters in FDR mss.; FDR to Harry B. Hawes, August 13, 1928; FDR to Howe, September 17, 1928; FDR to David S. Hawkins, August 9, 1928.

10. FDR to John A. McIlhenny, July 26, 1928, and numerous other letters; interview with ER, September 2, 1952; Lindley, *op. cit.*, 21.

11. FDR to McIlhenny, July 26, 1928.

12. Lindley, 231–232.

13. Warren Moscow, *Politics in the Empire State* (New York, 1948), 15.

14. Lindley, 12–13.

15. Howe to FDR, telegram, September 25, 1928.

16. Howe to FDR, telegram, September 26, 1928; Howe to FDR, two telegrams, September 28, 1928.

17. Edward J. Flynn, *You're the Boss* (New York, 1947), 67–68; Lindley, 14.

18. FDR to Smith, telegram, September 30, 1928.

19. New York *Herald Tribune,* October 21, 29, 1928; Lindley, 12.
20. Howe to FDR, telegram, October 1, 1928.
21. Flynn, *op. cit.,* 28; Lindley, 18; Farley, *Behind the Ballots,* 79.
22. PL, 2:646; New York *Post,* October 2, 1928; Lindley, 18.
23. ER, *This I Remember,* 44–45.
24. Lindley, 19–20.
25. Howe to FDR, telegram, October 2, 1928; New York *Post,* October 2, 1928.
26. ER to FDR, telegram, October 2, 1928; Howe to FDR, two telegrams, October 2, 1928.
27. John T. Flynn, *The Roosevelt Myth* (Garden City, New York, 1948), 269–270, 423. Flynn gives as his source of information Raskob and William Bray.
28. ER, *op. cit.,* 45, 367–368, gives the figures on Raskob's gifts and FDR's loan.

CHAPTER XVI

Victory by a Hair's Breadth

1. *Wall Street Journal,* October 15, 1928; New York *Times,* October 4, 5, 1928.
2. New York *Post,* October 2, 1928; see New York *Herald Tribune,* October 3, 1928.
3. New York *Times,* October 9, 1928.
4. New York *Herald Tribune,* October 5, 1928.
5. Lindley, *Roosevelt,* 21.
6. New York *Post,* October 5, 13, 17, November 1, 2, 1928.
7. New York *Post,* October 2, 1928; interview with ER, September 2, 1952; ER, *This I Remember,* 47.
8. New York *Herald Tribune,* October 4, 1928.
9. New York *Times,* October 11, 12, 1928; New York *Herald Tribune,* October 28, 1928; Lindley, *op. cit.,* 26.
10. Howe to FDR, October 22, 1928.
11. New York *Times,* October 5, 7, 8, 9, 1928. New York *Herald Tribune,* October 9, 1928.
12. New York *Herald Tribune,* October 9, 1928.
13. New York *Times,* October 9, 10, 1928; New York *Post,* October 9, 1928.
14. New York *Herald Tribune,* October 17, 1928; PPA, 1928–1932: 13–16.
15. Samuel I. Rosenman, *Working with Roosevelt* (New York, 1952) 16.
16. PPA, 1928–1932: 21; New York *Times,* October 17, 18, 1928.
17. New York *Herald Tribune,* October 20, 1928; Rosenman, *op. cit.,* 22; Perkins, *Roosevelt I Knew,* 44.
18. New York *Times,* October 22, 1928; Rosenman, *op. cit.,* 17.
19. Rosenman, *op. cit.,* 17–21.
20. PPA, 1928–1932: 30–36.

21. PPA, 1928–1932: 38–44.

22. PPA, 1928–1932: 44–51; New York *Herald Tribune*, October 29, 1928.

23. New York *Times*, October 30, 1928.

24. New York *Herald Tribune*, October 27, October 29, 1928; New York *Post*, October 27, 1928.

25. New York *Herald Tribune*, October 25, 1928.

26. New York *Times*, October 19, 1928.

27. John Godfrey Saxe to FDR, November 2, 1928; Moscow, *Politics in the Empire State*, 16.

28. New York *Herald Tribune*, November 3, 5, 1928; New York *Times*, November 2, 1928; Perkins, *op. cit.*, 44–45.

29. New York *Times*, November 5, 1928.

30. New York *Post*, November 6, 1928.

31. Van Namee to FDR, November 14, 1929, GP.

32. FDR to Fidelity and Deposit agents, telegrams, November 6, 1928; Rosenman, 26; Flynn, *You're the Boss*, 71–72; Farley, *Behind the Ballots*, 53; *New York Legislative Manual*, 847.

33. New York *Times*, November 7, 1928; FDR to T. F. Conway, November 8, 1928; FDR to Archibald Roosevelt, November 19, 1928.

34. Copies of form letters in FDR mss.; FDR to J. Bruce Kremer, November 22, 1928.

35. New York *Times*, November 11, 1928.

36. Welles to FDR, November 10, 1928.

37. Will Rogers to FDR, undated, *c.* November, 1928.

INDEX

Index